Charlotte Perkins Gilman

The Making of a Radical Feminist 1860-1896

Mary A. Hill

TEMPLE UNIVERSITY PRESS *Philadelphia*

Temple University Press, Philadelphia 19122

Published 1980
Printed in the United States of America

Library of Congress Cataloging in Publication Data

Hill, Mary A.
Charlotte Perkins Gilman: the making of a radical feminist, 1860–1896.

Bibliography: p.
Includes index.
1. Gilman, Charlotte Perkins Stetson, 1860–1935.
2. Feminists—United States—Biography.
HQ1413.G54H54 301.41'2'0924 [B] 79-22395
ISBN 0-87722-160-X cloth; ISBN 0-87722-225-8 paper

Photos courtesy of The Schlesinger Library, Radcliffe College.

TO SARA AND TOM

with affection and respect

Contents

Preface

MY purpose in this first volume—*The Making of a Radical Feminist*—is to trace chronologically the origins of Charlotte Gilman's feminist convictions and to explain some of the patterns of her early life. In a second volume I will provide a detailed study of Charlotte's later, more public life, using her rich correspondence with Houghton Gilman as further illustration of the intellectual-emotional complexities which predated and inspired her major work. In published form her writings thrust her into the forefront as a major intellectual of the women's movement in America. And in unpublished private form they show a very human self. By interweaving public statements with private letters, I hope in both volumes to show how her intellectual dilemmas related to her private ones, how her idealistic goals conflicted with practical demands, and how her keen professional ambition confronted—head on—her intense desire for love.

My indebtedness for this book extends to many: to my parents, who as dedicated intellectuals, inspiring teachers, and profoundly helpful friends, stood solidly behind my work at every stage; to many of my university colleagues and professors, most especially David Noble of the University of Minnesota, who first taught me that history means commitment; to Doreen Jackson, whose encouragement and support, strength and perseverance saw me through the toughest years of personal/professional development; to my friends in Montreal—particularly Freda Bain, Janet Rapoport, Barbara Jack, and Linda Copp—who first encouraged my women's studies involvement and concern; and to countless others who remain unnamed, yet who deserve my heartfelt thanks.

I am grateful to the members of Charlotte Gilman's family, whom I interviewed in Pasadena, California. Most importantly, I appreciate the patience and candor of the late Mrs. Katharine Stetson Chamberlin, who generously showed me family photographs and memorabilia, and shared insights into her mother's character that I could not have attained in any other way. Dorothy Chamberlin and Thomas Perkins, Jr., also provided helpful information and useful suggestions for further research.

I am indebted to the following libraries for permission to quote from material in their collections: the Stowe Day Foundation, Hartford, Connnecticut, for their letters of Mary Westcott Perkins and Isabella Beecher Hooker; the Bancroft Library of the University of California at Berkeley, for letters from the Charles Walter Stetson correspondence, the Rhode Island Historical Society, for Charlotte Gilman's letters to Martha Luther (Lane); the John Hay Library at Brown University for the Charlotte Gilman–Lester Ward correspondence; the Vassar College Library, for Gilman's correspondence with her cousin, Marian Whitney; and finally, the Arthur and Elizabeth Schlesinger Library on the History of Women in America, Radcliffe College, for its outstanding collection of Charlotte Perkins Gilman papers. The staff at the Schlesinger Library deserve a special word of thanks. Their generous response to my inquiries, their knowledgeable suggestions for further research, their encouragement through many years of contact and correspondence were all well beyond the call of professional duty.

The long-term process of research and writing was possible because of financial assistance from a number of sources. I received a Canada Council Research Fellowship for 1972–73, a Quebec Government Grant for the same year, a Bucknell University Summer Stipend for 1977, and a leave of absence with financial assistance for 1977–78. Many additional expenses—for typing, xeroxing, research assistance, and travel—were generously assumed by Bucknell University.

Judy Gilbert also deserves appreciation, not only for her first-rate typing skills, but also for her consistently warm and gracious support. Several research assistants, particularly Judy Peeler and Gloria Withim, lightened and brightened the investigative process, and tracked down numerous details. A number of Bucknell students rendered important assistance as well. Their questions and discussions, privately as well as in the classroom, their enthusiasm for the field of women's history, cheered my spirits and inspired my growth.

When I think over the number of colleagues and friends who have contributed in some measure to this book, I sometimes wonder who is left to read it. Despite my indebtedness to them all, I list only a limited number here. First, I want to thank those who provided useful criticisms of my doctoral dissertation on Charlotte Gilman several years ago: Mari Jo Buhle, Linda Gordon, Janet Rapoport, John

Rosenberg, Nancy Cott, Philip Withim, Catherine Smith, Phoebe Sheriff, Richard Twomey, Howard Zinn, and, of course, my two advisors from McGill University, Robert Vogel and A. R. Riggs. Carl Degler of Stanford University was particularly helpful as I completed my doctorate. His suggestions for further research, his willingness to facilitate contacts with Charlotte Gilman's family, and most importantly his encouragement—all strengthened my confidence and solidified my commitment to move from a theoretical to a more biographical approach, in short, to write a very different book. Sections of the second and more current manuscript received constructive readings from the following: William Chafe, Joan Scott, Donald Scott, Jacquelyn Hall, Peter Filene, Rosalind Rosenberg, John Kasson, Joy Kasson, and my editors at Temple University Press, Michael Fisher and Kenneth Arnold.

I owe a special debt of gratitude to members of my family for their support through a particularly critical but happy year. They read my work carefully, criticized it tactfully, and provided the kind of family atmosphere which freed me from extraneous responsibilities and enabled me to complete the book. Thomas Hill's close, steady attention to detail, nuance, and general interpretive meaning prevented countless errors and confusions; and Sara Hill's psychological insights helped to shape and inform my own. The cross-generational readings, particularly the mother-daughter exchanges which resulted, were among the richest, most rewarding aspects of this work.

Through the many years this book has been in progress, my closest supporters and companions have been my two children. To David and Noelle Porter, a very special word of thanks. In every phase of writing and professional struggle, they have provided the kind of mature understanding and genuine affection which I will remember and appreciate always.

Charlotte Perkins Gilman

The Making of a Radical Feminist 1860-1896

Introduction

IN *Women and Economics* (1898), Charlotte Perkins Gilman described the enigmatic "woman's conflict" this way: "We ourselves, by maintaining [an] artificial diversity between the sexes, . . . have preserved in our own characters the confusion and contradiction which is our greatest difficulty in life." In the year after *Women and Economics* was published, she privately described the enigmatic conflict in herself: "To prove that a woman can love and work too. To resist this dragging weight of the old swollen woman heart, and force it into place—the world's Life first—my own life next. Work first—love next. Perhaps this is simply the burden of our common womanhood which is weighing on me so."

Charlotte's struggle with the "burden of our common womanhood," or, more accurately, the burden of our common humanity, is the central focus of this book. Many years ago, when I first came across her published works—witty, insightful, radical feminist critiques—I was looking for a heroine, for closer contact with a woman who could articulate my own frustrations and explain women's problems in ways relating directly to my life. Her concerns were mine as well: how to reconcile family responsibilities with professional ambitions; how to be a responsive mother to two small children and still have time to teach and write; how to satisfy the human need for love and work. Undoubtedly, I was looking for historical roots as well, for intellectual precedents to feminist ideas of the 1960s, which to many even now seem unsettling and new. In any case, I had no notion then of what the research-writing process would involve: poring through Charlotte's diaries and letters, living through her roller-coaster vacillations, dissolving my sentimental admiration, grounding my respect. It led to a rich, enormously rewarding, decade-long involvement with her life. For as the heroine image disappeared, a very human woman came to light, a woman whose brilliance was matched by her complexity, and whose failures reflected so many of the ubiquitous destructive social forces she sought to understand.

* * *

With the publication of *Women and Economics* in 1898, Charlotte Perkins Gilman began to emerge as a major American feminist theorist of national renown. Lecturer, writer, charismatic wit, she was the "Marx and Veblen" of the woman's movement, according to Andrew Sinclair; the "most original and challenging mind which the movement produced," wrote suffragist organizer Carrie Chapman Catt; the "leading intellectual in the women's movement during the first two decades of the twentieth century," Alice Rossi recently asserted. *Women and Economics* reflected Charlotte's brilliance. It would be translated into at least six languages, go through more than a half dozen printings, and serve as a "Bible" for many suffragists and feminists for years.

Women and Economics sounded a responsive chord just when women seemed to need it most. For the 1890s was a decade of perceived national crisis, of economic upheaval, of surging political debate. Working-class needs stirred middle-class consciences; grass-roots politics merged with intellectuals' concerns; and a woman's movement soared side by side with broadly based campaigns for reform. Earlier in the century women had been expected to provide peaceful loving service to their families in respectful deference to the laws of a patriarchal God; yet by the 1890s, many women were turning heads and raising eyebrows.* They were demanding the vote in clamorous suffragist conventions, entering the work force in swelling numbers, seeking new opportunities, shaping new definitions of themselves. Charlotte's self-chosen mission—or accidental fate—was to goad them on: to analyze their entanglements, dramatize their subjugation, mock their opponents, radicalize their goals.

At a time when many women were already cracking the walls of "domestic enslavement," Charlotte was devising hard-line critiques

* "Many women" refers primarily to middle-class women (and not necessarily to a majority of those) rather than to black, immigrant, or working-class women. As historian Gerda Lerner puts it, "The history of notable women is the history of exceptional even deviant women, and does not describe the experience and history of the mass of women. . . . Women of different classes have different historical experiences" (Gerda Lerner, "Placing Women in History: Definitions and Challenges," *Feminist Studies*, III, no. 1/2 [Fall 1975]: 5).

of sexual inequalities across the board—economically, politically, psychologically, sexually. She turned to socialists for her revolutionary egalitarian ideals, to evolutionary theorists for "Natural Laws" to prove that justice could be humanly sustained, and to contemporary writers of all descriptions—economists, historians, anthropologists, sociologists, and theologians—for anecdotes and arguments to demonstrate the curse of androcentric power. In Charlotte's view, it could be proved beyond a doubt that the patriarchal family was the primary oppressive force in women's lives. The family ensured women's economic dependence, their nonvoluntary domestic service, their emotional subservience, their sexual submission. Each of these themes Charlotte integrated into a complex (albeit not consistent) feminist philosophy; and each she presented with a clip and style and drama that had a broad appeal. She wrote, "Of women especially have been required the convenient virtues of a subject class: obedience, patience, endurance, contentment, humility, resignation, temperance, prudence, industry, kindness, cheerfulness, modesty, gratitude, thrift, and unselfishness." Reject the "slave mentality," she advised. Women must demand equality and freedom. They must press not only for the vote, or work, or better pay, not only for political reforms or patchwork improvements, but also for full economic equality according to the socialist ideal, satisfying work outside the home, and sexual equality in love relationships with men.

* * *

Although in part it was the force of Charlotte's political-feminist ideas that first attracted me, it was also the fascinating contours of her life. Born in 1860 into an upper-crust New England family, Charlotte had the kind of rich cultural heritage—and the aggressive drive to match it—that help explain her eccentricity as a female intellectual. She was the great-granddaughter of the famed religious leader Lyman Beecher, and grand-niece of the influential female Beecher rebels, Catharine Beecher, Harriet Beecher Stowe, and Isabella Beecher Hooker.

In some respects, Charlotte seemed to romp through adolescence with inordinate confidence and self-awareness. But she suffered from bouts of insecurity as well, and from family strains that hurt. Her parents were separated; her father was distant and unsupportive; her mother, as single head of household, was overworked, economically hard-pressed, and stern. When Charlotte was in her young adulthood years, her life was plagued by a series of major crises: a miserable depression after her marriage to Walter Stetson in 1884; a "nervous breakdown" following the birth of her daughter Katharine in 1885; a divorce necessitated by temporary "insanity"; and a painful separation from her daughter necessitated by an itinerant public career. By the mid-1890s (Charlotte's mid-thirties), however, she began to experience some measure of success. She began to recover her health, renounce her "feminine" responsibilities, and preach the rebel views she had been harboring for years. By the age of thirty-six she was speaking on the cross-country socialist-feminist lecture circuit. By thirty-eight, she had published *Women and Economics* and several other shorter works. And by the time she was forty, as though to claim a private reward to match her public ones, she had found a second husband, Houghton Gilman, to whom she could turn for emotional and intellectual support. By 1935, the year she died, she had to her credit not only countless nationally and internationally applauded lectures, but some twenty volumes of published work besides.

For a quick overview of such major facts, crises, and successes, one can turn with confidence to *The Living of Charlotte Perkins Gilman: An Autobiography*, published posthumously in 1935. Having preached for years about what women should do to live more happily and freely, she had felt compelled to provide a glimpse of how she had lived herself. Just that, a glimpse. For as she began writing her autobiography in the spring of 1926, there was a carefully nourished public persona she wished to portray: the strong-minded theorist often sidetracked by emotional entanglements, but ultimately successful because of her dogged determination in pursuing selfless humanitarian ideals. She told her readers that her private life had been rather consistently depressed, her public work the major source of satisfaction. She liked to emphasize her disappointments in love relationships, not the self-affirming passions that had more than once engulfed her. She described her selfless suffering as though anger or defiance had never been a fundamental motivating force. Personally, she demanded her readers' sympathy. Professionally, she wanted their respect. After devoting almost half of her autobiography to the oppressive environment of youth, she mentioned her thirty-four year marriage (1900 to 1934) to Houghton Gilman in a sentence or two, and proceeded thereafter to describe celebrities, travels, and public triumphs as though emotional relationships had been unfortunate or insignificant distractions.

Charlotte's autobiography is a record of her oppression, her perseverance, her hard-won success. But she left another record as well, a far more human one. It can be found in leather-bound diaries dating back to the age of fifteen, folders filled with early drawings and adolescent fantasies, unpublished autobiographical short stories and essays, hundreds of effusive self-revealing letters—all of which she unceremoniously stacked in boxes, but nonetheless carefully preserved.*

According to the self-styled public image, Charlotte was a brilliant uncompromising theorist for the woman's movement—calm, cool, emotionally aloof. According to the private record, she was a woman complicated by a full range of human passions, by love and hate, by generosity and selfishness, by hard-headed determination and pig-headed stubbornness, by confidence and debilitating insecurity. Autobiographical projections notwithstanding, Charlotte did not find abstract theory a means by which to transcend her mercurial emotions; nor did she formulate her insights in a vacuum. She experienced women's conflicts fully, recorded the process, and saved almost everything she wrote.

* * *

Some time in the winter of 1973, I first began to read through Charlotte's private papers. It was an unforgettable experience, exhilarating, overwhelming at times, as rich as any I have known. I felt I finally had met her. I had touched the past somehow, poring through box after box of personal memorabilia, confronting directly her self-reflections and the on-going experiences of her life. It was as though she had sensed all along that someday biographers would want to know her, that they would be impressed by her precocious insights and shocked by her early anticipation of fame. For she did not just dash off quick reminders of significant events. She approached dreams and hopes and personal fiascos with the same literary flair and fervor she later gave to public writings. For instance, at the age of ten, she wrote—and then carefully preserved—the "Literary and Artistic Vurks of Princess Charlotte."† At the age of eighteen, she wrote in her diary, "Gentle reader, wouldst thou know me? Verily, here I am. . . . 5 feet, 6½ in. high, weigh some 120 lbs.

*Except where changes in punctuation, capitalization, and spelling have occasionally been made to enhance readability, quoted passages have been reproduced exactly.

†The Charlotte Perkins Gilman papers remained in her daughter Katharine Chamberlin's garage for some thirty years. They were purchased in the early 1970s by the Arthur and Elizabeth Schlesinger Library on the History of Women in America.

. . . Possessing great power over myself. *Not* sentimental." At age nineteen, she began the "Autobiography of C. A. Perkins." And at age twenty-one, she was pleased with the thought that some of her erotic, self-assertive letters to her closest friend Martha Luther might someday come to public view. She wrote Martha, "Incidental thought, wouldn't these letters of mine be nuts for commentators! *If* & *if* of course, but how they would squabble over indistinct references and possible meanings!"

In years and years of detailed record-keeping, Charlotte confronted personally, sometimes disastrously, almost every major woman's issue she publicly discussed. To read through her published works is to appreciate the power of her wit and sensitivity and intellect; to peruse her private papers is to view the underlying drama of her life: the passion and excitement of female friendship, the "insanity" of loveless marriage, the trauma of young motherhood, the nerve-wracking guilt of divorce. She seemed always to be searching for the "New Woman" ideal, for the experience of meaningful work, economic independence, equal human love. And elaborately, often eloquently, she described the process: the struggle to pursue a full-time career while raising a daughter and nursing a dying mother, to find a satisfying human relationship based on love and not just convention, to keep the public persona discreetly separate from the private self.

It seems understandable that in her autobiography Charlotte chose not to discuss her personal relationships extensively. Many of her loved ones were still alive, and she did not want to hurt them; many of her life decisions would not be publicly acceptable or easily understood; many she found difficult to understand herself. Whatever the reasons, she cultivated misperceptions that would last for decades: that she was a calm rationalist who believed simple truths could cure major human ills; that she was a man-hating feminist who wished to banish men from her emotional life; that she was a strong-minded professional who preferred the sanctity of work to the risks and disappointments of love. Privately, however, she described herself quite differently: "well, sometimes I feel like 'a heathen goddess come again,' a wonderful struggling mixed feeling, half shame, half pride of being—to most people's knowledge a stern cold thinker, a calm pleasant friend of men, dearly loved by women, the favorite of children—a widow—a celibate, a solitary—and inside—Ashtoreth!" *

* Ashtoreth was an ancient Semitic fertility goddess.

The public image, rational and cool. The private self, compelling in its emotional complexity. My biography rests on the assumption that the truth and power of many of Charlotte Gilman's theories come from her passion and experience, and that her historical significance stems not only from her brilliance, but also from the way she tried to live her life.

1860-1880

Chapter One

Preceptors and Provocations

CHARLOTTE was born into a family for whom conventional sex-role expectations didn't fit. Whereas most nineteenth-century women were taught to aspire to "true womanhood" ideals—to be pious and pure in self-sacrificing service to their families—Charlotte was taught, by example anyway, to be a self-assertive reformer instead. She was a Beecher. Among her relatives, calmness and conformity were the exception, innovative eccentricity the norm. Her Beecher great-aunts were fiery abolitionists when women were expected to be peaceful, physical fitness enthusiasts when they were supposed to faint, and prolific public writers when most women occupied themselves with private chores at home. All Beecher women paid lip-service to the "true womanhood" ideology; yet most reshaped it to serve their needs and expand their power.

Charlotte's parents were less successful and renowned than the Beecher ancestors, but no less eccentric by the standards of the times. Charlotte's father, Frederick Beecher Perkins, dutifully acclaimed the sanctity of the family, but hated its tensions, left his family when Charlotte was still a child, and preached (by example) that independence was preferable to patriarchal power in his home. Charlotte's mother, Mary Westcott Perkins, was unintentionally a rebel. Forced to raise her children by herself, she unwittingly taught her daughter about the false security and spurious deceit of wife-mother myths.

Most people in the nineteenth century accepted the rigidly defined boundaries separating men and women into their respective public-private spheres; they seemed to enjoy the benefits of the arrangement and to assume that associated hardships were either fate's decree or punishments for sin. Had Charlotte's family been a properly acculturated one, she might have adapted passively herself. Instead, she learned to challenge the "domestic ideology" her family preached but often subverted in practice, and to believe that the price for peaceful compliance was too high.

* * *

The roots of Charlotte's feminist convictions and reform-minded drive thus lie first in her family history, particularly in her filial connections with the famed Beecher clan. Her great-grandfather Lyman Beecher—apocalyptic preacher, community organizer, charismatic leader in early nineteenth-century political and religious movements—was its undisputed patriarch. Publicly, he worked to promote conservative ideals, to strengthen church and family influence in a rapidly industrializing and urbanizing America. And privately, he fathered Beecher rebels: Henry Ward Beecher, illustrious pastor of the Brooklyn Plymouth Church; Harriet Beecher Stowe, abolitionist enthusiast and author of *Uncle Tom's Cabin*; Catharine Beecher, fervent and effective advocate of "domestic feminism"; Isabella Beecher Hooker, nationally renowned suffrage worker; and several other zealous Beecher progeny besides. These were Charlotte's great-aunts and great-uncles: "world servers," she called them. They were the "Saints and Sinners" whose crusades and imbroglios not only secured the family prominence among New England's cultural elite, but also established it as one of the most energetic and influential in nineteenth-century America.

Perhaps best known of Lyman Beecher's children was Henry Ward Beecher—loved and respected as a distinguished authority on American morality, yet simultaneously vilified for his part in the titillating three-year scandal of his alleged liaison with the wife of reformer-publicist Theodore Tilton. A man of "splendid physique and abounding vitality," he could *"work enough to kill half a dozen ordinary men,"* wrote one contemporary. He was an abolitionist (albeit inconsistently), a president of the American Woman Suffrage Association, an enlightened conservative, an incurable optimist, and an avid defender of the "beneficent progress" of the new industrial order. "God has intended the great to be great and the little to be little," boomed Beecher with his forty-thousand-a-year income. A strikingly imposing figure—outspoken, eccentric, and at least moderately reformist—he promoted an exalted image of the Beecher birthright which a young ambitious Charlotte would accept fairly early as her own.

The Beecher influence was by no means confined to Lyman and his seven preacher sons. The Beecher women—Harriet Beecher Stowe, Catharine Beecher, Isabella Beecher Hooker—were also among Charlotte's first models, her first exemplars of literary excellence, political prowess, and keen-witted vitality. From her earliest childhood Charlotte remembered long visits in their homes, family celebrations, evening concerts, heady sermons and debates, and probably some whispered exchanges on Beecher scandals as well. At first, Charlotte's parents were included in Beecher gatherings simply because of the traditions of family loyalty. Supportive relationships, round-robin letters, marathon visiting tours—these were common among Beechers. By the time Charlotte was four or five years old, however, there were more compelling reasons for Beecher hospitality: Frederick left his family for increasingly extended periods of time; Mary needed help—financial as well as emotional. The Beecher women's Hartford homes became a favorite refuge, especially the homes of Charlotte's grandmother, Mary Beecher Perkins, and of her great-aunts, Isabella Beecher Hooker and Harriet Beecher Stowe. As a vital center for the Nook Farm literary community and for the local spiritualist cult as well, Isabella Beecher Hooker's home doubtless had an important impact on Charlotte's young mind; but it was Aunt Harriet Beecher Stowe's "wonder house" that Charlotte most vividly described: "A little river ran near it, tall trees made a thick wood behind, there were large gardens, and inside, a conservatory to the roof—with a gallery all around on the second floor, so that the bedrooms could share in its cool beauty. A little fountain played in the middle, rich drooping ferns draped the walls, with flowers and shrubs in pots."

While Charlotte later recalled Harriet Beecher Stowe painting "charming water color studies," her great-aunt's perseverance, energy, and bristling reform convictions also made their mark. In society at large, women were often described as weak and ineffective; but for Harriet Beecher Stowe, like most Beecher women, that image didn't fit. She raised seven children, coddled and supported (economically as well as emotionally) her husband Calvin Stowe, achieved national prominence with the publication of *Uncle Tom's Cabin*, and thereafter published, on the average, almost a book a year—novels, biographies, and essays.

Harriet Beecher Stowe, like so many women novelists of the nineteenth century, always paid respect to idyllic images of "domestic femininity"; yet she managed to project a radical message nonetheless. Some later critics would disdainfully dismiss her works as "domestic melodramas": her style and rhetoric seemed overly romantic, her images of slavery too conventional, her glorifications of mother-love too sentimental. True in part, but what about her underlying views? Not for a moment did Harriet Beecher Stowe advocate female innocence or domestic doldrums either one. Instead, she seized one of the few "career" opportunities available to women, condemned the barbarities of the slave-owning class with a vigor few could match, and subverted "true womanhood" ideology along the way. Romantic imagery notwithstanding, she dramatized slavery in ways which stirred the nation's conscience, acclaimed women's power in terms her generation could accept, and, in practice, if not in theory, fought for women's right to economic independence, creative work, and self-respect.

Catharine Beecher was another of Charlotte's great-aunts who in effect attacked "domestic femininity" even while glorifying it. Founder of the Hartford Female Seminary, authoritative writer, lecturer, teacher, organizer, temperance worker, and physical fitness enthusiast, Catharine Beecher was no more the frail weak-kneed maiden than was her younger sister Harriet. In fact, perhaps more than any other woman of her generation, Catharine Beecher was responsible for turning conventional clichés into a tactically brilliant feminist call to action: woman's domesticity and unique moral purity was woman's claim to preeminence and power. Again, some critics would condemn—or misunderstand—the strategy, saying that Catharine Beecher had written Dr. Spock–style home and hearth domestic manuals which only tightened women's chains.* Or, as the bombastic Victoria Woodhull put it, Catharine Beecher was trying to "clog the wheels of progress" and give man the same power over woman "as he possesses over his horses and dogs, and other chattel property."

Historian Kathryn Kish Sklar suggests an alternative perspective—that Catharine Beecher acclaimed a philosophy which permitted women to enhance their self-image as individuals and as a group, and ultimately to organize for action. In short, Catharine Beecher's rhetoric of "domestic feminism" had a "feminist" intent—to expand women's power in the only sphere society allowed them. By improving their health and fitness, women could silence myths about female frailty; by improving the efficiency and quality of housework, they could enhance their self-respect; by emphasizing their capacity for purity, piety, and love, they could extend their influence in the home, the schools, and even in society at large.

***Miss Beecher's Housekeeper and Healthkeeper* (1873), for instance, or *Principles of Domestic Science* (1870).

There was a serious problem in this philosophy, to be sure, one that would complicate the work of feminists for years: how to fight for female equality while stressing innate differences? Still, Catharine Beecher stirred Charlotte to think. For not only did she leave a rich body of feminist ideas to be absorbed and challenged, she provided a model of self-assertive independent living as well. Significantly, it was this aunt for whom Charlotte later named her daughter.*

While the work of Catharine Beecher and Harriet Beecher Stowe represented an early and preparatory stage of the nineteenth-century women's movement, their younger half-sister Isabella Beecher Hooker attained her prominence among the later, more pragmatic leaders who emphasized woman's right to vote. Isabella Beecher Hooker was a founder of the New England Woman Suffrage Association, an activist in the Connecticut Woman Suffrage Association, a lecturer, author, and nationally known suffrage crusader. Thanks in part to her eccentric friend Victoria Woodhull, she was also a spiritualist of considerable imaginative verve. She professed to perceive through séance and communion not only the imminence of woman's suffrage but also the proximate coming of a matriarchal government. In fact, Isabella Beecher Hooker sometimes may have thought herself to be the matriarch—politically astute, religiously zealous, and domestically devoted. And since Charlotte's mother, Mary Perkins, had chronic needs as well as fervent spiritualist convictions, she and her family were especially welcome guests at the Beecher Hooker home.

Although for the most part Isabella Beecher Hooker fostered close Beecher family ties, she also formed alliances which threatened Beecher tempers. She was a friend and staunch defender of the controversial Victoria Woodhull—editor of the *Woodhull and Claflin Weekly*, first female presidential candidate—a flamboyant and, to some, outrageous feminist. A spiritualist and socialist as well as a suffragist, an advocate of free speech (or unrestrained invective) as well as free love, Victoria Woodhull scored her first major victory when she persuaded the House Judiciary Committee to hold hearings on woman's suffrage, and a first major *faux pas* when she tried to vilify the Beecher name. For her, Catharine Beecher was a despicable proponent of female degradation and Henry Ward Beecher was an adulterous libertine. It was at a meeting of the National Association of Spiritualists in the fall of 1871 that Victoria Woodhull "exposed" the "free love" antics of woman suffrage friend and Beecher

* Katharine Beecher Stetson (Chamberlin) was named for Catharine Beecher and Kate Bucklin, a Providence, Rhode Island, friend.

family hero, Henry Ward, thereby causing "the greatest scandal of the day." Isabella Beecher Hooker defended Woodhull—who predictably but temporarily had gone to jail. Henry Ward Beecher, who spent thousands of dollars seeking exoneration in the trial for adultery precipitated by Woodhull's charge, publicly declared his half-sister insane. Alliances were formed and broken. The upshot was a permanent split in the Beecher family, a fissure in the woman's suffrage movement, and a strategic retreat by many suffrage leaders from frank discussion of politically significant and explosive questions of sexual morality.

Charlotte Perkins was an impressionable twelve year old when the Beecher scandal hit the nation's press and Beecher tempers reached the boiling point. Their wrangles stirred her curiosity, whetted her appetite for the piquant, and prompted a lifelong craving for contact with "movers and shakers" generally. The homes of most of Charlotte's contemporaries doubtless were more stable and secure, but to her they seemed staid, witless, and dull. Viewing elder Beechers with adolescent fascination, she learned to associate politics with drama, women with aggressiveness, sexuality with controversy, religion with flamboyant rhetoric, and reform with New England's cultural and intellectual elite.

* * *

As elder Beechers set personal examples and national precedents by resisting conventional nineteenth-century stereotypes, Charlotte's father, Frederick Beecher Perkins, was something of a rebel too, albeit a less successful one. Hard-working but erratic in his own style of Beecher nonconformity, he was a drifter, a man eventually submerged beneath the ebb and flow of other Beechers' notoriety. He loved brandishing ideas, but hated formal schooling. He attended Yale, but never graduated. He studied law but never practiced it. Finally, he graduated from Connecticut Normal School in 1852, taught for a short while in Greenwich, Connecticut, and then joined relatives and friends as assistant editor of various newspapers and journals—the New York *Tribune*, the *Independent*, the *Christian Union*, the *Library Journal*, among others. Also, under the pseudonym of Pharaoh Budlong, he published an impressive though uneven set of essays and fiction pieces—parodies of political intrigue, didactic reformist tracts, ardent if rather stylized love adventures—quixotic, witty, often forceful works. Though writing was his passion, economically it never was sustaining. Undaunted, he turned to library work—a reasonably attractive recourse for a man with his encyclopedic mind. He secured a position as assistant director of the Boston Public Library in 1874, moved to California in 1880 to become chief librarian of the San Francisco Public Library, and in 1894 returned East, where he worked on sundry editorial projects until his death in 1899. From Charlotte's point of view, he was impressive, intellectually engaging, somewhat overwhelming, but never the success he should have been. He was too irresponsible, too erratic in his work, and too intolerant of those with whom he disagreed. At the time of his death in 1899 (when Charlotte was thirty-nine years old), she wrote, "What a sad dark life the poor man led." "So able a man—and so little to show for it. Poor father!"

Though Charlotte was sometimes piqued at Frederick's failures, she admired his gall—his outspoken honesty, his impetuous compassion, his annoyingly obvious pride. In pre–Civil War days he had rescued a young black woman from mob violence in an anti-abolitionist community. Another time he had been irritated with authorities, thrashed a college professor, and got himself removed from school. At least he was courageous, Charlotte noted, even if he was unwise. He simply buckled down to no one: not to pious pundits, not to pretentious celebrities, not to any "smug, fat, young divine." Skilled in his use of words and wit, an aspiring literary counterpart to Charlotte's cartoonist-hero Thomas Nast, Frederick seemed to her a captivating iconoclastic model, even though he wrought havoc with his life.

In part, Charlotte admired her father because she was so much like him, in temperament and style, if not always in conviction. Frederick railed against injustices and inequalities, mourned the plight of the "deserving poor," and blasted the "recklessness, dishonesty, mad covetousness, [and] deliberate treachery" of profit-mongering monopolists and giant swindlers. Some of Charlotte's political enemies and analyses were different, to be sure. She was an 1890s socialist-feminist, he a romantic of the post–Civil War mugwump generation; both were idealists, optimists, committed rebels. Frederick's message was simply an older, more sentimental one common to his generation. Through honesty—in government, business, and the home—the honor of a more rural, pre-industrial, family-centered America could be restored. He sympathized with the "wretched poor," ennobled them in fiction, and admired the patient faith with which they silently endured their suffering. The hope of America, he believed, lay not in organized protest, as later reformers usually argued, but in the hearts and souls of individuals, rich and poor alike. "The reason of the wickedness of our politics is, that our voters are deficient in intelligence and goodness," Frederick wrote; "the only really noble standard is ourselves."

It was "honest good Government" Frederick wanted, not a "Democratic hat nor a Republican pair of boots." And it was honest, good individuals in honest, good families that would lead the way. That was a characteristic Beecher view, of course, especially after Catharine Beecher had popularized, refined, and shaped it through her prolific writings and educational campaigns. Under the moral leadership of ennobling, self-sacrificing women, she insisted, homes and families would provide the needed antidote to contemporary political and material corruption. Women were the most effective opponents of crime and selfishness, of industrial and urban upheaval, and thus would promote progress and ensure national integrity. For Frederick, for the Beechers, and for many reformers all across the country, the glorification of feminine domesticity seemed honorable and opportune. The home provided a sanctuary of moral virtue. At least one soothing refuge still remained.

It was a consoling enough message for any man to cherish: women would secure goodness and right in the home and thus ennoble and inspire men's efforts in the outside world. It was the message Frederick had been hearing since his childhood, and not just in the sometimes puzzling form his celebrity aunts presented it—worshipping domestic harmony while busying themselves with nondomestic work whenever they had the chance. He had also learned it at his mother's knee. Frederick's mother, Mary Foote Beecher Perkins, was devoted to the domestic private life her sisters publicly acclaimed. As one family member put it, Mary Perkins was "an anomaly, she was the only purely private Beecher." Wife of prominent Hartford lawyer Thomas Clap Perkins, sister of Harriet Beecher Stowe and Catharine Beecher, Mary Perkins had devised her own style of Beecher nonconformity: "During a long and blameless life, never did she deviate into public view by writing a story, article or book, making a speech, giving a lecture, preaching a sermon or conducting a public enterprise. Measured by the proprieties of that day she was the only lady in the family." In Frederick's view (nostalgic memories enriching his vision of the beneficent effects of homes), that was as it should be. He later wrote, "still I constantly feel, and fully know that that pure, calm, quiet, bright, loving, intelligent, refined atmosphere of my home silently and unconsciously penetrated and vivified my being." Like most preacher-teacher Beechers, Frederick thus advised women on the best means to attain the true womanhood ideal: before marriage they could have some outside interests; if single they might work; but a public life after marriage would only "satisfy imperfectly that divine zeal for useful exertion." Women should "find perfect gratification in their own homes, in their families."

The idyllic dream. The romantic image of perfect family life. Unfortunately, Frederick's adult experiences worked differently: tensions in his own marriage led to separation, then to divorce, then to years of single living. All the more reason to sustain the fantasy. Perhaps he felt there was a fairly simple explanation for his family misery: he had married the wrong woman; Frankie Johnson was his lifelong love, yet Mary Westcott became his wife.

Frankie Johnson had been Frederick's first love and for a time his fiancée. Then her family interfered, the engagement was broken, and the "slighted" Frankie Johnson married Frederick's uncle, James Chaplin Beecher. In search of consolation, Frederick then married his distant cousin Mary Fitch Westcott, who, conveniently enough, bore a close resemblance to his former love. "Her eyes are much the same color—and there was a simplicity and frankness of manner that was sadly reminding," Isabella Beecher Hooker wrote on hearing the news of Frederick's abrupt and unceremonious marriage plans. It hardly seems surprising that the Perkins marriage ended in divorce.*

While Frederick may have married Mary Westcott on the rebound, he was careful nonetheless to choose a woman who he thought embodied his ideals of womanhood: "Delicate and beautiful, well-educated, musical, and what was then termed 'spiritual minded,' she was femininely attractive in the highest degree." Daughter of Henry Westcott, a well-established and respected merchant in Providence, she was descended from a family which in prominence and nonconformity possibly matched even the Beechers. An early ancestor, for example, was Stukely Westcott, one of the original thirteen proprietors of Rhode Island, and one of Roger Williams' deacons "when being a Baptist took some courage." Mary's father was a religious rebel too, "a Unitarian when being a Unitarian took even more." Considering Mary's beauty, charm, and illustrious connections (and Frederick's reputation as a roving flirt), Isabella Beecher Hooker at first suggested that Mary "was too good for him." But on

* Many years later, after the deaths of both Mary Perkins and James Beecher, Frederick's first love was rekindled. In May 1894, Frederick married "the love of his youth, now his widowed aunt!" Charlotte later wrote, "By this combination my father became my great-uncle, my great-aunt became my mother, and I became my own first-cousin-once removed" (*The Living of Charlotte Perkins Gilman: An Autobiography* [New York: Harper & Row, 1975; 1st pub., 1935], p. 191).

second thought she added, "we hear however that she has flirted as much as he has and being thirty years old is not very unsuitable." *

The frail daughter of an elderly adoring father and his young and childlike wife, Mary Westcott had grown up with the cultural and educational refinements expected of young ladies of her class. Attractive and appropriately innocent in her "idolized youth," she was "petted, cossetted and indulged" by her family and charmed, courted, and adored by a "flood of lovers." Mary, like Frederick, was somewhat fickle in the nineteenth-century–style singles' competition, yet she had experienced at least one painful disappointment—the death of a particularly determined fiancé. For the most part, however, there was little in the undemanding and overly protective environment of Mary's youth to prepare her for adult responsibilities. Perhaps intuitively she postponed the day of reckoning: "Engagements were made, broken and renewed, and re-broken" until "at the extreme old maidenhood of twenty-nine," she married Frederick Perkins, on May 21, 1857.

If reality had matched prevailing myth, the Perkins would have enjoyed elaborate nuptial rites and subsequent domestic harmony. Instead, they began housekeeping "the very same day" of their quick, informal wedding. With his paltry income from various editorial positions, Frederick was unable to repay old debts, much less to provide a home for his "most passionately domestic of home-worshipping housewives." New debts mounted quickly and oppressively; Frederick was unable to hold a steady job; and Mary became ill during frequent pregnancies. Four children were born in eight years, two of them died in early infancy.†

Charlotte later assumed that a factor contributing to her parents' separation was the issue of sex and reproduction, the two being inextricably linked in pre–birth control America: "The doctor said that if my mother had another baby she would die. Presently my father left home. Whether the doctor's dictum was the reason or merely a reason I do not know. What I do know is that my childhood had no father."

Doubtless the causes for the breakup of the Perkins' marriage were more complex than guesswork on their sex-life would reveal. Facing the stark realities of debt, illness, and death, Mary and Fred-

* Mary was twenty-nine.

† The two surviving children were Thomas Adie Perkins, born May 9, 1859, and Charlotte Anna Perkins, born July 3, 1860. Thomas Henry Perkins was born on March 15, 1858, and died in April that same year. The fourth and final child, Julia De Wolf Perkins, was born January 29, 1866, and died the following September.

erick were forced to seek aid and comfort with their families and to adopt an itinerant style of life which in some respects only enhanced their troubles. In any case, judging from his fiction, Frederick treated family tensions, crying babies, and even human sexuality with a kind of light-hearted humor that Charlotte could never share. One of his collections of fiction pieces, *Devil Puzzlers and Other Studies*, was published when Charlotte was seventeen years of age; though it was probably not designed to reach or persuade his daughter, it may have been an effort to explain himself.

Among the more "comical" and extravagant of the short fiction pieces in *Devil Puzzlers* is "My Forenoon with the Baby," a sportive sketch of a male's impotence (his own?) when caring for a crying infant child (Charlotte?):

> A species of fearful contortion passed over his visage—his mouth opened to an extent unparalleled in my experience, occupying a space that left no room for the rest of his face, . . . [and] he discharged such a shriek as really hit me on the forehead and knocked me straight up again into a frightened perpendicular. It didn't stop either—it continued. I had no idea there was so much noise in anything. This was evidently a diabolic energy. A child would have to breathe, but this phenomenon didn't. Its whole being resolved itself into a shriek.

The "humor" of the piece results in part from Frederick's objectivity: in life and literature he could quit the scene. Charlotte's perspectives on child care would of course be rather different. In view of her mother's experiences with crying-dying babies, and her own later "hysterical" experience with motherhood as well, Charlotte may have felt that there was a particularly grim irony in Frederick's quips on human sexuality:

> I often ask, with Dr. Franklin, "What's the use of a baby?" He gave no answer; I do. A baby is providentially provided as an "awful example" for the warning of maids and bachelors, as terrific consequences universally follow great follies. It is the delirium tremens of matrimony. If you don't want to have it, let the causes alone.

Most likely, in his own marriage Frederick felt compelled to "let the causes alone"—especially so, given Mary's illnesses in pregnancy. But when he came to explaining why a man might leave the "consequences" too (or possibly why he left his family), his double standard was perfectly plain. For women, Frederick offered the hackneyed prescriptions: self-sacrifice is one's sacred duty and virtue is its own reward. But it was a rather different "instinct" which he proudly valued in himself: an "instinct for living out my life fully and freely, not so as to infringe upon the rights of others, but not stinting or distorting or amputating myself."

From Frederick's point of view, the separation from Mary had been a requisite self-affirming act. Having married unwisely, even impetuously, he refused to do penance with his life. Abstractly, he glorified the peaceful harmonies of home and family, but the tension-filled setting compared poorly to his romanticized ideals. And though Mary's innocent naiveté and charm had been appealing in the context of premarital flirtations, in marriage her immaturity, dependence, and submissive loyalty may have been offensive. Frederick probably felt sympathy and obligation toward Mary, but not respect or love.

In another short fiction piece, "The Compensation Office," Frederick again may have been reflecting on his relationship with Mary, this time with considerably more hostility. In the story, a woman, deserted by her husband, seeks compensation for and redemption from her suffering: "I, who have a loving heart, and a busy mind withal, am cruelly shut off from the happiness which I sought in marriage. . . . I remain alone in life, and am eating my heart in my sorrow." Momentarily, Frederick encouraged a sympathetic hearing, but then began to show the woman's source of grief: "How could I keep love alive in my heart, when I was left alone for years by the man who had promised to love and cherish me? How could I help becoming cold and distant myself, when the only human being who was bound to love me, left me alone?" The portrait that then emerges is of a suffocatingly grasping woman: "Whatever love might in former days have been in her heart, it did not now beam at all within her haughty eyes. She must have been supposing the regretful remembrance of it to be the possession of it." Moreover she had neglected her duties as a wife and mother. She had failed to provide "over-brimming fountains of love" to her family, to "cherish" her husband, "to guide, and attract, and instruct" her children "so as to make their home the centre" and herself the "queen and beloved source of their happiness." Frederick's message was the message of the era. A man must live "fully and freely," not "distorting or amputating" himself, but a good woman should turn the other cheek.

* * *

Whatever the reasons for the Perkins' separation, Charlotte had reason enough from the outset to be suspicious of the ideology her parents preached in theory but did not practice. Images of romantic love had been displaced by the reality of too frequent pregnancies; expectations of home-based security had disappeared in the context of her parents' itinerant, precarious style of life. On both counts, Charlotte often blamed her father. He had failed to fill the traditional family role of father-breadwinner; he was too irresponsible to settle down to steady work; he used relatives' hospitality to fashion a fancy-free escape from his own family responsibilities. Charlotte's early autobiographical reflections, punctuated by sarcastic quips, suggest resentment. For instance, when her parents moved first to Henry Westcott's home, Charlotte noted, "Father agreed to pay our board, and didn't." In 1862, her parents went to "Grandpa Perkins"; Frederick promised to stay there three months, "instead it was 9," she quipped again.* From 1863 to 1873 there were repeated moves between Apponaug, Rhode Island; Hartford, Connecticut; and Rehoboth, Massachusetts. Frederick deposited his family with reasonably sympathetic relatives and absented himself for increasingly long periods of time. By 1869, there was a tacit understanding of permanent separation, and several years later a filing for divorce. In 1873, Mary Perkins, now a single mother, moved to Providence. All told, she had been "forced to move nineteen times in eighteen years, fourteen of them from one city to another."

At times at least, Charlotte explained her parents' separation as though Frederick were the villain, Mary the martyred saint, the "deserted wife" who bore no grievances: "Absolutely loyal, as loving as a spaniel which no ill treatment can alienate, she made no complaint, but picked up her children and her dwindling furniture and traveled to the next place." Moreover, Mary, with totally self-sacrificing love, single-handedly assumed responsibility for the divorce: "thinking to set my father free to have another wife if he would not live with her, [she] divorced him. This he bitterly resented, as did others of the family. . . . Divorce was a disgrace."† Only as a kind of afterthought did Frederick get a bit of sympathy from Charlotte: "my father may have suffered too; but mother's life was one of the most painfully thwarted I have ever known."

While, for the most part, Charlotte seemed to identify and side with her mother, there were times when she could understand and

*These quotations are taken from the "Autobiography of C. A. Perkins," written January 14, 1880, when Charlotte was nineteen.

†In another unpublished version of the autobiography written in the 1920s, Charlotte implied that a reason Mary divorced Frederick was because he failed to send the family money.

share her father's point of view as well. Privately, for instance, she described her mother's tendency to "sicken" Frederick "with over much affection"—"saving the very hair she cut from her husband's head. . . . Yes, and even the parings of his nails!" Also, from long, hard experience, Charlotte knew Mary could be sternly cold as well as loyal, even cruel though "loving." Charlotte felt she had herself been "violently well brought up," subject to emotional chastisements and physical beatings which suggested underlying mother rage, not conformity to sentimentalized images of selfless, even saintly, mother love. Charlotte clearly recognized her mother's frailties: a certain severity that accompanied a supposedly submissive stance, a self-effacing pretense by which Mary manipulated other people and played upon their guilt. Always Charlotte would rail against such weaknesses in women—their pettiness, narrowness, and selfishness. But though she condemned, she also sympathized, and later wrote volumes showing why. Mary may have often been cold, stern, and petty, but from Charlotte's adult point of view she was not to blame; denied opportunities for a full and free and satisfying life, Mary had exercised her human will to power in the only realm available, in her home and in her personal relationships.

Chapter Two

Princess Charlotte 1860-1875

CHARLOTTE would always view her childhood years as ones of deprivation, discipline, and coldness. She felt that she was never cuddled or loved enough by either parent. With a father absent and a mother preoccupied, she had grown up in a hurry, and very likely developed in the process some lifelong fears about the insecurity of love relationships, and some persistent anxieties about herself. At the same time, however, Charlotte had learned some crucial lessons for her later feminist rebellion. Her brother taught her how to defy authorities with childish capers, how to survive teasing competitions, and why she should resent being "just a girl." Both parents taught her to challenge conventional family expectations—her father by taking his leave, her mother by default. Moreover, her father helped her to appreciate the fun of learning, the power of writing, and the fascination of the masculine world outside the home. And her mother showed her that women could, despite enormous odds, survive without the support of men. Rather significantly, it was during Charlotte's crucial adolescent years that Mary became marginally self-sufficient. And while she sometimes coaxed Charlotte to aspire to feminine norms of passive piety, she also preached, by example anyway, that women were not helpless, that men were not reliable protectors, and that children could fend for themselves.

* * *

Some of Charlotte's earliest childhood memories were unhappy ones. Most poignant is her autobiographical description of her mother's calculated coldness:

> "I used to put away your little hand from my cheek when you were a nursing baby," she told me in later years; "I did not want you to suffer as I had suffered." She would not let me caress her, and would not caress me, unless I was asleep. This I discovered at last, and then did my best to keep awake till she came to bed, even using pins to prevent dropping off, and sometimes succeeding. Then how carefully I pretended to be sound asleep, and how rapturously I enjoyed being gathered into her arms, held close and kissed.

It seems likely that Mary's coldness was, as Charlotte later believed, one of the most destructive aspects of her childhood. During most of those early years, Mary was painfully preoccupied —moving from house to house, from relative to relative; coping with her own nearly fatal illness at the time of Julia Perkins' birth and then mourning Julia's death; worrying over Frederick's absences, her own future, her contemporaries' scorn; and managing countless household chores besides. Mary's predicament was not unique, to be sure, though perhaps she exposed some of the conflicts between the myth and reality of motherhood more dramatically than most. Clearly Charlotte learned, and then vividly remembered, that idyllic images of mother love could often mask seething anger, frustration, and resentment and that blissful images of motherly self-sacrifice were a pernicious mirage. Charlotte "rapturously" enjoyed the affection Mary gave her—especially being "held close and kissed" covertly. "Mother loved us desperately," Charlotte would write, but Mary too often seemed cool, distant, and uncaring, and her "tireless devotion was not the same thing as petting." Like so many children, Charlotte had first experienced, as one contemporary writer puts it, "both love and disappointment, power and tenderness in the person of a woman."

Charlotte did, of course, have some happy memories of her mother. For instance, she remembered fondly her mother's "lovely tales" and "memorably delicious meals, new potatoes boiled in their jackets, all peeling and mealy, with a bowl of hot milk with butter and salt in it; and a whole dinner of 'hasty pudding,' first with milk, then with butter and molasses, then with milk again and so till we could no more." Mother had a "natural genius for teaching little ones," and loved helping Charlotte to "print letters in a little blank book," or reading to her "constantly" from "Object Lessons," from "The

Child's Book of Nature," and from *Oliver Twist*—at the age of eight. And there were other vividly remembered mother-daughter times as well, especially sewing for her dolls: "'over and over' it was, patchwork, making a little cover for the mahogany doll's cradle I had inherited from mother, whose father had made it for her. There was a mahogany bedstead too, a dining table with leaves that lifted, and a bureau, the cradle being as big as the bureau by the way." Charlotte didn't like the "flat-jointed, sawdust-stuffed bodies" of some dolls that she was given: "I wanted Beauty, with a Large B—not mere prettiness." Apparently she wanted dolls with the regal image she fashioned for herself. "My dolls were Queens, not babies, and I longed for appropriate surroundings for them, wondering why thrones and such things were not made for them 'of burnished brass and polished glass,' as I crooned it to myself."

Charlotte had other interests too. Especially delightful were the periodic stays at a country home near Rehoboth, Massachusetts, between 1870 and 1874 (when Charlotte was ten to thirteen years old). Both Charlotte and her brother Thomas loved the place. Thomas nostalgically recalled "the evening chorus of birds and insects, . . . the wind sounds, the water sounds; the scents of wet woodlands, warm scents of sweet fern, hay land, pine woods, sage brush." As Charlotte remembered, these were "years of healthy barefoot wandering in summer, and joyful tumbling in great snowdrifts in winter." It must have been a relief for Mary to stay there as well; at least the romping outdoor life helped keep Charlotte and Thomas out of their usual rounds of extravagantly imaginative mischief.

In the summer of 1864, for instance, Thomas, age five, explained to his believing sister the "mystery" of putting out fires with sand and offered to show her how to do it in the fine dry grass behind the house. The problem was the wind. And good intentions notwithstanding, "small handfuls of sand did not extinguish the fire as advertised." Some neighbors "came and made a line of buckets from the well," so the house was not hurt, Charlotte later wrote; "but the flames swept up to the graveyard behind our lot, and there burnt a little spruce tree with a nest of young birds in it, which made a painful impression on us."

Both the spontaneity and remorse were typical, but so were countless other pranks. Charlotte and Thomas were a handful. One especially memorable day, they filled their mouths with water and "squirted the same as forcibly as might be, over the passers-by—ducking swiftly out of sight." Pleased with the responses, they continued to perfect their squirting skills until, accidentally, they thumped the town mayor: "mother came up stairs, no cherubs ever slept more sweetly," but on that occasion the cherubs did not win. Another bit of "malicious mischief" was rolling "hoops in mud-puddles and then into the voluminous crinolines of passing ladies." Sweetly and earnestly the darlings apologized, and then, "immune," "re-muddied and re-apologized." Later, Charlotte sometimes emphasized the earnestness of her early childhood; but she also delighted in the "ingenious misdemeanors," the "Ishmaelitish resentment," and the precocious independence with which she and Thomas engaged in the spirited intrigues of adult-child warfare.

While some of the time Charlotte and Thomas were allies against the "fops and proudies" of the grown-up world, more often than not they were playing tug-of-war with one another, Charlotte often losing. In some respects she may have had advantages: she could sled out on thin ice where Thomas could not reach her, or climb the locust tree high enough so that Thomas would not dare to come. But still, from Charlotte's point of view, Thomas had the upper hand simply by being elder and male. He was immune from kitchen duties and was assigned the preferred tasks of gardening and hunting. He did not have to hear the carping about what "good girls" should say or do or wear. And then, while Charlotte worked alongside her mother—imitating, learning, resenting the never-ending domestic tasks—Thomas exploited his precarious advantage by badgering, heckling, and generally enraging her. The "continual teasing" was "infuriating," Charlotte wrote. "The effect on me was to cultivate a black and bitter temper, rebelling at the injustice of it, steadily resenting what I could not escape." It was enough "to quite arrest the natural affection between us." From Thomas' point of view, the envy was reciprocal. He later recalled, "I know that a secret consciousness of having to 'step lively' to keep up to my sister mentally must have led to much of the unkind teasing I visited upon her, however much the 'innate cussedness' of youth may have had to do with it." Charlotte was a force for Thomas to contend with, but for the moment she felt keen resentment about the inconvenience of being smaller, younger, and just a girl.

To make matters worse, Thomas seemed to have a preferred position with their father. For instance, Frederick brought him a "light shot-gun, with powder-flask and shot-flask too. . . . I dare say he brought me something as well," Charlotte wrote, "but it made no impression whatever." Gradually, Thomas was becoming a bread-winner of sorts: with "the gun, and his traps and snares in the woods, he brought home many a partridge, rabbit and squirrel," and kept chickens and raised fruits and vegetables besides. All the teasing notwithstanding, in the eyes of little sister, Thomas was a hero to be both envied and admired. When Charlotte was about twelve, she wrote:

> Dear Father,
>
> Will you please send the money for July, August, and September. You told me to remind you of The Princess and Goblin if you forgot it. My three kits are getting large and fat. *Thomas* drowned the old cat for she killed four chicks. *Thomas* has got a nice garden and furnishes us with potatoes, tomatoes, melons, corn, beans and squashes and pumpkins. We have apples and pears in plenty. Please write a real long letter to me. This morning *Thomas* found a chimney swallow in the dining room. He had come down the parlor chimney, the fireplace of which was open. I wish you would write to me often; Willie Judd and Thomas Lord write to *Thomas* and he to them but nobody writes to me but you. *Thomas* caught a little turtle about an inch big. *Thomas* has got his snares set again, and caught a partridge this morning. I enclose two pictures in hopes you will do the same.*

While big brother Thomas and gift-giving Father were Charlotte's heroes at this age—somehow privileged allies in tantalizing escapades outside a girl's domain—Frederick had the special clout. Appearing and disappearing in his enigmatic itinerant career, protected from daily family irritations, and conditioned to enjoy the authority almost automatically accorded men, Frederick seemed to Charlotte a far more fascinating model than her mother was, far more understanding and wise. Very likely, she viewed him as an ally as well, a kindred spirit who would protect her from her mother's anger and compensate for some of Mary's coldness.

After all, Frederick was safely distant from most day-to-day parenting responsibilities. He could afford to approach his children with a more relaxed affection than Mary usually could manage, and to stand a bit self-righteously as sensitive defender of the rights of children. "A whipping inflicted upon a child old enough to remember it," he later wrote, "is almost certainly a terrible mistake. No one knows how often it happens that a child's sense of personal insult or degradation, though incapable of expression, is every whit as quick and deep as a man's." Yet Frederick's theories would have been more impressive had he not used them as a subtle form of warfare with his wife. For instance, on one of his short visits, Mary

* Emphasis added.

asked him to whip Charlotte into line. She had been leaning over the bannisters on the top floor of their boarding house, and had managed, with a good deal of playful ingenuity, to spit on the landlady standing on the bottom floor. As Charlotte later put it, "If you were a mischievous child—she had the beginning of a bald spot on the crown of her head—what would you have done? Or at least wanted to do? I did it. It was too tempting—Down softly from story to story sailed the little white drop, and landed, spat! exactly on that bald spot." A roguish prankster like Frederick might have simply been amused, but, to comply with Mary, he reluctantly whipped his daughter gently and then immediately undermined his wife's authority by asserting—within earshot of the children—that he would never do so again.

From a romping child's point of view, then, Frederick was a kind of special guest: a kindly protector and playful wit, a mastermind of facts and figures, a whiz of foreign languages, a Mr. Virtuoso in an exotic outside public theater he would talk about and recreate for Charlotte through books and magazines. These last Frederick brought or sent her in abundance. Thomas, she may have figured, had access to her father through sports and hunting; her trump card in the competition was her mind. Since Frederick was a writer himself, perhaps she thought she could win him through writings of her own—fairy tales mostly—moralistic as well as playful ones, imitative variations of styles and themes and images from children's books she almost knew by heart. Not only might father take notice —and mother as well—but also quietly and resolutely she could rearrange the pecking order in her family, dramatize her own self-styled princess status, and claim her father's adoration by showing him how beautiful and strong and kind she was, and how very much she cared.

Thomas, in these fairy tales—the "Literary and Artistic Vurks of Princess Charlotte"—was rather easily dismissed. He was a roguish prankster, a bad, bad boy. He was so bad, she added with delight, that his father became absolutely furious: "His father was so angry with him that he did not know what to do with him." In her childish fiction, then, brothers are a pest, sisters good and beautiful, and mothers single, itinerant, and poor:

> Once there was a woman whose name was Mrs. Ferow: she was a widow and had two children, a boy and a girl. The girl's name was Jenny and the boy's was Sam. He was a very bad boy but Jenny on the contrary was a very good girl. . . . He passed three years in constant squealing, squalling, scratching and bawling; until his unhappy mother had been turned out of

> about sixteen hundred different houses because none of the neighbors could sleep nights on account of Squalling Sam.

If "Squalling Sam" and goody-two-shoes Jenny suggest some fear and guilt and wishful thinking about Mary's endless moves, another adolescent piece—"A Fairy Tale"—suggests some fear and wishful thinking about Frederick's plight as well. This time, however, the heroine, Princess Araphenia, takes action: She restores her father's home, though it takes whole armies to do it. And even more importantly, she restores father-daughter closeness, with Thomas and Mother totally left out.

In "A Fairy Tale," Princess Araphenia wants to come to the aid of her good father, King Ezephon, whose subjects have rebelled and occupied his lands. Confiding in her friend, the Fairy Emadine, Araphenia explains her need for "an army of true and loyal men to repel those wicked besiegers that surround us now." Araphenia then pays a visit to her fairy friend: "Emadine asked her whether she would like to sleep alone, or share with her? Araphenia said she would rather sleep with her." Emadine then explains her origins and tells how good fairies had granted her ingenious powers: "One gave me beauty, one wisdom, one wit, one unbounded riches, one gave the power of writing, drawing, reading, and speaking all languages under the sun as easily as my own; and the last, and greatest, that whatever I wished should be granted." So with portentous blending of physical, intellectual, and occult power, Emadine rescues women in distress. First, she saves "an unprotected female in the hands of twelve ruffians" who "were in the act of forcing her into the mouth of a deep dark cavern." And then she proceeds to make Princess Araphenia commander of the troops who restore the good king's empire.

What fantasy delights! In the first story, mother received the protective sympathy she deserved from the good, the very very good Charlotte. But since Mary was now the widowed victim, since her husband had safely died, she could then be appropriately excluded from the second tale, Charlotte emerging happily as benevolent replacement. Father is a good, kind king, but since his wit, language skills, and literary genius have been appropriated by Fairy Emadine, he clearly needs a princess' help. Women are not men's helpmeets, after all, but their conquerors, their leaders, their saviors. Some men are ruffians and need to be subdued. Others, like the soldiers, are "true and loyal" to a princess' needs. And still others—specifically father—are good but powerless. In each case the women reign supreme. And how do they do it? Through female friendships—collusive, intimate, and occult. Quite naturally, princesses and fairies confirm their tenderness and trust in bed.

Later, and rather simplistically, Charlotte argued that her early fantasies had merely helped satisfy her "thirst for glorious loveliness." However, she showed a rather well-developed taste for the macabre too. An artist of sorts as well as child-author, she also left notebooks of her drawings, drawings of peaceful country scenes, delicately graceful flowers, elaborately bedecked damsels in their princess-fairy glory, and also of ghoulish monsters winsome and engaging in their ugliness. Long-nosed demons represented a maliciousness Charlotte sometimes thoroughly enjoyed. The sexual imagery is obvious—alternately self-affirming and masochistic—as are the virtue-vice and God-Devil variations on the good and evil power-struggle themes. Yet whether sexual or moralistic implications seem more telling, Charlotte's childish fantasies provided a tantalizing theater for her passions and conflicts, an appealing antidote for the kind of guilt-producing pieties adults so often preached. For both splendid princesses and ugly monsters had their magic powers, and the beauty of her role as child creator was that she could reign supreme.

At the age of thirteen, however, fantasy was abruptly toppled from its throne—or so Charlotte later recalled. It was as though through autobiographical reflections she were continuing a very human kind of fantasy—that mother was the cruel parent, and she the misunderstood and martyred child. Mary insisted that the "dream world" cease:

> [I]nfluenced by a friend with a pre-Freudian mind, alarmed at what she was led to suppose this inner life might become, mother called on me to give it up. This was a command. According to all the ethics I knew I must obey, and I did. . . .
>
> Just thirteen. This had been my chief happiness for five years. . . . No one could tell if I did it or not, it was an inner fortress, open only to me. . . .
>
> But obedience was Right, the thing had to be done, and I did it. Night after night to shut the door on happiness, and hold it shut. Never, when dear, bright, glittering dreams pushed hard, to let them in. Just thirteen.

Charlotte's description of this blow to childish fantasy shows a strange admixture of resentment and pride. Alternately she was angry with her mother and delighted with her mother's affectionate support, alternately self-pitying and inordinately pleased with her own self-discipline and strength:

> To this day I marvel at the rigid power of that young brain, and the conscientiousness which could keep faith in a world

> none but myself could enter. I did it. Night after night I lay awake, (always hoping to keep awake till mother came to bed so as to know when she hugged me), and when the lovely crowding visions came I shut the door, I drove them back; I would not think of happiness, the one great happiness I had.

Though Charlotte remembered the dream world prohibition as the greatest disappointment of her thirteenth year, very likely it was the stark practical realities which she found much harder to face. In the fall of that same thirteenth year (1873) Mary moved to the female-headed household of her mother, Clarissa Perkins Westcott, and her grandmother, Clarissa Fitch Perkins. Eighty-five-year-old Clarissa Perkins was caring for her sixty-three-year-old bed-ridden daughter, and very soon Mary was caring for both. Charlotte remembered these elder women responding warmly to her as a child. "Grandma Westcott" especially had been an object of her "childish prayers and sympathetic letters." Now, too suddenly no doubt, Charlotte was expected to act as an adult, illness and deathbed scenes serving as her training ground. For so many young women of the nineteenth century, illness brought a rude awakening; homes served as the crisis centers in times of family trauma—not hospitals with professional nurses to alleviate the strains, not neat, sterile, distant places for the sick.

The experience was painful and abrupt. Grandmother and great-grandmother were both sick and dying. Thomas contracted typhoid fever at the same time. The "Irish servant promptly departed." And Mary was left "to get on as best she could." Great-grandmother Perkins died December 7, 1873, her daughter in March 1874. Very likely, this four-generational mother-daughter exigency tightened bonds between Charlotte and her mother. Although at times Charlotte must have felt resentful and hurt that Mary's attention was directed mainly toward others, she began also to appreciate the struggles Mary faced, to feel compassion and loyalty as she witnessed Mary's strength and vulnerability, and to feel a certain pride that she could help. But if, as seems likely, she perceived the death of loved ones symbolically as the death of childhood fantasies, the underlying feeling was the pain of growing up.

Still, it was at about this time that adult responsibilities would have been expected anyway, new regulations imposed. From the point of view of most parents in the 1870s, a girl's years of puberty were fraught with peril. Menstruation marked her entry into womanhood. Appropriate rules and regulations had to be imposed, danger signals watched for carefully, strict warnings frequently repeated.

Childish fantasies, it was commonly believed, would lead to worse indulgences, perhaps to masturbation, thought to be among the worst of sins. Negative attitudes toward female sexuality were commonplace, warping a girl's attitude about herself, undermining her confidence, and setting the stage for lifelong fears. Very likely, Mary simply echoed prevailing admonitions. Already Mary's coldness had planted seeds of insecurity in Charlotte; now her warnings deepened them. Keenly aware of the price she had paid for love, of the life-threatening consequences of the sexual embrace, Mary would not or could not paint a rosy view of womanhood. Perhaps she was simply trying to help Charlotte as she had done in her own misdirected way once before—"I did not want you to suffer as I had suffered." In any case, from Charlotte's point of view, the adolescent years marked the end of childhood innocence—the blow to childish fantasies, the stark encounter with death, the apprehensions about the perils of womanhood. Resentfully Charlotte recalled the "stern restrictions, drab routine, unbending discipline that hemmed me in."

* * *

During her crucial adolescent years, Charlotte viewed her mother as the stern disciplinarian, the authority who continually interfered with the things she most loved to do. Fortunately, however, Charlotte had other female models to relate to as well, her playmates' parents, for instance, or her Beecher relatives. To some extent they may have helped her sympathize a bit, and unconsciously to absorb some unintended lessons about inequalities of money, prominence, and power. Most of the women Charlotte knew were affluent; Mary wasn't. Most were settled; Mary moved around a lot. Most had conventional marriages; Mary was a divorced mother. Most enjoyed rather refined and leisured lives with maids, tutors, and butlers, whereas Mary was mother, maid, and household manager, as well as the educator and often even the bread-winner for her family. In some respects, Mary was a victim by the standards of the times. She had hoped for the safety, security, and domestic harmony expected by women of her class: the peaceful two-parent dwelling with the prescribed division of labor, a father presiding as esteemed patriarch, a mother (and maid) managing domestic duties in the home. Unwillingly she was a single mother instead—regretful, unhappy, and usually overworked.

While Charlotte sometimes probably felt sorry for her mother, identified with her, and resented her father for having caused so many worries, just as frequently she saw Mary as a pinnacle of strength—not a victim deserving pity, but a woman who proved more successfully than most that women could fend for themselves. For it was often Mary's strength that Charlotte was resisting, not her weakness, and Mary's independence that Charlotte often emulated as well as Mary's martyr stance. In fact, at the very time that Charlotte was facing adolescent growing pains, Mary was experiencing some growing pains herself, and becoming something of a rebel besides. She was picking up the shattered pieces of her life, calculating how to care for children by herself, and shaping alternatives that worked. Perhaps in unconscious rebellion against the rationalist rhetoric and unfulfilled promises of her Unitarian parents, she turned to esoteric spiritualist communion. And out of self-defense she challenged the imagined inviolability of the single-family private home. For a time, Mary had sought refuge with her relatives, their family constancy throwing into strong relief her own guilt-associated status as a single mother. But after the deaths of her mother and grandmother, Mary began to seek viable arrangements outside the family fold. In June 1874, just before Charlotte turned fourteen, Mary moved into the Swedenborgian cooperative housekeeping establishment organized by Dr. Grenville Stevens. For a woman of Mary's class and background, this was not an easy step, nor one which many of her contemporaries would approve of. Here was a group of religious nonconformists, a group of divorcées at that, cooperating on housework, communing in their mystic faith, and forming what would seem to many a threatening substitute for the traditional family model.

For a year and a half (from June 1874 through February 1876) Grenville Stevens' three-family Swedenborgian cooperative community was Charlotte's home. She may have heard too many of her father's jibes against religious mystics to be impressed with the spiritual communions of her mother's friends. They seemed to Charlotte to be "floating and wallowing about in endless discussion of proofless themes and theories." Nonetheless, there were ways in which Charlotte was impressed. For one thing, she saw her mother enthusiastically discussing ideas "as the important things of life, instead of gossip and personalities." And for another, she saw her mother developing more confidence and strength. For years, Mary had been depressed by her marginal social status and her financial predicament. Now she was finding some security with people who respected her, and comfort from a faith which inspired and reassured her. "I have always loved God in heaven but am just beginning to *realize* Jesus Christ," she later wrote to Isabella Beecher Hooker, one of the few relatives who could fully understand.

Mary was becoming a different person from the one she had been in the early years of her marriage. No longer as submissive or childlike in her own self-chosen community, she was beginning to achieve some control over important spheres of her life. For adolescent Charlotte, Mary's involvement in the Swedenborgian community could not have been more opportune. Mary had interests of her own outside her children; and Charlotte had new adult models to relate to, not necessarily ones she admired, but at least ones which made spats with Mary less intense. So many mothers, as one contemporary writer explains, are too closely protective and controlling of their daughters—far more so than they are with sons: mothers "identify more with daughters and help them to differentiate less." When they are insecure themselves, mothers often refuse "to allow their daughters to perceive themselves as separate people." In Charlotte's crucial adolescent years, Mary was inching her way toward self-sufficiency, and in the process—rules and regulations notwithstanding—allowing Charlotte some very necessary distance for the healthy processes of separation, rebellion, and self-development. The greater Mary's security, the more easily Charlotte could grow up.

In her autobiography, Charlotte explained her rebellion rather differently: her own precocious independence had not one whit to do with Mary's strength; Charlotte was the wise discerning child, Mary the foolish parent who deserved to be dismissed. In October 1875, Charlotte remembered, "one of the major events of a lifetime" had occurred. She had defied her mother—head on. Mary had demanded that she apologize to "psychic" Mrs. Stevens for having seen her eat a bunch of grapes belonging to the cooperative, and having "thought harsh things of her." To apologize seemed bizarre —"flatly dishonest, a lie." "Hence the ultimatum": "'You must do it,' said mother, 'or you must leave me.'" Charlotte had her mother trapped: "I am not going to do it,—and I am not going to leave you—and what are you going to do about it?" What a jubilant success: "I was realizing with an immense illumination that neither she, nor any one, could *make* me do anything. One could suffer, one could die if it came to that, but one could not be coerced. I was born."

* * *

By 1875, Charlotte was feeling her oats, Beecher style: "If I was a free agent what was I going to do with my freedom? If I could develop character as I chose, what kind of character was I going to develop?" And whom to turn to for advice? From Charlotte's point of view, her mother was the home-based antagonist too quick with negative advice, her father still the distant hero. Frederick's encyclopedic knowledge seemed so much more impressive than her mother's mystic prayers, his "masculine" world of books and learning so much more engaging than Mary's "drab routine." In any case, feeling self-assertive and adult-like in her rebellious stance against her mother, Charlotte decided to turn to her father for advice. She wanted to meet him on his own turf, to approach him with her own prototypically masculine concerns:

> Dear Father,
>
> Now I want to have a nice long talk with you. Here I am, fifteen years old, quite strong, moderately supplied by nature with members, and such, and instructed in the ordinary branches of study in a reasonable degree, with a taste for literature and art, a desire (as is general I believe among girls) for well, a great many things, *and* a lamentable blank in the direction of a means of livelihood. Now, I don't want to beg, borrow, or steal, I don't approve of that ordinary mode of mending the broken fortunes of young ladies in general, viz., advantageous matrimony, and the question is, in the words of a ranting Methodist preacher whom I once heard "What shall I do to be saved?" I have an inclination in the direction of authorship, *but*, I have doubts as to whether I could make it *pay*. I also have a leaning on the side of art; but have the same misgivings. I made a little spurt in Phonographic Reporting, (a lucrative profession, I have heard,) but doubt my own ability; I am very much interested in Physiological aspirations to be an M.D.; and more than all, and [illegible] worse than all, perhaps you will say, I confess to the *heinous crime* of being *strongly* attracted to the *Stage*!!!!! There! The murder is out, the cat has left the bag, the ice is broken, and Come one! Come all! This rock shall fly, from its firm base, as soon as I!!!!!!

It is a striking letter, both for its bumptious dramatic flair and also for its equation of salvation with professional success. Too young to have much chance to test her heady aspirations, Charlotte exulted in her narcissistic fantasies and, fears of censure notwithstanding, described her alternately diabolical and promiscuous mirror-images in another irreverently seductive letter to her father:

> "Unstable as water, thou shalt not excel" said the patriarch to his son. The words often ring in my ears, and I sometimes feel,

> as if there was not hope, and the irrevocable Word of the Lord had pronounced my doom. That is in my intervals of depression; few and far between you may think, but it is not so. I often feel hopelessly despairing, at my total inability to *work*. It is, the instability of character that has been the bane and poison of so many lives that might otherwise have been almost immortal. I really feel it father, and it distresses me. Why one day I'll sit down and write poetry, another time scribble and draw for ever so long, and again, go up to mother's room, shut the door, (in pity for the rest of the household,) stand in front of the glass, and give vent to the most extraordinary series of roars and shrieks that the human voice is capable of. When I feel happy, I contract my brows into a diabolical frown, when I have relapsed into the depths of despair, I assume a beautiful expression, and put on a beaming smile, when I am alone I laugh promiscuously. . . . I did practice fainting on two shawls, but it hurt, so I gave it up. *Now!* I want [a] good strong dose of advice, though I can't depend sufficiently on my present happy frame of mind to promise to follow it, and in the expectation of a speedy return to this protracted epistle, I remain your perplexed daughter.

Eccentric but refined old Frederick must have also been perplexed. Confronted—or verbally accosted—by Charlotte's emotional effusions, he may have thought she needed some lessons in restraint. New England–style communication was more cool and proper, demonstratively affectionate behavior rare. In any case, Charlotte later felt that Frederick had responded to her coldly, almost indifferently. Here she was exploding to him with her "shrieks" and "roars" of adolescent energy, and Frederick didn't even seem to care. A visit to her father in Boston, probably in February of 1876, was an occasion she would never forget: "I kissed my father in the Boston Public Library—not having seen him in years." Instead of being hugged and welcomed, she found herself "sitting there and being treated as a mere caller—I am about fifteen—and he put me away from him coldly and said I must not do that sort of thing there. I made a little vow, to the effect that if ever my father wanted to kiss me he should ask for it."

When Charlotte looked back at such events she grimaced, mourned, and confidently concluded she understood some of the sources of her lifelong insecurity. In so many of her later fiction pieces, she would describe her own youthful "appetite for petting, a fierce longing to be held close—close—and called tender names." No doubt neither Frederick nor Mary had given her the enthusiastic attention and support she wanted; almost certainly she felt disappointed, sometimes rejected, even humiliated, when her parents responded to her teenage histrionics with their characteristic reserve. Nonetheless, her adult recollections of the Boston visit were far more unhappy than her teenage perceptions recorded at the time. For whether or not Frederick kissed her, her diary shows she knew he cared: "Saw father. Had a nice long talk. Called me 'my child.' So nice!"

* * *

However frequent the kisses or the tender names, Charlotte was beginning to learn that the best way to catch her father's eye was not by using winsome smiles and coquettish appeals, but by proving herself intellectually precocious and worldly wise. She had not learned, as many girls did, that feminine dependency would bring respect, or that domestic women were particularly appealing. From Charlotte's point of view, Frederick preferred more successful literary women; and by sending her books and magazines he was telling her how she could become one—not piously or morbidly—but in a way consistent with her castle-building fantasies and whirlwind style. With Harriet Beecher Stowe and several other Beecher relatives, he had written *Six of One by a Half a Dozen of the Other*, a sportive novel about the musical-chair dating antics of a group of precocious youngsters like herself. And in "how to study" guides he preached that learning should be fun. "Have a good time" with books seemed to be the Beecher motto. As Edward Hale would put it, teenagers should choose the "most enlivening way" to learn, otherwise they will "go a-skating, or a-fishing, or a-swimming, or a-voyaging, and not a-reading, and no blame to them."

Charlotte was much more impressed with her father's free-spirited approach to education than she was by the local teachers or schools. In fact, she saw all too little of either: "my total schooling covered four years, among seven different schools, ending when I was fifteen." In part the problem was that she moved around a lot; and in part it was a problem of the times. Only after the Civil War did more than half of the nation's children attend any school at all, and in the 1870s four years' total schooling was still the average. After her family settled in Providence in 1873, Charlotte attended the Young Ladies School of Providence for a while, but the fact that she was absent twenty-three days in the winter term alone suggests that she preferred poetry to the pedestrian: "A tendency to versify, giving recitations in history, grammar, once even in arithmetic, in rhyme, was perhaps indicative of future powers, but no help in examinations." Her grades of 88 in spelling, 83 in composition, and 98 in deportment were mismatched with a 57 in grammar and a 69 in arithmetic.

Still, some school lessons were useful, though not the ones that teachers meant to teach. Instead, Charlotte learned about the pettiness of school authorities, their unfair power games, their uninspired mechanical routines—all of which suggests she was receiving subversive whispers and facetious gibes from Frederick on the sidelines. But at least she liked studying physics, or "Natural Philosophy" as it was then called: "Here was Law, at last; not authority, . . . but laws that could be counted on and *Proved*." Moreover, since they had "parallels in psychology," they could be usefully employed at home: "Friction produces heat, yes, in the bureau drawer that sticks and in the person pulling it." And finally there were shorthand lessons offered by the school; these too had some practical appeal. She would later use them to keep diary entries secret from her prying family and for playing chess by mail with her cousin Arthur Hale.

Far better than anything else at school, however, were the physical fitness classes, especially the exercise programs of energetic organizer-athlete Dr. John P. Brooks. He was a physician in town, the director of the Providence "Gymnasium and Movement Cure," and an itinerant physical fitness teacher in the local schools. There was a rather flat-sounding name for the cause Brooks promoted—the women's "health and hygiene movement"—but in point of fact it was rapidly becoming one of the most exciting parts of Charlotte's life, to say nothing of being one of the most impressively assertive aspects of the contemporary feminist campaign. Most current prescriptive literature glorified the disembodied woman—delicate, spiritual, and sexless. To those like Catharine Beecher, the Blackwell sisters, and other health mentors of the times, however, the sickliness and feebleness encouraged by the feminine ideal seemed absurd. They stressed women's need to develop stronger bodies, to wear looser clothes, to become freer and more active physically as a way of feeling more secure and confident about themselves. With Catharine Beecher's health treatises and John Brooks' practical coaching, and with a bursting energy she would have had to channel in some direction anyway, Charlotte forthwith "took 'to dress reform,' fresh air, cold baths, every kind of attainable physical exercise."

* * *

Whether to spite or to please her parents, or both, Charlotte had become a fifteen-year-old dynamo—energetic and ambitious, academically as well as physically. Already she "read rapaciously" and then reread the works of Charles Dickens, Sir Walter Scott, and countless others. She was running to and from the library with books and magazines, memorizing "miles" of poetry, taking drawing and painting lessons, and practising elocution stunts: Try pronouncing the word "strangledst," she would ask unsuspecting peers, "leaving off one consonant after another to the last 't' and then building it up again, sounding each one distinctly." Try keeping up with me. Years later she would remember that she had never received the warmth she had wanted and needed: "tenderness—never. Never from anyone, and I did want it." But for the moment anyway, she shrugged off the hurt and disappointment, flirted with her friends, and acted as though Mary's aloofness and Frederick's distance mattered not at all.

Chapter Three

Two Opposing Natures 1875-1880

CHARLOTTE'S diaries and letters from 1876 through 1880 (ages fifteen through twenty) often give the impression that she was sporting through life with lighthearted buoyancy. They show her enjoying calls and callers constantly, engaging in quick-witted debates with friends, reading voraciously, delighting in sleigh-ride parties in Roger Williams Park, and romping flirtatiously up and down the hills of Providence. She expressed some intense frustrations in her diaries, to be sure, but in the main she seemed confidently intrigued by the novelty of life. In contrast, a chapter of her autobiography entitled "Girlhood—If Any," begins with the following quotation:

> Sixteen, with a life to build. My mother's profound religious tendency and implacable sense of duty; my father's intellectual appetite; a will power, well developed, from both; a passion of my own for scientific knowledge, for real laws of life; an insatiable demand for perfection in everything, and that proven process of mine for acquiring habits—instead of "Standing with reluctant feet where the brook and river meet," I plunged in and swam.

The excitement and adventure of the plunge into the water, the first years of learning how to swim, are not quite the same in an adult's memory, of course, as they are for a child. The child tends to enjoy the novelty and sport of the moment, the adult to remember the long heavy pull toward more specific ends. It is not surprising then that, in her autobiography, Charlotte preferred to stress her mounting responsibilities, her conscientious approach to the "endless task of building noble character." "As I look over the diaries of the time," she complained defensively, "hardly anything is shown of the desperately serious 'living' which was going on."

Charlotte's autobiography is misleading in a number of respects. Remembering herself as a passive victim more than as a lively rebel sport, she often emphasized not her scheming self-assertiveness, but her self-righteous obedience instead. Not only does the autobiography tell of problems which actually disturbed her—her father's absence, her brother's teasing, her mother's rigid discipline—it also makes assertions which flatly contradict the diaries. For instance, Charlotte recalled that Mary would not allow her to read novels, yet Charlotte read them constantly, often *to* her mother. Intimate friendships were supposedly forbidden; yet Charlotte was busy sending valentines and coquettish letters to her girl friends, staying overnight with them from time to time, and enjoying flirtatious rounds with boys in Providence. It was as though the adult Charlotte tried to veto teenage frolics in her autobiography, just as her mother had done some fifty years before. Charlotte simply forgot what had occurred: "Girlhood, in the usual sense, I never knew." "Instead of flirtations and 'affairs,'—practically no young men came to the house except two who played whist with us," and they "solemnly asked" for her aunt when they called.

Almost inevitably, there is a self-serving dimension in autobiographical writing which warrants distrust. In Charlotte's autobiography, this most certainly is true. Seeking to fortify a public persona she had been shaping carefully for years—disciplined, honorable, humane—she depicted a noble private self. Seeking explanations for recurrent depressions and insecurities, perhaps exoneration from guilt over her own mothering practices, she produced a major scapegoat—her mother—thereby deflecting blame from herself. Moreover, autobiographies generally are "preoccupied with conflicts," with crises and negative experiences. As Gordon Allport puts it, "happy, peaceful periods of time are usually passed over in silence. A few lines may tell of many serene years, whereas pages are devoted to a single humiliating episode or to an experience of suffering. Writers seem driven to elaborate on the conditions that have wrecked their hopes or deprived them of satisfactions."

Even though they contain distortions, Charlotte's autobiography and diaries both provide essential data about her youth. To some extent, they reflect familiar conflicts between adult and childlike inclinations, the autobiography emphasizing Charlotte's earnest goals, the diaries and letters her fun-loving and self-assertive side. But they seem to expose another conflict she was experiencing as well—a conflict, as she later viewed it, between the "feminine" and "masculine" elements within herself, between her mother's "implacable sense of duty" and her father's more independent drive. In any case, by age twenty-one, Charlotte felt that "two opposing natures" in herself had been clashing for years and that it had been a "long tiresome effort to satisfy" them both.

* * *

On December 25, 1875, brother Thomas gave Charlotte a small leather-bound diary with the following inscription:

> Within this book, if *every day*
> You entry make of some import,
> On Christmas next, to you I say
> I'll give one dollar. *Naught if naught.*
>
> Each entry must upon the day
> Be entered, entered be.
> If this rule's broke and is not kept,
> Thou shalt get naught from me.

Charlotte accepted the proposal with "sincere thanks." On the first day she carefully recorded: "By the way, Thomas says he must read all this to be sure that the entries are made. I must look out." The next day she decided Thomas would be the one to look out: "Thomas is more than usually imbecile. That is for him to see, when he reads this." Another day: Thomas is "just unbearable." "Sometimes I almost detest him." He "needs squashing." He "whistled. I laughed. Thomas punched. I got mad. . . . Such a teaser. Such a sneezer!" Then, to snipe a bit against mother too, she wrote, "at home to sew and set the table. However, I don't sew, but pop corn." Housework, apparently, she always found a bore. "Scrubbed" was one day's entire entry. "Ugh! Made 17 Button Holes!" was another. And she was especially irritated when she was forced to "*Celebrate*" her birthday "by washing dishes and ironing."

After several months of this, Charlotte turned to matters of more consequence. The possibility of brother's teasing or mother's disapproval may have bothered her a bit, but the delights of teenage love were too enchanting to exclude. The infatuation of the moment was Mr. "Frog Prince," an actor in "The Frog Opera" at the local theater.

She had yet to meet him, but felt glowingly romantic anyway: "Oh be joyful! I *saw* my darling 4 times. And he saw me! And I blushed! What should I do if I was introduced? Bless him." Several days later she dreamed herself "into a state of beatitude before going to sleep" —Mr. Frog Prince on the sidelines. Only Cousin Arthur Hale could possibly compete, at least at times when brother Thomas was around to watch: "Everything fine and gay, lovely times, poetry and fun," she wrote. "A[rthur] kisses me goodnight, and Thomas looking on! A ha!" Charlotte's diary was rather thin that first year of experimental record-keeping, but she had kept her promise, let out some of her frustrations, and had some fun besides. Already there was an "earnest" bent appearing, but more often than not she expressed it flippantly. At the end of 1876 she wrote, "The last entry! What a wasted year. But I don't know—. Father here. Crambo." And then facing the "memoranda" page she wrote: "Of what shall I make a memoranda? Save that I hereby certify that my cousin Arthur says he isn't in love with me, and don't want to marry me, yet hangs around all the time and kisses me on all occasions. Dear boy! How nice he is!"

If discipline and disapproval were Charlotte's major problems, her early diary entries don't usually show how much they hurt. For instance, when her family was about to leave the Grenville Stevens cooperative, she wrote, "We leave here Saturday, loaded with 'Stevenish' opprobrium. 'Fiddle de dee'!" Or, after going to a party at the home of some relatives, she wrote, "Dance or not to dance? Charlotte versus mother. Drew, wrote, fun." Then, however, on April 18, 1877 (age sixteen) she wrote, "Oh dear! Oh dear! An invitation from Robert to a *College* concert and one from Edward to *Booth* in *Hamlet*. & I couldn't accept either! Mother didn't think 'twas best. Oh dear! Oh dear!" According to her autobiography, this encounter left a "ghastly impression" and a lifelong numbness to disappointment.

> One of mother's cousins, ten years older than I, invited me to a students' concert at Brown. Mother declined for me. . . . I made no complaint, being already inured to denial. But that same day another of those cousins, twenty years older than I, asked me to go with him and his sisters to sit in a box, and see Edwin Booth in *Hamlet*.
>
> Booth! *Hamlet!* A box! Nothing in all the world could have meant so much to me at the time. And mother refused. Why? She afterwards explained that having refused Robert, she feared that if she accepted Edward's invitation it would hurt Robert's feelings. How about mine? . . . The unparalleled glory offered

> and the pitiful inadequacy of the reason for its denial made a ghastly impression on my mind. Something broke. Perhaps it was like what is called "a broken heart." At any rate I have never since that day felt the sharp sting of disappointment, only a numb feeling.

Apparently, this was just one of the prohibitions that Mary imposed—fast and furiously. Whether she was punishing Charlotte for some of her own unhappiness, or simply continuing with restraints characteristic of the times, in Charlotte's view, Mary was increasingly unreasonable. She required a "submission to a tutelage so exacting that even the letters I wrote were read, as well as those I received; an account was always demanded of where I had been, whom I had seen, and what they said—there was no unhandled life for me." Mary was "rigorous in refusing all manner of invitations for me," and "forbade practically every pleasure that offered."

At times, Charlotte responded to her mother's prohibitions by obeying them, quietly and resentfully posing as the martyr. After all, that was what Mary did from time to time—demand sympathy as the mistreated wife and mother. Charlotte could imitate her nicely by suffering as the mistreated child, the dutiful daughter who had no choice but to obey passively. There was something strangely comforting about the process, feeling so clearly wronged, fuming against her scoundrel mother even while following some of mother's ways, perhaps identifying with some of Mary's troubles by punishing herself. The reward was tension-filled "peace and quiet"; the price was seething rage, then self-pity, then depression. As Charlotte later remembered, these were "steady years of self-enforced obedience to management I heartily disapproved of, and which was in some ways lastingly injurious."

In her autobiography, Charlotte stressed the negative effects of Mary's discipline, and the negative example Mary set, as though Charlotte and her mother both usually responded to life's problems unassertively. Of course, they did not always respond unassertively. Mary's reproofs may have set the stage for some of Charlotte's insecurities, but Mary's strength inspired her to resist—consciously and aggressively. Charlotte learned to "fight fire with fire," as she would put it, "to seek perfection in everything," so that Mary's "forbiddings were lost in the shuffle, as it were." Charlotte later regretted some of her self-protective, stoic strategies, but she also remembered embracing them with a sense of grandiosity which matched her Beecher heritage, a gamesmanship that suited her teenage fancy, and a self-control that meant she, not her mother, had control.

> The first step was to establish prompt and easy execution of decisions, to connect cerebral action with the motor nerves. . . . I deliberately set about a course of exercises in which small and purely arbitrary decisions were sharply carried out. . . . The essence of this method is in its complete detachment. There is no temptation to be overcome, no difficulty to be met, nothing but a simple expression of will. Such exercises, carried on thoroughly, do develop the habit of executing one's decisions, and make it easy when there is something serious to be done.
>
> With each trait to be acquired the Process was used; determination, self-suggestion, "making up the mind"—"I *will* think before I speak!"

At times Charlotte was a bit self-righteous about her self-training programs: "I was bent on doing my best, and eager for self-improvement." But she could also be more flippant. For instance, a friend approached: "Charlotte, I have heard that you said that I lied! You didn't, did you?" Charlotte had, and said so. "But you don't believe it do you?" Charlotte did and said so. Likewise, she taught herself consideration: "Now I don't care anything about you, yet, but I'd like to," she told a "poor invalid" little girl of the neighborhood. "Will you let me come and practice on you?" Apparently, the process was successful. She learned to like the girl she practiced on, and at least momentarily won the compliment she craved: someone "said that she did like Charlotte Perkins—she was so thoughtful of other people. 'Hurrah' said I, 'another game won!'"

Much later, Charlotte captured this Amazonian self-image in her novel, *Benigna Machiavelli*. The teenage heroine of the story mirrors the teenage Charlotte.

> What do I want to do in life?
> I want to be big—Big—BIG!
> I want to know everything—as far as I can.
> I want to be strong, skillful, an armory of concealed weapons.
> I want to be far more able than anybody knows.

Benigna Machiavelli is tactically brilliant and worldly wise: "I'm a Machiavelli, and proud of it. The Scotch name I have to wear outside, like a sort of raincoat, but my real name I always feel is Machiavelli, Benigna Machiavelli. I mean never to marry and change it."

Charlotte's teenage self-image was strikingly portentous. By the time she was eighteen, she already seemed to feel that her self-discipline was reaping rich rewards, and that she was headed for greatness. She was uncertain about her specific goals in life, of course, but the expectation-wish for prominence was so strong that she had to tell the world how powerful she felt. On January 1, 1879, she wrote in her diary:

> Gentle reader, wouldst thou know me? Verily, here I am. 18 years old. 5 feet, 6½ in. high, weigh some 120 lbs, or thereabouts. Looks, not bad. At times handsome. At others decidedly homely. Health, Perfect. Strength amazing. Character—Ah! Gradually outgrowing laziness. Possessing great power over myself. *Not* sentimental. Rather sober and bleak as a general thing. At present I am not in love with anybody; I don't think I ever shall be.

* * *

Her schemes for personal behavior well designed and executed, Charlotte decided, in the fall of her eighteenth year, to go back to school. Thomas was going to study at MIT (where he had failed the year before), her favorite Boston cousins (Edward Everett Hale's sons) were to study at Harvard, and many of the men she knew in Providence were students at Brown. Most women of her generation would not have expected a chance for higher education, but coming from the Beecher family, where female education was so highly valued, Charlotte set her hopes on the Rhode Island School of Design, just opening in Providence. Mary balked at first. She argued that a girl should "remain in her mother's sphere until she entered her husband's." Still, since studying art and painting was thought to be appropriately cultured and refined, and since Frederick agreed to foot the bills, Mary finally gave her blessing: "I Mary A. Perkins, do hereby agree and covenant never to badger my beloved and obedient daughter on the subject of going to the Art School, having given my *full* and *free* consent to her so doing." *

Father gave his written approbation too. "Go to the School of Design by all means, and learn all you can. You could not do a better thing." But then—unfortunately—he offered some disclaimers which must have hurt. It was as though he had to establish an appropriate fatherly indifference to neutralize his affectionate intent. He wrote that for the future, she could expect him to send books occasionally, some catalogues of books, some guidelines for her history reading, but very little else.

> As for writing letters, I don't expect ever to write anything except notes any more, & no more of those than I can help; but

* So said a notation in Charlotte's diary which Mary probably wrote, though possibly it simply reflected Charlotte's wishful thinking.

> I shall be pleased to help you about studying if I can. You may have the $5.00 for clothes, and you may tell me how much more you need for the winter, and I will furnish it *if I can*. If I cannot, you must go without. At any rate I can not myself get any new clothes; —however, such things are more important to you than to me, so figure away.

Possibly because of Frederick's coolness, more likely because of other family strains, the Rhode Island School of Design did not seem to have much impact. Charlotte enjoyed improving her skills as an artist, but she remembered the hikes back and forth to school more than the lessons when she got there, her athletic feats more than her academic or artistic ones. It was a "two miles' walk a day. In the coldest weather I'd start off so briskly that before long I'd have my mittens off and coat unbuttoned, smiling triumphantly at chillier people." And since classes were on the top floor of a five-story building, the stairs became a major challenge too: "in a month or so I was running up the whole four flights two steps at a time and beating the elevator."

One reason Charlotte remembered so little about the Rhode Island School of Design may have been that family problems kept her home during much of the winter of 1878–1879. As her family responsibilities increased, work at the art school slipped to second place.

Thomas was still Charlotte's hero—especially since he had gone away to school—and she had peppered her diaries with expletives to show it. "Oh! TOMMIS IS COME! Rah! Rah! Rah!" she would write. Or "Ouf! Ouf! Tommis is gone away!" Apparently his vacation visits had always seemed too short. Then, in November 1878, Thomas failed out of MIT. He had already been bounced out once the year before; this time it was for good. However glad Charlotte was to see him, she felt keenly disappointed with his news. "Thomas comes. And Oh, he comes to stay! Failed again! I wonder if he will ever amount to anything."

There had been a time when Charlotte had resented Thomas' preferred position as a male, but during the last several years she had sometimes felt more piqued with his irresponsibility than jealous of his opportunities. No longer did she have to worry about his becoming the favored hero of the family, or posing as Mary's male protector. In fact, just the opposite. From Mary's point of view, Charlotte was the more reliable of her two children: more supportive emotionally as well as financially.* Thomas was somewhat like his

*There is an interesting comment of Mary's in a letter written to Isabella Beecher Hooker the following spring (May 1879). Mary at that time was considering the possibility of moving to Hartford to live closer to the Beech-

father: irresponsible, ungainful, capricious. With Frederick increasingly distant and Thomas a disappointment and a worry, Charlotte may have tried to take the place of both. At times the responsibilities made her feel proud and important; at other times she felt resentful and exhausted instead. In any case, when Thomas came down with diptheria, home duties intensified, as did Mary's emotional demands; Charlotte tried some hard-line stoic resolutions to muster her strength.

> Having after much toil arrived at a state where pain and pleasure are nearly immaterial to me I now resolve to practice Duty for a while. Without the slightest doubt that as I progress it will grow easier and pleasanter till I shall never be tempted to forsake it. Of course some slips are to be expected, but I long ago learned not to be discouraged by them. A steady struggle if never willfully relaxed, is invincible in such matters.

Charlotte was only eighteen, yet already she sometimes viewed life as "toil" and "steady struggle," and told herself that her own pain and pleasure did not count. Then she became ill (possibly with diptheria). One of her first major depressions followed.

> If it were not for mother I had just as lief "go out" as not. As a tired child drops asleep, I could lay down my arms, and stop the endless battle in this world, without any feeling but calm content, but I won't, for her sake; and—I blush to own it, because I would be pointed out as an example of foolhardy recklessness.

With suicidal fantasies thus in conflict with her sense of "Duty" and "Right," and with her fears of disapproval as well, her situation worsened yet again. Now Mary became ill. Charlotte wanted to be the cared-for child herself, to receive comfort and sympathy, not to give it. When Mary needed nursing and comforting instead, Charlotte felt despondent, even resentful. She wrote, "Mother is scared and blue. Her throat *is* sore. I believe I have no heart." Or several days later, "Mother is very cross and fretty. As for me, I weep. Pretty business."

Fortunately, both Charlotte and Mary had relatively minor bouts of illness and recovered rather quickly. Thomas was their principal

---

er relatives. She wrote, "Thomas would hope to get some situation in Hartford where he could earn enough to pay his board. Charlotte would more than pay hers by her labor" (Mary Westcott Perkins to Isabella Beecher Hooker, May 26, 1879, SD).

concern. He had developed a lung infection that seemed so critical that Charlotte wrote her father asking him to come to Providence. It was a tension-filled nightmare scene, Thomas needing round-the-clock attention, Charlotte wanting some support. She felt nothing but indifference instead, first from Mary (preoccupied and worried) and then from Frederick too. Charlotte's sardonic diary entry reads: "Postman with letter from father saying he will come if it is necessary!" Not surprisingly, she responded with some self-destructive sullen tactics of her own. First she railed against Thomas and mother; then she turned the bulk of stored-up anger against herself.

> How blind people are! . . . One would think I was the worst of criminals to hear my accusations at times. And Thomas too! One would think he had enough to answer for without molesting me. I must really abolish all desire for comfort or any sort of happiness if I expect to have any peace. Things look black tonight. A person who has a good creed and does not follow it is a weak fool.

With rationality battling against emotional frustrations, and domestic responsibilities keeping her home from school, Charlotte found that reading aloud in the evenings with her mother was one of the few comforts she had. Mary seemed so much closer during these quiet reading times, and questions of the mind seemed so much more appealing than the endless family strains. "We were both permeated with cold chills" from the "mere contact" with "clear strong ideas," she wrote, "the even mythical possibilities of the human will." They "roused me from my enervating course of novel reading during these sick times. I long for science again."

* * *

Time and again, Charlotte seemed to respond to domestic crises by turning to her books. Undoubtedly she wished "to help humanity," as she later remembered, but reading was also a way to help herself, to alleviate introspective worry, to strengthen bonds with both her parents since she could not seem to reach them in any other way. With Mary, the contact through books was direct and emotionally intense. Mary and Charlotte especially liked reading sentimental novels together, "enervating" though they might be. They would "weep and snivel consumedly." As Charlotte later put it, "I break down, and mother reads and sobs while I stand by the stove and dry my handkerchief." With Frederick, however, the intellectual contacts were becoming more serious, more sober. Charlotte assumed he would not disapprove of her reading sentimental novels, since he wrote them himself. But she also knew he would expect her to taste stronger fare.

For years, Charlotte's strategy for gaining Frederick's interest had been to demonstrate her precocious mental skills, to follow his "masculine" example and become independent, creative, worldly-wise. As she rather piously recorded in her autobiography, she had written to her father at the age of seventeen explaining that she wished "to help humanity," that she realized she must "understand history," and "where should [she] begin?" Or, as she put it in her diary, "Have taken a fancy to work hard and be very smart," and to devour all the books in sight. "Let us call good reading solid food; novels candy, poetry fruit—and nonsense the peanuts of life." In any case, Frederick recommended that she study the works of Reform Darwinists: *Five Great Empires* by George Rawlingson, *Prehistoric Times* and *Origins of Civilization* by Sir John Lubbock, *Early History of Mankind* by Edward Tylor. All these provided the foundations of her understanding of "logic and important systems of ideas," she recalled. They provided the necessary tools for grappling with "the problem of evil, long baffling so many." Her autobiographical description continues:

> So I sat me down before the problem of evil, thus:
>
> "I will go back to the period of a molten world, where we can call nothing right or wrong, and follow carefully up the ages—see where it comes in." So I followed the process until the earth was cool enough to allow the formation of crystals, each square or pentagonal or whatever was its nature, and then if one was broken or twisted, I pounced upon the fact—"here it is! It is right for this to be a hexagon, wrong for it to be squeezed flat. . . . That is right for a given organism which leads to its best development.". . .
>
> As to pain—? I observed that the most important continuous functions of living are unconsciously carried on within us; . . . that just being alive is a pleasure; that pain does not come in unless something goes wrong. . . . God is good.

Charlotte was looking for relief, "something to be depended on when immediate conditions did not tend to produce right conduct," and something which would give a greater sense of purpose too. It was vaguely defined, of course, as it was for so many reform-oriented contemporary women. Thus far she had only her delightfully heady and ambitious dreams, inspired first by her "world serving" family models, and then secured by a pragmatic religious faith. "God was

Real," she decided, "under and in and around everything, lifting, lifting. We, conscious of that limitless power, were to find our places, our special work in the world, and when found, do it, do it at all costs."

Charlotte was becoming more religious and more serious in her reading programs, but she was still playful and rebellious and, like her father, something of a skeptic besides. Publicly, she preferred to stress her unique self-styled perspicacity, an "innate incredulity which refused to accept anybody's say-so." Privately, however, she realized that her father's promptings helped. In "reading all men's opinions," he had written her, "it is necessary to be careful and remember that they are opinions." Charlotte very happily did just that—even in pious talks with preachers. On one occasion, for instance, a local clergyman found her "holding communion with nature"—or so he apparently believed. Actually, Charlotte proudly quipped, there was no "communion" happening at all: "I was reading a tale called 'Drink in the Streets.' I smuggled it away while he appeared." And then "I tackled the old gentleman beautifully. He thought I was a convert sure, started finely on 'now is the appointed hour' etc., but I fear he found it a disappointed hour for him. He struggled manfully but I withstood him and really made him squirm. Fine fun."

Part of the "fun" of course was bantering about precocious views with friends, shocking them if she could, or at least trying to impress them with her *savoir faire*. And that was no small challenge, hobnobbing as Charlotte was with the daughters and sons of some of the most intellectually prominent families in the area: Ada Blake, daughter of Brown University physics professor Eli Whitney Blake; Esther Carpenter, who reportedly read Shakespeare with her father at the age of eleven and studied German, French, and Spanish in her teenage years; May Diman, daughter of history professor J. Louis Diman; Mary and Grace Channing, daughters of scientist and inventor William F. Channing, and granddaughters of the famed transcendentalist thinker and Unitarian clergyman William Ellery Channing; Charlotte Hedge, daughter of a prominent Unitarian minister in Cambridge; Harriet and Eliza, the children of Harriet Beecher Stowe; and finally, the Hale cousins in Boston, the sons of her uncle Edward Everett Hale. Never one to miss an opportunity, Charlotte managed to be fed, entertained, and warmly welcomed into some of the most intellectually stimulating families in New England.

Domestic responsibilities notwithstanding, then, Charlotte had plenty of time for seeing friends, and, apparently, the more money and brains they had, the better. For instance, in the winter of 1879 (the same winter Thomas was so ill and her own frustrations were so severe), she wrote in her diary: "Hurrah! Go to the Essay Club! . . . Make the acquaintance of my double, Miss [Ada or Alida] Blake, and Miss Carrie [Caroline] Hazard. . . . I shall diligently encourage the Hazards one and all. For why? They are agreeable. They are smart, i.e., intelligent. They are (two of them) noble youths. They have a country residence in Peacedale. They have (here we come to it) SADDLE HORSES!!!"*

Prosperous, cultured, and confidently upper class, the Hazard family suited Charlotte perfectly. Their saddle horses were superb, the elegance of their homes impressive, and their literary-intellectual discussions fascinating given her precocious tastes. The Hazard youngsters—with their tutors, foreign travel, and high-class private schooling—may have possessed more polish and refinement, but probably not more prodigious ego or more energy and drive. Especially encouraging was the Hazard attitude toward the women in the family. Hazard women did not sit respectfully on the sidelines as the men reflected on the problems of the world. They held their own, sometimes aggressively so, and had every reason for developing confidence and pride. The elder sister Caroline Hazard, for instance, was not only well educated and well respected in the community, she would later publicly promote progressive views of women's dignity and honor that she had very likely first learned at home. In a manner reminiscent of Catharine Beecher, Caroline

* Charlotte believed that she was welcomed into the Hazard family because of her close resemblance to Ada Blake, younger first cousin of Caroline Hazard.

Caroline Hazard's father, Rowland Hazard II, was superintendent of the Peacedale Woolen Mills, a scientist, a man of letters, and a philanthropist. Prolific author as well as respected business leader of the community, he was a theoretical and practical enthusiast of the profit-sharing system, which, on the model of the Rochedale cooperative establishment in England, he introduced into the Peacedale Woolen Mills. The system so impressed Hazard's friend and colleague, Edward Everett Hale, that Hale commended it as one which was "changing laborers who drudge into workmen who work for God." A man of "genius and poetic insight," Hale continued, Rowland Hazard worked "amid spools and spindles and yarns and webs," discussing "the highest problems of philosophy in the counting-room of a mill" (Edward E. Hale, *Roland Hazard Memorial* [Peacedale, R.I., 1891], pp. 34–35).

Caroline Hazard was four years Charlotte's senior, and a favored protégée of Brown University History Professor J. Lewis Diman. He sponsored lecture series and discussion groups for women in the community, offered ad-

Hazard would write, "There are three ways in which women are preeminent: They are the binders together of society, they are the beautifiers of life, and they are the preservers of morals." Women are the "great conservative force in society."

* * *

Charlotte's teenage education—autobiographical disclaimers notwithstanding—was quite a fascinating venture. It was not lonely or isolated, not always piously profound, and certainly not exclusively confined to books. A fun-loving youngster as well as an aspiring reformer, she liked the Hazards' horses as much as the Hazards' brains, and she enjoyed flirtatious social whirlwinds as much as intellectual debates. In fact, Charlotte worked almost as conscientiously on social skills as she did on academic ones, jotting down her progress in her diary, and planning trips to test her talents. For instance, just before she turned eighteen, she had been visiting the Hale family in Boston, and enjoying it immensely—especially swimming, sailing, and carousing with her kissing cousin Arthur Hale. "We understand each other now," she wrote, "and rest on a calm super-flirtatious ground." Sometimes Providence would seem rather disappointing to her after coming back from Boston trips, but, judging from her diaries, dullness was the exception, not the norm. "I am feeling very lonesome and unsatisfied just now. I am entirely deprived of any intercourse with the other sex, and it makes me one sided and unhappy. I don't think it is right." Fortunately, the lulls were temporary, and, for the most part, Charlotte busied herself pursuing male attention, though not always successfully. "He came, he saw, he conquered, but he quickly went away," wrote a very stoic Charlotte.

Without question, the Boston visits were the highlights of each year. Presumably her uncle Edward Hale's home provided some intellectual enticements, but Charlotte hardly mentioned them. She talked about "super-flirtatious" games instead, about Harvard class-day celebrations, and about all the teas, dances, and parties she attended. After one particularly dazzling vacation visit (age nineteen),

---

vice on tutorial or self-educational plans, and helped women make contacts with many of his colleagues. So well respected was Caroline Hazard among Diman's Brown University friends, that with their patronage she later published Diman's memoirs. She also became a social worker for the children of the laborers in her father's woolen mills, a prolific writer, and fifth president of Wellesley College. For the Hazard family in general, and for Caroline Hazard in particular, women's right to education was axiomatic.

she wrote, "I never was so courted and entertained and amused and done for in all my little life. It seems as if the memory of today would last me in solid comfort through all the ills that flesh is heir to. . . . Why to think of its being ME!" Or, as she put it in a letter to her younger cousin Houghton Gilman: "What joys were mine! I went sleighing, went to the theater, I went to parties, and I received calls. Bye and bye, when you 'are old and hideous, and the hairs of your beard are mostly grey,' as the poet says, you will understand the joys of such an existence."

Charlotte was so effervescent, so irrepressibly delighted with her teenage social rounds that there must have been times when her mother understood, tolerated, or perhaps even vicariously enjoyed them. In any case, Mary trusted Charlotte enough to take some independent jaunts of her own—to cousin Isabella Beecher Hooker's home in Hartford, to the Hales in Boston, to other relatives as well. Meanwhile Charlotte was left to "reign supreme" in Providence, to revel "in the solitary grandeur," and to "verily rejoice" when Mary returned. There were plenty of arguments with Mary, but Charlotte often won, noting the incidents calmly, sometimes flippantly, in her diary. For instance, she made it a point to "notify mother" about a sleigh-ride party. Mary "*strenuously complains*," Charlotte wrote, and then sported off gaily anyway. A week later: "Potter home in the wet at 4:30 A.M." from another sleigh ride fete. Or again, "little fight with Mama," or "Mother is abothering me." Doubtless Charlotte felt freer on her Cambridge visits, but she caroused in Providence as well, particularly with Sam and Jim Simmons, two Brown University students she had met. For instance, Sam would call to play whist: "Mother introduces her new rule of stopping at 10, but I smile on, and he prolongs his call until 11." Or when Jim invited her out: "Mother smiling, I go and enjoy it immensely. One continuous giggle." Fascinated with the intrigues and necessary calculations of nineteenth-century–style dating, Charlotte exulted in her "splendid" escapades, her "uproarious jollification" with recent conquests Sam and Jim, whom she viewed alternately as competitors, jokesters, and flirtatious "swains."

* * *

Over the last several years, Charlotte had become increasingly confident, in fact, inordinately pleased with herself: pleased with her "uproarious" ventures, her perspicacious friends, her consciously devised self-improvement feats. As she put it at the end of 1878, "My greatest fault now is inordinate egotism." At times, of course, she felt discouraged. They "all call me excitable and head strong; and all that," she wrote. "But I know that I am not. I ask in despair now how many more years of quiet self-control will be necessary." For the most part, however, she wrote of her "progress and considerable improvement," a self-evaluation Mary would have probably confirmed. In fact, Charlotte was becoming Mary's mainstay, often as energetically resourceful in supporting Mary as she was in subverting Mary's power. For instance, Charlotte helped her mother form a small day school for "young scholars" and, thanks to her art school training, earned extra money by selling flower paintings as well.* She and her cousin Robert Brown even initiated their own "joint enterprise"—"the Perkins and Co. Designers"—earning some three hundred and seventy dollars by selling hand-painted advertising cards to the Kendall Soap Company. So responsible did Charlotte feel on money matters that she even undertook to negotiate finances with her father, and to badger him, if need be, for rent payments he had promised. In one diary entry she quipped sarcastically, "Pleasing epistle from father stating that he can't send us any more money for some months. This is too redikelous." Or again, "My respected papa returns the rent bills mother sent him."

In some respects, Charlotte was becoming increasingly supportive of her mother, and increasingly annoyed with her father's penny-pinching style, his dry, infrequent letters, his distance. Charlotte felt especially close to Mary after Thomas left home. In the fall of 1879, Thomas had taken a position as railroad surveyor in Nevada, thanks to the advice and help of his uncle Edward Hale. Mary was proud, but she also was crushed. She still had a few close relationships with women—particularly with her half-sister Caroline Robbins,† who lived with Mary and Charlotte from time to time—but Thomas' departure seemed a stark reminder of earlier separations from Frederick, and of her own inability to keep the men she loved at home.

* Caroline Hazard bought one of her pictures for thirty dollars, which made Charlotte feel ecstatic.

† Caroline Robbins had become a widow several years before and probably commiserated with Mary through current family sorrows as well as joined her in coping with economic and domestic strains. Author of an 1876 book entitled *Poems and Anti-Slavery Drama in Prose and Verse,* Caroline Robbins wrote the sort of thing Mary seemed to like to hear: cathartic poems bemoaning slavery's evils (published post–Civil War), eulogies on the pious works of famous Beechers, sententious religious prayers, songs of troubled mothers weeping for their young. Although Mary Perkins and Caroline Robbins were no doubt mutually supportive in many ways, grief and misery may have sometimes been their strongest common bond.

Mary wrote to Isabella Beecher Hooker: "I suppose I ought to feel glad, but I find it hard to be reconciled to have him so far away, and exposed to danger and sickness, where I could not go to him. I don't take any kind of separations easy except death, and then I can bow to God's will."

At times, Charlotte seemed pleased about her relationship with Mary—the sense of special closeness, the companionship, the sharing. They enjoyed shopping together, playing chess in the evenings (Charlotte usually winning), sleeping together, and, of course, commiserating their way through sentimental novels. There were also times, however, when Mary seemed to be a burden, when Charlotte's sense of duty clashed too strongly with her hankering for independence, or when claustrophobic domesticity interfered with teenage frolics she preferred. So strong was Charlotte's resentment (in retrospect anyway—at the time she simply felt depressed), that she would later argue that mother-daughter relationships could be among the most oppressive of a young girl's life: The "dutiful daughter" becomes affectionate, considerate, and efficient, assumes the responsibility for household management, and relieves the burdens of her victimized unhappy mother, but in the process runs the risk of becoming a victim herself. Charlotte knew the feeling well. For even though Mary had managed her responsibilities as a single parent fairly well, Charlotte, like the heroines of many of her later novels, learned the requisite daughter skills, understood her mother needed help, and, at times at least, was overwhelmed by her mother's troubles and demands. Charlotte experienced the late winter of 1881 (age twenty), like the winter when Thomas was so ill (1879), as a particularly depressing one.

In January and early February of 1881, Charlotte seemed to take domestic chores in stride, finish them quickly, and then rush off to "jolly" sleigh-ride parties or sundry ventures with her friends. For instance, on January 15 she wrote, "Up in the broad bright starry moonlight and work thereby—Do all the housework, sweep kitchen, fill lamp and such, and do the whole ironing before 10:15." Or on February 20: "Fix everything as clean and cozy as could be. . . . Hop up and get dinner, 'chops and tomato sauce,' wash dishes, more buttons." Then, in late February, Mary became ill; Charlotte stayed home all day to nurse her, and before long was morbidly depressed. February 24: "I am no sort of good with invalids," she wrote. "Don't do a thing but loaf around and tend mother." Or several days later, "Feel discontented generally." By early March, even stoic resolutions failed to boost her spirits: "Being in a season of moroseness and depression I laboriously grovel through the work and then help mother make an old black silk for me." The next day she could write very little, she noted, "on account of causeless weariness and total lack of events." And on March 5: "Arise morosely in our 6th consecutive day of all pervading gloom."

* * *

Charlotte's moods alternated that winter of 1881, home-based responsibilities causing frustration and depression, nondomestic projects sparking her energy and drive, although usually with some underlying guilt. Charlotte seemed unable to comply easily and happily with the lessons her mother tried to teach—to be the dutiful daughter, to content herself with feminine concerns, to aspire to "true womanhood" ideals of passive pious purity. She was too fun-loving and vivacious for that, too resentful of her mother, too envious of her father, and too much of a Beecher besides. For while Charlotte could accept the notion that adult concerns must replace childlike "imbecilities," she found the conventional distinctions between masculine and feminine adult not to her liking at all. Femininity, like childishness, she hoped to overcome; it suggested her mother's dependence and vulnerability. Masculinity—meaning creativity, strength, her father's more worldly style of life—was the model she had chosen for herself. In any case, about a month after the domestic doldrums episode with Mary, Charlotte decided to sidle back to Frederick—cautiously and icily—to reclaim his attention if she could.

Aligning herself with Frederick was in some ways painful, to be sure. She had to disassociate herself from Mary, while sensing fully that her relationship with her mother had been among the closest of her life. Possibly Charlotte handled the conflict by viewing herself as a masculine protector; with her precocious strengths, she could alleviate some of Mary's suffering. The trouble was that Charlotte admired, even envied, what her mother feared—her father's independence, his fancy-free escape. Inevitably, Charlotte's feelings were confused. She loved her father and wanted to be like him; yet she hated him as well, not only for the suffering he caused her mother, but also for the rejections she had experienced from him herself. Charlotte seemed to ask for his affection and approval, but in cool hostile terms, designed to hurt.

> Dear Father,
>
> I am twenty-one this 3rd of July, have outgrown sundry imbecilities of which I wrote you at the age of fifteen; and am

rapidly turning into an unattractive strong-minded old maid. . . . Life looks broad and pleasant, with much to do for the general good, and personal pain or pleasure not worth counting on. . . .

I know of old that you are too busy to write letters, even if you cared to, but I *should* like to know whether you wish me to write to you, for I am anything but desirous to intrude.

Do you know,—I think I should have liked you very much—as a casual acquaintance.

1881-1890

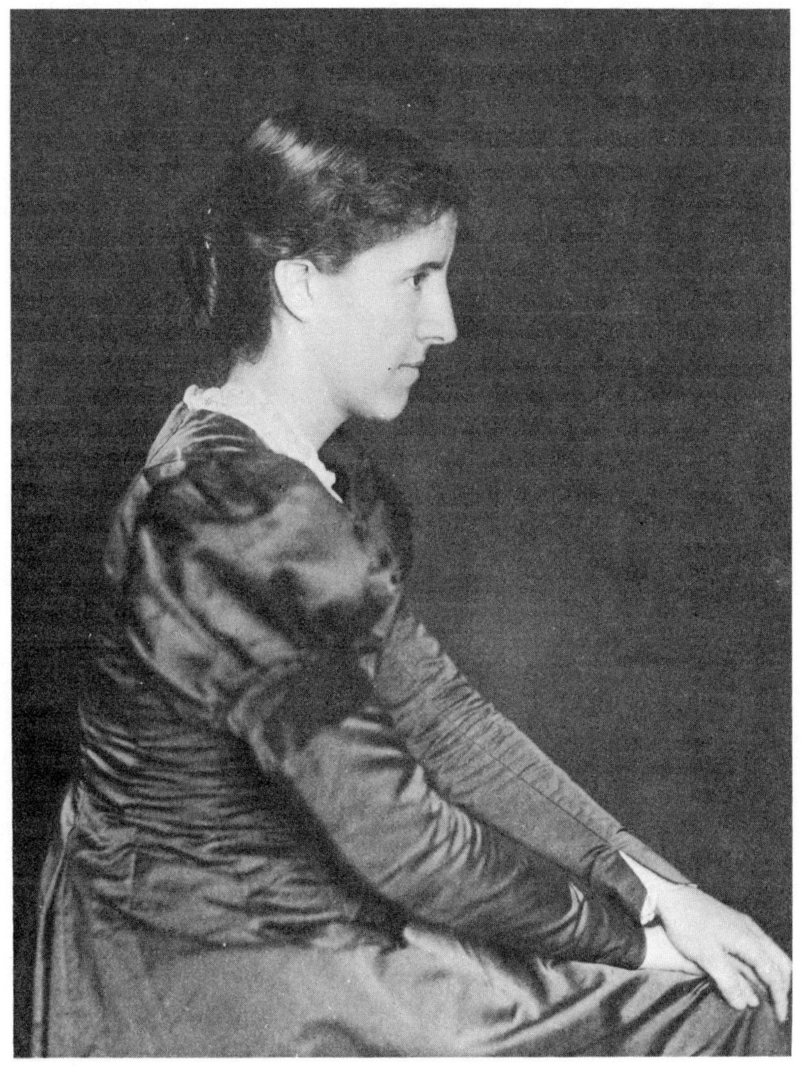

Chapter Four

Martha
1881

DESPITE the dispassionate facade she projected for her father, and despite some occasional heavy-hearted gloom, Charlotte saluted her twenty-first birthday in a mood of ecstasy and vindication, anticipating a long-delayed escape. She was pleased with the economic self-sufficiency which painting and teaching provided her, and also inordinately jubilant about her self-improvement feats. Physical fitness training, lecture clubs, language classes, history-science reading programs—all these kept her busy from 5:00 A.M. to 10:00 P.M. and thriving in the process. In the autumn of her twenty-first year she wrote, "I never knew before what it was to be busy *every* minute of a day. From the time I wake up at 5 with an instantaneous bounce out of bed; to the time when I sit in my little chair just long enough to review the events of the day and crawl into my sheeted Paradise, there is not a moment wasted. Little bits of idleness when I stop to play with Belinda [the cat] a second etc. are not wasted for they are necessary rest. And O I like it!" Even in her autobiography she proudly reminisced about the "Power and Glory" she had felt at twenty-one: "My health was splendid, I never tired, with a steady cheerfulness which external discomforts or mishaps could not dim. When asked 'How do you do?' it was my custom to reply, 'as well as a fish, as busy as a bee, as strong as a horse, as proud as a peacock, as happy as a clam.'"

Enterprising, vigorous, and peacock-proud, Charlotte had chosen William Blaikie's *How to Get Strong and How to Stay So* (1879) as her bedside Bible, her Atalanta-guidebook for the coming race.* At

*In classical mythology, Atalanta was a huntress who devised numerous

nineteen she had written, "Follow Blaikie every night with the greatest assiduity. I can put all my fingers on the floor, knees rigid and count 30." She also practiced other Blaikie-recommended skills —weight-lifting, gymnastics, even running the seven-minute mile. Physical fitness, Blaikie wrote, was the key "to sanity and mental power; to self-respect and high purpose; to sound health and vigorous enduring strength; to genial, attractive good-nature, and to sunny welcome cheerfulness." That message suited Charlotte perfectly. Like Catharine Beecher, Blaikie thought female frailty and feebleness was offensive, injurious, and absurd, and, almost one hundred years before Joan Ullyot wrote the popular *Women's Running* manual, he championed the cause some people assume is just a recent fad. "*Among American women running is a lost art*," Blaikie wrote in 1879. "Yet you will have hard work to find an exercise that will begin to do as much to make a girl or woman graceful as correct running. Girls should *all learn to run*." Like so many women in the contemporary women's health and hygiene movement, Charlotte did just that: "each day I ran a mile, not for speed but wind, . . . I could vault and jump, go up a knotted rope, walk on my hands under a ladder, kick as high as my head, and revel in the flying rings."

With William Blaikie's advice reinforcing that of Catharine Beecher, the Blackwell sisters, and other physical fitness enthusiasts in the women's movement, Charlotte had been developing her athletic skills for years. By the age of twenty-one, however, she wanted more systematic training, a group of friends to practice with, and a place where they could work. Besides, a gymnastics class designed especially for women would mean delightful get-togethers with her friends, not only to work on toe-touching and weight-lifting routines, but also to have dances, polka races, and some carefree socializing fun. So Charlotte and her friends began badgering Dr. John P. Brooks, the local gymnastics teacher, to help them start a women's class. They were scheming for a hall, Charlotte wrote Martha Luther, "with 'facilities' wherein we could wear abbreviated garments and elevate the massive dumbbell at our leisure. And a lady physician to examine us and tell what course we should pursue." Obviously, the goal wasn't physical attractiveness in conventional true-womanhood terms. She wanted a body that was useful, agile, strong, not a passive object she would wait for others to approve. To twenty-one-year-old Charlotte, organizing the gymnastics classes seemed another self-affirming coup.

Charlotte felt that somehow there had been a turning point when

---

schemes to avoid marriage, including outrunning her male suitors. She finally lost to Hippomenes, who used Aphrodite's assistance to distract her.

she had finally reached the age of twenty-one: "No long-tutored heir to a kingdom ever came to the throne with a more triumphant sense of freedom and power than mine when I reached my twenty-first birthday." Not only did she delight in her own physicality, she delighted in the effort to control her body as part of the larger effort to control her life. She locked her door "actually and metaphorically," sat up all night because it was forbidden, slept on the floor once, out on the roof another time (again, mother told her not to), and generally indulged in, or "wasted [her] substance in," equivalent "riotous—virtues."

The most satisfying and assertive demonstration of her heightened sense of freedom, however, was a passionately effusive correspondence with her close friend Martha Luther, a "gentle, lovely intellectual girl," an admirer and confidante. They had tried corresponding several years before. But the more sustained efforts began—dramatically and incautiously—just two weeks after Charlotte turned twenty-one. There was good reason for some momentary hesitation—a portentous awareness that her intimate loving correspondence with her girl friend might someday come to public view, and that "Philistines" could never understand—but Charlotte profusely, almost defiantly, poured out her private thoughts and feelings anyway. She wrote to Martha, "What horrid stuff these letters would be for the Philistines! Lock 'em up, and sometime we'll have a grand cremation." Or again, "Incidental thought, wouldn't these letters of mine be nuts for commentators! *If* & *if* of course, but how they would squabble over indistinct references and possible meanings!"

* * *

Martha Luther and Charlotte had been friends for several years. They had hiked miles and miles together. They had studied French and Latin together, exchanged short stories, commented on each other's literary feats, communed about their boyfriends, and squeezed and talked for hours. They felt a special sense of female bonding—winsome and covert—and Charlotte simply glowed: "Martha comes," she wrote in her diary. "I let her in unseen, she prowls up to my room, and we spend the afternoon in tranquil bliss. I trim her hat, and she hems my pillowcase. She returns as invisibly as she came, at which I am exalted."

Some bleak times may have solidified the friendship too, a commiseration that she and Martha shared, especially during the winter of 1881. The double tragedy in May Diman's family may have been of particular importance. May's father, Brown University history professor J. Lewis Diman, suddenly became ill in the fall of 1880, and died February 3, 1881. During visits, outings, and talks together, Charlotte tried to help May with her grief. Then, several months later, May Diman was critically injured in a horseback riding accident, and died April 29, 1881. Charlotte worked hard to conceal her sadness, sympathizing with a young fellow who wept openly at the funeral service, yet setting different standards for herself: "As for me I found I couldn't stand the music and took refuge in the 'sorrows of Amelia' and the 'rivers and lakes of Mane' which treatment enabled me to preserve the appearance of composure. Why should I sit and drivel to no purpose?" *

Only two weeks after May Diman's death, in the spring of 1881, Martha and Charlotte entered a "compact of mutual understanding," mutual consolation, mutual love: they bought "lovely little red bracelets with gold across," Charlotte wrote in her diary, to be worn as a "badge, ornament, bond of amour." They "agreed that neither would ever 'put on' any pretense of feeling, and never have the slightest falsehood or deceit." Then, several months later, Martha left Providence for the summer holidays. Charlotte wrote her almost daily, and somehow her letters have survived. Apparently, Charlotte did not save Martha's letters. But even the one-sided correspondence shows the intensity of mutual affection. As Charlotte later wrote to Martha, "Those years with you, that blessed summer of eighty-one —I doubt if most people have as much happiness in all their lives as I had then."

* * *

The letters begin casually with progress reports on playful antics involving boyfriend Sam Simmons, mother and Aunt Caroline vicariously enjoying the frolics from the sidelines. Charlotte had been on her way up to her house, saw Sam pop in just moments before, and decided to play coy: "'Well' said my aunt in tones of triumph 'there's a gentleman waiting for you!' 'Let him wait' said I coolly, and as they didn't know I had seen him, my indifference worked admirably." Momentarily she had the upper hand: "I proceeded to talk to the youth as little as I could, and crush him whenever opportunity offered." Poor old Sam—"'such *teeth*!' 'such *eyes*!' Such *manners*!"—he "didn't stand the ghost of a chance now." Except he did, of course, with a Brown University education to help him even up the score. Charlotte had been studying Latin privately, thought she was doing rather well, but then Sam played a trump

* In Henry Fielding's *Amelia* (1751), a beautiful, virtuous young woman bears her countless trials and tribulations with patience and humility.

card. She wrote, "Boasted to Sam that I had the 1st declension 'solid,' and he fell on me with a quick rain of 'Genitive plural? Accusative singular? Vocative plural?' etc. etc. which put me to shame in no time. But I am doing the same thing by myself now, and shall be ready for him when he comes again." Sam unwittingly had served as teacher simply by getting her goat.

If Sam caused Charlotte minor spells of insecurity, his brother Jim Simmons' style of gallantry was worse. Jim was smooth-talking and self-confident, Charlotte was aggressively competitive, so they argued constantly. They tackled the biblical prodigal son story, for instance, Jim taking the traditional position that genuine disinterested repentance had motivated the poor renegade. Charlotte considered his argument patently absurd: "'Why,' said I, 'if he had repented while he was in the midst of his splendor and merriment; seen his wrong doing, and gone home from sheer remorse, giving up pleasure for right, that would have been one thing; but to wait till he had nothing to look to, and was absolutely starving—why to go home was all he could do—mean-spirited wretch!" Jim's retort she found cool, firm, and humorless: "'Just so;' says Jimmy; *'this was given* as an example of genuine repentance, and you've got to take it so, no matter how his action looks to people.'" "*Wasn't* that fine."

Charlotte reacted as though a kind of double jeopardy had been involved. First, she wanted to believe that redemption comes primarily through suffering—a favorite item in her own strength-promoting faith. But secondly, and for the moment more importantly, she wanted approval and confirmation, not condescension, from her friends. When Jim used male prerogative and the authority of God and Church to win a point, Charlotte lashed back furiously: "I asked him point-blank 'what under the sun he came to see me for!' And he dodged and parried and struggled, but I insisted on talking about it." Poor old Jim must have felt perplexed. Girls were supposed to like knowledgeable men who had ready explanations, strong men who understood The Truth. But Charlotte was not among them. At the time she could not locate the source of the confusion. She felt bewildered, humiliated, then enraged. But she could at least partly isolate the problem when describing the incident to Martha; gradually she decided that what she wanted, needed, and deserved was equality and self-respect.

> But I declare I had rather he wouldn't [visit], than to feel this horrid, unsatisfied Sisyphusic* sensation, after a talk with

* Sisyphus was a figure in classical mythology who was punished for his trickery by being compelled to roll a stone to the top of a slope; the stone

> him. . . . Now it may be that he is so inapproachably good, that my eviler nature can not abide him, but I don't think that is it.
>
> He is not perfect enough to have that effect—nor am I so bad as to be abashed at goodness. It is simply that we don't agree on anything. My high ideals that serve me so well through work & rest, all wizzle up under the fitful gleam of "les Lunettes" etc., and he murders every theory whether mine or another, that I chance to bring up, so remorselessly that I feel when he leaves: first, confused in general, second, uncertain of any ground in earth, heaven, or hell, save rigid old school theology, third, doubtful of my own aspirations, and worse, of my own powers, fourth in a state of abasement and malevolence toward him, and fifth with that universal discomforture which results usually from petty sin. . . . Once and only once did I detect a glimmer of what I want—equality, and some benefit conferred on my side. You know I don't go to but few places,—T'was casual, but I noticed it, and was greatly reassured. You're a fine man Jim, but I am going to be 'er fine woman too, and you have got to admit that you want me, or I won't have *you* if I wanted you a thousand times as much as now!

Charlotte was not quite the sweet, easy, endearing sort of friend Jim Simmons probably was used to, and whether he was angry or hurt or simply baffled, he decided it was best to stay away. Charlotte felt a real sting of disappointment, but nonetheless reacted with a take-it-or-leave-it kind of spunk:

> And truly I bethink me he has absented himself for good and all. I do not care x x x x If he couldn't understand me, couldn't see how much I cared for, respected, admired him—if he must needs get angry and feel hurt when I was simply lumbering about in my own clumsy way to straiten things that are generically crooked—why he had better go. And truly, I feel freer and better without his influence. So I guess it will all turn out right, as honest efforts after truth always do. . . . Last fall I should have wept, mourned, repented, abased myself, and been a fool. *Now* I do not care. This is certainly a change, if not the growth I fondly believe it, and that is something.

But then Charlotte decided that somehow the change was a prerequisite for growth, that if she were really serious about progressing with her work, it was better not to think of men at all. Interestingly enough, she referred to the work-ambition in herself as though it

always escaped him near the top and rolled down again, to his perpetual frustration.

were a "he." Since she thought work-ambition would be threatened by her boyfriends, she felt compelled to dismiss them out of hand, to assure that the head (masculine ambition) would rule the heart (feminine affection)—with one significant exception. The one love she would pursue was Martha. She wrote her:

> Look you—I do not want men friends just now, not until my head sitteth more firmly on my heart, not until brain exercise has enlarged and strengthened that organ, and I am sure enough of my ground to venture off it. Then—! Imagine me puss at thirty-five—no, on the whole I will still keep my ambition in the background. He is but feeble yet, and I will carefully repress his futile character until he is strong enough to move mountains. So no gentlemen for me just now. I have friends enough, and one love. I have more work than I hardly dare to think of, I have thoughts, and talks, and studies, and look back amusedly at some ten weeks ago, when I told Sam my mind was unoccupied and that I intended to fall in love as a means of filling it!

By late August, teenage cupid games having been firmly exorcised, Charlotte relaxed a bit. Jim must have partially recovered too because he began to drift back casually from time to time—an old-shoe kind of friend. Charlotte wrote Martha, "What sayeth the Sage? 'Stand by your own instincts and the world will come round to you!' Lo I stood, and the world has reappeared. (You *might* be justified in inferring that Jim was 'all the world to me.' Tain't so!) But isn't it exhilarating?" She would still lean a bit too heavily on Jim's approval, but for the most part she had regained her composure: "You've no idea how different he seems to me now. I neither heroize nor fight him, but he takes a pleasing position at a somewhat greater distance, and remains there—a most agreeable object."

Meanwhile, Charlotte was also engaged in idea-tussles with Jim's older brother, Sam Simmons; he was a safer, less threatening friend somehow. In fact, she "luxuriated in dear Sam (as one might in dear *jam*, you know.)" Jim was more arrogant, more authoritarian, while Sam was usually more respectful, sometimes even complimentary. He liked Charlotte's diatribes, apparently, and on one particularly memorable occasion said just what Charlotte loved to hear: he pronounced "with a most deeply interested expression that *that was a new thought to him*! Now *that* is just what I want. To be the sort of woman, handsome, self-poised, well-read, keen-sighted, refreshing,—who men will delight to talk with, and always find meat."

So supportive did Sam seem, in fact, that Charlotte decided to consult him on a major current crisis—how to deal with mother. Maybe underneath she was vaguely formulating subsequent feminist laments—"The man free, the woman confined; the man specialising in a thousand industries, the woman limited to her domestic functions"—but for now she personalized the issue as a "frightful incompatibility" between her mother and herself. She explained the conflict to Martha and Sam both: "my rebellion and utter inefficiency in this runround sort of life, my gradually strengthening and now inconquerable desire for mental culture and exercise; my determination to drop my half-developed *functional* womanhood, and take the broad road of individuality apart from sex." Since Charlotte sensed an inevitable conflict between womanhood and personhood, she viewed her mother as her worst opponent. And predictably so. Mary was her first female model, her first source of confirmation and affection—of anger and condemnation too—the first person from whom Charlotte learned about herself. So it was not just a question of seeking "mental culture and exercise," but of wrenching free of Mary's well-intentioned grasp. Increasingly, Charlotte wanted to assert her independence, at least metaphorically. But since rejection of mother's lifestyle necessitated emotional rejection of mother too (and also of important dimensions of herself), Charlotte needed and asked for approval and support from friends. From her perspective there were two major obstacles to independence: the "surviving relics of over-driven heredity" in herself (the Beecher drive for sainthood?), and Mary's "inability" to live alone—euphemisms both, for guilt-producing loyalties and fears. So she asked Sam his opinion, and then restaged the conversational exchange for Martha.

> And what do you think [Sam] said? In the first place he took it beautifully, was as respectful and as deeply interested as heart could wish; saw the whole seriousness of his position too, in giving the casting vote perhaps to a young girl standing with her well controlled nature in her hand, waiting to let it go one way or the other—Admitted that, in almost as many words, said, he "saw that I was in a place where a very little urging would send me on in the way I was pointing," and realizing his responsibility, and knowing what he did of mother's life and my life—his advice would be "GO AHEAD!" And I'm *going*.

The "going" was symbolic, not real; a matter of attitude, not action. Though she had taken Frederick as her model and emulated his achievements, she was also painfully aware of the emotional havoc his independence had caused both Mary and herself.

> And so further. My father knew nine languages when he was thirty, and there is nothing to hinder me. Child you have no

idea of how much bigger I feel. *I have decided.* I'm *not* domestic and I don't want to be. Neither am I a genius in any especial sense, but a *strong-minded* woman I will be if I have to wade in blood as the ancient bravado hath it. I can work now to some purpose, wait with some patience, guard my health and strength with an end in view, and cultivate my beauty (don't laugh) to its utmost, as one strong weapon. Mind, I haven't let ambition so much as squeak yet; just as I crush a haunting thought out of my mind and cooly walk on feelings (ever blessed my education!), so do I keep that strong angel gagged and bound, pushing with articulate clamor from behind my outer brain and adding all his prisoned force to mine.

. . . What I want you see is to acquire sufficient *strength*, real literal *strength* of mind to be able to see clearly and *kill* swiftly any recalcitrance of the part of my heart in after years. (Here I pause a bit to sit on Ambition. Let him kick, by all means, he does very well where he is, but once out I should lose the power that all ungratified longing gives. . . .) And I'm *not* sleepy, and I want to write a *lot* more, and I *will* stop now, for I know that sleep is necessary to health, health to my immediate progress, progress to my ultimate end—and so goodnight.

Yours with the first free breath I ever drew
Charlotte Anna *Perkins*!

The violence of the metaphors—to cultivate beauty as a "weapon," to kill the heart for strength of mind, to gag and bind ambition so that "his prisoned force" invigorates the effort—all this seemed urgently required, since in reality Charlotte had by no means achieved the easy confidence and self-direction that she claimed. One relative, she told Martha, was "shocked and grieved at the independent stand I have taken in general, and my attitude towards mother in particular," and that bothered her enough. But when everyone seemed to open fire at once, she dissolved in tears:

They all opened on me at breakfast yesterday, Mother silent and pathetic, Aunt Mary outspoken & exhortive, and even Aunt C[aroline] chimming in with the crowd, as she always does. And I was fool enough to *cry*! O! I was mad. There I was, as cool and unmoved as I ever was, certain of my own ground and divinely indifferent to anybody's opinion, and yet my insufferable diaphragm all afloat, so that I couldn't talk at all! O! I was mad.

. . . But I, myself, undisturbed as the morn under clouds—I *know* I am right, defy the world, and in all my lofty isolation

> am conscious of a human love and tenderness always mine while you live.

Defiance, anger, crying spells—all reflected the intensity of family battle. After all, her self-sacrificing, domestic, and emotionally dependent mother had clashed irreconcilably with her cool, ambitious, independent father. Now these mother-father conflicts erupted once again, this time in herself. To some extent Martha provided a "lofty" isolated refuge, but the real peace-keeping maneuver, Charlotte decided, would be to strengthen her "self" and kill off the inclinations to remain "merely" a woman or to become a mother and a wife.

> I am really getting glad not to marry. For the mother side of me is strong enough to make an interminable war between plain duties and inexpressible instincts, I should rage as I do now at confinement and steady work, and spend all my force in pushing two ways without getting anywhere, & be [spoiled?] like my pa most likely. Whereas if I let that business alone, and go on in my own way; what I gain in individual strength and development of personal power of character, *myself as a self*, you know, not merely as a woman, or that useful animal a wife and mother, will I think make up, and more than make up in usefulness and effect, for the other happiness that part of me would so enjoy.

Martha apparently perceived some noble-martyr undercurrents in Charlotte's spinster plan, but, for the moment, Charlotte denied them out of hand.

> How do you make me out lonely? Neither do I think you have any particular ground for calling my plan high and noble, there's no great nobility in flying headlong for one's element over friends & foe. The relief and happiness to me is in the blessed certainty, the end of the long tiresome effort to satisfy the demands of two opposing natures in myself; and all I've done now is suppress the weaker one once and for all.

The "long tiresome effort" was not over, however, nor were opportunities to "satisfy the demands of two opposing natures" easily available to nineteenth-century women. Yet Charlotte revelled in her dream world anyway, fantasizing that she could play the husband role and still have work, love, and family, especially since Martha seemed so eager to play the role of wife: "I know you want to 'be loved and taken care of and helped,' I'm willing that you should, I want you to be, I intend to do a good share of it myself—but *I don't*!" So first she planned to "attain the character" she had envisioned for herself, to become "worthy of love" and "have it—needs must." But she never wanted love if it was condescending or overly protective, and certainly not if it denied her right to be free; "care I don't want unless I'm sick—'never trouble trouble till trouble troubles you'; and help I get from every quarter of the earth and sky."

The problem was she seemed to soar back and forth between them—earth and sky—clearly preferring celestial grandeur to mundane plodding with her friends. She could only "do great things while the fit lasts," she wrote Martha, so she hoped now to figure out some way to maintain "this exalted state of mind and work from it, till it gets to be the normal position." Don't worry, she continued. "Now I shall descend from my eminence with surpassing agility, and I shall continue to resemble other people in the most reassuring manner, so don't feel that I have fled to Parnassus without a goodbye." Still, she hoped to "be conscious all the time of how I *can* feel," even when depressions hit. She would experience a "wild delicious sense of boundless strength and continuingly mounting ambition" after midnight sessions with her girlfriends, or after "Sam's intelligent, soul to soul approval." But even when inspiration had "fallen like a cold popover," she still liked to fly: "It leaves me a trifle higher on average than I was before, and with every inspiration and subsequent drop, the flight is higher, the fall shorter, and the average rising with most gratifying celerity."

On one such flying trip, Charlotte stopped for a while not only to communicate with Martha, but to contact her brother and her father too, each in different ways. To Martha she wrote, "O my little love! I'd like to wind all round and round you and let you feel my heart." Then she started "making overtures" to Thomas, asking to renew "his acquaintance and correspondence." Apparently the effort was not terribly rewarding, so with her father she took a more obstreperous approach. She was "*demanding* encouragement and assistance," she told Martha, and would "await his answer with some interest." Meanwhile, her own independent source of flying fun was work. "And 'work' I say when the bent head turns and the tired eyes stray out of the window; 'work!' when my senses fail and the unconscious hand drops the colorfilled brush right into the paper—'work!' when I drowsily open my eyes after 6 hours sleep and would give the world for more,—and '*work!*' this much when I want to talk for hours to my little love, and must go and wash dishes *and* so forth."

Realistically admitting that it was "half from personal love," and half from her need to "talk," Charlotte was dashing off ten-, fifteen-, sometimes twenty-page letters to Martha. For the time being, mother and Aunt Caroline seemed "deaf and dumb" to her flying wonders, though Charlotte added unpersuasively: "Don't ever think that I look down on my relations, or despise and dislike them because they are not like me, it is only that we are not on the same road. Their level may be higher than mine, but as our Sage hath it, 'if I am the devil's child, I will live then from the devil.'" Confidently iniquitous, and also loving, trusting, and temporarily secure, Charlotte added, "Can't you cuddle me a little? My pet! Fancy me strong and unassailable to all the world beside, and then coming down and truckling to you like a half-fed amiable kitten!"

Already that was Charlotte's conscious goal: to develop a public image of strength and independence while surreptitiously enjoying an utterly compassionate nestling with her closest friend. Given Martha's absence, letters became the temporary source of consolation and support, both writing and receiving them. For not only did letters help to satisfy Charlotte's need for effusive and direct expressions of affection, but they also provided her with an open-ended opportunity to vent her frustrations, articulate her problems, and find relief in sharing the intensity of her alternating moods. Sometimes she felt exalted, she explained to Martha: "I wouldn't change with Shakespeare!" Then restrained optimism would follow: "The enthusiasm of a lifetime may only raise me two per cent above the average, but that's better than stagnation." And finally, she would hit bottom, but with a droll candor that helped her bounce back up again: "I formulate my ideas when I'm excited, write them down, and rely on them implicitly when I can't see an inch before my nose. My idea of faith."

With Martha standing by, Charlotte could meet minor slumps quite philosophically. In mid-August she wrote her: "The curtain wavers, and I don't feel so *satisfied*, but if I felt always as I did a week or two ago, earth wouldn't hold me. I am contented to be less happy at times, in order to be more so at others." Still it was hard work, apparently, "to hang on to preconceived ideas, dead against everybody else, without anything to hang on *to* save the remembrance of decision." Martha's letters were her bracers, Martha's love her inspiration.

> I look forward to 'em [letters] from day to day, go back to my work in the most dispirited way when it don't come, and when it does I carry it in my pocket and gloat over it ever so long, before reading, and put it hurriedly aside after the first perusal

> to get some work done before the second. I was a little dubious about writing the above, but even if the Philistines ever should see it, what care I! If I am not ashamed of having sentiments I am not ashamed of admitting them, and why shouldn't I love my little comfort when I haven't anything else to love?

Inhibited Charlotte was not, even if the "Philistines" sometimes had her scared. Her fantasies about future notoriety, her conscious delight in the scandalous potential of the friendship— these seemed to enliven her fervor, not restrain it. Martha was Charlotte's "little kitten," her "pussy," the dear "sweetheart" whom Charlotte hoped to love for life: "As for you I could spend hours in cuddling if I had you here. I can see all your manifold dearnesses, and I'd be willin' to bet five cents, if I was in the habit of tellin', that you will make up to me for husband and children and all that I shall miss. And if I can't do enough for mankind to earn myself a home in my old age, I don't deserve one. Oh! I am so grateful to the kind father or the just law that led us two together."

But if Charlotte had the confidence to scoff at the "Philistines," to state openly that her sensuous love for Martha was superior to the love of any man, it was not easy for her to ignore the dangers in the friendship. Essentially, there were two terrifying fears: that Martha might not really love her equally, and that, even if she did, it was temporary. One day some man would steal her.

Part of Charlotte's vulnerability may have resulted from her parents' coolness, their rebuffs, their awkward ineffectual ways of showing love. But Charlotte's fears were certainly exacerbated by Martha's sportive talk about her various flirtations, and also by her traditional attitudes toward marriage. Charlotte tried to woo Martha toward some form of sisterly commitment, always letting it be known—with good humor, anger, or heart-felt distress—that she regarded marriage as an unfortunate intrusion at best and impending doom at worst. Still, so long as marriage was only a distant possibility, Charlotte expressed her attachment to Martha as openly and erotically as ever: "As for your heart—with its everlasting hungry little corners, just dilute me and fill 'em up, and I will leak quietly away when an *interloper appears*."

Unfortunately, an interloper had appeared—Charles A. Lane, or "Halicarnassus," they called him in their letters—and ingeniously Charlotte began jostling for a way to beat him down. "It's a long lane that has no turning,"* she kept reminding Martha, half in jest, but

* Charlotte was referring here to a line of Robert Browning's poem, "The Flight of the Duchess." The narrator of the poem, whose wife and children

also deadly serious. The situation called for subtlety, which was not exactly Charlotte's style. But at least she tried some different strategies, hoping that somehow one of them would work. At times she was breezy and playful about Martha's "flirting with old gentlemen." Or she would try colluding and advising on the basis of her own former prankish courtship games. And occasionally, assuming that experience might effect a cure, Charlotte urged Martha to flirt to her heart's content: "Go ahead and enjoy yourself *heartily*. . . . Don't fret about him! The easy agility with which he will get over his penchant will be—more amusing than complimentary. And as for you, a little genuine experience of any kind is better than everlasting shadows, and brooding over misty might be's." Just remember, she continued, when "fat, fair, and forty," and "rereading old letters for a treat in *literary perfection*," such trivial incidents of youth will seem absurd.

But the wishful thinking had to end. Just after dismissing Halicarnassus so cavalierly, Charlotte received a letter from Martha that made it necessary to adopt another tone. Clearly the situation was critical, for whatever Martha may have said about Halicarnassus specifically, she must have mentioned her desire for marriage and motherhood, and perhaps even acknowledged that she could not share Charlotte's goals. Charlotte was feverishly ambitious, after all; Martha was fun-loving and gay. Charlotte projected fantasies of lasting female love. Martha felt conflicting loyalties toward men. Martha probably had sounded defensive and self-reproachful in her letter; that in itself Charlotte may have taken as an added danger signal in the friendship. For if Martha felt criticized and vulnerable instead of confident, or if she became apologetic when she really felt angry instead, very likely she would turn to other friends. So Charlotte tried to reassure her, partly with a firm reminder that Martha too had a right to be her "self," and partly with reassurances that the major concern was that their own love would last.

> I think you misunderstand me a trifle. I don't want you to be the same kind of humbug that I am, not a bit of it. You are to be your own sweet lovely self, marry all you please, and be loved and cared for to your heart's content. But be your home as charming as it may, I am to have a night *key*, as it were, and shall enjoy in you and yours all that I don't have myself. Halicarnassus will like me I know, and as . . . I never said that I was

---

are dead, anticipates no happiness in his future, and knows simply that all human situations, like all human lives, will someday end: "It's a long lane that knows no turnings" (l. 872).

> to make up to you for all this, but you to me, and that without requiring the slightest sacrifice on your part.

While Charlotte was trying to reassure Martha, however, she was also working hard to brace herself: "And if Halicarnassus *doesn't* like me or if you should up and die, in short if I can't have it—why I'll go it alone and be happy as a clam *nonetheless*." And then, as though she were writing a news dispatch to her father instead of a love-letter to her friend (and as though she were actually convinced), Charlotte continued, "I've dropped the heart business once and for all, it never was as strong as my head, and the sooner I squelch it altogether the more firmly shall I progress."

So that was Charlotte's characteristic self-defensive stance, or at least one variation of it. Another she had revealed only a few days before. The ambitious stoic-martyr was also just the poor defenseless child. Playfully, but also plaintively, she had mocked her need for verbal hugging with some baby-talk.

> Little kitten, little kitten . . .
> I love you this warm bright Sunday morning more than ever. But you don't answer letters worth a cent. When I take pains and writes lots of petty fings to 'moose my little girl, I like to have my little girl notice 'em. Likes to have her 'stonished at my 'ventures, and pleased when I remember every word of some folks' conversation to tell her. Hasn't said a word bout nuffin I said, 'ny more 'n if you hadn't got 'em! Long, fat, beauful letters! Bused!

Especially with Halicarnassus in the background, Charlotte's fear was that Martha might not really love her. Affectionate but scared, Charlotte sometimes was the strong and heartless initiator male, at other times the dependent childlike female, but always the loving disappointed letter-writing teacher, alternately instructing, scolding, teasing, begging, or angrily demanding love. On July 29 she wrote Martha: "Look you, I haven't answered your letter at all yet, and I had half a mind to let it go at that in retaliation, you unsatisfactory composer. I sh'd think you'd be ashamed. Here I show you my heart and you don't take the slightest notice, nor drop a word as to whether you enjoy the prospect or no." So with a curious blending of childlike twaddle and aggressive exhortation, Charlotte fought to keep the friendship going, fought for the romantic's dream of vital, candid, mutually trusting love.

> I'm disappointed. That mean owdacious postman stalked straight by, and I have no letter from Marfa! Don't care. I shall

> viciously quote from the Sage, (whom you may have divined is in my mind at present)—"It has seemed to me lately more possible than I knew, to carry a friendship greatly on one side, without due *correspondence* on the other"—shall I go on? It grows viciouser.
>
> "Why should I cumber myself with the poor fact that the receiver is not capacious?" . . . And see here pussy, "Friendship, like the immortality of the soul, is too good to be believed. (!) The lover, beholding his maiden, half knows that she is not verily that which he worships; and *in the golden hour of friendship we are surprised with shades of suspicion and unbelief.* (!) In strictness, the soul does not respect men as it respects itself (!)."
>
> "Let me be alone to the end of the world, rather than that my friend should overstep by a word or a look his real sympathy."

Love-letter imagery thus spun around in circles. Charlotte was the "little kitten" needing care and protection, then the virile husband prodding his more passive wife, and now the soul-searching philosopher suspicious of his simple "maiden." If the annoyance was partly tongue in cheek, its intensity was nonetheless apparent, emerging from confidence as well as insecurity, from trust as well as fear. For whatever inequalities Martha may have apologetically described—intellectual inferiority or less ambitious goals—Charlotte reminded her, again and again, that it was mutual respect, mutual dependence, and mutual appreciation that kept the friendship whole. In fact (as many men feel about their wives), Charlotte recognized that noncompetitive tenderness and generous support, not aggressive intellectuality, were Martha's most important gifts. In the beginning of August Charlotte wrote Martha:

> O you dear bewitching lovely little Frotty! You obtuse perversely misunderstanding thickheaded little idiot! What under the sun do I love you for, save that you are not like me! . . . Why the grand base of my towering pile, is the divine right of *each individual* to act out *his own nature*. You can do the other thing and do it well. You can be all that is sweet and delicious as well as intellectual, but I can't,—& you know it. If we were two rocks we should bump each other unmercifully, but now there is no possible contest between us, I think I may be a help to you, and you are my greatest comfort now and ever, a loving sister soul, who will see the need of my ascending and always have a nest.
>
> . . . Why *do* you talk about holding me back? Understand

> once and for all that you are my one stay and support,—my other self. . . . If I can return it in any way, in virile force, or anything which I have & you haven't, so much happier I, and if I can't I shall remain the most ungrateful & contented beneficiary you ever saw. Now is that plain? Are you convinced of your indispensability? *Will* you stop talking nonsense?

Martha was indispensable, yet unattainable. That was the problem. Charlotte knew, as a woman, she could never have such a lovely wife. So she resumed her self-defensive preparations, accumulating more shields and weapons as though the armory were not already well-supplied enough. This time she argued that she did not want Martha's affection in the long run anyway. The letter continues:

> I *am* certain of you pussy. Sure as death—for now. I'm not for ever, and I don't want to be. I should hardly care to turn my hand over if I thought I had such a friend as you for all time. No, I will keep you while I have you, and revel & luxuriate in the clear cool depths of your heart as I do in the sea, but if ever you grow, or I grow, on another path,—why there is bliss behind and hope before. It seems improbable to me that two souls *could* be so perfectly matched as ours seem now. There must be places in each that we don't either of us know about yet—undiscovered countries where we may go together, and may not.
>
> I shouldn't much wonder if Halicarnassus after all might be the stream to divide us. Apply our pet poem dear, imagine our finding the young affection deep in your heart, walking hand in hand over the pretty thing—and then—and then—And yet I know past all doubting, a knowledge greater than death can stir, that as I loved she will love me, duly. And better, far better! than I love her!
>
> Believe it, pussy. Every time that little cherub of ours sits down in that unsteady resting place, my heart, he is bigger than he was before. And able to keep his seat longer. You see I don't dare hope for years and years of it. Perhaps—perhaps, as I grow older, my mother's constancy may take the place of my father's fickle fancy—I shouldn't wonder. . . .
>
> Yours in a *calm ordinary, wellbehaved friendly* (not intimate) *masculine*! way,
>
> Charlotte Anna Perkins

According to the conventions of the times, Charlotte *was* masculine, of course. "Masculine" implied strength, independence, and ambitious commitment to one's work; "feminine" implied gentleness, kindness, and affectionate absorption in one's personal relationships. Thus Frederick's apparent emotional indifference to his family, and Mary's contrasting emotional dependencies, may have seemed representative and normal. Later, Charlotte would ridicule the oppressive terminology: "giving to the woman the home and to the man the world in which to work, we have come to a dense prejudice in favor of the essential womanliness of home duties, as opposed to the essential manliness of every other kind of work." Or again, in "our steady insistence on proclaiming sex-distinctions we have grown to consider most human attributes as masculine attributes, for the simple reason that they were allowed to men and forbidden to women." But, in 1881, she was plagued by dichotomies: head versus heart, strength versus gentility, male versus female. Not surprisingly, Charlotte tried to claim the former, to squelch the "feminine" within herself, to assume the "virile force."

To some extent then, Charlotte accepted traditional male-female inequalities, and even encouraged them in her relationship with Martha; but she also simultaneously railed against the personal, social, and political realities that seemed to force her to choose between the female and male "instincts" in herself, between the emotional involvement she thought was weakness, and the self-sufficiency she thought was strength. If, under these assumptions, marriage necessarily seemed ominous, female friendship seemed to her to be a haven of delight. Charlotte could receive love from Martha without having to assume debilitating domestic responsibilities, blunt her assertive style, or compromise ambition and thereby lose her self-respect. In short, Charlotte had turned with relief and uninhibited pleasure to the "female world of love and ritual," as Carroll Smith-Rosenberg has called it, the female love that provided positive and emotionally supportive extensions of the mother-daughter bond, and was an essential source of the "integrity and dignity which grew out of women's shared experiences and mutual affection." Close and intimate friendships between women were common in the nineteenth century, as were hugging, kissing, commiserating, communing, unashamedly sleeping together in one another's beds. Whether such relationships were sexual is often impossible to know. Charlotte argued hers was not. An equally important issue, however, is the quality of the female bond itself. In her autobiography, Charlotte publicly and proudly proclaimed the "deep personal happiness" she had known in female friendship. And, in a letter to Martha, she gave an unrestrained triumphant cheer: "The freedom of it! The deliciousness! The utter absence of 'how will he take it?'! Never again will I admit that women are incapable of genuine friendship."

What then might interfere with such affection? Males, perhaps, particularly "swains" like Charles A. Lane, but certainly not the competition of other women. Charlotte wrote of one of Martha's friends, "Glad she likes you, am perfectly willing that the whole world should worship, so that I reign supreme." Or of one of her own Providence girlfriends she wrote, "And she don't come between us, my darling, or interfere with my love for you, any more than a strong quiet landscape would interfere with my enjoyment of exquisite music." So why not extend the experience? Why restrict it exclusively to one another?

> Look here. Some sort of club—a society we must have. It is too bad for girls of this stamp not to know each other, and the meetings of ordinary society are at once impracticle to some of us . . . and insufficient at the best of times. Somewhat like that Essay Club, only *in earnest* we that can meet to tell all to write, and all to help each other. Comparative restrictions immeasurable, but a common ground. In unity is strength, and many a girl would not be ashamed to mend her life if she were supported by others she knew. We as a class—girls, think our higher aspirations untrustworthy, we don't show them to parents, we don't show them to friends, they don't accord with ministers—with the Bible either, perhaps, but there is an element of reform and growth among lots of the girls I know, girls who have no atmosphere to encourage it, and who will lose it altogether in a few years. *Growth* of generalities you know.
>
> . . . This may be wild. At any rate it is an idea, and ideas are worth having.
>
> . . . Truly the manageress and reformer worketh within me! Shades of Aunt Catharine!

Reformer she was indeed, though to some extent already a surreptitious one. She was fighting a host of conventions on the public front, yet leaving portions of her private life closed to public view. That was understandable. For even in the nineteenth century, female friendships were considered suspect or perverse. Charlotte exercised restraint in openly attacking such attitudes, but at least privately she dismissed them out of hand. She wrote Martha, "I think it highly probable (ahem!) that you love me however I squirm, love the steady care around which I so variously revolve, love me and will love me—why in the name of heaven have we so confounded love with passion that it sounds to our century-tutored ears either wicked or absurd to name it between women? It is no longer friendship between us, it is love. Why I feel it in me to be the *friend* of thousands, but you—!"

That was a passionate statement to be sure, but also an open declaration of her private thoughts on women's right to same-sex love. Then, as though she were aware that the principle might not particularly appeal to Martha (or possibly that Martha might not share her point of view?), Charlotte changed her pace abruptly: "Seems to me my letters might strike you queerly amongst all your merry-making, but then you know that I am not a somber 'mummy at the feast,' but would enter into your proceeding with all the fervor imaginable if I were there. . . . I feel quite sure that the tone of my thoughts just now must clash a little with yours. Who wants a sermon read aloud at croquet! Keep 'em till you feel sober pussy, indeed I will inform you with self-intimate candor that I should like to have you read them all over to me bye and bye! O my sister! If it ever is so, can be so! I am blissfully content to have you so much more to me than I ever can be to you—*just* what I couldn't stand in Jimmy! Why I never imagined in my wildest dreams such a heaven as this, it can't last."

The immediate threat was still the abominable Charles A. Lane, and Charlotte fought him furiously. She wrote Martha:

> Suppose you love that man as I think you do—fear you will. Suppose he's cold and proud enough to suppress his own feelings forever. You see, I take it for granted he has 'em, a dishonorable flirt else. Well now is that sort of thing going to satisfy you? Can you live and grow on an *uncertain* consciousness of a grand man's love? Can you wait for years without a word while he is trying to do something? My little girl! My little girl! If this thing came to pass you will need me in good earnest. If you can do it and be comfortable and happy go ahead. If you think it's good for you, pleasure aside, go ahead by all means. If you can't help it—why I love you still. But you shall not have to mourn that you never considered the question.

From Charlotte's perspective, Charles A. Lane was too cold and proud and emotionally reserved—just the qualities Charlotte disliked in her father, yet sometimes proudly claimed herself. But more importantly, she thought Lane would inflict on Martha—perpetually—just the sort of humiliation she had endured on a lesser scale with Jim. The letter continues:

> O my prophetic soul! What do I see before me! Martha married to Jim. Jim's keen powerful mentality a warping of Mar-

tha's unfounded ideas and affections—imperceptibly. . . . But it would be dreadful some twenty years hence to have you wishing that your heart had not carried you where you were no longer happy. To have you find that your heroic image of him was no longer so ever present as to obliterate "son thé, son grammaire, son theologe" etc. To find the grand virtues that you worship dormant for lack of use, the clear logical mind unnecessary at the breakfast table, and all that "undiscovered country" lying in the distance dimmer, grander, and more unapproachable than ever. Rather a lonesome life for my kitten, who likes you see to be the leading spirit, and yet coaxed and cuddled and taken care of. A side of you likes a side of him, but Oh! the others! Now to retract and qualify in my usual timid style. You *may* (!) see him differently. He *may* love you and all your little ways better than I do. As a husband and father he would be virtuous in the extreme—his universality of home talent would figure well in a house of his own. He would *let* you have as large a library as he could afford I doubt not, and everything else that money could buy and love could give —when he had it. And you would probably love him enough to scale all chasms, surmount all hills, and smooth off the face of nature as it were, to suit yourself.

But would you always suit? That firm immovable decision from which there is no appeal—straightening of the tall figure, "little bigoted curve of lip," with sidelong movement of the head, and stony reflected gleam in those careful gatekeeper "les lunettes"—how would all that seem when turned against you? Wouldn't it *hurt*? Love can do great things, but could all the love under God make Jim Simmons change those religious views of his? Do you want to be dragged into things; persuaded, convinced, and converted before you come to it naturally: to have a never ending contention; or to have an unmentioned gulf lying quietly between you, to have him pray *for* you, and not *with* you?

The diatribe over, Charlotte relaxed a bit, teased a bit, and resumed her jocose letter-writing style. Having been on a cleanliness campaign, she happily exclaimed: "And here's encouragement—Mother has praised me twice for clean hair, and says I really begin to smell sweet!" Or again, "Eat, drink, and be merry, for tomorrow you come home. (I wish you did,) and once I get my claws on you, farewell to your 'luxurious laziness.' *Now* ain't yer 'fraid!"

Charlotte kept her wit and sparkle, but was unable effectively to disguise the grimness of her mood. About a week later, she capriciously formulated a fantasy solution to the Halicarnassus dilemma that was meant to be funny, though probably Martha didn't think so. It will be such fun, Charlotte wrote, when

> we live in our big house, you & I, and by the way, I have settled your business finally. You are to marry, of course, you would never be satisfied if you didn't, and after a certain period of unmerited, *his*, happiness, your young man is to drop off, die somehow, and lo! I will be all in all! Now isn't that a charming plan? You can always have tender melancholy about you, during special fits of which I will thoughtfully explain that "she is thinking of the old un," and then it's more than likely that there would be some little Halicarnassuses which you would be too much occupied with grief to mind my experimenting on! Glorious.

This was rather obtuse humor, to be sure. But then, as though the fantasy had been entirely playful, comic, mutually refreshing, Charlotte continued as flirtatiously as ever, "Say, I feel ever so pretty. I have the loveliest new way of coiffuring—thus [sketch included]. It does not in very truth look *quite* so like an eccentric pretzel, but is soft, clinging, mysterious, and extremely pretty." In fact, such sensuous quixotic silhouettes embellished many of Charlotte's letters: "what fun it was to stop and bathe, and coil up the heavy masses of my lustrous hair! To buckle on that charming novelty, my blue dress; to scan the contents of my top drawer, and select a white mull neckerchief, just for a change! Then to sweep in trailing robes down the broad stairway, and strike wild chords of melody on the grand piano to relieve my troubled soul—I tell yer! O my! pussy! I do want you!"

Obviously, Charlotte felt quite sensuously attracted and attractive, and quite pleased with her long "trailing robes" of glory. Such glamourous pretensions might seem rather strange, given Mary's slender means and Charlotte's own obligatory penny-pinching style. Presumably Charlotte could have felt cowed by the *haute couture* of many of her friends, the Hazards, Blakes, and Channings, in particular. But in fact, since they preferred to share rather than to outclass, and since Charlotte didn't mind accepting gifts, they adorned her lavishly. For example, an 1880 diary entry reads: Ada Blake "brought me 7 pairs of four button GLOVES. All shades dressed and undressed. I walk home with her, and she furthermore bestows upon me a pair of black silk stockings and a silver beaded comb; balls on top. Lovely. I admire, exult, and gratitudinize in fine style." She "gratitudinized" again in a letter to Martha: "Lace, finer than finest tulle, cobwebby, etherial, delicately êcru, sprinkled not with *white* specks, but with delicious transparent, glittering little dew drops of—gum arabic I should judge, so that when you veil yourself therein the folds in shade are golden mist, and the folds in light all dots of fire. *Ecstatic*."

"Do women dress to please men?" Charlotte would later ask. An emphatic "yes" would be her answer. But at least at this stage of her experience her answer was "no," and it was the same among a good number of her friends. She wrote Martha, "dressed up yesterday for Cassie [Thurston's] benefit and my own delight; sending for her to come up stairs at about dusk, to find a pitch dark entry, closed door —burst of light, and me in satin and lace, with my hair high, a crescent of silver balls gleaming on top, long white gloves, gorgeous fan, etc. etc. I added a string of great pearls at the throat and that piece of creamy speckled lace for a veil, and if I didn't look nice I wouldn't say so. Cassie was smashed. And I have vowed a vow to wear good clothes in future whenever I can. *Won't it be nice*, little girl."

So there were flirtatious games aplenty—between women as well as between women and men. Charlotte was enjoying herself immensely, but with Halicarnassus lurking in the background, she was also deadly serious, very likely far more serious than Martha knew. For judging from Charlotte's letters, Martha was consciously or unconsciously misleading her; Martha implied that she was only practicing her feminine wiles on a passing male intruder, and outwitting him at that. Charlotte wrote: "He's devoted to you, but you don't care for him—just as it should be, my love! And you hope you showed it, but don't know whether you did or not—why you precious duckling, what earthly difference does it make! Just go right on and live your own life, do good and enjoy yourself, and *if*, in consequence of your being and doing certain things, divers menfolks are affected in certain ways—why you should say 'what difference does that make to me!' I hate to see you wandering off into the thousand devious ways of self-analysis and censure over occurances that will some day seem to you to be very trifles." No, "this strongminded old maid" found such "delicious tangles" an immense delight:

> That shawl device was inhuman—how he must have felt all the time he was getting it! As to being a flirt, you know you are! A most audacious one. . . . And O you *gay* deceiver! That gate scene—! To be confused and inaudible, and then look up at him with that frank smile and light turn of the conversation —why I can't imagine it done better if you were Circe herself.

> It is novelly, very, and great fun for me. So go on and slay your thousands, and I will absolve you every time.

Encouraged by Martha's fun-filled letters, Charlotte confidently dismissed the opposition, and with considerable Machiavellian finesse, urged Martha to protect herself and care not a whit for Charles. "Just open your big eyes, and tell him you are spoken for by a female in Providence, and can't marry just yet." "And as to that marauder's being pitifully unhappy—why so he ought to, to leave you. Wasn't *I* 'pitifully unhappy'? And ain't I now? Pity 'bout him! And now look here! If you go to abusing yourself, and being grateful to that thing because he spent most of his vacation in the pleasantest way he could think of, why, I'll cut your acquaintance. *Now* where are yer?"

* * *

By the fall of 1881, Charlotte's wit and banter had helped to exorcise the feckless Charles A. Lane, but there were still enough hooks and ploys and vagaries recurring in her letters to suggest some underlying fears. She kept assuring Martha (herself?) that confidence was warranted: "Say pussy, you've no idea how all my grand plans have folded their wings and turned into strong horses fit for immediate use. . . . It seals my faith in these roseate theories—to see them work so well." But she was also quick to claim her preference for and expectation of adversity: "Now if I were to live as the dream—alone with you—with a circle of souls like ourselves, and the quiet atmosphere of mutual love and perfect accord—why I question much if I should not develope the wrong way in such Elysian temperature. I must have something to brace on in order to push with any effect. *Ice boats*, my love, go fastest with adverse winds! *Fact*." And such adversity was by no means hard to come by. A sense of a "daughter's duty" would serve conveniently and well. For whereas a rebellious self-affirming stance toward Mary had flourished in the "Elysian temperature" of Martha's love, it was crushed by "adverse winds" when Charlotte tried to brace herself alone. The letter continues:

> It is rather grievous to me to have to come back to housework, but there is no reason that I know of why I should have my preference on the matter of work so long as it be necessary and useful, any more than in the matter of food. I think every person is bound to accept their immediate duties, when they are so indissoluble as mine are. I need not fret over obligations

> because I did not solicit them, mine they are, and I must shoulder them as best I can, my own happiness and advancement being *contingent*. . . . I now project to keep my temper and be pleasant with Mother & Aunt C[aroline] & to learn and grow under adverse influences, it is as *hard* a thing as I can do, and hence desirable.

The heavy tone, the celebration of distress, seemed to be last-minute preparations for Martha's homecoming. Some feeble jests and jabs at Lane only thinly disguised Charlotte's premonition of the *bete noire*'s victory. "'If I had a lover so noble and free, I wish he would send big fruit baskets to me!' . . . I fondly suppose that everything in trousers would give his head to marry you. *Don't* you let 'em! None of 'em! They ain't good enough! Not near!" But then she continued, "I have said full enough concerning your man I think. Still I will give you my benediction over again if you wish. But Ah! Remember clear and plain. When strong is love is burning, That its the longest kind of Lane, that never knows a turning!"

Martha may not have realized that her banter about Charles Lane had falsely kept up Charlotte's hopes. Surely truthfulness would have been more kind. Possibly, however, Martha still felt indecisive. Or perhaps she found it too downright burdensome to confront Charlotte directly with the seriousness of her intentions. In any case, even after she returned to Providence, Martha was still unclear. Charlotte's early October diary entry reads: "Go to Martha's. All alone. Stay till almost 8. Nice talk. ('No!')." (Did the "no" reflect Charlotte's wishful thinking?) October 27: "Martha there. We take walks and converse. Verily I love the damsel." On October 29, 1881, a dried pansy or rose was inserted in the diary. It remains there still. The entry reads: "Am closeted with Mrs. L[uther] and change my views a bit. Tell M. to go ahead. Kiss her." On October 30, she mentioned going to a "sermon of which I heard little being principally occupied in not crying. Walk home with M. . . . Write to Sam asking help, & to Cassie [Thurston]. . . . Speak to M. a moment—wishing her joy of her All Hallow'een. . . . O my little girl! My little girl." November 1: "Martha over. She hath a ring. I have a pain. Give her my blessing. Write to Sam and tell him all about it." November 5: "Pleasant, to ring at the door where you've always been greeted with gladness; to be met by the smile that you value all others above—to see that smile flicker and vanish and change into sadness because she was met by *your* presence instead of her love." On November 9, she wrote: "Letter from Sam. Kind but discouraging. . . . Am dully unhappy, but can stand it." November 13: "Go home with Mrs.

Luther. Spar with the enemy." November 15: "Spend an hour in the chilly twilight up at my window, and have my crucial struggle with my grief. Victory. Too utterly worn out to do anything in the evening but write down my 'state o' mind.'" The following day: "Walk in the dark sts. for an hour or so in dumb misery. Where is that victory?" December 18: "Jim comes home with me. We walk about, talking, for an hour or so and more when he comes in as they were all abed. He does not help me." On December 28, Charlotte attended a party; they played twenty-four games of whist: "A grand jolly unmitigated success. But it fills a mighty little place."

On December 30, 1881, Charlotte went to Martha's to return some books. Martha was out, so Charlotte left her a little poem:

> Some books and things for you dear, once kindly lent to me;
> I have had pleasure from them all, & now with thanks for great & small I bring them back to thee.
> I'm rather glad you're out dear, I write without a sigh,
> And miss the taste of bitter tears, the hopeless glimpse of dear lost years
> I'd have if you were by.

Charlotte's diary for the year 1881 ended with the following reflection:

> A year of steady work. A quiet year and a hard one. A year of surprising growth. A year internally dedicated to discoveries and improvements. A year in which I knew the sweetness of a perfect friendship and have lost it forever. A year of marked advance in many ways, and with nothing conspicuous to regret. I am stronger, wiser and better then last year, and am fairly satisfied with the year's work. I have learned much of self-control & consideration for others; often think before I speak and can keep still on occasions. My memory begins to show the training it has had, I can get what I want when I want it, pretty generally. Most of all I have learned what pain is, have learned the need of human sympathy by the unfilled want of it, and have gained the power to *give* it, which is worth while. This year I attained my majority—may I never lose it.

Chapter Five

The One Great Question 1881-1884

THE feelings that prompted Charlotte's extended self-evaluation at the close of 1881 continued into the New Year. On the flyleaf of her new diary for 1882 is the following inscription:

> My watchword at 21—1882 WORK!
> *Once and for all*; to Love and personal happiness—
> so called—NO!

Another beginning diary entry reads:

> I have on my mind this year three cares—(so far).
> 1. Others first.
> 2. *Correct* and *necessary* speech only.
> 3. Don't waste a minute!
> If I can form the ground work of these habits in a year it will be well. Furthermore I wish to form a habit of *writing* as much as I can.

* * *

On January 12, 1882, Charlotte was invited by a friend, Sydney Putnam, to visit the studio of a local artist, Charles Walter Stetson. Two days later she recorded, "I have a twilight tête-à-tête with Charles Walt. Like him. It's a new thing to be admired." The following week she wrote, "Mr. Stetson calls. We are left alone, and have a nice talk. I introduce myself as fully as possible, and he does the same. We shake hands on it, and are in a fair way to be good friends."

Aspiring artist Walter Stetson must have suited Charlotte's melancholy mood exactly. Sombre, dedicated, well-read Walter was a noble, heavy-hearted soul in a strikingly attractive body—broad-shouldered, vigorous, and physically imposing. Moreover he was a gentleman—protective, kind, intensely proper—something of a dreamer, possibly a wit, and a rather smug but unpretentious nonconformist too. And he had other impressive credentials Charlotte liked: parents who were itinerant out-of-pocket renegades, a similar education—in geographic mobility, in economic insecurity, in religious heterodoxy—and most important of all, an impassioned commitment to his work.

Two years Charlotte's elder, Walter was the son of Free Will Baptist Joshua Augusta Stetson (of the famed Stetson hat clan) and his wife, Rebecca Steer Stetson, of Gloucester, Massachusetts. Like Frederick, Joshua Stetson had an unsettled many-faceted career, serving first as a poorly paid missionary-clergyman through the Civil War years, studying medicine briefly, and then manufacturing and selling proprietary medicines in his later years. Walter remembered mainly the childhood deprivation in this "poor New England pastor's family," the life of hardship, the "ambulatory and precarious existence," the "constant changes, often uncongenial homes, and meagre salary—too often paid in kind." In 1870, however, the family settled in Providence, where Walter later finished his high school education. Subsequently, he decided to move out on his own, to earn his living as a painter, despite some family qualms. By the time Charlotte met him (1882), he had managed to finance a modest studio and to attain some recognition—at least Charlotte thought so—as a beleaguered though promising young artist. She later wrote, "He was quite the greatest man, near my own age, that I had ever known. He stood alone, true to his art, in that prosaic mercantile town, handicapped with poverty, indifference and misunderstanding. His genius was marked; although largely self-taught, his work was already so remarkable for its jeweled color that a dishonest dealer tried to suborn him to paint Diazes for him—in vain."

Ambitious, hard-working, precariously established, Walter must have been pleased by Charlotte's heart-felt admiration, and doubtless pleased as well by her spark and beauty. She was, as her brother Thomas would remember her, a "dark-haired and dark-eyed, very good-looking girl, demurely sober, with a rather wistful, far-away look, but whose face was unusually expressive of anger, delight, mischief, or other aroused emotion, and whose words and actions were apt to be accordant with and strongly expressive of the emotion aroused."

After all her agonizing over Martha, and after several months of self-imposed isolation from her friends, Charlotte was more than ready for some animated earnest conversations, and for some flirtatious antics also. Temporarily enjoying one of the "highs" of her whirlwind emotional career, the kind which usually accompany new infatuations, Charlotte must have been a conversational delight, leaping from concern to impassioned concern, Walter standing, rather dazzled, at the vortex. But if Walter took a more subdued and passive stance—momentarily at least—he must have been surprised and pleased to realize how much they had in common. A love for art, literature, history, science, a shared religious faith (intense, however iconoclastic), a commitment to a set of mutually ill-defined humanitarian ideals, an irritation and frustration with disapproving churlish parents—all these must have heightened the attraction. But then, suddenly, unwisely, Walter decided to propose, on January 29, 1882, only seventeen days after their first meeting. Charlotte carefully recorded, "I have this day been asked the one great question in a woman's life and have refused." Two days later she wrote "An Anchor to Windward."

> January 31, 1882
>
> This is for me to hold to if, as I fore-fear, the force of passion should at any time cloud my reason, and prevent or benumb my will.
>
> Now that my head is cool and clear, now before I give myself in any sense to another; let me write down my Reasons for living single.
>
> In the first place I am fonder of freedom than anything else.—I love to see and be with my friends, but only when I want them. I love to have pleasant faces in my home, but only when I want them.
>
> I like to have my own unaided will in all my surroundings—in *dress, habits, diet, hours, behavior, speech*, and *thought*.
>
> I *increasingly* like to feel that my home is *mine*, that I am free to leave it when I will, and for as long as I will.
>
> I like to select for myself, to buy for myself, to provide for myself in every way.
>
> I like to start out in joyous uncertainty of where I am going, and with no force to draw me back—like it beyond words.
>
> I like to go about alone—*independently*.

The sense of individual strength and self-reliance is sweeter than trust to me.

I like to be *able* and *free* to help any and everyone, as I never could be if my time and thoughts were taken up by that extended self—a family.

If I were bound to a few I should grow so fond of them, and so busied with them that I should have no room for the thousand and one helpful works which the world needs. As it is now, or rather as it *will be*, I can turn to any one in distress and give them my best help; my love, my time, my interest and sympathy.

I am cool, fearless, and strong; and have powers which can do good service in proper circumstances if I can only trust in them and coming opportunity.

It is a matter of futurity in any case, and I am willing to risk my life—yes, and another's too, to prove the question.

It is after all, a simple case, for I *mean* to do right, and if I am on the wrong track, I shall do a lot of good work anyway, and merely miss a few year's happiness.

For reasons many and good, reasons of slow growth and careful consideration, more reasons than I now can remember; I decide to *Live*—Alone.

God help me!

According to her autobiography, however, Charlotte was a bit less resolute when confronting Walter face to face: "[I] said that I had no present wish to marry him, but that it was possible that I might in time, and that if he so desired he might come to see me for a year and we would find out—which he was willing to do." And which he did—relentlessly, possessively, devoutly—intending to trounce the competition in the process. Even brother-sister-type friendships seemed a threat to Walter; yet gradually he managed to persuade Charlotte to take the blame for his jealousies and fears. Reverting haltingly but steadily to the all too familiar childlike role, she began to assume that he had the right to reprimand her, to restrain her friendships, to restrict her fast-paced independent life. He was offering her love, the greatest gift that could be offered to a woman. And despite her shrewd suspicious stance with Charles A. Lane, she failed completely to question whether leadstrings might be attached to Walter's nicely packaged honorarium, or whether associated protocol might fetter her footloose style. Confused but flattered, she turned to Sam Simmons for advice. For instance, a little over two weeks after Walter's proposal she wrote, "Sam comes. Real good talk. . . . He helps me—a little." Two days later, she seemed considerably annoyed with the mounting pressure. "Mr. Stetson arrives. Very unhappy to find me engaged [with Jim Simmons], and won't stay to tea. . . . Why can't they all be friends like the Simmonses?"

For all her Machiavellian pretenses, Charlotte began to lose control, to become anxious and depressed. The previous summer, she had had a minor case of doldrums after arguments with Jim. She had written Martha, "The impetus is slackening already, and now comes the part I dread, a purblind indifference, a view of only my own nose." But this time, instead of letting her "trusted head cometh forward in the nick of time," instead of unraveling her tangled thoughts in a self-respecting way (as she had done with Martha), she began intensifying her program of self-discipline, reinforcing her introspective fears, and binding herself to "high ideals of the grand and pure." Indicative of her sombre inclinations is the following poem written not long after Walter had replaced Martha as Charlotte's closest friend:

IN DUTY BOUND

In duty bound, a life hemmed in,
  Whichever way the spirit turns to look;
No chance of breaking out, except by sin;
  Not even room to shirk—
  Simply to live, and work.

An obligation preimposed, unsought,
  Yet binding with the force of natural law;
The pressure of antagonistic thought;
  Aching within, each hour,
  A sense of wasting power.

A house with roof so darkly low
  The heavy rafters shut the sunlight out;
One cannot stand erect without a blow;
  Until the soul inside
  Cries for a grave—more wide.

A consciousness that if this thing endure,
  The common joys of life will dull the pain;
The high ideals of the grand and pure
  Die, as of course they must,
  Of long disuse and rust.

That is the worst. It takes supernatural strength
  To hold the attitude that brings the pain;
And there are few indeed but stoop at length
  To something less than best.
  To find, in stooping, rest.

Given such an energetic pursuit of no-win duties, such an application of "supernatural strength" to ensure a "hemmed in" life, Charlotte began to waver about her spinster vows. Yet still she clung to "high ideals" which momentarily and ironically protected her. For the same earnest conscientiousness that inspired the stoic martyr talk, inspired some free-spirited aspirations too. Desperately, pathologically almost, she wanted to be "good," and, in a manner characteristic of a child, she turned to others for a rating of that goodness. After all, she had met a man (like her father?) whom she respected and admired. Strong, forceful, and liberal intellectually, he evidenced no Jim Simmons–style religious dogma for her to chafe against, no flaws of character that would justify resistance. And he was passionately attentive besides, in just the ways she felt her father never was. Almost, but not quite, succumbing to a hero-worshipping respect, she wrote him: "O my Friend! My friend! What can I say to thank you for your noble confidence! How can I live purely and grandly enough to justify—God helping me to *glorify* your love! . . . You are the first man I have met whom I recognize as an equal; and that is saying a good deal for me." Then, with a simulated echo of her former bluster, and with a muffled protest against "feminine" emotional dependence as well, she continued to resist Walter with at least marginal success: "I would call you grandly superior, but that I am fighting just now against a heart-touched woman's passion of abnegation."

Partly it was Walter's firmness, partly Charlotte's extravagant respect, that exacerbated her self-abnegating tendencies. Walter's sense of purpose seemed well defined, hers mercurial. Far more importantly, she interpreted the rules of male-female interaction in ways that almost guaranteed that he would win. (In fact, for the most part, she took the rules from contemporary canons of church and state.) She thought she had to choose between feminine emotionality and masculine ambition, between acceptance of inferiority and the heady risk of facing all life's battles on her own. During the previous summer, with Martha to support her, she had assumed that she could resist the "force of natural law" and adopt the rebellious-single-woman role instead. She wrote Martha, "if I am the devil's child, I will live then from the devil." But with Walter, she began displaying requisite attitudes of a "feminine" adult, acknowledging Walter's sublimity, her own persistent vice: "The difference between our lives is this: You have lived purely and grandly from an inward impulse, a noble spirit that would be heard. I have seen certain characteristics to be good and desirable, and then *beaten them into* a nature where evil (of some sort) was predominant."

For all her apparent self-contempt, however, for all her near-capitulation, Charlotte still insisted on her right to debate the issues, pursue honest dialogue, and pummel Walter with trajectories deflected from the battle raging in herself. On February 20, 1882 she wrote him:

> I am thinking deeply just now. And the more I think the more appalled I am at the gravity of the subject. I dare not let myself dwell for an instant on the sense of *double* responsibility, the fact of two lives being implicated. From all that I have read, seen, and heard, that is a fatal step; it instantly weighs on the conscience of the arbiter; and hopelessly complicates a case already confused. No sir! You and your life are not the subject of discussion just now, it would be the last of my regnancy if they were. But I am studying mine with breathless care, backward as far as I can see, and forward as far as I can see, and forward in two directions, with the formula that has been my dependence for years—"if I do this this will happen and if I do *that*." And the fruit of my meditation thus far is this conclusion: that it is an open question which life I can work best in.
>
> That if I were to try the path you open to me I could not reconsider—I could never try my own; but if I first *prove* my own—if I find on fair trial that I cannot do as I think—perhaps —therefore that it is right for me to give a fair chance to feelings and instincts which are certainly wellfounded; to risk the loss of a few years' possible happiness rather than to risk the endurance of a life-time's possible pain. I am not a tenderhearted child; neither am I an impulsive girl; but a clear headed woman who is weighing a life time in her hand. The question under any circumstances is a hard one (it weighed heavily on my lost friend, though she had only to consider whether she loved or no, and had my best love and thought to help her) but situated as I am it is absolutely cruel.
>
> If I were out and free, if I had my home to live in and my work to lean on, if I knew as I then should just what I was losing (I *dare* not count the *gains*!), it would be much easier. But

> just look at it! Here I have every force in nature driving me towards you, and the resisting force is sapped by the underlying possibility of mistake *and presumption*. It is no easy thing to refuse one great work on the ground—self-asserted and unproven—that I can do a greater.
>
> I am beset by my childhood's conscientiousness, and by this new humility which you have taught me; so that at times it seems well nigh absurd to lay so much weight on my own opinion. There is *nothing* else you see, nothing else against the precedent of centuries.
>
> Here is a force—the strongest known to human nature which says "yield!" and I stand quietly against it. The voice of all the ages sounds in my ears, saying that this is noble, natural, and right; that no woman yet has ever attempted to stand alone as I intend but that she had to submit or else repented in dust and ashes—too late! That needless suffering at the best, or miserable failure at the end . . . ? I have nothing to answer but the meek assertion that I am different from if not better than all these, and that my life is mine in spite of a myriad lost sisters before me. Cool, isn't it?

It was a remarkably self-righteous, downright misleading statement for the niece of Catharine Beecher to have made—to suggest that only she among the "myriad lost sisters" stood firm against the "precedent of centuries," that she was serenely "different from if not better than" all other women. Walter may have given lessons in a "new humility," but as yet she had not learned them well. Perhaps she preferred to stand alone, consciously or unconsciously ignoring the rich legacy of women's writings she could have drawn on—the works of Mary Wollstonecraft, George Sand, Margaret Fuller, Frances Wright, Angelina or Sarah Grimké. If she were not yet familiar with their lives or writings, she still had the Beecher women models, whose work she had read, recommended, and admired for years. Charlotte must have learned, however inadequately, that countless women had asserted women's right to creative independence, that scores of sisters had used their reform commitments, their writing talents, their brains, to confront the politicos and pundits who taught women passively to accept their powerlessness.

Perhaps it is understandable that Charlotte conveniently forgot. To her, these seemed exceptional women, exceptional in talent, in ambition, in stamina. Thus, while she was dead wrong to proclaim the uniqueness of her independent stance, she was absolutely right to suggest that the "precedent of centuries" sanctioned the wife-mother role instead. Most of the books that Charlotte read (and Frederick recommended) told about the lives and works of men. Men seemed to be the thinkers and doers, the writers, rulers, and creators of human culture. Women usually were wives and helpmeets. Women loved. Men achieved. And if at times Charlotte had claimed a "masculine" ambition in herself, or tried, in the words of one psychologist, to take the "flight from womanhood," the rewards had not made the effort seem worthwhile. So long as she had been relatively secure in a loving female friendship, she could comfortably disclaim the need to marry. But now that the close relationship with Martha was over, where and how was she to satisfy her human need for love? Many years later, Charlotte would still be railing against this hellish choice. In a short story—"Three Women"—she wrote: "I have seen the effects of this choice you require—the choice between living and loving. I have seen what it means to a woman to have love—and lose life. And what it means to have life—and lose love." Unfortunately, it "is the woman's problem and must be faced."

In February 1882, that was the problem Charlotte thought she faced herself, and even then it angered her. Undoubtedly, she wanted to "shrink" from the "dismal trial," just as she claimed in notes to Walter. Not surprisingly, she complained about the "terrible" and crushing "struggle." But so long as she was still relatively independent, still debating what to do, she managed to send some staccato verbal blasts at Walter that suggest a clean, healthy, self-assertive rage. Of course, to blame Walter for the conflicts was hardly fair. He was no more responsible for sex-based social inequalities than she. But at least (thus far) she refused to blame herself.

> I have just spent ¾ of an hour in writing to you, and written nothing. It is not the first time either. You see I am not free. If you were the friend I wish you were I could write letters that keep you warm in winter. If you were such a friend as I have already, I could write most amusing and graceful epistles.
>
> If you were still what you are, and I were—what I *wish I was* —I could write like Sappho herself.
>
> But now—.
>
> I am crushing my heart under foot, and the exercise is not conducive to a free and easy demeanor. . . .
>
> I knew of course that the time would come when I must choose between two lives, but never did I dream that it would come so soon, and that the struggle would be so terrible.
>
> . . . When we first met I was happy with the simple joy of

> anticipated friendship. I showed you my life and my nature, and held glad hands to you because you were so alike. I was gloriously happy! It seemed as if I was at last to find what I had hardly known enough to long for—companionship. And now—why did you? O why did you! . . . Forgive me. I ought not to complain of being offered the crown of womanhood even if I may not wear it. And in the bottom of my heart I do not regret it, it is only at times that I shrink from a trial which in very truth *does* try me like fire. It is no more than fair that I should tell you this, for you must not think me higher than I am.

The next day she continued:

> How can I offer even the warmest friendliness to one who asks for love? I feel helpless and dumb. The feeling of delighted companionship with which I met you so gladly at first fades to insignificance before the look in your eyes that asks for more than I dare give. . . .
>
> Through you I am learning humility, through you I have learned to pray—and praying I am with a constant cry for help, a looking upward and inward for strength to bear this ordeal.

Charlotte was sending a strange double message. Defiant at times, she was also the proverbial female in distress—supplicating, "helpless and dumb." If she was "looking upward and inward" for strength, she was also pleading with a strong-armed male to help her out. Generously, Walter was willing to explain what she was doing wrong, since she had as much as asked him to. From his perspective (and according to the "cult of true womanhood" canons of the times) more lessons in humility were needed. He suggested she was living with a "proud and joyful heart" for her selfish pleasure. Defensively, momentarily, she retorted that such arguments were "mean and small," which they were. But they were also just the kind to score success. Had Walter only proclaimed her duty to become a wife, she might have boldly answered there were other duties too. But when he suggested she might be selfishly happy in her independence, he had her in a no-win bind. For a while she claimed the single life would be sufficiently unhappy to prove she was not selfish. But the more she reflected on that possibility, the more she resigned herself to a life of hardship either way. Walter had exposed her selfish faults. If he sometimes blamed and punished her (her parents helped to show he had that right), at least he could comfort and protect her too:

And I think of the hours of hopeless grief
Which I know that I must see
Till I long to turn from my journey wild
And throw myself like a tired child
Into arms that are waiting for me.

The resistance had been irksome and exhausting. By early March 1882, she decided it was superfluous and ill-advised as well, or so she led Walter to believe: "I am beginning to wonder how I ever lived through this winter, before you—; beginning to see how tired I was, how depressed and pessimistic. You want to give me something! You are giving me back myself."

That enthusiastic declaration was only partly true, however. To Walter she implied that she was abdicating slightly, but to girlfriends she suggested that she was not so sure. In late March she wrote a letter to a Cambridge friend, Charlotte Hedge, which says in part: Walter "thinks me queer among women, and I am rapidly giving him first place in my esteem. But the longer I live, and the more I know of myself; the more firmly I am convinced that I am not meant for that class of work(!) with all its utility and happinesses. I do not pretend to know just what I am going to do, but a life of comparative freedom and great activity I insist on with the force of natural instinct and corroborative reason. Time will show."

While Charlotte plummeted into the doldrums under Walter's loving gaze, she could still gloat about her buoyancy and spunk when she was on her own. Sportively she tallied up her ventures: painting, reading, and teaching; working ten to twelve hours a day; walking or trotting about Providence, over thirty miles a week. Her letter to Charlotte Hedge continues, "I've been a good little girl this winter, only that I should rob sainthood of its virtues by the bragging I do." Even an accident inspired parody: "I, the strong and impregnable; I, the budding athlete, and Chief Performer at the Providence Ladies Sanitary Gymnasium; I, the surefooted and steady eyed, ignominiously tumbled over a chair, and so injured myself that I was laid up for four days." Mournful and isolated Charlotte may have been at times, but her letter suggests that she could still be supported by her friends. "I have been blessed with more callers than I have had time for in all winter, and with bananas, *strawberries*, oranges, candy ice, and flowers in abundance. Should like to do it again sometime."

Once the shock of the marriage proposal had worn off a bit, and she felt revived by contacts with her friends, Charlotte occasionally approached even the stolid Walter with some of her characteristic playful reverie. The first of May she wrote him:

Because t'is Spring I needs must sing
My joy I cannot smother,
The grass is green, the sky is blue,
And I am I and you are you
And we have found each other!
Then what care we for Fate's decree
It must be one or t'other,
And if we live or if we die
Still you are you and I am I
And still we have each other.

And in June she wrote him love poetry, a bit more seriously but with obvious reserve.

With body & heart & brain, dear love,
"From the center all round to the sea,"
I love you dearly tonight, my love,
A *little* as you love me.

When I'm at my highest & best, dear love,
When the world looks fair and free;
I feel it rise in my heart, dear love,
A *little* like yours for me.

Several days later, Charlotte got a letter from her father, which presumably discussed the possibility of her marriage. Carefully and very formally she responded: "Yours of the 9th received, perused, and listened to. I am very much obliged to you." Then, as though she felt compelled to depreciate her own capacities in order to engage his interest (as she had done with Walter, only in a manner that was more straightforward and cold), she continued: "I have wanted for very long to have someone's judgment set against my own which I could obey without feeling as if I was running on 'sleepers.' Now it dawns on my aspiring mind that you know more than I do! And . . . if I were in your place and had a daughter, that I should like to have her follow my suggestion in a case like this." To some extent, Charlotte seemed to appeal to her father by complaining of Mary's meddling interference. But if she was trying to prove her independence by being hostile to her mother and sternly aloof with her father, she nonetheless unwittingly revealed dependent needs. For she requested not only binding rules from Frederick, but also his vindicating judgment. The letter continues:

> But your rule binds heavily—there is much in my intercourse with any friend which I should *not* desire mother to see. Not

> that I am ashamed or afraid, there are other people wise and good whom I shouldn't object to as spectators, but somehow I can't show things to Mother. I can't be easily myself in her company. She always used to read my letters, written and received, and I never knew what it was to write a letter till I was twenty-one and rebelled. May I not take you for my invisible judge? Perhaps it wouldn't do though, for I hardly know you enough to tell what.

In point of fact, Charlotte probably knew Frederick far better than she realized. She could read his books, even if he did not send her letters, and there was plenty of rich romantic imagery in them to feed her fantasy for months. One of his books that may have attracted her attention was *My Three Conversations with Miss Chester* (1877). Perhaps it was partly a fantasy about his ideal love (perhaps his first love, Frankie Johnson Beecher, as pictured from the bachelor quarters of a rather unhappy divorcé), but it seems a plausible fantasy to have had about his daughter too (Frederick's adult version of Charlotte's "A Fairy Tale"). In any case, the novel might easily have been read as an advisory piece, as though Frederick were saying, somewhat formally but very passionately: "Here, my daughter, is my portrait of the perfect woman's life."

The heroine of the novel, Miss Irene Chester, is Frederick's ideal woman, "namely, the embodiment of health and strength, under the lovely feminine limitations imposed by the laws and graceful lines of womanly beauty." She is well read, accomplished, fiercely independent, and a whiz at chess besides: "indeed she was the only lady player I ever saw who marshalled the mimic ranks with a man-like and purposeful decision and force of combination." Unmoved by the flattering attentions of most of the socializing boors around her, she is also keenly suspicious of the advances of the captivated narrator. Angrily she accuses him of trying to put her "volition into a state of subjection" to his own, thus inspiring him to defend his honorable intentions. He loves her, he declares, but wants a partner not a slave. As a wife, Miss Chester would be "truly a help," but "not in the assumption to herself of daily drudgeries, and in details and the freeing me therefrom . . . but in thinking with parallel and coequal vigor, in the same field of thought; in writing, talking, studying, the same pursuit. What a limitless dream of true union and interfusion of spirits!" Having thus explained his marriage goals in terms of dream-world ecstasy, the narrator then quotes a favorite German scholar to "prove" that wedding bliss in fact can be attained: "and thus the quiet and loving woman and the strong and bold man; do in their synthesis and unity arise into truth and perfection, such as our humanity may attain, before we arise into the heaven of Our Lord. . . . And not twice within the small life of man is that to happen; nor, truly, oftener than once in the lives of millions of men."

Whatever Charlotte thought of Frederick's books, she gradually began to share his "once in the lives of millions" point of view. Only three months after sending her advice-seeking letter to her father, she was ready to accept the "crown of womanhood." On September 8, 1882 she wrote:

As my reward there came
Such love as women seldom find.
Strong; tender; kind;
Passionate; worshipful; adoring; wise;
Ah! the deep sweetness in
those dear blue eyes!

He loves me. I am throned
Highest of earth in that great heart.
We, though apart,
So near each other live
that scarcely speech
Is needed to interpret each
  to each.

Thus safely inured to a "gladness superhuman," to a "wealth of giving," to a "humble deep surprise," Charlotte began to compare the "Joy and Duty" of marriage with the "free if friendless, strong if frozen" life she had before. A groundswell of poetic effusions followed, Walter keeping pace with Charlotte by sending remarkably passionate, though mawkishly sentimental love declarations of his own. Then, as though he wanted to capture and express his love with a grand finality, Walter began to paint Charlotte's portrait. As a poem in one of his love letters suggests, she sat patiently while he toiled each day to achieve the artistic perfection her beauty had inspired. But his description of the process creates a chilling image, strangely reminiscent of Edgar Allen Poe's "The Oval Portrait." In Poe's story, a painter tries to catch the essence of his beloved on his canvas. He too creatively pursues the artist's challenge. But at the moment he finally fixes the spark of life upon the shining canvas eyes, he discovers that his patient wife is dead. Walter's poetry suggests that his efforts as a painter, and as a lover as well, were oppressively intense.

These many days I've tried to fix the face
Of her I love on canvas, that it might
Remain to tell of her, and glad the sight
Of those to come with intellectual grace.
Most patiently did she sit, and I did trace
    And study the marvellous eye that's dark and bright;
    The curve from the wide clear brow's fair height
Along the cheek to the eloquent lip's red place;
    And then down the delicate smooth chin
To the supple throat, until it was so lost
In the [illegible] and heaving breasts' cream white high
  mounds.
    But Oh! today 'tis not more like to her with in
My soul, nor like to what her soul surrounds,
Than 'twas when first my brush the canvas crossed.

O what in me the fault, on what the sin,
    That dulls my sight or warps her image fair
    Until my hand may not her loveliness declare—
For which I've prayed 'eer since I did begin?
Ah, Lord, and hath it always suchwise been,
    That ne'er within my heart I yet did bear
    An image true of all her shape so rare,
Tho' sure I know her spirit dwells therein?
    What then the hope for eminence in Art
When what I love 'er as my very soul
Is not seen clear, is scarcely understood?
    And while I cannot fix the smallest part
Of her great loveliness what can console
And what of all my life and Art is good?

Perhaps there was some "fault" or "sin" dulling Walter's sight that autumn of 1882. For as he was busy painting, writing, and worrying about his eminence in art, his sovereignty as the all-knowing 20/20-vision lover, there were complexities in Charlotte's life and personality he could not possibly have grasped. Her unrequited love for Martha was first among them. On October 8, 1882, less than two weeks after Walter's ill-starred portrait-painting efforts, Martha Luther married Charles A. Lane. Charlotte had had nearly a year in which to prepare for the wedding, a year in which she apparently saw Martha almost not at all. However she may have felt—betrayed or rejected, angry or defeated—she explored no such feelings with her pen. If her diary entry the day of Martha's wedding is any indication, she probably felt compelled to keep silent with Walter and to adopt a guise of rank indifference to the whole affair: "Really enjoyed myself. Help Martha change her dress," then home to "read and write."

If Charlotte turned to Walter on the rebound from Martha's neglect, she also seemed to think he could relieve the sense of deprivation her parents had caused as well. It was as though she felt Walter could compensate for years of childhood solitude, years of hankering for Mary's cuddling or Frederick's warmth. Usually she was in that kind of dejected mood when she wrote Walter, a listless melancholy tone pervading almost all her letters, as though in mournful protest that the more life-affirming sparks she had sent to others failed to kindle a response. In any case, several weeks after Martha's wedding, Charlotte wrote another "love poem" to Walter.

My lips are my lover's
This hand you may hold;
It is proud of your pressing, This girdle enfold
With your strong loving arm. To my cheek
  lay your own
And kiss as it likes you all else;
  this alone
  I reserve for my lover

They were kept from first childhood
Not even the mouth
Of my mother touched mine in
My earliest youth.
And when in the forest in flickering light
My lover first kissed me I answered
the rite
With the freshness of childhood

Superstitious say you?
The logic is small;
To be chary of one thing and
generous with all.
To reserve one small piece and
make public the whole—
And yet I am glad from the
depths of my soul
I kept these for my lover.

C.A.P.

During December 1882, Charlotte occasionally felt aglow with the "flickering light" of love, but she seemed just as frequently to feel depressed and numb. December 31 was a case in point, New Year's Eve, a time for sober self-reflections. She had had a "long happy evening" with Walter, she decided, but it must have been a strange sort of happiness indeed, for that same diary entry continues: "My last act in the old year was to kneel at my bedside in shame and repentance, with hot tears and self-abasement. From which I rose resolved to pray no more for a season but to work again."

From January through March 1883, "happy" times continued—regular Sunday-evening quiet talks, occasional long walks, love letters in between. There were even a few marriage-planning sessions, still without commitment, still just fantasies, but serious enough for Charlotte's mother already to have offered assistance from the sidelines: "She thinks we'd better marry & come here to board. (I don't)." But if Mary's first offer had been wisely and quickly rejected, her second suggestion seemed more appealing: "Mother proposes a grand new arrangement to which we joyfully accede. We take the house and things, downstairs tenement that is, & live here for the present while she goes out west" to visit brother Thomas.

Pressures—from Walter, from Aunt Caroline, from mother, and probably from friends—were mounting, but Charlotte still felt she had some veto power. From her perspective, selfish resistance was intolerable, but altruistic-sounding arguments still served relatively well. Ultimately they would work against her, but temporarily they afforded some protection: "If I have any personal volition let it lean entirely toward right-doing; & desire to add such force as I have to the Power for Good." To a degree, Charlotte debated her own conflicting goals and needs clearly, but at times she seemed to feel she had lost control: She was watching and "longing to *do right*" as "two strong natures" fought for regnancy:

O God I wish to do
My highest and my best in life!
Stop not for hindrance or strife
Be Wise, and Strong, and True.
And can I also be a wife?
Bear children too—? . . .

Can I, who suffer from the wild unrest
Of two strong natures claiming each its due,
And can not tell the greater of the two;
Who have two spirits ruling in my breast

Alternately, and know not which is guest
  And which the owner true;

Can I, thus driven, bring a child to light
  Who from the hour of birth until he dies,
Will hear still more these strong opposing cries;
Will have my passionate longing to *do right*
  To reach the soul's most perfect Paradise.

As Charlotte searched for soul perfection, she accepted Walter's sympathy, at times his comforting protection, even occasionally his rules and regulations. When, on April 5, a friend gave her a beautiful new copy of Walt Whitman's *Leaves of Grass*, she noted, "I am obliged to decline as I had promised Walter I would not read it." But a crisis followed (according to diary entries that are tantalizingly laconic). April 8: Walter "is not coming any more. Went at 11:15. (Simply to anticipate the parting & save pain) Dear Love! Shall I come back?" If this represented a last-ditch contest of wills, a final confrontation with the agony and disapproval she thought a spinster stance would bring, perhaps it served as a trial-run resistance and, as such, an appropriate prelude to final promises and vows. April 10: "My pain & sorrow is all behind and underneath as yet. The least line of kindred thought in poetry brings all the ache and tears, but by myself I *won't* think about it." April 26: "Find that Walter has been here, expecting to find me not, and left note, and sonnets. Answer." April 28: "Mother tries to talk to me about Mr. Stetson, & blames him somewhat. I refuse to give any information." April 29: "Write to Walter; not to send, he does not wish it."

Characteristically, work was the self-prescribed antidote in crisis times—reading, teaching, painting—"not a wasted moment." She was also helped by earnest discussions with her friends, with Grace Channing mainly, and with Connie Pitman, another friend in Providence: "Call on Connie Pitman. I learn much about the *horror* of modern society. I knew it before, but this was face to face." And she turned again to favorite authors too, punctuating her diary with brief reminders of their healing power: Thomas Carlyle—"A grand pleasure;" Christina Rossetti—"Cry a good deal." It was as though she thought that by reading furiously, by confronting human injustices in society at large, she could eliminate her own lesser worries and happily direct her energies and talents toward serving all mankind instead: "O my *God*! Help me to live according to thy *laws*! Teach me to live. That I may grow each year Better; and help all those I meet and know and those who read or see what I have done. And those who know of me to find their lives Better as well. And easier and more light. O God I have been weak! I have been *weak*—. Help thou to make me strong! I *will* to do the right!" Discipline, piercing ambition, intense moral commitment—these must overrule emotional distractions, coldly, stoically, relentlessly. And since she had already successfully persuaded Walter of her Amazonian determination—enough for him to keep his distance for the moment anyway—now she penned a letter to her brother Thomas, as though to consolidate her lofty isolated stance:

> I always think of you much, am proud of you, and glad indeed for your happiness. But I seem to be singularly barren of natural affection. "Brother" brings no answering thrill to my heart. Perhaps because we had so little genuine loving intercourse when we were together. Fun we had in plenty, and a large fund of common intelligence; but I can never remember any companionship [nor?] beautiful ideas. And now that I have so outgrown myself that fun in general grates, (American fun I mean, mere made of nonsense—well you will understand if I say that I no long[er] care for parodies.) There is nothing left but the common intelligence. And your intelligence is so broad and real, and so far away from mine that I feel uncertain how to approach you.
>
> As I grow and grow I care more and more for right living, not of a pious kind—I yoke myself with neither creed nor Bible, but such living as will most conduce the progress and happiness of self and all self touches. I have ideas and theories which time will develope, and I work.
>
> Bye and bye when I know much more and hold such place in society as I will hold, perhaps I might write you letters that would be of some use.
>
> But now I am only acquiring knowledge, with scarce enough to impart; and my "ideas and theories" change and change as the years go by so that I have become gradually more taciturn about them.
>
> "Speak what you think today in hard words, and tomorrow speak what tomorrow thinks in hard words again, though it contradict everything you have said today;" says Emerson. Also, "With consistency a great soul has nothing to do." Which I believe; but where rules may be followed it is safer to test well before promulgating.

That was May 13, 1883—a solemn cheer for the virtue of inconsistency. And May 14—a resounding cheer for Walter's perseverance: "Walter calls! O I was *glad* to see him!" During the next several days, she apparently felt enough "happy" sadness to allow a bitter-sweet rapprochement. May 15: "Write note to Walter. Am unhappy. . . . The first night I have cried because I couldn't help it. That is couldn't help *wanting* to." May 17: "Walter comes, bless his heart! Happy evening."

According to her autobiography, Charlotte had "demanded a year's complete separation, to recover clear judgment, but could not secure it. [Walter complained a lot, no doubt, but Charlotte couldn't stand the tension either.] . . . Then, at one time when he had met a keen personal disappointment, I agreed to marry him." That was Sunday, May 20, 1883. In the morning she had taught a Sunday school class on Socrates and Mohammed, and then gone to church: "the grandest preaching I remember to have heard. Grand! and his prayers were *prayers*." Thus fortified by heavy doses of religion, shaken by Walter's discouraged mood, and tired of her own intransigence, magnanimous Charlotte agreed to marry. From her perspective, it was a binding promise; veto power was finally relinquished: "After that, in spite of reactions and misgivings, I kept my word, but the period of courtship was by no means a happy one."

* * *

As Charlotte busied herself with the thankless task of squashing qualms about her pledge to Walter, however, she also busied herself devising moral principles to suit, and securing a sympathetic audience on which to test them. Several months before, she had started teaching some "little scholars" in the Sunday School program sponsored by a local chapter of the Union for Christian Work. Her "sermons" dealt with questions she was raising anyway—personal dilemmas writ large: "Belief in God, and the Use of It," "Justifiable Lying," and "Does Courtesy Necessitate Deceit?" (Did she ask herself if a promise to love happily, unquestioningly, and endlessly was in some way deceitful?) Plan for the good, honorable life, expel the fear of pain or failure—this is what she and her "little scholars" had to learn. "No evil can befall a good man," she told them. That "means, you see, that if you are wise and brave and honorable in all ways, the outside things that happen to you can not *hurt*; that there is really no evil but what's inside of us. . . . It's not what's done *to you* that makes you anything; it's what *you do*." So be confident, for even the laws of evolution justify an optimistic point of view: it is "one of Nature's laws, or God's Laws, that things *shall* grow up and improve. . . . the most important thing for you to remember is that wrong doing is punished and right doing rewarded just as surely as night follows day. In order to be happy you *must* do right." But the formula is clear, straightforward, simple. Right-doing assures the happiness of others. Wrong-doing means selfishness unleashed: "As you know [selfishness] is the ruling motive in most lives; the root of most sin and misery; indeed I believe of all sin and misery. Tell me *one sin* that cannot be traced back to Selfishness."

Open spats with Walter, Charlotte had decided, were unjustified and selfish, but spats with the Sunday School director were quite another matter. The director thought she should be teaching Bible stories. She liked sportive practical religion more, and did not hesitate to explain the matter openly to her "little scholar" friends: "I could have rebelled I suppose, and left the class," she told them, but she had won a compromise instead: "A part of my lesson will be on the regular subject; and the rest of the time we will use as we please." So combining irreverent playfulness with her own style of religious ardor, she continued casually enough: "But though I agree with you that Solomon was 'a little off' on some subjects; though I can despise Jacob and laugh at Jonah and criticize Job; I do *not* see anything funny in Jesus Christ."

Charlotte was proud of her Beecher flair for preaching, her easy teaching style, the spirited class response. And if she used "sermons" to help resolve some private quandaries, she used them to boost her spirits too. For instance: "Boy's Room. Tell 'em stories, very much interested." Or again, "Boy's room. Same little ruffians I had last time come and *ask* me for more books! Show 'em animals and 'uncivilized races!'" So much did they like her, and so rarely had they found Sunday School classes interesting and fun, that as her teaching jaunt came to a close in the spring of that year (1883), they fussed and complained delightfully: "They are averse to the idea of losing me. Say they will have no one else—I *must* come. Pleasant."

Charlotte probably stopped teaching because she preferred a more lucrative kind of work, not because of disagreements with the Sunday School director or the "little scholars'" parents. That spring (about the time of her formal engagement to Walter), she was offered a ten-week position in Camp Walten, Maine, as governess for a little boy named Eddie Jackson. The news was "received with disapprobation by Mother and Aunt [Caroline]," no doubt by Walter too, but Charlotte was thrilled with the prospect anyway. Primarily she wanted money. Her mother was paying her to do housework, but as Charlotte paid room, board, and personal expenses, there was little left for all the household gear and gadgets, all the hope-chest finery and furnishings she hoped to buy before the wedding. Besides, a governess position was regarded as a perfectly appropriate way for single middle-class young ladies to make some money—one of the few available in fact. And from Charlotte's perspective, the work would be refreshingly brainless, facile, and mild. After the first two or three days of on-the-job training she wrote to Martha Luther Lane, "The men folks fish and hunt, the women folks knit and crochet and chatter, and I (neuter you observe!) Write & Draw & Paint and make myself generally useful."

Then the novelty wore off. Mary had objected to Charlotte's leaving because she needed help at home, Walter because he didn't like the time they had to be apart (or her relative independence). Charlotte soon objected to the work for reasons of her own: the dull monotony of the daily domestic routine, the frustration of dealing with a balking bawling child—his mother hovering, spoiling, defending on the sidelines—the relentless task of harnessing her temper, of staying tight-lipped, cool, and calm. Martha suddenly became Charlotte's sounding board again, not on the intimate private kinds of issues which might leave her vulnerable, but on issues which called for clean-cut rage. After about a week's experience as a governess, Charlotte wrote Martha,

> [T]he people here have grown highly obnoxious to me, and the boy in especial is abhorrent to my every—antenna. If it perplexes you to reconcile this with my former buoyant content remember that I am always apt to be pleased with my surroundings, and that character is a slow book to read. You know how fond I am of children & children of me; so you will believe it to be no light matter that could cause me to heartily dislike a child.
>
> *Selfish. Rude. Lazy. Dishonorable* weak. Timid. And more than I care to mention.
>
> I have no wish to give him pain, but I do want to get away from him; and to have to be around all day and every day with a youth who has neither respect nor love for me is *hard*. Don't you think I'm naturally inclined to be obliging and patient? Well this boy taxes both. Always his will and never mine, unless one prefers sultry resistance. So I just bear his exactions as long as I can, and then balk and let him think me as "horrid" as he pleases.

Initially, Charlotte had been considering the governess position for the entire coming year; but Eddie Jackson's family, no doubt for good reasons of their own, relieved her of any decision-making guilt:

"take it on trust dear that the winter looked like Purgatory to me; to be endured with hope of the Paradise beyond, and because it seemed meek and selfish to back out, *wasn't* I glad of release!"

There was a kind of free-flowing ease in Charlotte's letters to Martha, a sense of release in having someone on whom to vent frustrations. But there were undercurrents of strain as well. Charlotte had not written to Martha for months, probably not since that prolific summer of 1881. Through all the headaches and deliberations over Walter, she had not shared her thoughts or asked for help. There was too much hurt, too strong a sense of having been ignominiously exposed. She had been so forceful in proclaiming all the reasons for her spinster vows, so relentless in thrashing Martha for capitulating to a male; it was difficult enough to face her own reversals privately, but a bit more than pride could handle to admit them to her friend. So she teased and taunted Martha for her wife and mother domesticity instead, playfully, but with enough droll humor to let her stored-up irritation show: "I confess I'm a little astonished at your doctrine," Charlotte wrote her, "devouring beef & lamb, . . . pale ale, & flaxseed tea. . . . I myself could hardly keep that up all day. Do you mix 'em, or take them consecutively?" Still, Charlotte was warmer than she had been, for the letter continues, "Bless your little heart Martha, you're a comfort. You and your good husband and little fat-legged baby—I like to think of you."

Thinking back on the last several years of friendship, the estrangement, the sense of playing second fiddle to Charles A. Lane, Charlotte seemed to feel a certain spurious satisfaction in the recent role reversal. Cuttingly, unnecessarily, unpersuasively she acted as though Walter's love meant that bonds with Martha mattered not a whit: "I'm glad you want to see me, pussy, and so do I want to see you. But there is a man in Providence whom I should not stay away from for an extra minute even to see you! Now doesn't that show some change, some advance in my power of loving since I saw you last? I tell you dear there is no question now except one of time and means. Not even to you can I show my heart now, but you know it well from your own. Happy? Happy beyond words. You know, little girl, you know."

But if Charlotte felt she had to flaunt her indifference, to use Walter as her subterfuge, she also seemed to feel a warm nostalgia as she wrote to Martha, a sense of compatibility, intimacy, and mutual understanding that was absent in her relationship with Walter. So despite disclaimers that Walter's love replaced her need for Martha, Charlotte asked Martha to be not only a supportive confidante on issues Walter would misunderstand, but also an ally to protect her from his disapproving anger. Charlotte wrote: "Don't you think really dear that things must have been pretty bad for me to feel almost that I *couldn't* stand it? Do cuddle me a little; I don't want to tell Walter all about it, because it would make him angry—furious, and do no good. But I want you to get 'real mad' at these folks who have not been good to your best friend; just call Eddie names please, and say you don't think much of Mrs. Jackson for letting him grow up so! It comforts me already to think of it."

The summer months with Eddie Jackson passed all too slowly, Martha's long-distance comforting marred by resentments and regrets, the correspondence with Walter marred by irritations too. The summer's sojourn had been a disaster, and the return to Providence did not improve matters. Acknowledging her own disappointments, confronting others' I-told-you-so reactions, scanning the winter's prospects—all these seemed to leave a dull and gnawing ache. Rather quickly she plunged into her usual Providence routines—gym classes, literary clubs, teaching, writing, painting, running—but nothing seemed much fun. In early November she wrote: "Whereas I, Charlotte A. Perkins, am at this time 23 years old and not content, I desire to know *why* not! What have I done so far to fulfill my duties as a member of the world? If I were dead tomorrow what were lost? What do I mean to do and be? Why am I unhappy now? I have promised to marry Charles Walter Stetson. I love him? Yes. And by love I mean that I want him more than anyone else on earth? That and more. . . . Now love is more than *wanting*. *Love* is the infinite desire to benefit, a longing to give not merely a hungry wish to take." So back she flew to the moralistic self-sacrificing stance, as though efforts to achieve some fun-filled satisfactions would be fruitless anyway. Dutifully, almost morbidly, she summarized the characteristics she hoped to instill in herself:

1st *Absolutely unselfish*
And that means? To find my happiness in the pleasurable sensations of others rather than in my own. To consider others, think of others, think first "will he or she like it?" rather than shall I.
Do I do this now? A little.
As much as I can? no.
From this hour I rebegin.
2nd *Wise*. And that means? Foresight and memory and sure decision in the present. To use Reason in action, God given Reason, and do a thing with regard to its consequences.
3rd *Strong* . . .
4th *Brave* . . . Power to do right regardless of consequences.

5th *Pure*
Purity is that state in which no evil impulse, no base thought can come; or if forced in dies of shame in the white light. Purity may be gained by persistent and long continued refusal to entertain low ideas. . . .
6th *Truth*
Truth is simply the expression of what one is.

. . . Unselfish, True, and Wise; Strong, Brave, and Pure—if I am these I do right by my husband, my children, my God, and mankind. . . . Having no lover it is my duty to God and man and myself. Having a lover it is my first duty to him.

With such exacting saintly standards (and Walter's prodding—he asked her to be more gentle and calm), Charlotte lost her sense of humor; she could scarcely remember anything she had done to make her feel acceptable, much less desirable or proud. The end of the year (1883) diary entry reads:

And this year gone?
Weakly begun, ill lived, little regarded.
Some things have I done and learned, but
nothing to what I would have.

My clear life-governing will is dead or sleeping. I live on circumstances, and waves of misery sweep over me, resistless, unaccountable; or pale sunshine of happiness comes, as mysteriously.

I would more gladly die than ever yet; saving for the bitter agony I should leave in the heart of him who loves me. And mother's pain.

But O! God knows I am tired, tired, tired of life!

If I could only know that I was doing right—!

The diary entry for January 1, 1884, continues in the same despondent tone.

With no pride, with little hope, with uncertain occasional happiness, with no glad energy and living power; with no faith or nearly none, but still, thank God! with firm belief in what is right and wrong; I begin the new year. . . .

One does not die young who so desires it.

Perhaps it was not meant for me to work as I intended. Perhaps I am not to be of use to others. I am weak.

I anticipate a future of failure and suffering. Children sickly and unhappy. Husband miserable because of my distress; and I—!

> I think sometimes that it *may* be the other way; bright and happy; but this comes oftenest; holds longest. But this life is marked for me, I will not withdraw; and let me at least learn to be uncomplaining and unselfish. Let me do my work and not fling my pain on others.
>
> . . . I think if I woke, dead, and found myself unchanged—still adrift—, still at the mercy of passing waves of feeling I should go mad. Can the dead so lose themselves I wonder?
>
> And let me not forget to be grateful for what I have. Some strength, some purpose, some design, some progress, some esteem, respect—and affection. And some Love which I can neither see nor believe in when the darkness comes.
>
> I mean this year to try hard for somewhat of my former poise and courage. As I remember it was got by practice.

That was scarcely an auspicious beginning for the New Year, the year in which she planned to marry. In part, her willingness to explore, to acknowledge, to dwell upon the morbid implications of her decisions must have been inspired by the suicide of a close neighbor friend, Conway Brown. That same day, January 1, 1884, she wrote, "*Conway Brown shot himself yesterday*. . . . He told me last summer that he had times of horrible depression. And had often thought of shooting himself. What mental misery it must have been to make him forget his parents and all the other ties that bound him to earth! I can sympathize with him; mental misery is real; and in a season of physical depression might well grow unbearable. How needful to live so that in such times there is enough real work to look back upon to preserve one's self respect! The only safety is within."

There was desperation in Charlotte's writing now. Her former confidence was too often ravaged by a sense of hopelessness, her obdurate faith in the healing power of hard work too often shattered by uncertainties as to whether her self-styled therapy would work. Yet, sporadically, it still seemed to. For although there were only four months remaining before the wedding (it was set for May 2, 1884), and despite mounting anxieties, Charlotte managed to flip and sport about at quite a rapid and impressive pace. Alongside doleful entries during the last months before her wedding (and supplementing her autobiography, which depicts her misery too), there still are diary entries that show some drive, and some fairly healthy anger too.

Characteristically, Charlotte jotted down survival strategies in her trusted diary. First among them, she decided, should be a physical fitness retraining program. She had been feeling lethargic, sometimes sickly, so on January 2nd she mapped out a "course of diet, by means of which, and other changes, I trust to regain my old force and vigor." The diet would include oatmeal, biscuits, milk, and oranges, and "not too much of that." Of course, she rescheduled exercise classes too, writing in her diary that same day: "First evening at the gymnasium. Delightful to be there again. . . . I have not lost so much strength as I feared, can still go up the rope and on the rings, etc. Off on vaulting of course." She was off on other proofs of prowess too, her weight-lifting, toe-touching, mile-running exploits, all the reassuring signs that she had mastered the skills outlined in Blaikie's *How To Get Strong and How to Stay So*. Five feet, six-and-a-half inches tall and weighing some 120 pounds, she could pick up a girl her own size, she gloated, and "*run* with her easily as could be"; she could run "40 laps, vault 6 (on one side only) and lift 3 rings on the ladder!" Neither the skills nor the health maxims were new, of course; she had preached and practiced them for years: "Good *air* and *plenty of it*. Good food and plenty of it. *Good* exercise and plenty of it. Good sleep and plenty of it. Good clothes and as few as possible." But in the months before her marriage, there was nothing so enthusiastically, so ecstatically recorded in her diary as her physical fitness feats: "exercise hilariously," "cavort wildly," or "gym, enjoying it intensely and doing more than usual."

Meanwhile, Walter was preoccupied with some independent projects too. For professional reasons, and some worrisome monetary ones as well, he had arranged to have the Providence Art Club sponsor an exhibit of his paintings in the early part of March. There was still time for the regular Sunday evening *tête-à-tête* with Charlotte, and time for love notes almost daily, but otherwise Walter was so anxious to finish up his paintings that weekday visits were necessarily abbreviated and sporadic. Very likely, Charlotte did not mind at all. For with Walter absorbed in work, also a bit harried and depressed, Charlotte felt less overwhelmed by his attentions, less defensive, and thus could act more sympathetically and generously than usual. So she popped into his studio from time to time (to the dismay of priggish neighbors), tried to reassure and cheer him, and sometimes even helped by serving as his model. Most of the time she was scurrying about with her own hectic time- and energy-consuming schemes; perhaps for that reason alone, she could sometimes act as though she felt relaxed: "Sit and sew demurely while he paints; with occasional kisses in between."

Several weeks later—frantic weeks for Walter—the art exhibit opened. Friends poured in, sales seemed likely, and his reception was a grand success. Charlotte served as hostess and was proud of what she wore: "Carrie's black silk, white Spanish tie, ruching, & lace in sleeves, yellow ribbon, yellow beads, gold comb, amber bracelet, yellow crest on bonnet, yellow flowers." Yet almost immediately, irritation and estrangement undermined her festive mood. Perhaps because of overwork, or disappointment with the art show, or vague premarriage tensions that would have surfaced anyway, right in the midst of Walter's "successes" (Charlotte had been dutifully and enthusiastically recording Walter's sales), she complained: "Walter. Am lachrymose. Heaven send that my forebodings of future pain for both be untrue." The day after the exhibit closed, March 12, 1884: "stop and see Walter, and still miserable."

Whatever the reasons for the downward pitch, judging from the diaries, Charlotte allowed herself little time to wrestle with emotions. Instead, she immersed herself in a nonstop dizzying swirl of doings: daily rounds of calls and callers, whist and casino games with relatives and friends, afternoon teas with Grace Channing and the Hazard sisters, helping her mother with the day school program, keeping up with housework, darting over to the seamstress for endless fittings for her wedding dress, shopping for household miscellanea, sewing clothes and linens, rushing constantly. If, with such a schedule, she sometimes forgot her troubles, she also inadvertently and awkwardly forgot Walter's birthday (March 25). He was relatively understanding, she, embarrassed and annoyed. It was "not for lack of thought of him," she complained a bit defensively. That was just her way. She almost always forgot birthdays and anniversaries.

Meanwhile, she and Walter were planning for the small three-room apartment they would rent, choosing colors for rugs and wallpaper, ordering fixtures and "lovely curtain stuffs." Charlotte was by no means one to observe passively on the sidelines, autobiographical disclaimers notwithstanding.* In fact, quite often she seemed to take control. On February 13 she wrote, "stop and see Walter a little while; and tell him various plans of mine." February 29: "joying in my little house and plans in general." And in March: "Stop in and see my house, which is being painted and the stairs put on. Demand a door to the outside part."

During her engagement to Walter, Charlotte retained far more objectivity than she was sometimes willing to admit. Her letters to Martha concerning the governess position provide one clue that

* Diaries thus counter her autobiographical portrait of herself as the selfless acquiescent maiden quietly admiring while Walter planned their home: the "young artist" alone "had made it beautiful. 'Do it just as you choose,' I told him. 'I have no taste and no desires'" (*The Living of Charlotte Perkins Gilman: An Autobiography* [New York: Harper & Row, 1975; 1st pub., 1935], p. 85).

she confidently hid feelings she knew Walter would disapprove. Her diaries reveal another, a well-worn "female strategy" of coy pretense: Walter "was hurt at the gaiety of one of my letters. I shouldn't have sent it," she noted, as though next time she would wisely keep such letters to herself.

Charlotte had too many absorbing projects, and was too obstreperous besides, to lapse quietly into the pure-and-pious-lady mold Walter may have tried imposing on her (or she tried imposing on herself). Even in the last few months before her wedding, she was still grinding through German and French grammar books, preparing Sunday School sermons, writing poetry and fiction, and reading avidly. From January through April (1884), she read (or at least read "in") works of Rossetti, Carlyle, Shakespeare, Thucydides, Longfellow, and Emerson, to name a few. She also read John Stuart Mill's *The Subjection of Women*. This hardly was fare for the self-denying soul. In addition, she subscribed to two feminist-oriented papers, *Alpha* and the Boston-based *Woman's Journal*, and even tried sending articles and poetry to each. The previous December she had gotten a letter from the *Woman's Journal* accepting her poem "In Duty Bound." That was just the "first step," she decided, "the entering wedge. No pay, but it's a beginning." Then *Alpha* published another poem—"One Girl of Many." Sentimentally addressing the "fallen woman" theme, she by no means suggested that women should aspire to the all-trusting feminine ideal.

> All that life held of yet unknown delight,
> Shone, to her ignorance, in colors bright:
> Shone near at hand, and sure. If she had *known*!—
> But she was ignorant: she was alone. . . .
>
> Only one girl in many.
> 'Tis a need
> Of man's existence to repeat the deed.
> Social necessity.
> Men cannot live
> Without what these disgraceful creatures give
> Black shame, dishonor, misery and sin;
> *And men find needed health and life therein!*

* * *

Charlotte experienced a raging internal battle as the wedding day approached: intense anger—diffuse, sometimes misdirected—countered by incapacitating guilt. Her compassion for, or identification with, the passive female victim did not disguise her budding hostility toward men, her disgust with their duplicity and lust, her resentment of their power and independence. But if the most important current reason for her hostility was Walter himself, and her fear of becoming his wife, she could not admit that even to herself. Since to her, Walter represented pure and noble manhood, he deserved love and sympathetic understanding. To be angry with him was unjustified and selfish.

Assuming then that any tension or unhappiness hinged solely on her own faults and foibles, Charlotte devised a strategy of "intensive self-denial from within." As she put it in her autobiography, "there was no natural response of inclination or desire, no question of, 'Do I love him?' only 'Is it right?'"

Again, we come upon a favorite theme of her autobiography: she was the defenseless dispirited young woman swept along by circumstances beyond her control. Perhaps she felt that she would win the sympathy of readers if she emphasized her weakness, but that she would be held accountable if she described her perspicacity and awareness instead. So long as she was ignorant, she could not be blamed. To acknowledge elements of self-awareness, however muddled, would be to admit that some responsibility also lay within herself.

Some of the responsibility was hers, of course. She had failed to resist conventions she later forcefully condemned, even though she partly understood the consequences at the time. Still, the matter is one of emphasis only. For Charlotte's decision to marry Walter—despite her obvious unhappiness, her fears, her ambitious goals—speaks volumes about the marriage pressures most women of her generation faced. She, like so many women with far less opportunity for independent choice or understanding, finally accepted what she thought must be her fate. As she later wrote, "marriage is the woman's proper sphere, her divinely ordered place, her natural end. It is what she is born for, what she is exhibited for." She had thus experienced and perceived what Simone de Beauvoir would later echo:

> One is not born, but rather becomes a woman. No biological, psychological, or economic fate determines the figure that the human female presents in society; it is civilization as a whole that produces this creature.

Chapter Six

The Crown of Womanhood 1884-1887

On Friday, May 2nd, 1884, Charlotte put the finishing touches on her wedding dress, trimmed her bonnet, arranged "great stacks of flowers," and then flew about nervously trying to seem calm. At about 6:30 that evening, she and Walter Stetson were married, his father, Joshua Stetson, presiding. "Aunt C[aroline] was hearty in her congratulations," and Walter's "parents were kind and affectionate, but Mother declines to kiss me and merely says 'good bye.'" Charlotte continued in her diary:

> I install Walter in the parlor and dining room while I retire to the bedchamber and finish its decoration. The bed looks like a fairy bower with lace, white silk, and flowers. Make myself a crown of white roses. Wash again, and put on a thin drift of white mull fastened with a rosebud. He meets me joyfully; we promise to be true to each other; and he puts on the ring and the crown. Then he lifts the crown, loosens the snood, unfastens the girdle, and then—and then.
>
> O my God! I thank thee for this heavenly happiness! O make me one with thy great life that I may best fulfill my duties to my love! to my Husband!
>
> And if I am a mother—let it be according to thy will!
>
> O guide me! Teach me, help me to do right!

The next day she wrote:

> Up at 8:20 or so. Get a nice little breakfast of omelette and chocolate. Lie on the lounge in the soft spring sunshine and am

> happy, Happy, Happy. Walter stays quietly at home with me; and we rest and love each other. Get johnny-cakes and frizzled beef for dinner; wash dishes, Walter wiping; . . . put my boy to bed, (he is well worn out with a long winter's work,) . . . O I am happy! May I do right enough to merit and deserve!
>
> *Thank God*

Charlotte and Walter had planned only a short weekend honeymoon at home. They lounged about, read together, arranged things in their new apartment, trying awkwardly, self-consciously, to create an atmosphere of wedded bliss. Charlotte's way was to tackle kitchen duties and to loaf (though neither was her style). On Sunday she washed dishes and made bread while Walter read to her. On Monday, the honeymoon over, she fixed an elaborate breakfast, napped three hours while Walter worked, and made dinner when he came home at two. "Then loaf a bit, wash dishes and fix bedroom. He feels dizzy; and I put him snugly to bed and then write. Am happy."

The next week was more or less the same. She shopped, called on friends, lazed about, and tried to teach herself to cook. (Her mother had done most of it at home.) Tuesday she made a "most delectable dinner of veal fried in batter and new potatoes. Very very delicious," she wrote. "Am tired later and am put tenderly to bed." But she was "turning out [to be] a superior cook," she decided, and was pleased that Walter noticed.

For all her earlier jibes against domestic work—she had told Martha it was an insufferable bore—Charlotte now seemed to think not only that love meant giving, but that woman's love meant cleaning, cooking, and managing the housework. Being a man, Walter had other kinds of work to do; in fact, marriage added further purpose to his public, professional commitment. He had no time or energy, inclination or know-how to concern himself with pots and pans, mops and brooms and such. That was Charlotte's province. There was one day (or one moment of one day) back in 1882 when he had thought differently. Aware of her keen ambitions, but unaware of practicalities, he had written, "I hereby take my solemn oath that I shall never in future years expect of my wife any culinary or housekeeping proficiency." But if promises came easy, they faded from his memory when he faced the reality which (as Charlotte later remarked) very quickly and "rudely breaks in upon love's young dream. On the economic side, apart from all the sweetness and truth of the sex-relation, the woman in marrying becomes the house-servant, or at least the housekeeper, of the man." Spontaneously, only one week after their wedding, Charlotte wrote in her diary: "I suggest he pay me for my services; and he much dislikes the idea. I am grieved at offending him, mutual misery. Bed and cry."

Several weeks later, she got a letter from her brother Thomas that probably helped matters not at all (from Walter's point of view). Thomas wrote, "Realizing the great need of all young married people—the need of a quantity of advice and instruction of sundry and various kinds—I take great pleasure herewith transmitting a sufficient quantity thereof to not only supply your own needs, but peradventure several generations of your predecessors." Then, as though he knew precisely what was at issue, he "continued continuously thereon and thereafter" and proceeded to sketch a broom on one side of the page and Webster's unabridged dictionary on the other. The first was "woman's alleged sceptre," the second "Woman's (real) sceptre," he quipped. "Either may be construed in several ways. You can suit your own taste. *Mine* is to consider one to typify cleanliness and the other conversational ability—some would suggest force of arms and fluency of invective."

Walter may have been concerned or irritated, but in either case he was not dumb. In fact, he seemed quite supportive. For example, he began reading the story of Atalanta's race "for" her. And when she faced a "vast accumulation of dishes," wisely he came home and helped. Actually, Walter assumed a lot of household chores, though in part it was because Charlotte complained so much of feeling tired and sickly. "Bed. Am disgusted with myself—numb—helpless," Charlotte wrote after several weeks of marriage. "Tomorrow God helping me I will begin anew!"

Charlotte sometimes found that intellectual activity helped to boost her spirits, so she began reading again, talking "earnestly" with friends "on foreordination and free will," and studying "obstetrics diligently." But for the most part she seemed absorbed with housework, physical ailments, and Walter's kind attentiveness. July 3: "Scrub out house and stairs. . . . Go over to Mother's, darn stockings and talk." June 13: "Feel sick and remain so all day." June 14: "Walter gets breakfast. . . . Walter helps much. . . . Read and eat candy while Walter draws me in bed. Am happy."

But the next day, and in the days that followed, Charlotte felt differently: "Am sad: last night and this morning. Because I find myself too—affectionately expressive. I must keep more to myself and be asked—not borne with." June 25: "Get miserable over my old woe—conviction of being too outwardly expressive of affection." June 26: "still miserable and feel tired. . . . Am miserable some more but he persuades me to believe that he never tires of me."

These were remarkable statements for a nineteenth-century bride to have made—sensuous, even demanding, though apologetic. At least Charlotte was *trying* to adhere to appropriate "true womanhood" ideals of virtue and purity. But if some healthy gusty inclinations sometimes interfered, she piously and consciously tried suppressing them. "Purity," she believed, "is that state in which no evil impulse, no base thought can come in; or if forced in dies of shame in the white light. Purity may be gained by persistent and long continued refusal to entertain low ideas." Since Walter had probably worked long and hard to exercise restraint as well (sexual repression was not confined to women, after all), there must have been debilitating, irksome strains in their relationship—a sense of awkwardness, repulsion, fear—all well-supported by "Victorian" strictures concerning the sinfulness of sex.

For many nineteenth-century couples, the marriage adjustment must have been a rough one. For Charlotte, it was probably rough enough to intensify depressions she was feeling anyway, or at least so her later published writings would suggest. "One of the most pitiful errors of our views on this matter," she later asserted, "is letting young girls enter this relationship without a clear understanding of what they are undertaking." "Gaily to the gate of marriage they go, and through it—and never have they asked or answered the questions upon which the whole truth of their union depends." That was to become one of Charlotte's passionate convictions: a woman has the need for and right to a fulfilling love relationship, not love as the be-all and end-all of her life, but as a vital and critically important part of it. Charlotte may not have held such views before her marriage, nor may she have asked "questions upon which the whole truth" of a love relationship depends. But her diary entries only weeks following her wedding, her oblique references to thwarted passion, her mounting discontent and illness suggest a vague fear of being trapped in marriage without the satisfying experience of love.

In any case, whatever the fears or disappointments, an already difficult situation soon was exacerbated, perhaps irreversibly, by the fact that Charlotte became pregnant. On August 3 she wrote, "feel sick all day." August 8: "Sick still. . . . I eat, but lo! it remaineth not within me but returneth to upper air." Her mother brought flowers —"Dear kind thoughtful little woman!"—helped clean the house, washed the dishes, talked and tried to cheer her up. And Walter intensified his domestic efforts too, preparing meals, shopping, cleaning, comforting for hours. Walter was patience and tenderness personified (or so Charlotte recalled); but he also was undoubtedly somewhat piqued by what seemed to him to be irrational, even irresponsible behavior—"hysterical" crying fits, interminable doldrums, unreasonable demands. To him, firmness and masculine assertiveness seemed appropriate when feminine emotionality got out of hand. "Dismal evening," Charlotte wrote, "for I feel unable to do anything and am mortally tired of doing nothing. Get out on roof. Humbly ask if I can sleep there tonight and am told 'No you cannot!' Serves me right for asking. Bed? I guess so." Fortunately, her mother came and comforted her with pears and flowers.

Mary must have felt some rather intense anxieties, as well as conflicting loyalties, as she worried over Charlotte's pregnancy. Her own had been so frightful, so nearly fatal. (If Mary shared her pregnancy images and recollections, that, by itself, could have generated a good deal of Charlotte's dread.) But to make matters worse, Thomas wrote saying he needed Mary's help. He had been living in the West for years, had a wife and child, and was making an urgent appeal on the basis of his family's health. Of course Mary felt compelled to go, despite her apprehensions over Charlotte. And if Charlotte managed to encourage Mary's trip, she also felt disappointed, perhaps even abandoned, at just the time she especially wanted Mary's warmth. On September 18, Charlotte wrote, "I go up to mother's for the last time." And three days later: "sicker than I've been since any part of it. Walter . . . does everything."

For the next several months, in fact for the entire fall and winter that Mary was gone, Walter served as nursemaid, and Charlotte withdrew into a kind of self-denying lethargy. For the most part, she even put aside her diary-writing, summarizing, at the year's end, her mood of "happy" wifely acquiescence:

> My journal has been long neglected by reason of ill health. I am now better, and hope to keep it regularly and to some purpose. . . . [Walter] has worked for me and for us both, waited on me in every tenderest way, played to me, read to me, done all for me as he always does. God be thanked for my husband! . . .
>
> This last year has been short. I have done little, read little, written little, felt and thought—little to what I should have. I am a happy wife. I bear a child. I have been far from well . . . perhaps humbler. Ambition sleeps. I make no motion but just live. And I am Happy? Every day almost finds me saying so, and truly. And yet—and yet—"call no man happy until he is dead." . . . I should not be afraid to die now; but should hate to leave my own happiness and cause fierce pain. Yes I am happy.

January through March 1885 were months of continuing illness and depression. Only occasionally did she feel much spunk. She played chess from time to time, ran errands (somehow she remembered Walter's birthday), sewed sheets and baby clothes, and wrote letters to her mother. She also read some, notably the forthright woman's paper *Alpha*, but wrote very little. Mostly she was ill. January 15: "I get so tremulous and teary that my boy stays with me." January 29: "very hot and nervous evening. . . . [Walter] puts me to bed in a blanket." January 30: "Bed in blanket. Get frantically hot and nervous and kick out of it. Bad night, lame all over." February 2: "I *must* be strong and not hinder him. . . . Feel so downcast that I take out my comforter, Walter's journal, and get new strength and courage thence, learning how good and brave he is."* February 4: "Am very very tired and lame at night which displeaseth and grieveth my Walter. I didn't *mean* to!" February 17: "So hysterical indeed that Walter decides to stay with me." February 19: "A well-nigh sleepless night. Hot, cold, hot; restless nervous hysterical. Walter is love and patience personified; gets up over and over."

Katharine Beecher Stetson was born on March 23, 1885. Charlotte noted the event in her diary.

> This day, at about five minutes
> to nine in the morning, was born
> my child, Katharine.
>
> Brief ecstasy. Long Pain.
> Then years of joy again.
>
> Motherhood means—Giving.

If motherhood meant giving, it meant dependency as well, a sense of childlike vulnerability which Charlotte could neither control nor understand. Nancy Chodorow suggests such feelings are rather common: "The experience of mothering for a woman involves a double identification. A woman identifies with her own mother and, through identification with her child, she (re)experiences herself as cared for child." Chodorow believes that pregnancy and childbirth are almost inevitably threatening to a woman's sense of self, a "challenge to the boundaries of her body ego ('me'/'not-me' in relation to her blood or milk, to a man who penetrates her, to a child once part of her body)." Since mothering so often involves "the excitation of long-buried feelings about one's own mother," Charlotte may have

* Walter Stetson's journal may still be among the rich collection of family papers owned by the Chamberlin family, but at the time this was written, it was not available for research.

experienced what one writer described quite incisively: "as a mother suddenly I found myself a child again."

For the first two months after Katharine's birth, Mary stayed with Thomas, and Charlotte had a nurse to help, but was still "pretty well used up by the loss of sleep"—the lament of new parents almost everywhere. "I wonder what people do who know even less than we do about babies! And what women do whose husbands are less sufficient." Yet even with Walter's support, Charlotte felt irritated, cheerless, weepy—an exasperating contrast to romanticized wife and mother expectations she had sometimes harbored. May 2: "The first anniversary of my wedding day. I am tired with long sleeplessness and disappointed at being unable to celebrate the day. So I cry . . . dress myself in black silk, jersey, and yellow crepe neckerchief. Haven't been 'dressed' in months."

Two days later she received a telegram from her mother: "She starts [home] today. I shall be glad to see her!" Charlotte had kept Mary informed about her pregnancy, Katharine's birth, and various discouragements and ailments. Now she seemed more than willing to let Mary take control. On her mother's first visit after arriving in Providence, Charlotte wrote: "am very tired and depressed in the morning. . . . At about noon mother comes, bless her, and thereafter all goes well. She worships the baby of course; and to my great relief and joy declares her perfectly well. We have a happy afternoon." For the next several weeks, Mary came almost every day—relieving tensions, taking charge of Katharine, managing the house while Charlotte rested and gratefully observed. In fact, this was one of the few times that Charlotte expressed (in her diary anyway) some real appreciation for her mother: "Mother over early. She takes all the care of the baby day times; washes her today with infinite delight." "So nice to have mother here."

Mary doubtless remembered enough of her own tear-filled frustrating times with babies not only to work calmly and efficiently, but also to help Charlotte dispel some guilt-producing illusions about mothering, and learn some hard-headed survival tools instead. In ways not possible during more rebellious years, Charlotte may have felt much stronger mother-daughter bonds with Mary. Some were negative, of course—bonds based on mutual suffering, on learning to accept the disappointments of being a wife and mother. But others were more positive—bonds based on practical assistance, on mutual emotional support, on tenderness. In fact, the example of Mary's strength and the gift of Mary's love may have been Charlotte's major comfort.

At the time, however, it did not always seem that way. The more generous Mary was, the more guilty Charlotte seemed to feel for disappointing her, for complaining, for not adapting smoothly. Mary seemed patient and giving (Charlotte forgot that Mary had not always seemed that way), Charlotte mean and selfish by comparison. Yet there were some other dynamics operating too, more rebellious ones, which were temporarily obscured. For if at times Charlotte viewed Mary as a model she should emulate, at other times Mary was the exemplar of "virtues" Charlotte almost spontaneously abhorred. For years, Charlotte had described the "warring elements" within herself—"feminine" domestic instincts fighting "masculine" ambitious ones. Now she faced a major showdown, a consummation of her self-fulfilling prophecy of misery: "Here was a charming home; a loving and devoted husband; an exquisite baby, healthy, intelligent and good; a highly competent mother to run things; a wholly satisfactory servant—and I lay all day on the lounge and cried." "Motherhood means giving," she simplistically assumed; yet nothing "was more utterly bitter than this, that even motherhood brought no joy." "I would hold her close—that lovely child!—and instead of love and happiness, feel only pain. The tears ran down my breast."

In part then, it may have been a condemnation of domestic virtues, as well as a condemnation of herself for not possessing them, which so intensified Charlotte's misery during the first few years of marriage. She thought anger or resentment of mothering responsibilities was inappropriate, unjustified, the opposite of mother-love. But since anger and resentment kept cropping up even as she tried to squelch them, at times she lost her self-control. Gradually (but not consistently), she became what one writer has called a "paragon of Victorian femininity"—"helpless, housebound, and ineffectual." As she put it in her diary when Katharine was five months old, "Every morning the same hopeless waking . . . the same weary drag. To die mere cowardice. Retreat impossible, escape impossible." She may have found it easier to explain the crisis to Martha than to Walter, but in effect she made a desperate appeal to both: "I let Walter read a letter to Martha in which I tell my grief as strongly as I can.* He offers to let me go free, he would be everything in the world for me; but he cannot see how irrevocably bound I am, for life,

* The letter, written in August 1885, is not in the Martha Luther collection, and may not have been preserved. In any case, Martha's response did not seem very helpful. Charlotte's diary reads: "I wrote her my heart and she answers with not overwise head" (Diary of Charlotte Perkins Gilman, Sept. 5, 1885, AESL).

for life. No, unless he die and the baby die, or he change or I change, there is no way out. Well."

Crises, quarrels, and crying spells followed, the diaries chronicling complaint after miserable complaint. September 14: "Cry more after breakfast. An oppressive pain that sees no outlet." September 25: "Dreary days these. Only feel well about half an hour in all day." These were months of severe "hysteria," perhaps temporary "insanity" as well.

> I could not read nor write nor paint nor sew nor talk nor listen to talking, nor anything. I lay on that lounge and wept all day. The tears ran down into my ears on either side. I went to bed crying, woke in the night crying, sat on the edge of the bed in the morning and cried—from sheer continuous pain. Not physical, the doctors examined me and found nothing the matter.

One of Charlotte's major lifelong complaints was that no one realized how sick she was. No one sympathized enough. Little was known about mental illness in the 1880s, she explained, and many "openly scoffed" at her tears and "laziness." "Earnest friends" suggested that she use her will power, but from her point of view she "had used it, hard and long, perhaps too hard and long; at any rate it wouldn't work now." People did not seem to understand that her "mind was exclusively occupied with unpleasant things." Still, while Charlotte insisted that quips and scorns of friends and relatives had exacerbated her sense of failure, she also willingly acknowledged that the blame heaped on her by others could not match the blame she heaped upon herself. Her autobiography suggests that she never fully overcame her sense of guilt. "Eight years of honest conscientious noble-purposed effort lost, with the willpower that made it. The bitterness of that shame will not bear reviving even now."

> Feeling the sensation fear, the mind suggests every possible calamity; the sensation shame—remorse—and one remembers every mistake and misdeed of a lifetime, and grovels to the earth in abasement.
>
> . . . Prominent among the tumbling suggestions of a suffering brain was the thought, "You did it yourself! You did it yourself! You had health and strength and hope and glorious work before you—and you threw it away. You were called to serve humanity, and you cannot serve yourself. No good as a wife,

> no good as a mother, no good at anything. And you did it yourself!"

But while Charlotte carefully recorded anger with herself, what she failed to note in her autobiography was that she had blamed Walter too and that she had by no means lost her ability to say so—indirectly, but publicly and well. For despite her illness, she prepared an article for publication, entitled "On Advertising for Marriage," that was printed in *Alpha* in September 1885.

The major theme of the article is that men irresponsibly and far too rapidly push women into marriage. Men are attracted by women's femininity and charm, but care not a whit for their real personalities and concerns. Men pursue, flatter, and then propose, Charlotte wrote, without having "genuine sympathy and appreciation"—not of her "sexual nature! Heaven defend us! [Men] have studied that long and well, but the *rest* of her, the 'ninety-nine parts human!'" Charlotte seemed to feel that "beauty of the body and its sexual attraction" had inspired Walter's passion, but that her complex character was well beyond his ken.

> If a man sees a fair woman before he knows her; feels the charm of her presence before he begins to understand her character; is first aroused to the necessity of judging by his strong inclination; surely he stands less chance of a cool and safe decision than one who begins knowingly, learns a character from earnest letters, loves the mind before he does the body. And that first love would improve and be more to him yearly, growing ever richer, stronger, and more lovely with advancing age.

Charlotte's self-styled therapy, then, was to analyze the faults and foibles of her marriage, and to direct some of her energy and roaring anger into arguments which left self-respect intact. Her article was an attack on Walter (without saying so, of course). He had proposed seventeen days after their first meeting, had pursued her persistently thereafter, and had never come to know her for who she really was.

In part that was true, though there was another side as well. Surely one reason Walter failed to understand her, though admittedly he did not take much time to try, was that she had such difficulty being honest and direct. Only in the first few months after she met him did she openly reveal her complexities and contradictions. Thereafter, her letters were deferential and uncharacteristically sweet. She apologized, kept her peace when issues bothered her, and, at least, tried to display "feminine" humility instead. In short, by attempting to be gentle and submissive and loving according to prevalent "feminine" ideals, by trying to outgrow "devil's daughter" fractiousness and become a "lady," she had disguised herself, as women so often do, and then blamed Walter for misunderstanding her.

* * *

By autumn 1885, Charlotte and Walter had reached an impasse. Unhappiness and irritation led to attack and counter-attack, then to screaming arguments, crying fits, and "hysteria." Grace Channing offered Charlotte a temporary respite by inviting her to spend the winter with the Channing family in Pasadena, California. The Channings had moved there when tuberculosis threatened Grace's health, and, under the circumstances, a trip West seemed to offer prospects of relief for Charlotte's "illness" too: "We propound discuss and decide the question of shall I travel? Yes, I shall. . . . Hope dawns. To come back well!" So with mother and a maid left in charge of her baby and the house, and armed with "tonics and sedatives," Charlotte set off alone to cross the continent.

First, she visited her brother in Ogden, Utah, obviously not too sick for some prankish retributive horseplay. She decided to surprise him: "He came to the door in his shirt-sleeves, as was the local custom, holding a lamp in his hand. There stood the sister he had not seen in eight years, calmly smiling. 'Good evening,' said I with equanimity. This he repeated, nodding his head fatuously, 'Good evening! Good evening! Good evening!' It was a complete success."*

Thomas had gone West in the fall of 1879 to work as a mining engineer first in Nevada, and then in Utah. In his own way, he may have been rebelling also—against straight-laced New England relatives or some not-so-straight ones, against the demands, accusations, or perhaps self-fulfilling prophecies of his mother; probably he was rebelling against Charlotte too, since from his perspective she was the successful one, the family dynamo. In any case, he had quit school (involuntarily), moved from job to job, settled in a mining town in Utah, and proceeded to become the strange hybrid, a New England–born-and-bred, rough, tough Westerner.

If Charlotte was impressed, perhaps she was envious as well, tasting a bit of raucous frontier living, and contrasting it to her own domestic hell. To make matters worse, but a lot more fun, Thomas gloated in ways designed to shock. For instance, he took her to a dance at the town hotel in order to show her examplars of the local culture: one man had killed someone, he proudly noted, but people

*It had been six years since Charlotte had seen Thomas, not eight as she remembered.

did not seem to care; another man "had been scalped three times—the white patches were visible among the hair"; still others, whom Thomas inveigled to play whist, were tobacco-chewing swashbuckler types whose frequent use of the cuspidor rather challenged Charlotte's pseudo-prim repose.

From Utah, Charlotte went to San Francisco to pay a visit on her father, whom she had not seen, in fact probably had not heard from, for several years. Like Thomas, Frederick moved around a lot, and just recently he had accepted a position as head of the San Francisco Public Library. To some extent, Charlotte still unconsciously viewed him as her mentor, her masculine ally as she faced the "warring elements" within herself—mind versus emotion, ambition versus commitment to one's family—those vaguely defined dichotomies she assumed were tangling up her life. Since she may have felt that Frederick had rejected emotional involvement because of his ambitions, because he preferred public work to private disruptions, perhaps she thought he would appreciate her conflicts as well. But Frederick's choices had been different, his attitudes conventional: For one thing, child care and domesticity were not a male's concern; and for another, he rather liked the double-standard image of the loving-serving wife. Quite likely then, Frederick did not offer Charlotte the advice or affection, and most certainly not the collusive sympathy, that she craved. For whatever he said, whatever his response to her chronicle of troubles, she later could recall only his cold indifference and her own all-too-familiar disappointment. She wrote, father "took me across to a room he had engaged for me for a day or two. Here he solemnly called on me, as would any acquaintance." Then, as though to prove she had not wanted his affection anyway, she politely told him, "'If you ever come to Providence again I hope you will come to see me.' . . . To which he courteously replied, 'Thank you. I will bear your invitation in mind.'"

From San Francisco, Charlotte then went to Pasadena. The flowers were "a-glory," she later wrote, the Arroyo Seco "wild and clean." "The vivid beauty of the land, its tumultuous growth of flowers and fruit, the shining glory of the days and nights, gave me happiness and health." "Callas bloomed by the hydrant, and sweet alyssum ran wild in the grass. Never before had my passion for beauty been satisfied. This place did not seem like earth, it was paradise." Health and stamina seemed to be returning.

> Kind and congenial friends, pleasant society, amusement, outdoor sports, the blessed mountains, the long, unbroken sweep of the valley, with snow-peaks at the far eastern end—with such surroundings I recovered so fast, to outward appearance

> at least, that I was taken for a vigorous young girl. Hope came back, love came back, I was eager to get home to husband and child, life was bright again.

That was Charlotte's autobiographical reflection, but her first letter to Martha Lane during the winter visit was a bit more qualified: "I have not written to you for so long because of—circumstances. The mere writing itself is still an effort; and then my mental condition has made me oblivious of even my best friends. In despair of ever getting well at home I suddenly undertook this journey. It has already done me an immense amount of good, and I expect to return in the spring as well as I ever shall be. Perhaps that is not saying much."

This letter was written in early January 1886. Charlotte had been in Pasadena only a few weeks, Christmas celebrations were barely over, and the noise and stir alone had been enough to wear her out. Still she was optimistic. The Channings "are all very kind to me," she wrote, "and I gain rapidly." She described her enjoyment of the mountains, valleys, and plains, the flowers, fruits, and foliage. And lightly, momentarily, she expressed some feelings of affection for her daughter too, as though thinking about Martha's child, Chester, helped her love her own: "I wish he was near enough for me to see more of him, for I know he is just the child I should love and enjoy. Dear bright little face! It makes me homesick for my own baby." (Charlotte's sense of pain and guilt were so intense that the statement has a certain poignancy despite its cliché sentimental cast.)

Charlotte's visit with the Channing family was just what a perceptive doctor might have prescribed. Rigorous conversationalists and intellectuals, supportive and congenial friends, the Channings welcomed Charlotte almost as a family member. They helped her forget domestic responsibilities, stop her introspective worries, and be more accepting of herself. Grace's father, Dr. William F. Channing, was the leading spirit of the group. He was a writer, a medical doctor, a geological surveyor, a former abolitionist, an active social reformer, and a co-inventor of the telephone, for which Alexander Graham Bell had gotten all the credit. Moreover, he had provided the stimulation, if not the direct encouragement, necessary for his daughter Grace to grow up thinking that women could be doers and achievers too.

Grace Channing had been one of Charlotte's favorite friends in Providence. An avid reader, a generous confidante, Grace was also an aspiring novelist and poet, one of the few "thinking companions" who shared some of Charlotte's literary goals. But if there were many things the two women had in common, there were substantial differences as well. Grace was often weak and sickly, Charlotte was the physical fitness enthusiast; Grace was more self-effacing and quiet, more "delicate, shrinking, and spirituelle," whereas Charlotte (by nature anyway) was more raucous and aggressive. If Grace was (as one literary critic put it) "like some fine plant of the north flowering amidst the riotous hues of the south yet in consonance with it," Charlotte was more like the Arizona cactus, beautiful and flowering at times, but also prickling, towering, and, some would have argued, overbold. Grace, then, was the "womanly woman," the champion of women's long-suffering, self-sacrificing beauty, their nobility in face of illness, poverty, and death.* Charlotte usually preferred the fighting, rebellious kind of woman. Or, to put it in male terms, Charlotte preferred a Julius Caesar-type martyr to a Christ-like one.

But whatever the differences of style or fantasy or personality, Charlotte and Grace put their heads together that winter of 1885–86 and began improvising plays. They started out just spoofing and bantering with one another, then reshaping and practicing the lines, then writing out the dialogue, recruiting friends, and producing amateur, but quite successful, shows. Charlotte was ecstatic. She wrote to Martha Lane: "You can see I am not so sick as I was. . . . O but twas fun! To write a play and give it ourselves, all in a real theater, to a real audience, who laughed and clapped and enjoyed it. We enjoyed it more. It's a pretty good play. We're going to try and sell it."

Momentarily elated with success, Charlotte proceeded to review her winter's progress rather optimistically: "Have painted a very little here, learned much, made a few friends, gained what I came for—health, and written a Play!" But her concluding comments were rather sombre: "My California winter is about done. Shall start for home in a week or two more. I look forward with both joy and

* See particularly Grace Channing's *Sister of a Saint and Other Stories*. The beautiful martyrdom of Grace's heroines may have reflected goals she adopted for herself. When, several years later she found herself (her own illnesses notwithstanding) caring not only for a husband, a child, and a house, but also for two invalid and ailing parents, she wrote to her father-in-law: "But I do firmly believe the German saying: 'Out of Love can man do all things.' I am trusting my strength will last so long as my father or mother need me. After that I will make it last for Walter's sake!" (Grace Channing to Joshua Stetson, Dec. 22, 1896, BL). That was Walter Stetson she was referring to, to move the story ahead. Following Charlotte's divorce in 1894, Grace and Walter were married.

dread. Joy to see my darlings again, and dread of further illness under family cares. Well. I have chosen."

* * *

After returning to Providence in the spring of 1886, Charlotte wrote in her diary, "Am trying to get accustomed to life here. It will take some time." Katharine seemed to be her major worry. "Baby exasperating about her nap." Or, "Manage to paint two sheets of notepaper under great disadvantage from Miss Katharine." Charlotte occasionally enjoyed some playful romping with the child. But when she also wanted to think, paint, write, or be alone, toddler Kate would still be going strong—playing, laughing, fussing, screaming—Charlotte fuming in dismay. Walter helped a lot with child care, but tensions mounted: "Do not feel well during the day. . . . Get hysterical in the evening while putting K. to sleep. Walter finishes the undertaking and sleeps with her. When I am nervous she never does sleep easily—what wonder." Again and again Charlotte recorded that "Dear Walter" had given patient cooperative assistance; but she also noted there was "always the pain underneath," always an awkward resistance as she tried to say "I love you" to her "Dear Tender Heart."

While Charlotte appreciated Walter's help, she sometimes resented his independence more. It would be hard to guess how many hours she and Walter shared child-care duties, and how many hours she stayed alone with Kate. But very likely, as the breadwinner and the male, Walter spent most days painting at his studio, though he helped Charlotte when he could. Charlotte, by contrast, spent most days caring for Katharine and doing housework, though she wrote or painted when she could. Walter liked his professional responsibilities, and was relatively calm and confident. Charlotte hated her domestic work, was frustrated and ambivalent, and cried a lot. At times she tried to feel the appreciation she thought a wife and mother ought to feel, but at other times she expressed resentments fully, or so her fiction suggests. For it was about this time, the fall of 1886, that she wrote a little fiction piece, entitled "Allegory," that could easily be viewed not only as an attack on the inequalities of marriage, but also as a hate-filled blast at Walter.

"Allegory" describes a lifelong power struggle between two brothers—unequal from the start. The stronger despised the weaker, "made a mould for his brother and kept him in it," and then flaunted his own superiority: "'I am strong and thou art small.' And the weaker brother bore it, for he loved him well." The stronger gained experience and know-how in sports and warfare, wrote "great books," grew "exceedingly wise" and virtuous, and then ridiculed his imprisoned brother for being cowardly, ignorant, and bad. At times the weaker brother started to resist, but since the stronger "laughed at him and cursed him . . . he came back and re-entered the mould; for he loved him well." Finally, the weaker grew despite himself: "the mould broke continually, . . . in the end it broke utterly, so that he could bear it no more." The stronger "lifted his hand against him in deadly warfare, and the end thereof who can tell?"

That was just what the situation with Walter had come to, "deadly warfare" with terrifying consequences. "Hysterical" at times, Charlotte was a verbal virtuoso at others, in expressing anger anyway. For she had struck not only against the domestic "mould" she saw as maliciously constraining, but also against Walter, who she thought put her there, flaunted his undeserved superiority and power, and then mocked and cursed her efforts to break free. Sometimes she still busied herself staying "content" within the mould—for she "loved him well." More often she exploded—either against Walter, or, in more rational moments, against male-female social expectations she knew were not Walter's fault. As her poem, "The Answer," written that same fall makes clear, she saw herself in a life and death struggle.

A maid was asked in marriage. Wise as fair,
She gave her answer with deep thought and prayer.

Expecting in the holy name of wife
Great work, great pain, and greater joy in life.

Such work she found as brainless slaves might do;
By day and night, long labor, never through.

Such pain—no language can such pain reveal;
It had no limit but her power to feel.

Such joy life left in her sad soul's employ
Neither the hope nor memory of joy.

Helpless she died, with one despairing cry
"I thought it good! How could I tell the lie!"

And answered Nature, merciful and stern,
"I teach by killing. Let the others learn."

Charlotte knew perfectly well that many of her experiences, as well as her ideas, paralleled those of other women. It was probably that kind of confidence (as well as unhappiness) that inspired her to send "The Answer" to the *Woman's Journal*, official organ of the American Woman Suffrage Association. She already had contacts with the Boston-based suffrage organization through her Beecher relatives. Perhaps it was partly because of family connections that they published it. But Alice Stone Blackwell, then an editor for the *Journal*, must have also liked her work, because she gave Charlotte immense encouragement: first prize for "The Answer," a year's free subscription, and also a regular flow of congratulatory letters as Charlotte sent her other articles and poems. Alice Stone Blackwell, daughter of the famed Lucy Stone and Henry Blackwell team, and niece of the pioneering women doctors Elizabeth and Emily Blackwell, had been collecting, editing, and writing many of the crisp hard-headed articles that had spearheaded the women's movement for several years. Since Charlotte had been studying them carefully, and was now writing her own, it was not a question of whether but of when she would begin to participate more directly in women's political affairs, meet more of the leaders, and attend their annual conventions.

Her first suffrage convention was this same fall, 1886, Lucy Stone and Henry Blackwell presiding. In her diary, Charlotte described Lucy Stone in modest terms: she was a "lovely motherly sweet little woman with a soft quiet voice." Apparently, seventy-one-year-old Lucy Stone's appearance came as something of a surprise, for there was nothing "sweet" and "soft" about her reputation. Hard-working, forceful, a reformer to the core, Lucy Stone had been an abolitionist, a temperance worker, a captivating leader of the women's movement for over twenty years. Along with Henry Blackwell, Julia Ward Howe, and others, Lucy Stone had helped found the American Woman Suffrage Association and, even more importantly perhaps, had helped found, edit, and largely finance the weekly *Woman's Journal*, which Charlotte turned to constantly for pointers and cues.

Meanwhile, by the early winter of 1886, Charlotte was waging a two-front public-private battle, her published articles and verse reflecting her efforts to use analytic tools, her diaries reflecting her more fitful outbursts. For instance, in an article, "Why Women Do Not Reform Their Dress?" she analyzed some of the sources of her anger. It was plain to her that dress reformers had to face "friends' constant disapprobation, ridicule, [and] opposition," and that their nonconformity in dress caused "an uneasy sense of isolation and disagreeable noticeability, loss of social position, constant mortification and shame." She concluded that women had to combat their "miseducated sense of beauty and fitness." Those were feelings

Charlotte explained theoretically, but also felt keenly, as her diaries make clear. For instance, she got furious with her cousin Robert Brown: he "makes an ass of himself by his loudmouthed contempt of women's rights and other justice. It is hard to be despised by such men as that." And since she apparently could not fight Walter on the women's issue directly (he was far more supportive than most males in the 1880s would have been), she attacked him in other ways instead, like sauntering over to his studio and carping at his art work. In fact, one time she criticized his painting "so harshly from a moral point of view that he smashes it and burns it." Tears followed, as did profuse apologies, as did carping sprees again.

In fact, tensions seemed to increase all the time. The more Charlotte worked at painting, writing, or even housework, the worse the fights. Her painting created competition; her writing meant that private problems were publicly exposed (indirectly, but accurately enough to antagonize Walter); and housework fed resentments which brought on exasperating scenes. With all this going on, Charlotte's diary entry at the end of the year was remarkably optimistic.

> I leave behind me tonight a year of much happiness, growth, and progress; also of great misery. But the happiness and progress are real and well founded; and the misery was owing mainly to a diseased condition of the nervous system. It is past, I hope forever.
>
> I have become a person more in harmony with my surroundings; better fitted to live peacefully among my friends; and yet have not lost a keen interest in the world's work. I can write and paint better than before; and think as well when I am strong enough.
>
> But I certainly have lost much of my self-abandoning enthusiasm and fierce determination in the cause of right. Perhaps it is as well for the ultimate work done. I do not feel so. I feel in some ways lowered—degraded—traitor to my cause. But I am not sure, it may be a lingering trace of the disordered period just passed. When I know myself to be *well* in all ways I can better judge.
>
> I have written half a play this year and a little good poetry. Also some painting and drawing which has been very profitable to me as work. This is an immense gain on last year and that before. At any rate, I feel happy and contented with my home and family; and have hope and courage for the New Year.
>
> May it be fruitful and good!

Early in the year, in February 1887, Charlotte found a new opportunity to test her commitment to the "cause of right." Having established some reputation for herself as a contributor to the *Woman's Journal*, she was asked by Alice Stone Blackwell to manage a suffrage column for a Providence labor-oriented weekly newspaper called the *People*. On February 20, 1887, she noted that she had had a "good talk" with a certain Mrs. Smythe, who was "another victim" with a "sickly child" and an ignorant husband who was "using his 'marital rights' at her vital expense." That same day, she decided to accept Miss Blackwell's offer.

Charlotte's feminist writings were taking her in new directions, to contacts, albeit indirect ones, with political activists rather different in style and purpose from the reform-oriented thinkers she had been accustomed to. Reform Darwinists, Social Gospel leaders, academic and religious proponents of progress in the name of justice and right—these Charlotte had studied and admired. Most of her friends and cousins had reform inclinations, or reform-minded fathers anyway—William Channing, Rowland Hazard, Edward Everett Hale. Most of her author-heroes proclaimed the necessity for progressive social change. They used "law of nature" arguments, usually "scientific" evolutionary ones, to defend their view that man had an ethical, moral, and religious responsibility to use intelligence and reason to improve society in accordance with God's design.

But Charlotte must have noticed right away that articles in the *People* had a different and more radical cast. In the first issue of the paper (1885), the editors had openly declared their intention to "advocate co-operation and the rightfulness, the duty, and the benefits of labor partnerships, or trade unionism as it is sometimes called," and to publicize "the difficulties, dangers and privations with which all classes of workers have to contend." The founding of the *People* reflected a national trend: a rapidly expanding protest spirit, rising tension, strikes, violence. Openly committed to providing a pro-labor analysis of contemporary politics, the *People* was sponsored by a Rhode Island chapter of the Knights of Labor, a national organization founded in 1869 by Uriah Stephens, and boasting, by 1887, more than a half a million members across the country. According to some, the mounting labor pressure resulted partly from the Haymarket tragedy of 1886. For more than any other single event of the decade, it dramatized, in brutal form, what the conflict between capital and labor really meant.

The Haymarket incident was the culmination of a series of labor disputes at the McCormick Harvester factory in Chicago, Illinois, in the winter and spring of 1886. A lockout of some 1,400 impoverished workers in February was followed by a strike, by intermittent violence, and finally by a mass protest meeting called for the evening of May 4. A bomb exploded, the police opened fire, several people were killed, and over one hundred were severely wounded. Eight political activists were convicted of conspiracy to murder; their inflammatory speeches were said to have caused the violence. The press vilified their anarchist connections and called for retribution; three of them were later hanged. It was the cause célèbre of American radicals of the 1880s, sensitizing many to the grotesque inequities in society, but also intensifying popular suspicion of those who challenged the majority's complacency.

Very few contemporaries of Charlotte's class and background were enthusiastic supporters of the Chicago labor leaders. One of her heroes, political cartoonist Thomas Nast, condemned them. Even many labor leaders chose to look the other way. Still, the incident was symptomatic, and the restive labor spirit too contagious to be easily subdued. High rates of unemployment, the grim monotony of the factory scene, the below subsistence wages, child labor, unsafe working conditions—all these were attracting the attention not only of male intellectual and organizational reformers but also of the women's rights proponents whom Charlotte was coming to admire.

Like many of her contemporaries, however, and like many feminists before her, Charlotte would take a rather circuitous route toward identification with the labor cause; and in 1887 she had just begun. Only vaguely did she understand working-class grievances and programs; and only rarely had she learned about their life-conditions either from experience or from books. Upper middle class in a good deal of her outlook and training, she had developed her political perspectives not from the Henry George, *Progress and Poverty*, kind of reading, certainly not from activist pro-labor tracts, but from the more rarefied Darwinist and Reform Darwinist debates instead. In fact, she had become something of a Reform Darwinist herself. She was impressed by evolutionary analyses of the causes of human inequality, needless suffering, pervasive social ills, and she had her "fierce dedication to the cause of right." But in part because she had experienced too little beyond books and family life, she could (as yet) only vaguely relate her ideals and theories to the practical realities of modern industrial life.

When Charlotte was asked to write a suffrage column for the *People*, it seems likely that she had no clearly formulated views of the Knights of Labor, or even of the labor movement generally, but that she had strong pro-labor sympathies nonetheless, and ones which her identification with the women's movement were strengthening all the time. Still, for the moment, it was women's issues—middle-class ones at that—which she knew and thought most about, and which her *People* articles reflect.

On March 5, 1887, the editors of the *People* introduced Charlotte's suffrage column by saying, "since the vast majority of women are workers, it must concern chiefly the working women." Probably they meant women working for miniscule pay and long hours, women of the labor movement, women organizing to better their wages and working conditions. Charlotte spoke of other kinds of working women instead: career women whose public achievements were unrecognized, or housewives who were confined to unskilled, involuntary, unpaid domestic work at home. For instance, in her first column, she bemoaned the neglect of women's inventions: By 1886, women had received 1,935 patents, but some people said they never invented anything. (She borrowed the idea from the soon-to-be-prominent muckraker Ida Tarbell.) Her second article pointed out that "woman can take an interest in the world's work and housework too; can take her place as citizen and not lose her place as wife and mother." By March she had warmed up to the issue which most bothered her: "Men have for so long exercised political power in the world that they have come to look upon it as a masculine attribute, like the beard. . . . Then they have the habit of all the ages to make them feel superior to women; so it will naturally take some time for them to recognize our equality." Women are not emotionally inferior, she continued. "Men call us emotional because they know us mostly in emotional relations, they meet only that side of our natures."

Occasionally, the suffrage column discussed other political and economic issues, and sometimes rather forcefully so. For instance, in August there was an article on the unjust inequalities of women's wages: "In Massachusetts there are more than two hundred thousand women who earn their support, by work outside of their own homes, at less than ½ the wages paid men." There were reports on working women's demands for equal pay for equal work, for "equal opportunity to learn and practice diversified industries," for equal power in the labor movement. And by September, the writing sounded like that of a labor-oriented suffrage pro: "Twenty thousand women Knights of Labor are organized, in the city of New York alone, for mutual protection. Like the fabled Amazons, they are ready to assert and defend their rights, but not, as they did, with the sword. Organized labor demands the ballot for them."

Those were strong-sounding statements, increasingly radical ones at that, if only we could be certain whether Charlotte wrote them, or whether the *People* reprinted articles from other journals when

Charlotte did not have time or energy to write.* Nevertheless, a number of the articles probably reflect political perspectives Charlotte was beginning to develop, but not, as yet, ones that she could call her own.

Most of the articles Charlotte wrote for the *People* focused on an issue that, at this juncture, seemed paramount to her: the conflict between marriage and career. Marriage, she told her readers, "is what you are born for, trained for, taught for; it is at once your destiny and desire, your hope and your necessity." But she felt that women needed work as well as love: "Let girls learn a trade or profession as well as boys, and have an individual independent life of their own; then they will not have to spin webs for a living." Charlotte did not claim that her ideas were original. On the contrary, she was busy finding pithy passages of celebrities to quote, passages of her aunt Harriet Beecher Stowe, for instance, who was ending her career just as Charlotte was fitfully beginning hers. Charlotte quoted her aunt: "Every woman has rights as a human being first, which belong to no sex, and ought to be as freely conceded to her as if she were a man—and first and foremost, the great right of doing anything which God and nature evidently have fitted her to excel in."

That was Charlotte's view exactly: Women, "first and foremost," must secure their rights as people, be independent, develop their own integrity. If they do not, if they marry first, their nuptial vows are simply meaningless. It was almost as though Charlotte were using the *People* column to test—theoretically and publicly—her own private emotional dilemma: in "the marriage ceremony the bride is made to promise to 'love and honor.' But she sometimes finds that neither love nor honor is possible."

* A number of these articles for the *People* suffrage column were unsigned.

Chapter Seven

Strangely Changed 1887-1890

IN the winter of 1887, the situation on the home front was moving rapidly from bad to worse. Confident and intellectually excited when she approached women's problems in the abstract, Charlotte still resorted to crying fits when she confronted daily tasks at home. After "wearing" days of mending, caring for "that bewitching damsel" Kate, and getting supper "as usual," she repeatedly collapsed: "Kate tires me out in the sleep going; and I get real nervous and shaky. Walter gives me a warm bath and puts me to bed."

Still, at times, Charlotte practiced what she preached. For instance, she wrote an article called "An Appeal for a Ladies Gymnasium." It reflected not only her physical fitness principles for women (and a long heated squabble with the director of the Providence Gymnasium), but also a pragmatic therapeutic program for herself. Several years earlier, she and her friends had been allowed to use the local gymnasium for their classes. But later, when the director closed it to them, Charlotte opened fire: "Am horrified to find that [he] don't mean to have a ladies class till the new building is open. I reason with him," publicly, as well as privately, she might have added. That was in the fall, 1886. By January, 1887, for whatever reasons, the director had capitulated, and Charlotte resumed her how-to-get-strong-and-how-to-stay-so schemes. "Still feel poorly," she wrote in her diary, but "depart at 6 for the gymnasium. Speedily make friends; and resume my old position. Find myself happy to the verge of idiocy at being there again. Am as light apparently but not as strong as of old. . . . Home happy." Repeatedly the gym provided a welcome respite. Even after getting discouraged with Walter's disapproval of her child-care methods, off she bounded for her "jolly time at the gym in the evening. I seem to slip into my old position of inspirer very easily. And the girls like it." She also started thinking she might "try teaching gymnastics next winter."

Charlotte must have noticed the striking contrast between her dullness at home and her relative spunk when she had a chance to get away. The energizing programs at the gym, the lively debates at her women's "parlor meetings," the collaborative scurry at the local suffrage headquarters, the political buzz and stir at the *Woman's Journal* office in Boston (which occasionally she visited)—all these seemed to boost her spirits, promote her self-respect, and provide her with the kind of work she liked to do. All these, presumably, Charlotte might have managed to continue and extend, but too often she stayed home and cried instead. Elaborate theories notwithstanding, perhaps she felt, as one historian has put it, that outside work "was hardly a socially acceptable escape from a lady's situation, but [that] sickness, that very nervous condition brought on by the frustrations of her life, was."

In any case, Walter must have been increasingly perplexed, discouraged, sometimes furious, especially since he tried so hard to help. For instance, when she "started a course of reading on women" in early winter, Walter repeatedly went to the library to find books for her. Margaret Fuller's *Woman in the Nineteenth Century* was among them, and he even read it to her since she wasn't feeling well. Very likely, Walter had genuine respect for Fuller's feminist perspectives. He may even have argued—theoretically anyway—that of course women should enjoy equality with men. Certainly he had been amply, if not always peacefully, exposed to such a view, and Charlotte never seriously complained that he rejected it. But Walter (like Charlotte) must have also respected a fair number of the tried-and-tested masculine and feminine ideals. He must have felt piqued that his wife resented wifehood, and even more annoyed that despite all she had—his concurrence on woman's suffrage, his household help, a maid several times a week, and a mother to care for Kate while she went on her suffrage jaunts—Charlotte was still not satisfied.

Walter eventually decided that whatever the source of Charlotte's "illness," the "course of reading on women" was making her feel worse. He said she should stop. Angrily she acquiesced, and at the same time probably concluded that his forcing her to do so was proof of something she had long suspected: that he did not care enough about the women's issue, and, if that were true, he did not care for her. Several weeks later, with his "consent," she started her reading program again, but by now the tensions in the marriage were acute, beyond the control of either one.

On Valentine's Day, Walter wrote Charlotte a "poem." Presumably, he hoped it would boost her spirits, though reading it now, it is rather hard to imagine why he thought so. In the poem he talked first about what the experience of marriage had been like for him the preceding few years: it had brought "dull pain" and "fear" and "debt and wrong," as if he felt his misery should heighten her sense of obligation. Then, he proclaimed how much he loved her anyway, implying that his martyr-like forgiveness should somehow cancel any complaints she might have. And finally, apparently forgetting his reading of Margaret Fuller, he assured her that weakness was a form of loveliness, as though his protective all-engulfing love should be her major source of hope.

> Thro all the surging sound of debt and wrong,
> 'Mid all unrest and all dull pain,
> I hear the music of a tender song
> And rise from fear a man again.
>
> Love sings the song, and sings, dear Love, of you,—
> Sings till my joy grows great and clear,—
> Till I can breathe my love, my vows renew,
> And homage pay to wifehood here.
>
> You comfort in your weakness dear and wife,
> Far more than all the world in might;
> So for the power you are into my life
> I call you loveliest Love tonight!
>
> What tho' you grieve and feel your work undone!
> What tho' my life seem all distress!
> Hold fast to Love—to love, and all is won!
> Thenceforth our days are pleasantness!

Troubled by his own sense of inadequacy in reaching Charlotte, Walter responded in the only way he knew: he offered comforting protection, kindness, and reassurance that patient love would bring a cure. Understandably, he preferred trustful gentleness to angry blasts on women's issues, but he also encouraged apologetic deference rather than self-assertion, and to that degree he may have made her "illness" worse. Neither Charlotte nor Walter could have understood the double-bind progression of their relationship: the more he loved and comforted, the more she blamed herself for failing him;

the more he protected, the more she chafed against his strength; the more he tried to calm her, the more desperate she became.

Many years later, in the short story "Making a Change," Charlotte sketched her muddled but defiant confrontation with the guilt-producing myth of the blissful wife and mother love. Julia, the heroine of the short story, "was more near the verge of complete disaster than the family dreamed. The conditions were so simple, so usual, so inevitable." Already upset by her husband's disapproval of her child-care methods, Julia was kept "awake nearly all night, and for many nights," by her screaming child: "the grating wail from the next room fell like a lash—burnt in like fire." Unfortunately, Charlotte's heroine was "hypersensitive" not only to noise but also to the "duties" of motherhood: "If her nerves were weak her pride was strong. The child was her child, it was her duty to take care of it, and take care of it she would." Julia's husband, preoccupied with economic and professional responsibilities, "had not the faintest appreciation of her state of mind." She "lifted her eyes and looked at him; deep inscrutable wells of angry light." Her "wild visions of separation, secret flight—even of self-destruction—swung dizzily across her mind." If she suffered from "insanity," the diagnosis was simple and direct: "When people say they are 'nearly crazy' from weariness, they state a practical fact." Desperately (melodramatically), Julia tried to kill herself. The mother-in-law arrived in the nick of time, understood her plight, and helped her plot a method of escape. The mother-in-law and Julia then formed a pragmatic, secret alliance, Julia pursuing her professional career, the mother-in-law establishing a day-care center which not only solved Julia's problem, but also met the older woman's need for satisfying work. When Julia's husband first discovered the work projects they had developed on the sly, he was furious. But finally and reluctantly, he recognized women's rights outside the wife and mother sphere, forgave them, applauded them, and enjoyed marriage harmony and happiness thereafter.

In the story, Charlotte fantasized—or advised—a happy solution for the "hysteria" of young wives and mothers. Her own reality, however, was immensely more complex. Only the desperation, not the resolution, had been autobiographical. On March 7, 1887, she wrote, "A very hard night. Katharine down with my cold, way down. Walter sends for doctor, and tells mother, who arrives speedily. But it don't do me much good, for Kate will go to no one but me. I hold her all day, as I did about all night." March 13: "I have a crying fit while trying to make Kate go to sleep and am all used up." March 20: "Bad day. Getting back to the edge of insanity again. . . . Put K to sleep and feel desperate. Write my 'column' though." March 22: "Try the spare room again, but Miss Kate howls for me in the night, won't let her father touch her. . . . Write a little historical 'piece' in Monday's Journal. Cut out a lot of suffrage articles." By April, Charlotte's only happy diary entries were about her suffrage work, and even those were rare.

Exhausted by unexpressed feelings of hostility, neither Walter nor Charlotte could avoid the crisis scene that followed. It was an April evening. She was "approaching to frenzy," as so often was the case, and old friend Jim Simmons happened on the scene. Walter had always felt a certain twinge of competitive masculine hostility toward this long-term confidant of Charlotte's, but especially now he resented even well-intentioned interference. Walter was smouldering and overtaxed. Jim was relaxed, comfortably distant from the pressures, and casually supportive. When Walter had tried to be affectionate and understanding, Charlotte reacted with hysteria and tears. But when Jim tried quietly and simply to reassure her in ways Walter had tried all day, she happily and peacefully responded. The contrast was appalling: she was hostile to her husband, appreciative and sensible with Jim. Walter rushed out of the house in a rage—envious, resentful, virtually hysterical himself. Jim stayed, talked, and comforted her some more. When Walter came home later in the evening, he again witnessed Charlotte's calm rapport with Jim; by the time Jim left, family roles had been reversed: "Walter breaks down, and I soothe him and love him and get him to sleep."

To Charlotte, that evening's temporary "recovery" may have seemed worse than the disease, and she did not hesitate to take the blame for Walter's misery. Like her fictional heroine Julia, Charlotte turned to her mother for comfort and protection: She moved into Mary's house and let the "baby-worshipping" grandmother take charge of Katharine. But that could only be a temporary arrangement, and Charlotte knew it. Mary sympathized and may have even understood Charlotte's feelings. But there was no way she could help her "plot a method of escape." From Mary's perspective, Charlotte had to learn to bear it, to take responsibility for her decisions and behavior.

Still, Mary and Walter both recognized Charlotte's sense of desperation, her acute "illness." In fact, they may have feared a suicide attempt. They recognized that she needed outside help, medical assistance, preferably the best available. Dr. S. Weir Mitchell was the man they chose. He had treated several other Beecher women for parallel "nervous ailments," and was well respected as one of the best "nerve specialists" in the country. So when friends offered financial assistance, and with Walter and Mary applying well-intentioned emotional coercion, Charlotte agreed to travel to Philadelphia for Mitchell's six-week "rest cure." She was desperate enough to listen to her family's admonitions, but lucid enough to thrash Walter in the privacy of her diary:

> I have kept a journal since I was fifteen, the only blanks being in these last years of sickness and pain. I have done it because it was useful. Now I am to go away for my health, and I shall not try to take any responsibilities with me, even this old friend.
>
> I am very sick with nervous prostration, and I think some brain disease as well. No one can ever know what I have suffered in these last five years. Pain pain pain, till my mind has given way. O blind and cruel! Can *Love* hurt like this? You found me—you remember what.
>
> I leave you—O remember what, and learn to doubt your judgment before it seeks to mould another life as it has mine.
>
> I asked you a few days only before our marriage if you would take the responsibility entirely on yourself. You said yes. Bear it then.

At least temporarily, Charlotte seemed to feel relieved that others would "take the responsibility entirely." That was precisely what Mitchell thought was best. Her self-assertiveness, most certainly her kind of self-reflective arrogance, had to be "cured." Almost immediately after she arrived in Philadelphia, Mitchell prescribed his standard therapy: complete bed rest, daily massages, plenty of food, and no outside stimulation—no books, no conversations with friends, only consultations with staff and doctors. Overfed, relaxed, and freed from the taxing pressures of "inappropriate" ambition, the "hysterical" woman would begin to accept life's blessings calmly. She would become more loving, giving, gentle with her family, and more peacefully content herself—or so the expert believed.

If Mitchell was, as Charlotte later viewed him, hopelessly insensitive to her complexities and needs, he was also merely prescribing a treatment reflective of nineteenth-century attitudes toward middle-class women generally. Women who for some reason were discontent with domestic roles, particularly professionally ambitious women, almost invariably suffered emotional confusions. Pressured to conform to "true womanhood" ideals, they were frustrated by occupational discrimination, by social disapproval, by family complaints, and by self-imposed guilt as well. Yet, whatever the conflicts, Mitchell seemed convinced that these women had caused them by their own behavior. Later, Charlotte would assume that Mitchell had been personally prejudiced against her: finding her too ambitious and arrogant like other Beecher women, he had dismissed her "long letter giving 'the history of the case,'" as mere "self-conceit." In point of fact, however, Mitchell's treatment reflected a far deeper prejudice: that in a woman, ambition itself was selfishly destructive. It negated her capacity for the gratifying and essential experiences of love. In Mitchell's fiction as well as in his practice, he did not hesitate to show his disapproval, sometimes condemnation, of the nonconforming "hysteric" female type: she was inappropriately aggressive, dominating, even predatory; she strangled the emotional lives of others, used her illness as an excuse to shirk responsibility, and manipulated friends and family to heighten her own control.* Mitchell's rest cure, then, was designed to help such women. In an atmosphere of rest and quiet, they could learn to be more passive and warm, and thus more "feminine" and healthy. He seemed to assume that Charlotte, like so many other nervous, unhappy women, needed to learn that domesticity was the cure and not the cause of her disease.

After several weeks of remaining prone and passive, Charlotte returned home with the following Weir Mitchell prescription: "Live as domestic a life as possible. Have your child with you all the time. . . . Lie down an hour after each meal. Have but two hours' intellectual life a day. And never touch pen, brush or pencil as long as you live." The effect was nearly disastrous.

> I went home, followed those directions rigidly for months, and came perilously near to losing my mind. The mental agony grew so unbearable that I would sit blankly moving my head from side to side—to get out from under the pain. Not physical pain, not the least "headache" even, just mental torment, and so heavy in its nightmare gloom that it seemed real enough to dodge.
>
> I made a rag baby, hung it on a doorknob and played with it. I would crawl into remote closets and under beds—to hide from the grinding pressure of that profound distress.

*Dr. S. Weir Mitchell's *Roland Blake* is particularly revealing as a psychological study of his attitude toward the energy-absorbing woman. It was published in 1886, just a year before he treated Charlotte Stetson. See also Ann Douglas Wood's "'The Fashionable Diseases': Women's Complaints and Their Treatment in Nineteenth-Century America," and Regina Morantz, "The Lady and Her Physician," in *Clio's Consciousness Raised*, ed. Mary Hartman and Lois Banner (New York: Harper Torchbooks, 1974).

Thus, decades later, did Charlotte describe the post-rest-cure months of terror. Yet, only three years later, in 1890, she wrote an even more poignant autobiographical account. The short story, "The Yellow Wall-paper," written in the first person, is a fictional version of a "case of nervous breakdown beginning something as mine did, and treated as Dr. S. Weir Mitchell treated me with what I considered the inevitable result, progressive insanity." The story symbolically describes her own decline into mental illness. "The story was meant to be dreadful, and succeeded."

In "The Yellow Wall-paper," an "hysterical woman," overprotected by a loving husband, is taken to a summer home to recover from nervousness, and told to rest and sleep and try to use her "will and self-control" to overcome her miseries. The room her husband John assigns to her is covered with a yellow-patterned wallpaper. "The color is repellent, almost revolting; a smouldering unclean yellow, strangely faded by the slow-turning sunlight." Unhappiness occupies her total vision. The yellow wallpaper constantly forces its ugliness upon her mind: "The pattern lolls like a broken neck and two bulbous eyes stare at you upside down. . . . Up and down and sideways they crawl, and those absurd, unblinking eyes are everywhere." Ugliness is her new reality. "It makes me think of all the yellow things I ever saw—not beautiful ones like buttercups, but old foul, bad yellow things."

Even though the woman feels desperate, almost delirious, her physician husband tells her there is "no reason" for her suffering; she must dismiss those "silly fantasies." "Of course it is only nervousness," she decides. But "it does weigh on me so not to do my duty in any way! I meant to be such a help to John, such a real rest and comfort, and here I am a comparative burden already! . . . [and] such a dear baby! And yet I *cannot* be with him, it makes me so nervous."

The woman tries to rest, to do as she is told, but suffers doubly because her husband will not believe she is ill. He "does not know how much I really suffer. He knows there is no *reason* to suffer, and that satisfies him." She thinks she should appreciate the protective love he offers. "He takes all care from me, and I feel so basely ungrateful not to value it more. . . . He took me in his arms and called me a blessed little goose. . . . He said I was his darling and his comfort and all he had, and that I must take care of myself for his sake, and keep well." Yet it is impossible to talk to him "because he is so wise, and because he loves me so." Efforts to discuss the problem only bring a "stern reproachful look" and back to bed she goes. "Really dear you are better," her husband keeps telling her. "Can you not trust me when I tell you so?"

John offers tender love, but, in accordance with his medical expertise, enforces the inactivity that deepens her despair. She is "absolutely forbidden to 'work' until [she is] well again." She is not even allowed to write: "I must put this away,—he hates to have me write a word." So she asks if several friends may come to visit her, but John says "he would as soon put fireworks in my pillow-case as to let me have those stimulating people about now." He is certain that only rest will restore her health, so "he start[s] the habit by making me lie down for an hour after each meal."

The first stage of the breakdown is one of self-blame. The woman tries to follow her husband's orders and stop the fantasies he tells her are unreal. When a physician of "high standing" (who is also one's husband) assures "friends and relatives that there is really nothing the matter with one but temporary nervous depression—a slight hysterical tendency—what is one to do?" So "I take pains to control myself—before him, at least, and that makes me very tired." Gradually, however, the woman starts to believe in her fantasies. "There are things in that paper that nobody knows but me, or ever will. Behind that outside pattern the dim shapes get clearer every day. . . . I didn't realize for a long time what the thing was that showed behind that dim sub-pattern, but now I am quite sure it is a woman." As though suddenly aware of her imprisoned sister's fight against the strangling wallpaper, she trusts her own perceptions and acts wildly but assertively.

> I wasn't alone a bit! As soon as it was moonlight and that poor thing began to crawl and shake the pattern, I got up and ran to help her. I pulled and she shook, I shook and she pulled, and before morning we had peeled off yards of that paper.

The protagonist begins to creep and crawl within her madness. She detaches herself from the perceptions of others. Her husband faints from the shock of her defiance. And, in a climactic scene, she creeps over his prostrate body and exclaims triumphantly, "I've got out at last . . . in spite of you!"

* * *

In "The Yellow Wall-paper," Charlotte presented insanity as a form of rebellion, a crucial turning point toward independence. Her fight for and with the woman in the wallpaper may have symbolized her eagerness to fight for and with other imprisoned women. But the bizarre, nightmare fiction also portrayed the violent anger that accompanied the fight to free herself, the desperate struggle that ultimately resulted in the breakup of her marriage. Many years later, she would tell the tale more coolly: "Finally, in the fall of '87,* in a moment of clear vision, we agreed to separate, to get a divorce. There was no quarrel, no blame for either one, never an unkind word between us, unbroken mutual affection—but it seemed plain that if I went crazy it would do my husband no good, and be a deadly injury to my child."

While "The Yellow Wall-paper," then, exposes some of the behind-the-scenes horror that led to the separation, Charlotte's autobiography provides a less sensational account: the separation resulted from miserable depressions, but she could not imagine why they had occurred. She and Walter had always known love and understanding, never disastrous clashes on domestic issues or outside work. She experienced "grey fog" misery, never hate-filled explosive arguments. In fact, despite all of her later radical critiques on the destructive effects of the institution of the family—political inequity, economic exploitation, psychological submissiveness, sexual subjection—and despite (or, in part, because of) her personal anger, Charlotte chose to ignore, in her autobiography anyway, some of the radical convictions that had helped dissolve her marriage. Never had she intended to challenge the institution of the family. Circumstances simply forced her hand: "If I had been of the slightest use to him or to the child, I would have 'stuck it.'" But it seemed better for the child "to have separated parents than a lunatic mother," better to leave a husband, sane, than to stay, insane. Later, Charlotte would suggest pragmatic steps other women could take to save their marriages, to integrate feminist convictions with family life. But she preferred not to discuss directly the complicated feelings that had accompanied her own efforts, or to acknowledge the anger—painful, often misdirected, and threatening in its implications—that had motivated her decisions.

To a degree she may simply have been attempting to be fair, knowing that if Walter was a villain, he was a victim as well: he was forced to withstand her fury as though centuries of patriarchal dominance were of his own design. Still, absolving Walter from responsibility was as misleading as denying her own, just as emphasizing rationality obscured psychic provocations. Rational awareness strengthened her personal rebellion, but emotional violence lay

* The decision was made five or six months after Charlotte had gone to Philadelphia for Mitchell's treatment. The separation did not actually occur until a year later, the fall of 1888.

beneath the rational façade. As Margaret George has said of Mary Wollstonecraft, because "her feminism emerged as a product of her life experience, she had to try to live it, not through an objectively rational plan, but in the driving spontaneity of her decisions, choices, and actions." Like Mary Wollstonecraft, Charlotte was aware of the kind of life she did not want and could not tolerate. "What she did want had to be discovered in the trials of living. To be discovered too, was who and what she was."

* * *

What is most striking about Charlotte's life, particularly from 1884–1888, is that she had the energy to pursue any of the activities she found most satisfying, that she had enough time, space, and self-respect to keep in touch with even vaguely formulated goals. She was "ill," yet stubbornly ignored the admonitions of her family, refused their well-intentioned offers of security, rejected the advice of nerve specialist S. Weir Mitchell, and proceeded to devise an independent plan of action. She believed that self-assertion, in her case, the need to read, write, exercise, work, and jaunt about with politically committed friends, was crucial to her mental health. Lacking the support or even the understanding of most of her community in Providence, and having no income or well-defined plans for work, she prepared to move herself and Kate to Pasadena in the fall of 1888. Pasadena not only meant renewed contacts with the Channings, it was also the one place she had been happy since her marriage—by escaping marriage.

Considering the nineteenth-century code of womanly behavior, the decision was remarkably courageous. But Charlotte was raised with a Beecher code of nonconventional behavior too, and Beechers were never known for peaceful acquiescence to fate's decree. Their political-literary virtuosity, their public-private scandals, their *savoir faire*—these were part of Charlotte's family heritage. There was also the example of her father, an iconoclast, renegade, itinerant scholar who had bounced from job to job. Charlotte felt hostility toward him at times, but she also felt that behind his self-protective coolness was a kindred spirit who rejected claustrophobic family pressures too. Even her mother had unwittingly demonstrated some of the advantages of single living. And though Charlotte resented Mary's domesticity and narrowness, even occasionally her protective warmth, she also had seen Mary coping fairly happily within a community of women, almost none of whom depended on the wherewithal of men. In short, while separation and divorce would have been unthinkable in most families, Charlotte grew up suspecting that it sometimes might be best.

Back in the summer of 1881, that summer of intensely self-revealing correspondence with Martha Luther, Charlotte had already explored her need for independence. In those frank, defiant letters to Martha, she had described her eccentricities, aired her fantasies, disclaimed her need for men, and explained the reasons why. All along, Charlotte had sensed a conflict between masculine and feminine responsibilities; but now she felt there was a conflict between self-assertion and an abdication of her rights, however vaguely defined. In 1881, it had been Martha Luther with whom she explored her subversive views. More recently, it had been Grace Channing. Grace wrote regularly and profusely during the winter of 1887–1888 (the winter following Weir Mitchell's treatment). But even more importantly, in the summer of 1888 (the summer before Charlotte left Providence), Grace came East and helped with preparations for the move.

Grace was well-prepared for the task at hand: supporting, comforting, coaxing, tolerating Charlotte. Grace had a gentle self-sacrificing style, for one thing, and endless patience. But she also shared some of Charlotte's aspirations, and even may have offered some critical advice—if her published work is any indication. For the project Grace had recently undertaken was editing the memoirs of her grandfather, the famed unitarian minister, Dr. William Ellery Channing. Significantly, *Dr. Channing's Notebooks* (1887) begin with Channing's thoughts on freedom: "Freedom is not merely a means. It is an end. It is the well-being of a rational nature. To take it away is to violate the essential law and aspiration of that nature. . . . Forego everything, rather than invest another with the power of determining your actions, or transfer to him the empire which belongs only to our own minds."

It could be argued that Channing's words were directed primarily toward men. The male's need for independence and integrity was usually thought to parallel the woman's need for love. But since the Channing family had supported women's rights for years,* it seems more likely that Grace keenly felt the relevance of Channing's principles both to women's situation in general and, what is important

* One of William Ellery Channing's sons, William Henry Channing (Grace's uncle), was a particularly enthusiastic proponent of the women's movement. Along with R. W. Emerson and J. F. Clarke, he edited the *Memoirs of Margaret Fuller Ossoli*.

here, to the dilemmas Charlotte faced. Grace probably did not quote Channing maxims to Charlotte directly, but when she found Charlotte fuming about Walter and complaining about conflicting goals, very likely she paraphrased them for her: "Love is not giving ourselves away. We are too great to be given away." "Do we not feel a man to be great in just proportion as he forms himself,—retreats into himself for guidance and adheres to what his own soul pronounces to be good?" While at times Channing seemed to think that the "essence of love" was the willingness to suffer joyfully, he also believed that true love allowed integrity and self-affirmation: "Are we not to account that love the truest which respects our freedom, which lays no chain upon it, which encourages it, which leaves us free to act from our own minds?"

Respectful, encouraging, unconstraining love was precisely the kind Charlotte felt Grace (and Martha) gave her. Charlotte wrote, "All that winter Grace Channing kept my spirits up with her letters, with talk and plans for work." Then, when Grace came East in the summer of 1888, she and Charlotte spent several months together in Bristol, Rhode Island. They wrote another play, "gathered background for later work," and cooperatively tackled all the mundane considerations—and confronted all the grisly implications—of Charlotte's plan of action. Grace's level-headed generosity and confidence survived even Charlotte's panic times—whether they were angry outbursts against Walter or "hysterical" tirades against herself—and Grace's know-how and assistance assured that moving, cooking, packing, sorting, and cleaning would get done.

Grace worked on other arrangements as well. Charlotte had inherited some property in Hartford; Grace helped her sell it to the Hazards for two thousand dollars, pay off her debts, and portion out the rest for moving, packing, and travelling expenses. Also, they found an elderly dressmaker who agreed to lend a hand with Kate and housework chores in exchange for fare to California.

During these last frenetic days of preparation, Grace was a constant ally, and Walter may have simply tried to keep his cool. Reluctantly, he had accepted Charlotte's decision: she seemed starkly resolute despite her "illness." Still, there were plans and decisions that they had to talk about, jobs around the house they had to share. What their feelings were, one can only guess. Avoidance mechanisms must have operated in full gear as they dismantled the house together, rummaged through memory-laden goods, packed, sorted, and divided their possessions. There must have been numbness sometimes, tenderness and tears at others; moments of agonizing regret followed by stark indifference; an attempt to forget, a rush out of the house, an absorption in details so that naked truths were blurred.

Grace was a superb diplomat, sympathetic to Walter as well as Charlotte as she tried to ensure that a supportive female friendship would not make Walter feel outnumbered or left out. Despite their crackling quips and the sometimes grating façade of politeness and gentility, Grace tried to buoy up their spirits, respect their privacy, and, with matter-of-fact composure, help get things done.

With comparable composure, Charlotte described the day of separation: "So I set forth on October 8th, with Katharine, Grace, this inadequate dressmaker, a large lunch-basket, my tickets and all my remaining money in my pocket—ten dollars."

On arriving in Pasadena, Charlotte found that the Channings had engaged a "little wood-and-paper four-room house," right near their place on the corner of Orange Grove Avenue and Arroyo Drive. "It stood in a neglected grove of orange trees rich with fragrant blossoms, roses ran over the roof, tall oleanders stood pink against the sky." Her first impressions were of the vivid California beauty, the luxuriant plant life, the outrageously cheap and lavish local food supply. "To California, in its natural features, I owe much," she wrote. "Its calm sublimity of contour, richness of color, profusion of flowers, fruit and foliage, and the steady peace of its climate were meat and drink to me." She described the "nerve-rest of the steady windless weather," the calm supportive friendship of the Channings, and the "long hours in a hammock under the roses."

Facing the "preliminary necessity of getting strong enough to do any steady work," Charlotte sometimes claimed the rest she needed; but she had too many practical responsibilities to allow herself to rest for long. For one thing, she had to earn money. After several weeks of unpacking and arranging things around the house, she started painting again. She tried to sell flower pictures to local women, gave drawing lessons, and took in sewing and mending. For the moment that would provide enough to pay the bills. But there was also Kate to attend to, and endless housework, despite the "dressmaker" she had brought to help. The woman "proved in all ways useless," Charlotte complained. She refused to cook, sew, dust, or even wash the dishes—"said it coarsened her hands!" "Summing up the wide variety of things she would not do, I finally told her I would ask but one service—that she mend and put away the clean clothes. And the moron would roll up and put in the drawer unmended hose!" Apparently the "maid's" capacity for instinctive protest and ingenious resistance to housework matched Charlotte's rather well; but that little irony was missed.

There was another irony about the situation which Charlotte very likely did not miss: she was now "free" to manage almost everything alone—housework, Kate, finances, herself. In Providence, she may have disliked the tensions she felt with Walter and her mother, but at least they had been around to help. In more ways than she expected, the separation seemed to make things worse. Not only did it multiply responsibilities, but it also forced her to confront her fears. Realistically and not just resentfully, she had to deal with her uncertainties about Kate's future, about social ostracism and economic insecurity, about how in the world she would manage, especially if she remained depressed. In Providence, there had been a sense of finality about the decision: they had "agreed to separate, to get a divorce." But now that she faced some of the difficulties of life alone in California, and especially because Walter pushed her, she wavered. She had been writing Walter several times a week and receiving letters in return. By December, they had agreed to try a reconciliation.

Walter joined Charlotte in Pasadena at Christmas time. Especially after all the depressingly cold and wet New England winters, the California beauty seemed to boost their spirits, at least temporarily. Their backyard was a botanical delight, "Katharine is just blooming," Walter wrote his mother, and Charlotte seemed cheerful, though a bit distracted: "Charlotte is very busy with housework, reading, writing, giving drawing lessons, and taking lessons in French. In fact I think she is trying to do too much. I have induced her to have a woman come evenings to wash the day's dishes. That will be some help." *

The Channings helped as well. They offered Walter a room in their home to use as a studio for painting; they introduced him to friends, began arrangements for an exhibit of his art work, and coaxed, encouraged, and advised, just as they had with Charlotte. Grace was especially helpful to him. She took long walks with him when Charlotte was too "busy," posed for his paintings, listened to his complaints and plans and disappointments, and helped soothe his jangled nerves. Apparently, Charlotte felt no jealousy in this three-way friendship, and, by April, the Channings had invited the Stetsons to "combine and dine" with them. Walter wrote, "We pay a small sum weekly and Charlotte helps wash the dishes. . . . Our cooperative dining works very well indeed. I think it is pleasant all around."

* The dressmaker had left, and Charlotte had not had funds enough to hire another maid.

The busier Charlotte was with work, and the busier Walter was with Grace, the happier everybody seemed to feel. In May, Walter wrote, "Charlotte is better than ever." And in June: "Charlotte wrote her mother today and told her that she had not been so well since 1884. I had thought so. Today she has been with her class, which has increased. I do not think she finds it *very* hard work, and surely she is much interested in it; besides today she made seven dollars and a half by it—her afternoon's taking." That was not bad for teaching a class in modern literature—"some ten or twelve ladies, at five dollars a head, ten lessons," Charlotte crowed to Martha Lane. "Very successful so far."

However Walter had felt earlier about Charlotte's political or literary prospects, he seemed confident enough to boast about them now. "Charlotte is doing good work and will, I venture to say, make a name for herself that nobody will be ashamed of." In fact, if Walter's letters are to be believed, Charlotte was already a Pasadena success—at least among reformers. "There is almost always somebody here. Everybody seems to like to come, and Charlotte has a long list of disciples among the young women. They simply adore her. Not only the young women but the older ones also. It is astonishing how much she has changed for the better in every way. She never was so well or so calm. She is doing lots of good work and making no end of friends without any effort."

Charlotte seemed rather pleased as well, not only with her own successes, but also with Walter's liaison with Grace. "Walter is very happy here, but has done little pecuniarily so far. Still we think the prospect is good, and he is painting steadily. He and Grace are great friends, which gives me sincere delight. Katharine flourishes amazingly, like unto a 'green baize tree' as it were. We are all very content with our hegira."

Not only did Charlotte seem undisturbed by Walter's attentiveness to Grace, she also may have felt relieved. Apparently, she simply wanted to be free of him. The longer he stayed, and the better established she was in the community, the more she preferred to live alone. In part, it may have been her growing confidence, particularly in work, that encouraged her to make the final break, though characteristically she emphasized her "wretched health" instead—the crying fits she still experienced, the occasionally incapacitating doldrums: "By Christmas Mr. Stetson joined me, hoping that the change might have so bettered my condition that we might even yet reconsider; but it was no use, a dragging year followed." Likewise, in a letter to Martha Lane (written in August 1890), she described the "illness" which still troubled her: "the weakness of brain which has so devastated my life for the past five years still holds very largely; and while I can do considerable work of a kind which dominates me at the time, or which necessity demands, yet ordinary labor or obligation goes neglected."

But if Charlotte emphasized her "wretched health" as one obstacle preventing a reconciliation with Walter, she also felt that another rather basic one was that she never loved him in the first place. In fact, she now seemed to think that the only real experience of love she had ever known had been with Martha. Charlotte wrote her, "No one has ever taken your place, heart's dearest. No one has ever given me the happiness that you did, the peace, the rest, the everpresent joy. I do not forget. Neither do I remember, for the immediate past is still so vital a horror, and all the antecedent years so low. . . . I felt in your yesterday's letter that the time might yet come when we should again be much to each other. If it is so, how gladly will we hail it! If not we have a memory blessed past most realities."

Meanwhile, Walter was feeling family pressures to go back to Providence. His mother was very ill, and it seemed "almost cruel not to start at once," he wrote her, "but really I *can't*. I am not staying for my own selfish pleasure, although I have taken no pains to conceal that it is pleasant here. It seems to me my duty to stay." By the fall he had acknowledged the final break with Charlotte—"No, Kate and Charlotte will not return with me"—but he still seemed willing that his parents think that Charlotte was a predominant concern: "Charlotte is full of the new magazine which is to be called the Californian. . . . It seems that the more work of this sort Charlotte has to do, the better she is. She thinks herself well now, and if *she* thinks so she must be."

Walter stayed in Pasadena for several more months, all the while apologizing to his parents, and complaining enough to assure them that "selfish pleasure" was not what kept him there: "I have been rather out of sorts, not sick, but tired and feeling as if it were useless to try to do anything. Charlotte is beginning to feel her last months' strain. Grace Channing is sick in bed with a slight congestion of the lungs. Kate is cross." He acknowledged that family tensions were getting on everybody's nerves, but, without telling why, he explained that nursing Grace was high on his list of California duties: "I have learned how to concoct nice little dishes of a sort to surprise. By that means [Grace] has done very well at eating, what with Mrs. Channing's too. Besides I know better what she likes, or how she likes it, than they do, so I have, I flatter myself, been of some use. I like to do it."

Early in January 1890, Walter was "called suddenly to the bedside of his dying mother." Seven years before, when he had met some "keen personal disappointment," Charlotte had agreed to marry him. This time, a personal crisis served to hasten, or at least to clarify, the break. Charlotte wrote to Martha Lane, "Walter has gone East. He got a telegram last Saturday week, saying 'come home at once quickest way. Mother is very low.' He started Sunday and I got a telegram yesterday saying 'arrived last night. Mother was buried Thursday.' So there is trouble enough if one would grieve. The sad joyless old woman dying without one glimpse of her last born and best loved; and he not even seeing his mother's face! And no wife to comfort him."

But if there was a sympathetic note or two in Charlotte's letter, for the most part she seemed cool, almost intentionally indifferent, not only to Walter's grief and to what was now their final, openly acknowledged separation, but to Martha as well. Charlotte seemed to enjoy momentary reminders of past feelings of closeness to Martha, but she also seemed to need to prove her independence. Work and success were first priority considerations—naturally, since she had crushed the heart in favor of the mind.

> I haven't any heart but a scar; and I get nothing out of it by patient application but pathetic and agonized squirms. So I will hide the thing away again, in the cavity where it rattles about and hurts itself as I go on my path. Thank goodness it doesn't shriek and tear round as it used to! Don't imagine that I am still a melancholiac. Out here they think me "so bright! So clever! so goodnatured!" and I am sent for to officiate at church socials and similar festivities. And I never had so much praise for beauty in my palmiest days as I have here. I am considered *beautiful*—really! That would have been a great pleasure nine years ago wouldn't it! And I have good friends here; and plenty of work to do. I like my work, I am getting *very* fond of Kate; I look forward as I always shall, to doing great things sometime. But earthquake countries build their houses low—I don't venture to *feel* much about anything. Withal I improve in health of mind and nerve, slowly, slowly, but still so that it shows. . . . Now I guess I will shut the door of my heart again; and hang on it "*Positively* no Admittance except on Business!"

Sometimes pleased, sometimes morbid, Charlotte openly described to Martha the self-condemnation that accompanied her pride: as the self-styled devil's daughter, she was beautiful and bold and brilliant, but "wildly, darkly, strangely" soulless. She had changed dramatically—for the worse—she warned Martha. But

Charlotte must have also understood that the goals she had shared with Martha back in 1881 were simply being reaffirmed. Then she had described them confidently, assuming Martha understood; now she wrote about them apologetically, as though she knew that the process of implementation—compassionate, self-respecting, and heroic, but also pigheaded, egocentric, and destructive—was beyond Martha's ken.

> You knew and loved me once. You do not know me now, and I am not at all sure that you would love me if you did. What you cling to so tenderly is a sweet memory, a lovely past; as many a man or woman cherishes a lost love.
>
> Time and experience make us grow and change, in varying degree; and while you have changed only in a calmer wisdom, a sweet maturity, grown only the lovely lines marked out already in your character, an orderly wise kind loving woman, an ideal mother, a contenting wife, and with all literature and learning before you to rise in as you choose and can—I have grown and changed wildly, darkly, strangely beyond a mother's recognition, beyond my own. The girl you knew, the woman you loved died some years past, died in long slow unutterable pain.
>
> I believe you had some knowledge of it at the time.
>
> Whether she who now writes is a better woman or as good or worse is a matter of scientific interest perhaps, but one which I consider seldom. A change—a difference—a distance incalculable, an impassable gulf, lies between me and your old friend. We may be friends again, new ones, but I do not dare to hope it. So utterly unstable, rootless and windblown is my life, that all calm restful rooted things are my admiration and despair. And they do not generally like me, which is self-protecting natural instincts on their part. But this I will say of my love for you. Through the first year or two of my marriage, in every depth of pain and loss and loneliness, *yours* was the name my heart cried—not his. I loved you better than any one, in those days when I had a heart to love and ache. And now always in the future of wealth and fame which I dangle before my own eyes as an incentive to life and effort, I always think first of you as a sort of haven; to gorgeously befriend you—(only audacious fancies!) and to beg some of your sweet family influence for Kate. . . .
>
> Grace Channing saved what there is of me. Grace Channing pulled me out of living death, set me on my staggering feet,

> helped me to get to work again, did more than I can say to make me live, and I love her, I think, as well as any one on earth. But it is different. With you I *was happy*, and that is a word I have forgotten. Those years with you, that blessed summer of eighty one—I doubt if most people have as much happiness in all their lives as I had then. I do not forget. But neither do I remember, because it hurts. . . .
>
> You do not understand. Unless we could live together again, or indeed if I wrote daily and vitalized each letter with my present self, we can come to no contact whatever. Write so I cannot. Meet we cannot, now. But time may turn the wheel to our old gladness again—"When you and I asked nothing of the world but room and one another!" or may turn it to something better. Can there be anything better? Different let me say. You ask me to "reassure you." This is but a sad reply, and yet I have no better.

Charlotte's letter contains those strange but familiar conflicts: she was emotionally effusive while promising to lock emotions out; she viewed herself as unworthy in personal relationships, and an Amazon in public ones. It was sometimes as though she pursued work to compensate for loneliness, to escape from feelings of rejection, and to vindicate herself.

Meanwhile, with Walter gone, and Grace a bit freer, she and Charlotte started working on plays again, presumably trying to blunt some of the discomfort of their awkward situation in the process: Charlotte still resented Walter, Grace liked him better all the time, yet they wrote plays together about women's relationships with men. Their play, "A Pretty Idiot," may not reflect attitudes about Walter specifically (at least none Charlotte would openly admit), but it does probably reflect some of her residual resentments.

The pretty idiot in the play is Jean Churchill, a strong-willed female author who is simultaneously chased and ridiculed by a Mr. Harrington Dyke. Early in the play Miss Churchill describes her notion of the ideal woman: "strong, free, self-reliant, independent—with both intellect and muscle—having a career of her own—ambitious—able to meet you on your own ground!" Characteristically, Mr. Dyke responds, "Heaven forbid! You are describing a man!" His notion of the perfect woman, by contrast, is one who has "sweetness—gentleness—patience—amiability, above all the capacity for great absorbing self-sacrificing all-enduring love!" The pretty idiot proceeds to outwit Mr. Dyke and then fall in love with a man who respects her talents as an author.

Both Grace and Charlotte might have argued that Walter respected women's talents. After six years of married life with Charlotte, he probably was a more sensitive and well-informed proponent of women's rights than most (one of the reasons Grace had come to like him?). Of course, he had not always been so. Double-standard sex-role expectations were deeply rooted in his family, his community, his culture, and like Charlotte he had learned through hard experience. Charlotte may have been willing to acknowledge his good intentions (Grace kept reminding her if she forgot), but still she seemed to need to exorcise the stored-up anger, and to expose the "feminine" stereotypes that she felt he had used to curb her work. "The Test Case," another short story written about this same time, also provides clues to Charlotte's self-perceptions and experiences.

"The Test Case" presents a story within a story. The heroine, a young precocious New England woman, decides to "test" her friends' attitudes toward women by telling them a tale of "tragic love." In the tale, she describes a young man's efforts to avoid marriage to a beautiful and talented young woman. His worry was this: "he was a rabid reformer" whereas "she cared for nothing but love and music." He loved her "in a way," but he "didn't want to marry her." The woman, unfortunately, was insistent: "She had no scruples of any kind; she loved him and him alone, and meant to marry him, that was all. Of course it was only a matter of time." Engagements were made, broken, and remade, "and after a while he felt his honor engaged, and then he stuck to it and married her." He was miserable; his reform ambitions dwindled. Family responsibilities—especially for a crying child—wore on his nerves. He "nearly went insane." So much for a not-too-subtle tale. The heroine then asks for her friends' reactions. Of course the woman is categorically to blame, they argue; "she led him on till he *couldn't* refuse—in honor!" Fine, quips the heroine, but what if the sexes were reversed? A female reformer with a male in pursuit? In that case, the heroine explains, when a woman "of the most brilliant promise" is ruined by a marriage she does not want, no one blames the man. He is a "real genius! And his wife is a nervous hypochondriac! . . . It's a wholly different matter when you change the sex!"

In "The Test Case" Charlotte lashed out at some of the social attitudes that make women feel guilty for wanting freedoms men regard as natural rights: attitudes toward mental illness (hypochondria in women), toward marriage (woman's duty), toward a career (man's right); such attitudes seemed to her so absurd, so unfair. Believing that "hysteria" (hers or others') was often caused by the strains of family life, that her own reform commitments had been skewed by marriage, she seemed enthusiastic and relieved to face her "first year of freedom": "I wrote some thirty-three short articles and twenty-three poems, besides ten more child-verses." If to some extent she was still using her writing to understand and justify her own decisions, she was also ready to expand her insights on women's issues generally, to join other reformers, and to allow her political commitments to become more radical, more rigorous, more securely based.

1890-1896

Chapter Eight

The First Year of Freedom 1890

CALIFORNIA in the early 1890s was an ideal training ground for rebels. It was a vital center of contemporary protest thought, a relatively supportive community for radicals and nonconformists, an engaging political environment in which Charlotte could broaden and intensify her sense of alliance with nationally based currents of reform. She would work not only within the women's movement, but, at the same time, with other political activists—socialists, Populists, Nationalists—whose organizations and friendships encouraged her to express and enlarge her passion for reform.

* * *

From the perspective of most of Charlotte's reform-oriented friends, the 1890s was a decade of storm and protest, of deep and prolonged depression, of shocking inequalities of wealth and power. The garish opulence of the new class of multi-millionaires, with their marble mansions and royal entertainments, threw into strong relief the poverty and misery of workers in the slums. The "Eastern Establishment" was under attack. So also was the crass materialism of the age, the "conspicuous wealth" and "conspicuous waste" of business and political tycoons, the brutal processes of industrial capitalism which denied so many the basic necessities for a decent self-respecting life.

In 1890, approximately seven-eighths of American families controlled only one-eighth of the national wealth, and in the land of opportunity, the annual income of all nonagrarian wage earners averaged only four hundred and eighty-six dollars. Factory workers' weekly hours averaged about sixty. Nearly two million children below the age of fifteen were wage earners. At least 15 percent, possibly 20 percent, of the wage-earning population was out of work. Prices were relatively low, the cost of living rather stable, but vast numbers of Americans—even by the standards of the day—could be considered poor.* Anger and disillusionment were rampant. Grievances were of long standing. And the intensity of the protest mounted with each farm or labor meeting, each strike, each political campaign.

The heroes of the protest were many: the rebels of the great railroad strike of 1877, the Haymarket martyrs, the western miners, the activists in the Farmers' Alliance, the Knights of Labor, the farm and labor leaders clamoring for "people's rights" all across the country. In June 1890, there was a meeting in Topeka, Kansas, to organize a new People's Party. Railroad agitator James E. Weaver, "Sockless Jerry" Simpson, Ignatius Donnelly, and Mary Ellen Lease, with her "raise less corn and more Hell" philosophy—all were present at this colorful gathering. It was an impressive focusing of energies and insights, a radicalizing preparation for the 1890s battles in the interests of the common man.

Many middle-class Americans were supportive. They were not always enthusiastic about strikes and grassroots protests, but some, at least, were stirred to sympathy by books. Edward Bellamy's *Looking Backward* (1888) and Henry George's *Progress and Poverty* (1879) were hailed as stunningly persuasive indictments of the era. "The march of invention," Henry George wrote, "has clothed mankind with powers of which a century ago the boldest imagination could not have dreamed. But in factories where labor-saving machinery has reached its most wonderful development, little children are at work; . . . amid the greatest accumulations of wealth, men die of starvation, and puny infants suckle dry breasts." Like many of the rebels of his generation, George offered "remedies" that were amazingly simplistic—a single tax amounting to 100 percent on unearned increments in the value of land—but his sympathetic account of poverty conditions both reflected and augmented the growing protest.

* It has been estimated that an income of $1,500 to $2,000 a year, provided one exercised economy, was enough for a family to live quite comfortably as members of the middle class. Ten, even five, thousand dollars a year enabled one to live with few major economic worries. An income of $486, however, the average annual income of nonfarm workers, was not adequate to provide even the basic necessities of food, shelter, or clothing.

Jacob Riis' *How the Other Half Lives* (1890) was another protesters' call to action, another attempt, through vivid human-interest writing, to awaken Americans to conditions of urban poverty some would just as soon forget. By describing the look, feel, and smell of sweltering tenement houses, by telling how a couple lived on three dollars a week, Riis showed what poverty statistics meant in terms of human lives. By the mid-1890s, it was already known that more than two-thirds of the one-half million inhabitants of New York lived in 90,000 tenement houses; but Jacob Riis dramatically exposed the problem by conducting readers on a tour.

> Cherry Street. Be a little careful, please! The hall is dark and you might stumble over the children pitching pennies back there. Not that it would hurt them; kicks and cuffs are their daily diet. They have little else. Here where the hall turns and dives into utter darkness is a step, and another, another. A flight of stairs. . . . All the fresh air that ever enters these stairs comes from the hall-door that is forever slamming, and from the windows of dark bedrooms that in turn receive from the stairs their sole supply of the elements God meant to be free, but man deals out with such niggardly hand.

Protest works proliferated as frustration intensified. Helen Campbell's *Problems of the Poor* (1882), Hamlin Garland's *Main Travelled Roads* (1891), Lincoln Steffens' *Shame of the Cities* (1904)—these were but a few of the more dramatic indictments of what such writers saw as the indignities suffered by the many, the atrocities perpetrated by the few.

Most dramatic and successful among these protest books was Edward Bellamy's socialist utopian novel, *Looking Backward*. In part it was a fanciful romance; perhaps that explains some of its popular appeal. Bellamy dramatized the inequities of contemporary America by contrasting them to an ideal state he thought to be attainable, and then proceeded—many said pragmatically and persuasively—to show through fiction that a socialist alternative could work. He projected a vision of America transformed—twenty-first-century America—utterly equal, just, and cooperative, utterly free of poverty, crime, war, misery, ugliness. The American capitalistic structure had been eliminated, by peaceful means of course, and the needlessness of human suffering had been demonstrated beyond a shadow of a doubt, by logic, by reason, and by practice. Bellamy had not been a serious student of Karl Marx or of any other scientific socialist intellectual, but he had written the American-style socialist manifesto nonetheless. As Christian Socialist W. D. P. Bliss later wrote, "It is doubtful if any man, in his own lifetime, ever exerted so great an influence upon social beliefs of his fellow beings as did Edward Bellamy." He had made socialism respectable among the middle class.

In *Looking Backward*, in *Equality*, and in articles in the *Nationalist* and the *Nation*, Bellamy argued categorically that the state must secure complete control of the means of production. No compromise solution was possible. Nothing else would end the crisis situation. The state would have to be highly centralized, of course, with industrial officers and state-appointed managers. In fact, it would be organized rather like an army—efficient, forceful, but beneficent always. It would arrange for the production and distribution of goods and services according to needs, not profit, secure economic equality and satisfying jobs to everyone, and thus eliminate competition, selfishness, greed, and other ugly by-products of the cutthroat laissez-faire economy. The environment, not human nature, not man's depravity, was the problem, Bellamy explained. For when people are nourished within the classless society, it will become obvious that they are peaceful, cooperative, and loving—by nature.

The message must have been compelling, for by 1890, *Looking Backward* was sweeping the nation, selling at a rate of 10,000 copies a week, and rapidly becoming one of the most widely read political tracts of the period. Bellamy-inspired Nationalist Clubs were flourishing across the country—158 in 27 states, 65 in California alone—and countless social and political reformers began to extol the Nationalist cause. Charlotte's uncle, Edward Everett Hale, was prominent among them, as were William Dean Howells, Hamlin Garland, Julia Ward Howe, Frances Willard, W. D. P. Bliss. Nationalists joined forces with Single Tax Club members (Henry George's inspiration), the Fabian societies, and various socialist, feminist, and labor organizations. Opinions and interests differed, of course, but social and political commitments were often passionately shared. W. D. P. Bliss explained the faith quite simply: "Nationalism means essentially the application of ethics and equality through government to business. Its development means the development of righteousness to business. Its development means the development of righteousness in the social order. And righteousness *is* Christianity."

* * *

For Charlotte Stetson, as for so many of her contemporaries, Bellamy's message seemed to hit the mark. For years, she had aligned herself with reformers, read their attacks on Social Darwinists' laissez-faire perspectives, and identified personally as well as intellectually with their Reform Darwinist point of view. She especially admired their Social Gospel message, their emphasis on social morality rather than individual salvation, their concern, however paternalistic, for the working man's welfare. The Channings, the Hazards, the Hales, the Beechers, and especially her father—all these provided her with personal inspiration, reading lists, and books. Most of her author-heroes were evolutionary theorists to the core, reformers who maintained a religious faith in God's omnipotence while insisting nonetheless that society and its improvements were the responsibility of man: Sir John Lubbock, for example (*Prehistoric Times*, 1865), or E. B. Tylor (*Primitive Culture*, 1871, and *The Early History of Mankind*, 1865). Like many people of her class and heritage, Charlotte had learned from thinkers more than activists, men who emphasized religion, science, and keen educational training as reformers' tools, not farm and labor meetings, strikes, or galvanizing fights. But even if her intellectual mentors were rather aloof from—sometimes even opposed to—the grassroots protest movement of the 1880s, they were rebels nonetheless. Among middle-class Americans anyway, they were in the vanguard of reform—providing Bellamy with useful arguments and preparing converts to his protest thought.

Whatever Bellamy's genius may have been, it was not originality. And Charlotte knew it. He has "no style," she wrote Martha Lane, and he has "not invented much. Few people do." But he has, she continued, "put in popular form the truth of ages, and done it at a time when the whole world was aching for such help." Partly it was Bellamy's optimism that attracted her; his plans seemed so logical, so rational, so passionately attuned to the rights and needs of the common man. She liked his "largeness of thought," she wrote, "the daring imagination, the careful practical planning of detail, and the immense human love."

By 1890, then, Charlotte was a convert to the Nationalists' cause. From her point of view, they had exposed the "artificial habits of life," the senseless profit-based mentality which had made people "indifferent if not inimical to each other." They had devised alternatives—on paper anyway—in which "everybody would share and nobody would suffer." And they understood that "our natural impulse to love each other would be encouraged and developed by *the very instincts which now suppress it*!" "The Nationalization of Land and the Nationalization of Industry. They belong together, these two. They cover the whole ground." At a time of national crisis, Bellamy seemed to offer remedies which were simple, peaceful, and profound. Under Nationalism, Charlotte wrote, "class distinctions would disappear, and social instincts would unite instead of separating us."

Those were hardly ideas that some of Charlotte's high-brow kinfolk would have cherished—particularly her uncle Henry Ward Beecher, with his "the great will be great and the little will be little" philosophy. But despite some firm upper-class loyalties and preferences, many of Charlotte's relatives—notably Edward Everett Hale, Catharine Beecher, Harriet Beecher Stowe, and even mugwump father Frederick—all, in one fashion or another, championed the underdog and deplored oppressive inequalities. In some respects, Charlotte may have been more aware than they of what penny-pinching meant. She had shared some of her mother's financial stresses; now she faced her own. But problems of poverty are relative. Though Charlotte had seen hard times, she was not working class, and that rather significant distinction she apparently forgot. Attracted to Bellamy's theories about the classless society, she sometimes spoke as though she were utterly without prejudice herself: "Being born without any proper sense of class distinction, and always talking in terms of shocking intimacy with whoever would talk to me, I am now utterly lost and bewildered! I can't say for the life of me what 'class' I am! I have friends who own whole villages and friends who don't own the shanty they live in; I have friends who make dictionaries and friends who can not half read them." Therefore—or so she claimed—she had no upper-class pretensions: "No, I can state from sad experience, that it don't do to treat people as equals! You soon get to feel that they *are*; and then you find that they are *not*, and then when you [try] to classify them, and find your washer woman more of a lady than your hostess at a ball—you never again can get life straightened out on the good old lines, as sharp and clear as sumptuary laws!"

That may have been impressive thinking in the abstract, but it was not entirely representative of Charlotte's feelings or convictions, nor, in fact, of those of most reformers that she knew. It was one thing to sympathize with the "downtrodden," but quite another to respect or understand them. Theoretically Charlotte was an egalitarian, but in fact she was sometimes a racist and a snob. For one thing, she was offended by the Californians' lack of taste and breeding, their coarseness compared to the upper-class New Englanders' cultural refinements. But there were other people she found even less acceptable—immigrants, for example, or blacks, or Jews, or those whom she viewed as culturally or racially inferior. To be fair, it should be mentioned that racist and ethnocentric views were common to Charlotte's generation of reformers. But to be blunt, her grand theories on equality and love contrasted rather starkly with her condemnations of those she regarded as the "lesser folk."

In point of fact, neither Charlotte nor most of her Nationalist friends were able to shed the condescending paternalism that marked the movement from the start, the authoritarian sternness that seems inimical to the egalitarian ideals they professed. Bellamy had put his faith in a highly centralized system of government, a military-type structure at that. Clearly he intended that his socialist state serve the interests of the masses, but history shows that a socialist state can develop in very different ways as well, ranging from bureaucratic decision-making, to conscripted armies, to totalitarian socialism. Some political thinkers, notably those writing in the 1950s and 1960s, have severely criticized Bellamy for failing to recognize the authoritarianism underlying his dreams of justice.

Such criticism could also be applied to some of Charlotte's writings. Following Bellamy's example, she argued—at least occasionally—that the most splendid model of human brotherhood in action was the army. Soldiers impressed her—their community spirit, their support for one another, their loyalty to wounded brothers on the field. "The tradesman naturally loves his kind as much a[s] the soldier, but the tradesman soo[n] finds his own interests and his comrades' interests conflict—with the soldier they are identical." Nationalism, then, would be "an arrangement just as simple, just as possible, as the formation of an army," with cooperative, not exploitative, relationships as the central goal. That was the theory. Usually Charlotte realized that armies did not work that way in practice, so she switched her argument around. "Army discipline" was "destructive and immoral," she wrote. It taught men "to suppress all their best and noblest instincts and cultivate their worst, for the purpose of destroying life." In fact, she sometimes felt that military and police forces were so oppressive, so brutal and violent, that they must be evolutionary relics of an earlier barbaric stage, soon to "become extinct forms of human energy" as "civilization" progressed —among whites, that is, not blacks. Still, consistency was not Charlotte's virtue. For however anti-military she may have sometimes seemed, she could never abandon her authoritarian stance, and especially to persons of other races, it continued to apply with unabated force. The progress of blacks would be facilitated by some form of regimentation, she believed, even to the point of advocating a system of military conscription to "uplift" them.

Unfortunately, like most Nationalists, Charlotte was more effective in describing conditions which deprive human life of dignity and meaning than she was in projecting viable solutions, more eloquent in proclaiming principles of human equality than she was in confronting inequalities right beneath her nose. The utopian vision had reinspired her reform commitments, but by no means assured that she would or could devise impressive strategies for social change. Religious faith, the laws of God and nature (i.e., Nationalism), would somehow bring about the just and peaceful world. As Charlotte later put it, "The human race is one with universal law." "That which we used to grope for in the assurance that God was 'on our side,' we may now lay hold of as established fact." God was rational, clearly understandable, beneficent, the creator of laws of progress working for the cause of good. "The 'will of God' means health, intelligence, normal development, beauty, joyous fulfillment of all life's processes; and economic measures which promote such things must be in accordance with it."

Such religious idealism was widely shared by many of Charlotte's Nationalist contemporaries, their "good intentions" blurring their authoritarian and racist views, their advocacy of socialist principles emerging as extensions of their Social Gospel faith. (The Social Gospel movement had had its beginnings in the 1870s, but with the merging of religious and economic thinking in the 1890s, it had come of age.) Nationalists envisioned a future society based on cooperation, not competition, on respect for social welfare rather than selfish individualism; a society, in short, in accordance with the will of God. Washington Gladden and Josiah Strong, two of the leading exponents of the Social Gospel movement, saw a fundamental contradiction between capitalism and Christianity: the environment, not evil individuals, caused sinful behavior; only a society committed to serving social needs could ensure genuine Christian morality. Walter Rauschenbusch, also a Bellamy enthusiast, and later author of *Christianity and Social Crisis* (1907), argued that the expropriation of wealth by the few, and the consequent pauperization of the many, was in direct opposition to the teachings of Jesus. The *Dawn*, a Christian Socialist paper initiated by W. D. P. Bliss, published articles by Daniel DeLeon, Washington Gladden, and Richard Ely—all supporters of the notion that Nationalism was merely applied Christian ethics. Thus, religious leaders taught economic theory, and prominent economists (John Commons and Richard Ely) preached religious views, each supporting one another. For both groups, Nationalism offered guidelines for a viable economic and political system, as well as for an ethical way of life.

* * *

By 1890, Charlotte was an avid supporter of, indeed contributor to, this conglomerate Nationalist perspective, and was a lively witty one at that. In April, the *Nationalist* published her first major poem, "Similar Cases," which was immediately hailed as an evolutionary, ethical, religious, literary gem. It was just the sort of "poetry of vivid purpose" Nationalists relished—a vigorous blast against the senseless idiocy of defenders of the status quo, a mighty "thrust at the spirit that is content to argue against reform by appeal to precedents." Professionally, it was Charlotte's passport to the Nationalist lecture-writing circuit; and, on a more personal level, a rather welcome confirmation of success. Her uncle Edward Everett Hale wrote her: "I have been dying to write you to make my congratulations on the poem in the April *Nationalist*. It is perfect. If I told you all I say of it and all that other people say I should turn your head. The idea was an inspiration, in itself,—and the execution is perfect." Similarly, William Dean Howells wrote her, "I have been wishing, ever since I first read it—and I've read it many times with unfailing joy—to thank you for your poem in the April *Nationalist*. We have nothing since the Biglow Papers half so good for a good cause as 'Similar Cases.'"

Charlotte was elated, of course, and decided it was time to boast a bit to Martha Lane. In fact, Charlotte must have suggested (as comeuppance?) that she and Martha exchange samples of their current writings, Charlotte sending "Similar Cases," Martha sending a play and a children's primer she had written. It was as though this were the perfect opening for Charlotte, the perfect excuse for lashing back at Martha for gripes and irritations that had been harboring for years. Martha's primer was worthless, Charlotte decided; the play was just about as bad, and so—with no words wasted—she proceeded to ridicule them both. "It may be essential or at least advisable to put a child through all that stuff, but I am a heathen, I don't see it." Charlotte continued:

> Your play my dear is better than the primer!!!
> Did I read the play?
> Yes I read the play.
> It is a fine tale!
> Did the man wed the girl?
> Yes the man wed the girl.
> The same man.
> The same girl.
> The same old tale.

Charlotte seemed to delight in the sniping, to enjoy chiding Martha rather than accepting differences both always knew were there. "How I would like to shake you and talk to you like—an uncle about all these matters. You're living too much in one place." It was as though Martha had suddenly become the witless parent, Charlotte the ambitious, rebellious, disillusioned child no longer needing affection and support: "Here is a long neglected letter of yours—April 23rd, pricking me sore. . . . I'm exceedingly enraged at you my dear!" Martha had been studying spelling and handwriting, and had apparently suggested Charlotte's should improve: "But now look here! Aren't you tempting fate to revile my handwriting? Don't you imagine O devoted one! that whereas that handwriting is already rare and difficult of attainment it will be withheld altogether if you scoff? To what Cimmerian darkness of primers and spelling books would thee then sink!" Moreover, Martha had not praised "Similar Cases" nearly enough: "I'm glad you thought my poem funny. I herein boastfully enclose a copy of a letter showing it was thought rather more of by some!" Charlotte then copied Howells' letter for Martha's perusal: "Now who wants to throw inkstands? and *his* handwriting is far worse than mine!!! In sober sadness though, isn't that a delightful letter? I am so pleased too to find the man thinks well of Nationalism in spite of its 'flabby apostle'(!)"

Actually, Charlotte was far more pleased with Howells' praise than she was with Howells' work. She had read only parts of *A Hazard of New Fortune*, she explained to Martha: Howells "never was a favorite of mine you know. His work is exquisite, painfully exquisite, but save for that Chinese delicacy of workmanship it seems to me of small artistic value. And its truth is that of the elaborate medical chart, the scientific photograph." Apparently, Martha viewed Howells as "an apostle of truth;" but grumbling that Martha cared more for "artistic pleasure" than passionate reform, Charlotte decided Howells was to blame: "As far as I have seen, the waste horrors of our high class life, which he so fearfully portrays, awake no other emotion in the class portrayed than a pleased surprise at their own reproduction. Like a child with a looking glass."

Some of Charlotte's letters to Martha were so sarcastic, so arrogant, that whatever the political or literary disagreements, longstanding personal dissension was also clearly involved. Political views were bound up with each one's lifestyle choices, and cerebral conflicts reactivated feelings of vulnerability and risk. This was especially apparent as Charlotte and Martha began arguing about the work of socialist-feminist writer Olive Schreiner. Author of *The Story of an African Farm* (1883) and, later, *Dreams* (1891) and *Woman and Labour* (1911), South African feminist Olive Schreiner was already one of Charlotte's heroines. She was a free thinker, an unconventional "New Woman," a religious skeptic, an ardent reformer, a woman who shared her passions with her pen. To Charlotte,

Schreiner was among the most impressive pioneers of the women's movement, and Martha among the most stupid of fools for not appreciating Schreiner's work: "What you say of 'The African Farm' is a revelation to me. I do perceive between us more abysmal gulfs than I had thought. Are you just where you were when we parted, or have you grown to be an integral part of our present social world, and content therein! Read if you can find it Olive Schreiner's 'Hell.'"

Irritation, resentment, a persistent need to jab and wrangle—with such feelings, Charlotte decided she might not want to visit Martha even if she had the chance. Grace Channing and her mother were planning to go East (in part because of Walter?), and invited Charlotte to go along. In talking to Martha about the possibility, Charlotte seemed to pass from elation, to hurt, to indifference, and to conclude by boasting about her own career successes as though Martha's friendship mattered not at all: "If I do get East—and get to see you, *what* a time we shall have! Talk? . . . But I begin to wonder whether you will want to see me as much as you think. To hear me rather. My latest departure is in public speaking."

The "departure" professionally was *to* public speaking. More personally, it was *from* Martha, and Charlotte seemed to need to make that clear. She could flaunt success, reestablish distance, and try to prove she was not dependent on Martha anymore, but in the process she still showed dependence on the approval of friends for confidence and validation.

> I guess I told you of my first adventure in this line—with the local nationalist club. That was my first speech to a mixed audience, and they were so pleased they got me to *repeat* it, to a larger evening audience!
>
> Certain grandees from Los Angeles were present, (acquaintances) and they besought me to repeat the address at their house to a large invited party. Which I cheerfully did. . . . Then the 1st Nationalist Club in Los Angeles, hearing of my power, invited me to give them an address, which I did, and they were tumultuous in their applause, and begged for a repetition. Also they sent me a most appreciative letter some time since, enclosing five dollars! Said they didn't often pay, but mine was the best address they had ever had, and should be paid for however inadequately!

* * *

One of the women in the audience at that first Nationalist Club lecture may have been feminist writer and activist Harriet

Howe. She had been a member of the program committee of her Los Angeles Nationalist Club; Charlotte's name had just "been flashed across the country" because of "Similar Cases," so Harriet's committee decided to "have such a vital person to speak." Forty-six years later, Harriet Howe recalled:

> I shall never forget those first impressions. A slender woman, seeming on the platform even smaller than she really was, with —Eyes! Such eyes, magnetic, far reaching, deep seeing, nothing could be hid from such eyes, and a Voice, clear, compelling, yet conversational, easily reaching to the farthest end of the hall, entirely devoid of effort.

Already Charlotte showed a special flair for public speaking, an ability to reach people forcefully and directly. And no wonder. She was speaking from heart and mind together, her feelings of personal defiance amplifying verbal blasts against status quo mentality as though public and private issues were inextricably combined. It was unthinking conformity she railed against, that "steady undying force which urges us all to troop like sheep, to live like slaves, to die like any helpless cattle—*the impulse to do what we have done before, to do what others do—to do what we are told*—to accept and submit and swallow whole what we have given to us." In one of these early lectures, Charlotte summarized her personal-political Nationalist objectives: freedom, integrity, and self-respect.

> We know, I say, what human life might be.
>
> Give us health, and pessimism is gone.
>
> Give us happy industry—work that we love, the creative output of a willing soul and idleness and crime are gone.
>
> Give us love, pure happy freely-given love, love which does not ask "support" on one side or "submission" on the other—and immorality is gone.
>
> With health and work and happy love, intemperance would go, and Death itself would draw back to his normal limits.

The first time she heard one of Charlotte's lectures, Harriet Howe was ecstatic, and wanted to invite Charlotte back again to speak. She consulted the chairman of the Nationalist Club's program committee. Howe wrote, "To my delight he was almost as enthusiastic as I was. 'Sure,' he agreed, 'invite her again, soon, she's a mighty smart woman. Ought to be more like her.'" So back Charlotte came, speaking at first to both men and women in the club, and later to some women who decided to form a separate group. Harriet Howe appreciated the program chairman's approbation of Charlotte's lecture—"Wise Mr. Steward, of blessed memory," Howe wrote. But she also was angry at her male colleagues' condescending stance. Like women political activists of the 1960s, female nationalists of the 1890s had their own separate needs and interests, and sometimes felt they had to go their separate ways. Harriet Howe put the matter this way:

> The women in this Nationalist Club were treated with the usual condescension with which men treat women in all matters supposed to be over women's heads. The women tired of that treatment, so a woman's club was formed with a small nucleus which grew steadily. The first thing I urged them to do was to study Cushing's "Manual" or Robert's "Rules of Order" and so prepare themselves to speak easily and correctly in public.

If Harriet Howe's account seems rather trivial—here was a group of women attempting to perfect their parliamentary skills—the phenomenon she was describing in fact had portentous nationwide implications. All across the country, women's groups were forming, and not just to learn Robert's Rules of Order or to resist the insults of well-intentioned men. Through such clubs, women began to talk together more, to feel greater confidence than they could in groups with men, to learn more organizational and debating skills, to become more politically engaged. Charlotte could scarcely have started her political career at a more opportune moment, a time not only of farm and labor protest, but also of intensifying efforts and increasing expertise in the women's movement. The suffrage fight was part of it of course, but that was just one among many manifestations of the rising tide of resentment, of reform activism, of women's demands to have their voices heard. Women were joining the Women's Christian Temperance Union, the social purity movement, the social settlement movement, the women's trade union organizations, the countless women's clubs which, in 1890, merged into the General Federation of Women's Clubs. In short, the protest and rebellion of the 1890s was not confined to men. Women were active, assertive, innovative. They were emerging as crucial catalysts for reform and, in the process, also establishing firm bases for what was becoming a feminist movement of international dimensions.

While to a large extent the women's movement resulted from deliberate strategies and conscious efforts, there were also significant socio-economic forces—some progressive, some not—that were working in its favor. Educational opportunities were expanding (by 1900, 80 percent of colleges and universities admitted women). The birth rate was declining (between 1810 and 1900 it would be cut almost by half). The divorce rate was rising—in fact by two and one half times between 1890 and 1910. (Voluntarily or not, women were more "independent.") The increasing number of public schools and the longer school day and year decreased child-care worries, and improvements in household technology decreased some housework cares—though probably less than one might think. By 1890, some women were using sewing machines, eggbeaters, and canned goods—these were the most common "modern conveniences" available at the time. But since most women still faced coal stoves, not gas or electric ones, scrub boards, not washing machines, brooms, not vacuum cleaners, the real change for most middle- and upper-class women came from the availability of cheap domestic labor—a result, in part, of the influx of more than thirty million immigrants between 1820 and 1920.

Clearly many such "progressive" changes served the needs not of the majority of women, but of the more affluent. Since middle- and upper-class women had more time and energy for professional activities (the number of women in the professions would increase by 226 percent between 1890 and 1920), for clubs, for political involvement, not surprisingly some sectors of the women's movement reflected primarily middle-class concerns. But not exclusively. For while there was a recognition of progress for some, there was also an awareness—often a keen and bitter one—of the difficult, sometimes appalling conditions many women faced. This was especially true of "social feminists" such as Florence Kelley, Jane Addams, or Helen Campbell, women who were Populists or Nationalists themselves, or women who were concerned with or directly encountered the tough realities of the economic market place. For while it was clear that the numbers of women in the paid labor force was increasing (there would be four million women of working age by 1890, five million by 1900), women were usually holding the least skilled, lowest-paying jobs. Even in the same jobs, they were earning far less than men (approximately 53 percent of what men were earning). To be sure, some women had found "prestigious" jobs in nursing and teaching, but a far greater percentage had less satisfying work: some had low-paying jobs as stenographers, clerks, typists, and salespersons; more than a fourth of women laborers were factory workers—the lowest-paid and least secure level of the industrial system; and the largest single group of wage-earning women—two million of the five million women workers in 1900—were domestic servants.

In short, women reformers were beginning to expose problems that concerned male protestors rarely, if at all: the fact that few women had either job opportunities or income levels to approach those of contemporary men, and that most women's work was still essentially domestic—poorly paid, if it was paid at all, yet regarded as "feminine" by nature. Eighty percent of working-age women were still not in the paid labor force in 1890; the ones who were wage earners usually were young and single. Even as late as 1920, almost 90 percent of the female work force was unmarried, the bulk of them under the age of twenty-five. Married women were increasingly busy—with their clubs, their volunteer associations, their reform activities. But almost all of them were dependent on their husbands for their spending money, indeed their livelihood, and almost all of them assumed their main responsibilities should be at home. "In large generalization," Charlotte Gilman would later write, "the women of the world cook and wash, sweep and dust, sew and mend, for the men." Women had no choice, but were simply defined as naturally responsible for the care of home and children. A vast percentage of the "feminine energy of the world is still spent in ministering laboriously to the last details of bodily maintenance."

While the women's movement reflected women's diversified efforts to move into the public sphere—to win the vote, to participate in social reform, to improve women's educational and job opportunities—it also reflected a concern with more private family-oriented issues. The "social purity" movement of the 1890s is but one example. Sharing the Nationalists' view that human love was a predominant ideal, social purists often emphasized the corruption of male-female love relationships, and the destructive effects of social diseases, as significant political concerns. Like many of their reform-minded contemporaries, they felt disillusioned with the decay and misery of American society, but they also seemed to feel that sex was a major source of evil, and that "moral reformation" would provide a cure. Unfortunately, social purity proponents are sometimes best remembered for their repressive prudishness, their excessive moralism, and their self-righteous hypocrisy. According to some historians, social purists were the new abolitionists—abolitionists of white slave traffic, of prostitution, of sexual license. Reverentially respecting law, order, and the sanctity of the family, social purists were the exemplars of Victorian virtue, the priggish straight-laced ladies with repressive reactionary goals—or so popular commemorations would have us believe.

But such a characterization is seriously misleading, for social purity covered a multitude of sins. For one thing, it was a diversified movement with a broad range of issues and concerns. For another, as contemporary historians usually acknowledge, purity workers conducted some rather self-affirming feminist campaigns. They promoted sex education, which for many women meant expanded power. They developed programs in social hygiene, child rearing, vocational training. They were concerned with "moral education," which at least for some meant preaching the triumph of love over lust, and proclaiming women's right to make decisions concerning their own bodies, and thus the right to control fundamental aspects of their lives. Indirectly, at least, they urged women to pursue or reject the sexual embrace according to their own interests, rather than exclusively according to the demands of men.* Admittedly more radical than some, Charlotte Stetson put the matter briefly: "If there is any real law . . . it is each woman's law unto herself."

* * *

When Charlotte joined the California lecture circuit in early 1890, she did so as a social purist as well as a Nationalist, and the rebellious implications pleased her. She wrote to Martha Lane, "Now I am helping to organize a Social Purity society here, with good success. I may get to be a dangerous person to know, so you had better hedge a little, hadn't you?" From her point of view, Nationalists provided some profound guidelines for reformers: "Nationalism has struck a great tap root in striking at our business system. The root of the struggle between man and man." Still, there was "another root as deep—possibly deeper" that Nationalists did not fully understand: "the struggle between man and woman." Nationalism was the "most practical form of human development," but the equality of the sexes, the existence of equal male and female love, was "the most essential condition of that developement." Love and human sexuality, the "causes and cures" of immorality, the "immeasurable extent of disease and death which have been brought upon us from this evil alone"—these were issues Charlotte wanted to discuss, but guardedly and appropriately always.

True to the Victorian code, Charlotte spoke about sexuality discreetly enough to convince most people of the "purity" of her ideals. She moaned about pervasive immorality, flailed against contempo-

* Carl Degler argues that nineteenth-century women (presumably including many social purists) were probably not so rigorously anti-sex as was formerly assumed. Historians have too frequently relied on prescriptive data, he maintains, thus distorting the actual attitudes and experiences of women themselves. See Carl Degler, "What Ought to Be and What Was: Women's Sexuality in the Nineteenth Century," *American Historical Review*, LVIII (Dec. 1974), 1467–1490.

rary sins, and listed them as follows: "Jealousy, suspicion, infidelity, and overindulgence, vices public and private, natural and unnatural, married unhappiness, single uncleanness, disease, insanity, crime and death." She spoke about the "wretched falsehoods of license and excess," the pernicious "overdevelopment" of sex—that "lowest form of love."

There, in a nutshell, were some of the perspectives of the social purists that sealed their fate as the prudish prissies of all times. But the fact was that many of the social purists felt free enough to talk about some lusty loving inclinations too, about sexual needs as well as sexual fears, and Charlotte did not hesitate to join them. "Sexual attraction," she asserted, was "the highest holiest force in nature, our most perfect happiness and glory, the closest link between God and Man" and yet "a thing we blush to mention to each other!" The real "evil" was to conceal the facts of sex: "we have hedged it about with lies, and bound it down with laws, and smothered it with shame and loathing," and allowed the "rigid conventions of society [to] hamper and confine our daily lives and crush out all happy human intercourse between men and women." Inconsistencies notwithstanding, Charlotte lamented "sexual sinfulness," but affirmed the joy of sex: "On the rightness, the happiness, of the relation of the sexes hangs the rightness and happiness of all life to most of us; and on the strength and purity of that relation hangs the best hope of future generations."

While some of the women in the audience may have considered these ideas inappropriate or too avant-garde for comfort, others found them scarcely shocking at all, a bit bluntly worded perhaps, but compelling. Many of Charlotte's early lectures—"Nationalism and Love," "Nationalism and the Virtues," "Social, Domestic, and Human Life"—treated human love as a political concern. "[G]reat success," she wrote in her diary after one such lecture. "Some of the women cried, and they actually clapped at times!" Or again: "And they call those earnest deepfelt definitions of the [f]aith that is in me —'Bright!' and call me 'Bright!' I suppose they would say the same of John the Baptist and the rising sun!" Harriet Howe must have been one of those enthusiastic followers, for years later she still spoke glowingly of the "magic" impact of those early lectures:

> Her object was to persuade women to think for themselves instead of accepting what they were told to think. For years I had been harboring heretical thoughts on many subjects, chiefly on the degraded position which women held without seeming to be aware of it, and the inevitable effect this must have on the children born under such conditions and of such un-

> thinking mothers; but I had never dared whisper these views because even a hint of such ideas in those days was regarded as more than eccentric. And now here stood this scintillating soul on a public platform and hurled my very inmost thoughts at a small audience which received it with uneasy, hesitating satisfaction. . . . It was magic. It was an EVENT. I sat enthralled. I knew at once that I had met the greatest personality that I had ever seen, or likely ever would see. This was, and still is, true. And she had given me the greatest of all gifts,—the courage of my convictions.

Charlotte must have felt an energizing thrill not only in making her demands, but in knowing they were shared, in hearing applause for ideas which were heartfelt and hard-earned, even if still troubling at times, and still associated with personal regrets and memories. She seemed to thrive on flailing her own eccentricities and on challenging love and marriage myths directly. But not surprisingly, she exercised some caution too: "Now some of you are squirming a little again," she wrote in the quiet of her living room; "you are suspicious of Free Love, the moment any one hints at bettering our domestic life." No—"Free Love" is not the goal: "I believe in permanent monagamous marriage as the best thing for our race." The "passion of love"—that is, the "noble ideal" of marriage—not the "monstrous degradation" most women stupidly accept: "We women have remained in the patriarchal age of development, perpetuating in the family a 'patriarchal home.'" So "let me say again, a hundred times if it is necessary, that *housework* has nothing to do with love." Instead of marrying freely and equally, women lose their integrity because of economic dependence and destroy their capacity for love because of their need to wheel and deal to win a man: "Our lives are bent from birth to attract a male—for thus we make our living." Women's responsibility, then, is to remove the "antagonistic pressure of our economic dependence on men," to redefine our "duties" as wives and mothers, and to reaffirm our duties to ourselves.*

> We hear a great deal of these holy and wonderful duties of ours. Holy and wonderful they are; but they are only feminine functions—not *human* ones! We share our maternal instinct, and our mating instinct, with the other animals—away down the line until you come to the uni-sexual things, and the egg-laying

* While most of the quotations in this chapter are taken from 1890 lectures and diaries, several from 1891 are included when they seem especially pertinent.

creatures which never know their young. Womanhood is a fine thing, but it is not Humanity—any more than Childhood is Humanity. The dominant soul—the clear strong accurate brain, the perfect service of a healthy body—these do not belong to *sex* but to *race*!

* * *

By the end of 1890, Charlotte had produced a rather impressive array of subversive writings on the fraudulence of love and marriage myths. Her early pieces in the *Woman's Journal*, her plays, her autobiographical short stories, her Nationalism lectures—these were campaign documents for the women's movement, trial runs for her ideas, and also exhortations for herself. Particularly her early lectures—twenty- to thirty-page documents written carefully in longhand—stand as unpolished yet forceful expressions of opinions that in later published form—in *Women and Economics*, in *Human Work*, in *The Home*—would bring her national acclaim. For the moment, her lectures brought her contacts with activists in Nationalist clubs, single tax clubs, church groups, and women's organizations throughout the Los Angeles and San Francisco areas. There she met other women who were questioning their "feminine" responsibilities, women who had fallen into wife and mother roles without clearly choosing them, women who were alone, without an income, or without a means of satisfying work. The more she saw, the more she recognized her "calling," her vocation, her passion: to understand the whys and wherefores of women's situation, to organize within the women's movement, and to preach the idea that self-respect, satisfying work, and economic independence were women's basic rights.

But if Charlotte felt confident about her political commitments and insights, she must have sometimes felt they were not as personally therapeutic or absolving as she hoped they would be. In fact, writing and lecturing sometimes made her depressions worse—concentrating on problems all the time, her own or other people's, explaining, exposing, dwelling on the negative aspects of life that she hoped to purge. In any case, her diaries of 1890 suggest persistent anxieties: "Am pretty miserable just along here." Or: "Am really miserable," or "Tired." As she put it later, "'Tired' always means that ghastly below-zero weariness, and it was a frequent item." She was consulting various physicians and taking medicine to calm her down, but it was sometimes as though she pursued unpleasantness deliberately. Writing "The Yellow Wall-paper," a major 1890 project, may be a case in point. Writing it meant recreating nightmares, reviving shapes and forms of madness, perhaps even reexperiencing some of the ghastliness of insanity itself. Two days after finishing a draft, she wrote in her diary, "overdose of acid phosphate gives *terror*." But still she liked the piece, and not just because of its literary value, but seemingly in part because of the horror itself. She wrote Martha Lane, "When my awful story 'The Yellow Wall-paper' comes out, you must try & read it. Walter says he has read it *four* times, and thinks it the most ghastly tale he ever read. Says it beats Poe, and Doré! But that's only a husband's opinion. I read the thing to three women here however, and I never saw such squirms! Daylight too. It's a simple tale, but highly unpleasant."

Despite the satisfactions of working with the women's movement, then, Charlotte still struggled in her private hell. There was loneliness to contend with, tangled feelings over Walter, persistent regrets about Martha, anxieties about her relationship with Kate. To make matters worse, in the fall of 1890, Grace Channing decided to go back to Providence. For whatever reasons, Charlotte decided not to go along. She encouraged Grace's trip; probably she encouraged Grace's liaison with Walter; but she seemed to feel hurt nonetheless, almost as though Grace's leaving meant reexperiencing the sense of abandonment she'd felt when Martha married Charles A. Lane. Charlotte wrote Martha, "Grace has left me. . . . I miss her rather more than I do most people. But I never really *missed* anybody but you. Still you went, and now you are not there! Those were the good days. But like everything else taken out of my life I do not regret it—it leaves me stronger and more independent, better able to do world's work."

"Work"—that had been the watchword for 1890, and the pace had been frenetic. Depressions notwithstanding, she had written two to four journal articles a week, spoken at countless meetings, taken French lessons occasionally, and had even tripped off to the gymnasium when she could. Domestic responsibilities—attending to housework and caring for five-year-old Kate—must have taken up her time as well, but diary entries barely mention them. Despite the memories they brought to mind, public efforts inspired her confidence, personal relationships continued to bring mostly pain. On December 31, 1890, Charlotte summarized the year as follows: "A very quick but very hard year; cruelly hard since Grace went: A year of great growth *and* gain. My whole literary reputation dates within it—mainly from 'Similar Cases.' Also the dawn of my work as a lecturer."

Chapter Nine

Woman Supporting Woman 1891-1893

In February 1891, Charlotte was invited to Los Angeles to give a lecture in honor of Susan B. Anthony's seventy-first birthday. It was a gala occasion, a celebration of the endurance and vitality of the women's movement, as well as a tribute to one of its most respected and best-loved masterminds. Temperance, dress reform, social purity, abolition, woman's suffrage—these were some of the causes Susan B. Anthony had been promoting—door-to-door, state-to-state—for almost forty years. She "will go down in history," Charlotte thundered, "as having seen the one first need of humanity today—Freedom and Justice for women!" But she must also be remembered—here Charlotte's tone must have changed abruptly—as a pioneer in the women's movement who had paid an extraordinarily heavy price:

> And have any of you ever thought of the personal cost to these early reformers—the women I mean? . . . Now these women—these leaders—these first ones who fought for us so long unthanked—what did they give up? They had to triumph over their woman-hearts and woman-bodies, and become human beings; they had to sacrifice in large measure the approbation and kindness of the other sex. Do you think this is a light thing? It is a terrible thing. Do you think they have not felt it? I know they have. Their heads knew they were right and they went ahead, but there were times when their hearts ached for the common woman's need of praise and petting—ached just as yours have ached perhaps and may again. . . . It is always

> upon the first ones that the worst fate falls. Theirs the unthanked labor, the distrust and scorn, the contumely and bitter opposition.

At times, that was also how Charlotte viewed herself: as an "early reformer," she had lost the opportunity for "praise and petting," suffered "distrust and scorn" and heartache, and sacrificed her happiness because she had fought so hard for women's rights. Madness, "bitter opposition," and the loss of affectionate relationships with men—these were the negative costs of the rebel woman's fight. But there were positive rewards as well—and Charlotte knew it. There she was—Southern California, 1891—speaking at a Susan B. Anthony celebration, in fact speaking constantly all over the area, and even achieving some national acclaim. Almost wherever she spoke—Nationalist clubs, social purity meetings, suffrage or reform organizations—women laughed at her jokes, applauded her exhortations, shared their grievances, insights, and experiences, and then introduced her to ever-widening circles of politically oriented friends. Charlotte may have received disapprobation and scorn from some quarters, but she was getting personal and political support from many of her women friends: from Mrs. Emily Parkhurst, organizer of the Pacific Coast Women's Press Association (which would soon become one of Charlotte's major interests); from Mrs. Caroline Severance, well-known "mother of women's clubs" in the Los Angeles area; from Dr. Kellog Lane, staunch Nationalist co-worker, physician, and personal confidante; from Harriet Howe, aspiring feminist activist and writer; and from Adeline Knapp, who, for a while at least, became the closest and most loving of them all.

In short, women were backing her, advising, coaxing, boosting her spirits, and she was cheering and praising them in return. In fact, the emphasis in many of Charlotte's writings was becoming distinctly positive: there was less self-pity, more self-affirmation, less hostility directed against "enemies," more stress on cooperation with one's friends, less anti-male anger, more pro-female love. It is time women were "united as a class—woman supporting woman," Charlotte declared. "It is time we learned the one great secret of all human improvement—*working together*." Previously women did not recognize their potential, their power, their capacity to move beyond the home:

> She walketh veiled and sleeping,
> For she knoweth not her power;
> She obeyeth but the pleading
> Of her heart, and the high leading

Of her soul, unto this hour.
Slow advancing, halting, creeping,
Comes the Woman to the hour!—
She walketh veiled and sleeping,
For she knoweth not her power.

"That is but a brief expression of what seems to me the position of women today," Charlotte wrote, but she felt convinced that the time had come for change: "We stand at the threshold of a new life, in the doorway that opens up from the Home to the World." Contact with the California women's movement was altering Charlotte's outlook. It was heightening her respect for her female friends, deepening her understanding of them, and strengthening her personal as well as political attachments to them. She was becoming a "woman supporting woman" who sometimes found with women the "praise and petting" she was looking for. "Women are human and so am I," she later wrote. "I know women best, and care more for them. I have an intense and endless love for women."

* * *

In the spring of 1891, Charlotte met Adeline E. Knapp*—an aspiring journalist, reformer of sorts, and co-worker in the Pacific Coast Women's Press Association. On May 11, Charlotte wrote in her diary: "Was introduced to Adeline E. Knapp . . . and like her." Ten days later: "Go and lunch with Miss Knapp. I love her . . . feel better—thanks to Miss Knapp." May 23: Miss Knapp "stays here all night." May 26: "She is a fine woman, and we are fond of each other." June 2: "A wretched night, only made bearable by Miss Knapp's tender helpfulness. She is a dear woman." June 7: "Miss Knapp near supper time. We are very happy together."

Not since the summer of 1881, that summer of intense exchange with Martha Luther, had Charlotte felt such powerful affection, such trust, such passion and romance. "My girl comes," she confided in her diary. Or "Take a moonlight ride, first with Kate, then only with each other." Charlotte and Delle were together almost daily, or wrote passionate letters when Delle was out of town. Later, Charlotte described those letters to Houghton Gilman: they own "most fully the really passionate love I had for her. I loved her, trusted her, wrote her as freely as I write to you." There was a cer-

* Charlotte referred to Adeline Knapp as "Dora" in the autobiography, for reasons which will become clear. Diary entries refer to Adeline Knapp as "Delle."

tain stigma attached to such a relationship, of course. The stigma was not so troublesome as to block her passions at the time, but several years later she did seem to feel compelled to describe the friendship—briefly and nonapologetically—to her future husband: "I told you that I loved her that way. You ought to know that there is the possibility of such letters being dragged out some day." Likewise, in her autobiography, Charlotte acknowledged her relationship with Delle simply and directly: Delle "certainly did love me, at first anyway." She was a "friend with whom I had sincerely hoped to live continually."

Some of Charlotte's closest friends, Houghton Gilman and Martha Luther in particular, saved the letters they received; very likely Delle did not. Consequently we are left mainly with elusive diary entries: July 24: "Two dear letters from Delle. Write to her in the morning, also now." July 25: "No letter from Delle today." August 3: "Write to Delight. No letter." August 25: "Bad day. Am very lonesome for Delight. Write to her." August 27: "Write in the afternoon two sonnets for Delle—'To the Conquered' and 'To the Conquerer.'"

Whatever the storms and passions of the emotional alliance, at least it is clear that Delle provided the kind of practical support Charlotte needed most. Delle was "most generously kind with money," helped with housework, attended to errands Charlotte found a bore, and nursed her when she felt depressed. Delle was playful and affectionate with Kate. (Many years later Katharine still remembered horseback riding trips with "Miss Knapp.") And finally, but by no means least in this catalogue of friendship gifts, Delle helped Charlotte start proceedings for a divorce.

Divorce would be a messy business, as Charlotte well knew, with legal and emotional conflicts, with Walter complaining, Grace Channing urging her more quietly, and the press nipping at her heels. Charlotte had been talking about divorce for years, since 1887 in fact, and had done nothing. But when she finally had a friend, particularly one with whom she "hoped to live continually," she initiated a formal suit (one month after meeting Delle). First, she went to California luminary Charles Lummis—newspaperman, author, western enthusiast, and mentor to many of her political and literary friends. He had been wrestling with some personal and legal divorce matters too. Charlotte wrote: "Call on Dr. Lummis and ask advice about divorce. Get it. Get letter of introduction to nice lawyer and go to him." But even with Delle's support, Lummis' advice, and a "courteous gentleman lawyer" to help, the problem still was to find grounds, and then to make them stick. Neither "desertion" nor "failure to provide"—grounds Charlotte and Walter had agreed on—were acceptable under California law. After the first day's unproductive efforts, Charlotte wrote in her diary: "Then I write to my love." Likewise, several months later: "Letter from Walter enclosing one from Grace—reproaches at the delayed case. Delle cheers and comforts me."

Almost from the outset, then, Delle accepted critical familial responsibilities: child care, domestic chores, strains with Grace and Walter. But only three months after Delle and Charlotte met, they confronted another, more difficult concern, one which would be far more stressful (possibly ruinous) for their friendship: Charlotte's mother planned to come to California and live in Charlotte's home. Mary had not been well, and brother Thomas, busy with his own family and career, "wrote that he could no longer keep her—it was my turn." What tangled feelings crossed Charlotte's mind and heart we can only guess: anger with Thomas for what may have seemed like selfish irresponsibility, anger with Mary for a whole backlog of grievances Charlotte had never been able to confront successfully, also sympathy with Mary, then guilt, then frustration, then panic, and finally self-pity—all of which made Delle's position unenviable, to say the least. But whatever Delle's feelings, whether she was loving and generous or reluctant and scared, she apparently offered Charlotte full support, for they agreed to move from Pasadena to Oakland, to set up housekeeping, and to live together there. Almost immediately, Charlotte borrowed money for Mary's trip, journeyed up to Oakland, searched around for inexpensive boardinghouse accommodations and, by mid-September, had settled matters rather comfortably. "I have a lovely room with Delle, and mother one with Kate," Charlotte noted rather confidently. But reflecting on the built-in tensions of the situation, she also jotted down some resolutions:

> On Friday, Sept. 18th, I came here to live with Dora [Delle]. . . . Mother is with me also, and Katharine, of course. The pleasure in the new relation is that I now have some one to love me, and whom I love. . . . It is a Home. The duties of the position are these; First as always to live higher daily, to be loving, tender, thoughtful, courteous, wise, dignified, true, gracious. To do right by mother and by Katharine, to help Dora [Delle]. To maintain the position it is necessary that I should earn twenty dollars a week. Let me now consider ways and means.

The ways and means were lecturing and writing, but since these never brought earnings that could match the carefully transcribed fantasy calculations, Delle's help was a blessing. The help was mutual, Delle supplying funds from time to time, Charlotte providing professional advice, wit, and literary know-how in return. Delle was a "clever writer," a "hard worker," and a "good speaker," but by comparison with Charlotte she was still a novice in literature and politics who, according to one contemporary, had "not yet mellowed into that state where she can rise above her personal prejudices." Very likely, Delle was ambivalent about some of her political perspectives, and, being mercurial at times, she probably echoed the views of others when she did not share them, or even imitated other writers' literary style.* Later, Charlotte would be highly suspicious of Delle's integrity and character (in her autobiography, Charlotte called Delle a literary vampire), but for the moment Charlotte enjoyed Delle's ostensible heroine-worshipping support. The two of them started attending Nationalist Club meetings together, all the while Charlotte coaxing Delle to imbibe the appropriate "revolutionary" views. "Delle is beginning to feel much roused on these questions," Charlotte recorded proudly.

Whatever the discrepancies in their political perspectives, the loving friendship with Delle gave Charlotte real pleasure. October 29: "A lovely evening with Delle. God bless her!" October 30: "Another pleasant evening with Delle." Or on Thanksgiving Day: "I am exceedingly thankful. For Delle, Mother here, Kate, improved health, outlook in work." Predictably, there were rough times too—spats and scenes and crying spells—supportive friendship and noble resolutions notwithstanding. On Christmas Day, Charlotte wrote, "Celebrate by a fit of hysterics in the morning, and am laid up thereby." Even though her physician friend Dr. Kellog Lane suggested Charlotte might not be able to "stand the strain" of the "present family arrangement much longer," Charlotte seemed determined to keep trying. First, she wrote a sermon on "Pain," reminding herself that God speaks through pain as well as pleasure. The next day, she tried the sermon therapy again, writing and then giving a talk on "The Human Will." Of course the strains remained: "Still pretty weak," she wrote. "Delle nurses me all day." On the last day of the

*Delle seemed particularly impressed by Charlotte's brand of utopian socialism, suggesting in didactic fiction pieces that the cooperative egalitarian socialist society should be viewed as analogous to the healthy body organism, each cell and organ feeding, supporting, and generously serving all the others. See, for instance, *One Thousand Dollars a Day: Studies in Practical Economics* (Boston: Arena Publishing Co., 1894). It seems likely, however, that Delle was less sympathetic to Charlotte's views on women's issues, though she may not have said so at the time. In any case, several years later, Delle publicly opposed some major suffragist-feminist goals.

year Charlotte wrote, "I am by no means well. Two fits of wretchedness in a week is bad. Still the year shows some gain. It is the anxiety etc. about mother that is wearing on me now. That must be borne. May next year help more!" Charlotte's concluding self-reflections, unlike the abbreviated daily diary notes, were sombre and long.

> For this new year unknown whose steady wing
> Joy, Peace or Pain may bring, I plan one thing.
>
> In this new year which finds me still so weak
> From loss the past can speak, one thing I seek.
>
> For one thing shall my soul's hands lift and reach,
> Praying the year may teach more perfect speech.
>
> Clean, honest, wise, correct, strong, gentle too—
> Courteous as angels, set in order due, perfectly true. . . .
>
> I wait the coming year too sad for fear,
> Too old for hope, too wise for real despair,
> Wait it in patient prayer.
>
> It matters little about me if so I be
> Able to make the effort of one soul
> Help on the whole.
>
> Only not too much pain! Oh not again
> That anguish of dead years—
> Terror and tears!

Early in the new year, Charlotte and Delle decided to move to another boarding house, "a large and pleasant one, on a nice street, with a good yard behind it, an excellent place for Katharine." Mary was ill, and there was cleaning, sorting, and packing to be done, so Charlotte decided to have her mother board with Dr. Kellog Lane, who generously offered nursing help. Charlotte hoped this arrangement would relieve her of some of the worries, resentments, and adjustment strains that produced her "wretchedness." At first, she assumed that the boarding house would at least provide the meals, though there would still be household and child-care chores. But then, abruptly, the lady who kept the boarding house announced that she was leaving; if Charlotte was interested, she would have to assume management responsibilities herself. Probably for financial reasons, Charlotte "decided to take it as it stood, and keep boarders as she had done." Not that she wasn't busy enough already. She was writing, lecturing, scurrying about to meetings, cooking, cleaning, trying to get settled, and seeing to boarders' needs besides: "9 people in the house—8 to cook for! . . . I can't have mother yet!"—though it sounded like she thought she should. Then Kate got the measles: "Measles galore, no sleep, no regular meals, housework allee samee." And two days later, scrawled across two pages of the diary: "Just work and measles." It was a relief that her mother stayed with Dr. Lane.

Several weeks later, Mary learned that she had cancer, though doctors may have been suspicious for some time. Naturally, she moved back in with Charlotte: "She likes her room and bed and board, seems very comfortable," was the calm and simple diary entry. But later, Charlotte described the situation more darkly:

> I did all the housework and nursed mother till I broke down; then I hired a cook and did the nursing till I broke down; then I hired a nurse and did the cooking till I broke down. Dr. Kellog Lane said I must send mother to a hospital. This I could not bear to do. "If you say definitely as a physician that I shall die, or go crazy," I told her, "I'll do as you say. But if I can possibly stand it I want to go on, I do not wish to have it said that I have failed in every relation in life."

Apparently, Dr. Lane agreed: "She concludes to do nothing for me at present. Says I had better break down honestly now than be bolstered up and break more extensively later. A wise physician."

Harriet Howe, who was boarding with Charlotte at the time, claimed she had never been aware of the "heavy ordeal" Charlotte went through until she read her autobiography many years later. Howe wrote, "It is difficult to reconcile the gay and gallant courage with which she did all tasks and met all problems, with the serious and even pitiful, conditions described in the book [the autobiography]. . . . She was at all times a gay companion, although often over-wearied and would change one occupation for another to shift the strain, but always equal, apparently, to any situation." Despite all the responsibilities, Harriet remembered Charlotte's *joie de vivre* and playful repartee rather than her anguish, and concluded that "the dissimulation she must have used to conceal from her sympathetic household her true condition is now proved to have been no less than heroic."

> To support and nurse a dying mother would be enough for many women; to support and rear a child would be enough for almost any woman; to take over a house full of boarders would be more than enough for the majority of women. Yet she

> cheerfully assumed all three of these responsibilities, because they were necessary.

Harriet's recollections of Charlotte's cheerfulness contrast sharply with some of Charlotte's rueful autobiographical descriptions. Yet there is probably truth in both accounts, sadness and spunk somehow co-existing. Charlotte sympathized and grieved with Mary, but she was busy—enthusiastically so—with projects of her own. She was overworked, but well liked and admired, and certainly delighted to be so much in demand. For instance, she had written a prize-winning essay called "The Labor Movement" for the Alameda County Federation. The compliments and publicity it brought her not only boosted her spirits, but also helped to expand her contacts in the area, secure even more lecture invitations, and improve her income besides. She was of course spending many hours by her mother's sick bed, but she was still writing, and writing well. September 30: "Up till 12:30 watching mother and writing in my room. Doctor—Mother's last day down stairs—I think about now anyway." October 25: "Am feeling first rate these days—full of plans to write, sew, build, etc. The creative instinct rising and promising well for work when the strain is off."

Bounding about feeling "first rate" (at least occasionally) while her mother was ill and dying, Charlotte must have felt some deep pangs of guilt—always her nemesis. Undoubtedly she felt compassion and affection for her mother, but she felt resentment and anger as well, and then, predictably, self-reproach for her own irresponsibility and selfishness. Characteristically, she tried to analyze the problem in feminist political terms, to formulate calmly and rationally the principles involved. Then she would lecture publicly about them, try to persuade other women to see how ridiculous their guilt-oriented obsessions were, and in the process coax herself to remember precisely the same thing. For instance, "A Daughter's Duty" was the title of one of her lectures at about this time; possibly she even wrote it while sitting at her mother's bedside. Most certainly it can be viewed as a persuasive, even acutely insightful piece about daughters' responsibilities to mothers, an issue of importance to countless women; but it can also be viewed as anger unleashed.

> The mother has other children, other friends, other interests, and means of support—she does not blame the daughter. But society does, the mother is a martyr, the daughter a renegade. Why? Had this daughter, no girl, but an adult woman, no rights as a woman?
>
> . . . She studies for years, fitting herself for work she loves.

> Her father dies. Her mother claims her daughter's duty—says she cannot spare her, and the girl who might soon have been earning both fame and fortune, retires into the shelter of the home, to wash dishes for the "boarders," and "take care of her mother" at no salary whatever!
>
> . . . A duty is a duty, but there is more than one way of doing it! A girl can take care of her mother as an independent householder and wage earner, providing her with the same delicate generosity let us hope with which the mother once "supported" her; or she can take care of her as a subordinate, a nurse, a companion, upper servant. Why is not the first better?
>
> . . . The object of this is to suggest to the Daughter that she is also an Individual and a Human Being, and has duties as an individual to herself, and as a human being to her race, as well as the duty of a daughter to her mother.*

Charlotte's analysis of mother-daughter conflict was both optimistic and rebellious, but it did not entirely reflect the way she felt. On issues such as work and wages, she could practice what she preached with a reasonable degree of confidence. But there were other issues that challenged her self-respect and independence. Anxieties about her mother's coolness, fears of her mother's disapproval—these still weighed too heavily. How did her mother feel about her lifestyle? about her relationship with Delle? about her child-care methods with Kate? For even if Mary did not criticize at all (and it is possible that she did not, since she also had been a single mother in a primarily female community), Charlotte still could have worried. Particularly troublesome was the divorce issue. Charlotte had a tendency to sympathize with her mother as the victim mistreated and deserted by her renegade husband. That tendency was intensified by Mary's approaching death, and by Frederick's refusal to visit, despite Mary's pleas. But Charlotte's affection for her mother was entangled with anger toward her father, which in turn triggered anger toward herself. No matter what Mary said, and no matter how persuasively Charlotte preached about a daughter's duty to herself, her father's actions had too closely paralleled her own, and rational analyses could not eliminate the self-reproach.

To make matters worse, it was at just about this time that the San Francisco *Examiner* decided to give full-page coverage to the divorce proceedings. The suit had been dragging for months. Charlotte's

* While most of the lecture is autobiographical, some of the details are not. Charlotte's father had not died, and probably Mary had no other easily available sources of support.

efforts in the California courts had been so fruitless that Walter decided to initiate proceedings in Rhode Island. "This was more honest than my getting it," Charlotte wrote, "for I was the one to break off." Walter's application reads: "She hath willfully deserted your petitioner for the period of three years." That may have been more honest, all right, but it was rather hard to swallow, and it also was not quite the message her mother liked to hear. Still, Charlotte tried to keep calm about the situation. For instance, she told an inquiring reporter the "simple facts, that there was no 'story,' simply a case of broken health and mutual understanding, and that I was doing my best to keep it from my mother who was dying upstairs—to save her worry; and would he please not spread it about. Foolish woman! The result was a full page in the *Examiner*," and lengthy coverage in eastern papers too. "The worst of it was some singularly discerning friend sent clippings to mother, so that her last days were further saddened by anxiety about my future. Whatever Charlotte's major worries, whether they were Mary's anxiety and disapproval or her own anger and self-contempt, the press scandal triggered another painful depression. Several days later Charlotte wrote in her diary: "It appears that I am sicker than I thought." "I am very weak." December 29: "Gave out in the morning. Rode on cable car with Hattie [Howe]. All mixed up this week. Sick—sicker."

That was not so surprising, given the *Examiner's* report of Walter's charges:

> Yesterday morning's dispatches from Providence, Rhode Island, told the story of G. Walt Stetson's efforts to secure a divorce from Charlotte Perkins Stetson, a writer of renown, now residing in Oakland. The husband . . . accused his wife of not wearing corsets or even waistbelts, . . . of devoting her time to the doctrines of Bellamy, and of running after fads and fancies in social and dress reform—all to the exclusion of sewing buttons on his shirts and making wifely remarks about his respiration upon his return from "the lodge."
>
> He said she followed gymnastics until she became very muscular. G. Walt is not a muscular man, and somewhat undersized, so his complaint seemed to hint that his wife was rather the head of the household before she picked up her dress reform duds, her Bellamy writings and her muscular development and put off for California, leaving in her husband's memory nothing in the nature of connubial bliss more distinct than an impressionist daub. . . . The divorce has caused no end of talk, and the peculiar allegations have set the tea tables a 'titter.

Having provided plenty of nuggets for tea-table titter himself, the reporter then ostensibly quoted from the interview with Charlotte.

> The fact that the proceedings have been brought is no news to me. It was understood and agreed upon between both of us. . . . There is not the slightest ill-feeling between Mr. Stetson and myself and there has been none. . . . We are the best of friends and will remain so. . . . Walter never said what he is reported as saying. . . . All there is to it is I wanted to devote myself to my profession and earn my own bread and butter, and I could not do it in double harness. . . . I shall not contest the suit. . . . It was brought with my consent and wish.

Doubtless Charlotte hated having private matters blazoned across the country, but she must have been pleased that her own public statements seemed clean and to the point, not at all apologetic, spineless, or flat. A Philadelphia paper quoted her as saying, "When two grown persons conclude that they cannot live together and want to separate that is sufficient, is it not? They can separate if they desire to do so. Further than that, it is a private matter and no one's business."

But the issues were too hot for Charlotte to be let off quite that simply. According to the press, Walter had brought charges for good reason. One paper quoted him as saying, "she had too much literary work to attend to to pay much, if any, attention to me." Or again, "In the name of dress reform, her husband charges, she felt constrained to sacrifice conjugal relations." The Los Angeles *Times* produced a letter, purportedly from Charlotte to Walter: "Do not deceive yourself, dear. My life is too precious to me to waste any more of it like those seven years we spent together."

Walter managed to respond publicly to some of the charges: "I am pained that the press seems so eager to speak ill of a woman of so much genius and sincerity of purpose." Or in the San Francisco *Examiner*, "I have always taken an interest in her success, and have regretted that our separation became necessary." Nonetheless, the *Examiner* continued its attack. Five days later,

> There are not many women, fortunately for humanity, who agree with Mrs. Stetson that any "work," literary, philanthropic, or political, is higher than that of being a good wife and mother. . . . Either all her reasons have not been made public (which is probable), or she is wanting in those powerful instincts which render the love of husband and children necessary to woman's happiness.

That was the *Examiner's* Christmas gift, December 25, 1892, and several days later, when Charlotte penned her New Year's reflections, she was obviously feeling the effect: "It has been a year of great and constantly increasing trouble. Poverty, illness, heartache, household irritation amounting to agony, care, anxiety, grief and shame for many many failures." Even the relationship with Delle seemed to be collapsing, for Charlotte continued: "My last love proves even as others. Out of it all I ought surely to learn final detachment from all personal concerns. The divorce is pending, undeclared, mother still lives. There is only to go on." Several hours later, however, her mood had shifted slightly. Delle and Harriet had rallied round, and Charlotte seemed more confident. The January 1 diary entry reads: "The bells and horns, the steady booming of one big whistle, the scattering explosions, announce the new year. Hattie and Delle and I are sitting up in Delle's room. We have just had a nice [s]upper with delicious coffee. . . . May last year's misery be less, and new strength through me flow. More power to see and to express the blessed truths I know. And a little less pain if you please! I can do more if I suffer less."

A considerable part of the strain on Charlotte during these winter months of 1892–1893 was illness—everybody's illness, including her own—and she had always hated playing nurse. She wrote, "There were six sick women in that house at one time, and they used to come tell me their troubles, mostly in the middle of the night." Then, to make matters worse, Kate got the whooping cough: "Up at three with Kate . . . This too!" There are some diary entries which suggest that Delle was still supportive—"Delle gets supper and bathes Kate," or "Delle gets me some coffee, and breakfast for all of us. I write 'The Modern Mother'"—but tempers were near the breaking point. January 13: "A fuss with Delle." January 16: "grand row with Delle. She is in a wretched condition of health." The next day, another "fuss at dinner time," followed by a "pleasant evening," followed by the "pleasant" news—several days later—that Delle was leaving town. In "high feather" Delle abruptly announced that she would be going to Hawaii. She had been assigned as correspondent for the San Francisco *Call* to report on the proposed annexation of Hawaii. Undoubtedly Charlotte felt proud; Delle was the first woman ever to represent a large daily newspaper on such an important assignment. But there must have also been relief on all sides, since Delle would be gone for several months.

Meanwhile, no matter what the homefront troubles, Charlotte worked steadily. In early January, after going to a lecture by English socialist theosophist firebrand Annie Besant, Charlotte wrote, "very interesting. . . . Joy in life—Get up! It is time to begin! Plenty of time ahead—glorious world—let's start." And start again she did—in a fury. The end of the month's diary entry reads: "Have done about fifteen pieces of salable work this month—, three lectures, three poems, nine articles of one sort or another. Received $40.00 therefor so far. Fair work for an overworked invalid." Sometimes she was pleased with the quality and pace of her lecturing and writing, but she was less confident about her personal situation. In fact, the worse home problems became, the harder she was on herself: "Unless I learn my desired virtues *now* I never shall. Difficulties are nothing. The power to live rightly is outside of these difficulties. Unless I can, all will claim the same exemption."

"Difficulties are nothing" indeed. Mary's condition worsened daily, and, though there was often a nurse to help, Charlotte stayed up nights, worked days, and seemed surprised that she felt tired. By mid-February she was lecturing infrequently. She continued to write, but mostly she stayed home, comforting her mother, helping her in and out of bed, making sure to be available in case of crisis.

To make matters worse, Mary kept asking for Frederick to visit, in effect to say goodbye. He was living in San Francisco at the time (just across the bay from Oakland), but, for whatever reason, he refused to come. Charlotte's account suggests, if nothing else, the intensity of her anger with her father.

> Divorced or not she loved him till her death, at sixty three. . . . She longed, she asked, to see him before she died. As long as she was able to be up, she sat always at the window watching for that beloved face. He never came. That's where I get my implacable temper.

Frederick's treatment of Mary had been an explosive source of Charlotte's anger for years. Current mother-daughter bonds only strengthened it. For over a year now, Mary and Charlotte had been together, talking, sharing anecdotes, learning more about each other's lives. Among other things, Mary probably talked a lot about family matters, her own experiences in marriage, in pregnancy and childbirth. Perhaps she speculated on reasons Frederick left his family—that another pregnancy would have ended Mary's life. Or at least it seems likely that Charlotte thought about such problems, for the more time she spent with Mary, the more she sympathized, and the more hostile she felt toward her father. One writer suggests that often for a woman "her mother's death reinforces her dedication to freedom from oppression," and for Charlotte that may have meant women's freedom from the sexual dominance of men. Only three days before Mary died she wrote: "Sit up til two in the morning with mother—the nurse gets four hours' sleep. Write short powerful paper—'The Sex Question Answered'—for the World's Congress. Nothing seems to seriously affect my power to write. This paper has been done in short laborious efforts during these wretched days, and finished last night by mother's death bed." The next day, Charlotte tried writing a lecture "giving reasons for assuming women's dependence to be conducive to sexual immorality." She put the matter this way: "The essential indecency of the dependence of one sex upon the other for a living is in itself sexual immorality."

Charlotte was saying, in effect, that, as a relation of dependence, marriage itself was sexually immoral. And she was saying it in her behavior as well as in words. Like her mother, she had chosen an alternative: a relatively cooperative approach to housekeeping,* to child care, to family responsibilities, an emotionally supportive environment among female friends. For the last several years, Charlotte's relationships with women had become the most central of her life, the bonds with Mary strengthening them even further. With Mary, there were so many shared feelings and experiences: the common fight against illness—Mary's against cancer, Charlotte's against depression—their traumas in marriage and pregnancy, their disappointments in men, their passionate sympathy, affection, and respect for women. Charlotte's sense of special closeness to women dated back to the friendship she had had with Martha Luther, of course, but before that it was grounded in the love she had felt for Mary, all the strains and stresses notwithstanding. For female friendships often seem to be deeply rooted in the mother-daughter bond itself. In part they may represent a lifelong search for mother-love that was never fully satisfied in childhood. But more positively, they also represent a reaffirmation of experiences of mother-daughter warmth—enormously important sources of many women's sense of security and worth. In any case, especially during these final months with Mary, Charlotte turned to women for support.

Since Delle had been in Hawaii the last few weeks, Harriet Howe had been Charlotte's closest friend, "running errands," sharing

* Since she was burdened with the responsibility of her mother and daughter both, Charlotte seemed to feel in 1893 that a cooperative approach to housework was a godsend. In later years, however, she came to believe that domestic concerns—cooperatively handled or not—almost always weighed so heavily on women that they could not enjoy effective or creative outside work. She later argued, therefore, that a professional, not cooperative, approach to housework would be necessary if women were ever to achieve equality with men.

housework, and also sharing some of Charlotte's grief. Harriet remembered the "quiet sunny afternoons" when "this beautiful and gracious mother talked to me of family history" while Charlotte "took a little needed rest." Later, Harriet recalled Charlotte's words as they "both watched her slowly dying mother." Charlotte had whispered, "If this should come to me, in future years, I will *not* go through with it. It is needless."* After so many hours by Mary's bedside, after long talks, walks, hours of comforting, and a week after Mary's death, Charlotte recorded simply, "Sleep with Hattie." As she put it in her autobiography, Harriet had been a "warmly devoted friend who came to live with me."

Charlotte's diary, March 6, 1893: "Mother sinking all day. The laudanum ceases to take effect by nightfall and her cough grows worse. Dr. Kellog in about 7:30 can find no pulse. Orders chloroform to quiet the cough. I go out with Hattie and get it. Give it to her till after 11. Every time she rouses it is only to cough terribly. Try and rest a little then but am soon up again. She passed away at 2:10 very quietly. The nurse and I wash and dress her and clean up the room —all done before 5. Then we try to eat—try to sleep. I don't succeed." The next day's diary entry is equally stark: "Father over in the afternoon."

* * *

During the last few months of immense pressure—nursing Mary, caring for Kate, looking after the boarding house—Charlotte's reliance on her friends intensified, enriching the relationships in some respects, threatening them in others. Perhaps at this juncture Charlotte was too dependent, had too many needs, or was too preoccupied to be able to give fully. In any case tensions and jealousies had been developing. There was a *menage à trois*, in fact, which in less traumatic times might have been avoided. Delle's trip to Hawaii had solved the problem for a while, but, a month after Mary's death, Delle returned to San Francisco. On April 4, Charlotte wrote, "And tomorrow Delle comes back.—I wonder."

At first, everything seemed fine. April 5: "The dear girl—looks splendidly, and I am absurdly glad to see her. . . . Sleep with Delle. She has been to Hawaii, as special correspondent, apropos of proposed annexation. Has done fine work." With no apparent difficul-

* When, many years later (1935), Charlotte was dying from cancer, she chose to commit suicide, rather than to force herself or her daughter Katharine to endure the last few weeks or months of needless suffering.

ties, Delle, Hattie, and Charlotte together worked out housekeeping arrangements and bestirred themselves with political engagements. Within a month, however, tensions were explosive. May 3: "Trouble with Delle over the yard—and other things. . . . Hattie gets supper mostly." May 11: "All along lately hard times with Delle. Am too exhausted to attend committee meeting. . . . Delle goes without me. . . . Dreadful time with Delle." The next day they went to a Woman's Alliance meeting, and Charlotte wrote, "Home utterly exhausted—scene with Delle all the way up from ferry to house in the car." And the following day, "Delle comes home. She decides to leave the house. I have so desired since last August—and often asked her to."

Delle left, but only temporarily. The diary entries of the next several weeks tell of shopping trips she and Charlotte took together, Women's Press Association meetings, several evenings at the theater, visits with mutual friends, fights, then reconciliations; as yet neither one was ready to make the final break, though doubtless each made preparations. Charlotte's characteristic strategy was first to remind herself that work could take the place of friendship, and then to figure how to manage economically without Delle's help.* May 31st was resolution day.

> Age—near 33. Probably forty years' time before me. Desired to accomplish in that time—the utmost attainable advance of the human race. . . . Means of accomplishment the perception and transmission of truth, applicable truth. Most immediate necessity, the maintenance of self and child.
>
> . . . To maintain self alone would require,

Furnished room	$ 5.00
Meals	15.00
Clothes and extras	10.00
per month	30.00

* Charlotte apparently opposed women's economic dependence on each other as well as on men. All of the funds Delle had provided, some $1,000, Charlotte regarded as a loan, which she was able to pay back slowly over the years, though apparently not at Delle's insistence. There is an interesting and very amicable letter from Delle to Charlotte, March 10, 1894, requesting that Charlotte please send her $100. Delle was low on funds, and needed to pay off some of her own debts; but she made it clear that she held Charlotte under no further financial obligations. Delle wrote, "Any amount you may deem yourself owing me I shall consider more than cancelled if you can devise some way of lifting this responsibility."

> Ten dollars a week would do me well. One good day's work a week would take care of me, one to rest, five to give.

She continued to make resolutions on June 1st, 1893.

> Rise at six. Be through housework at nine. Write from nine till twelve. Be through lunch work at two. Nap. Go out till five-thirty. Be through supper work at seven. Free writing must be done evenings. Go to bed by ten if possible. Take a tonic. Eat well. Simply train and work for a year and a half. . . . Will have time enough then to take a good rest. Write $5.00 worth a day.

Later in June 1893, she expanded her list of goals.

> W. P. A., I am on Child Labor committee and also on education. I wish to ascertain and present information on these subjects. Try to keep up the general ideal. Ebell; Furnish four more sociological papers. Ec Club; Write papers, read, discuss, exhort, work. Pa. Assn., Organize and push the general society. Plan for the work at large. Visit local groups as desired. Make it go. St. Council, Help organize. Help push. A large slow thing this. Should be a City council also.

In July, the arguments between Delle and Charlotte grew worse. July 6: "Delle comes up and spoils the rest of my evening. She and her affection!" July 12: A general "disturbance with Delle. She undertakes to be out within a week." The next day, Hattie and Charlotte tried to dissuade a mutual friend from "entering upon any housekeeping arrangements with Delle. Hattie is a mere rag because of it." A few days later: "Her behavior has been such as to gradually alienate my affection and turn it to indifference. It is a great relief to have her go." A relief indeed. It was a crisis requiring full-scale philosophic exhortations: "Talk with Hattie; seeing newly and with great clearness what abnegation and sacrifice stand for in moral evolution. What we call Self—(the personal inclination)—Personality—is the echoing fading force of the Great Life in its material limitations. The fresh life must come direct, (through the mind?) not through inherited inclinations. Therefore to hold personality in abeyance and act *direct* from God is to help evolution." Such incantations notwithstanding, there was yet another flare-up about a week later: "Says my behavior to her was 'like a servant girl's.' Says she will never enter my house again."

That, apparently, was the final scrap, though not quite the end of friendship. For the next year or so, Delle and Charlotte worked together politically and enjoyed socializing among their mutual literary friends, but the old trust was long since past.

In her autobiography, Charlotte did not hesitate to describe the friendship with Delle as one of the most loving ones that she had known, but her explanation of the break was not entirely persuasive: It was all Delle's fault. Delle had been a liar, a hard drinker, and a cheat. Moreover, she had been "one of those literary vampires who fasten themselves on one author or another with ardent devotion, and for the time being write like them." * Delle's published writings —stylized, unoriginal, and seemingly unthreatening—along with Charlotte's diaries and Harriet Howe's reflections, suggest deeper strains as well.

One of them was the relationship with Hattie Howe—the competition, the elusive jabs of jealousy, the jousting for affection. All along, there had been no love lost between Harriet Howe and Adeline Knapp, though, from Harriet Howe's point of view, it was not a question of jealousy, but of treachery instead. Years later, Harriet gave her version of the fiasco:

> There seemed to creep in a vague coolness amongst us for which we were unable to account, as nothing whatever had happened to warrant it. . . . It seemed that one of our number was in the habit of visiting in the separate rooms of each of us, in the evenings, and discussing critically with each occupant the other members of the household, and then going to the next room and reporting what she herself had said, pretending that the remark came from the first person visited instead of from herself. †

According to Harriet, Charlotte had calmly and efficiently stopped the "troublemaker" by talking quietly to each of the boarders. She

* For the close friendship between Delle and Charlotte to have developed, one would assume that they at least tacitly agreed on women's issues. But perhaps they did not. Several years later, Delle publicly expressed her disagreements with some of Charlotte's central arguments. In 1899, Delle wrote, "The woman who expends herself for home and children does no more, and she should certainly do no less, than do the birds of the air, the creatures of field and forest. These are services performed not for her husband, but because of her human nature. She is entitled to maintenance while performing them, not because of her usefulness to her husband, but because of her incalculable usefulness to the nation." It would be to "depart from social sanity to believe that the average wife and mother should become a wage-earner" (Adeline Knapp, *An Open Letter to Carrie Chapman Catt* [Berkeley, Calif.: New York State Association Opposed to the Extension of the Suffrage to Women, Nov. 10, 1899]).

† Harriet Howe's account did not identify the "troublemaker" by name, but it seems probable that she had Adeline Knapp in mind.

asked each of them to inform the other as quickly as possible "exactly what had been said and by whom, and so forestall all hurt feelings." The "method worked like a charm," the disturber was baffled, the boarders thereafter were merely amused.

Charlotte did not view matters quite that way. According to her autobiography, she had been crushed, not calm, efficient, or amused. She wrote of Delle:

> The kindest thing I can say of her character is that she had had an abscess at the base of the brain, and perhaps it had affected her moral sense. I do not mean to describe her as "immoral" in its usual meaning; she was malevolent. She lied so freely as to contradict herself in the course of a conversation, apparently not knowing it. She drank—I saw her drunk at my table. She swore freely, at me as well as others. She lifted her hand to strike me in one of her tempers, but that was a small matter. What did matter was the subtle spreading of slanders about me, which I cannot legally prove to have come from her, but which were of such a nature that only one so close could have asserted such knowledge. Also, I do know of similar mischief-making from her in regard to others. At any rate that solace ended not only in pain but in shame—that I should have been so gullible, so ignorant, as to love her dearly.

Delle's version of the story is, unfortunately, the one most difficult to ascertain. In a brief note, May 1893, Delle wrote: "I left Mrs. Stetson's house for Mrs. Stetson's good. Very ill temper and unreasonable conduct having rendered it impossible for her longer to endure it. I would have remained had not my remaining sense of decency driven me away."

Charlotte was often aware of the "very ill temper and unreasonable conduct" Delle described. Throughout the 1890s Charlotte was still having her "grey fog" times, her bouts of "hysteria," her explosions of anger and hostility which friends hadn't necessarily caused, but which were furiously directed against them anyway. Her own explanation—one she gave to Houghton Gilman several years later—was that characteristically she was terrified of relationships that offered the possibility of dependence, intimacy, and trust.

> To most people, meeting them as I do, I can behave nicely, and as you have observed they mostly like me. I can be nice and kind and patient, and steady and cheerful and all sorts of nice things.
>
> But as soon as any one comes near me and takes hold, I wobble awfully. . . . And I don't like it. It makes me unreason-

> able. It makes me feel—where I don't want to feel; and think—where I don't want to think. It sort of wakes me up where I'm dead, or where, if I'm not dead, I ought to be. Now, I can't afford to be fond of anybody in that sort of way—man woman or child. I can't afford to want things. . . . I'm *not* a nice person to be close to. I do very well at long range."

Charlotte's self-assessment may have been painfully precise. Personal relationships had always meant disaster—with Martha, with Walter, possibly with Grace. More recently, she was under such strain with respect to her mother, Kate, her career, and her pocketbook, there would have been little reason to expect success. She wanted support, but, anticipating disappointment, perhaps angrily and unwittingly she began to court it, to make accusations and defensively to assume that blame lay elsewhere in order to claim the victim status for herself. Overburdened with responsibilities, overly dependent, Charlotte faced another fear as well: a substantial collection of her very candid passionate love letters might still be in Delle's possession. However confident Charlotte may have been of her own feelings and convictions on the controversy-laden issue of female love, she still was not confident enough (understandably) to disclose them publicly. Delle would create quite a scandal, consciously or accidentally. And as Charlotte began to trust less and argue more, she probably became increasingly aware of her own insecurity and vulnerability. It was a vicious circle. Anxieties intensified and she began to "wobble awfully." Intimacy brought memories of hurt, love brought panic, and warmth soured into anger.

* * *

There were any number of reasons why the relationship with Delle Knapp ended in disaster, but what were the reasons Charlotte thought it could succeed? Fortunately, one of her public lectures—"Socialism and Morality"—indirectly provides some clues. Written in January 1893, a month of intense involvement with Delle Knapp and Hattie Howe, it suggests that far more important to her than the failure of her relationships with women was her awareness of the importance of sexual freedom in women's lives. As usual, her lecture by no means reflects a guilt-free approach toward sexuality; nor does it directly mention women's love for one another. But it does show her contempt for the hypocrisy and immorality of current norms of love and sexuality. And even more importantly, it suggests that her experiences of love in the early 1890s—experimental and nonconventional—were integrally related to her emerging theoretical conviction that unrestricted nondependent love was a fundamental human rights.

The lecture begins: "Right conduct on our part is such as helps in the line of growth. . . . 'Moral' means 'purpose' you know. . . . And the purpose of man's actions—of man's living—is to make man better." What then makes man bad? First, private ownership of property, the economic dependence of one person on another, the opportunity of the "stronger to prey on the weaker," the consequent "stunted poor, the bloated rich, the outcome of sickness, feebleness, and deformity, physical, mental, and moral." Even more importantly, evil results from the "economic dependence of the woman on the man. . . . We have forced one whole half of us to get its living by the exercise of sexual functions—one whole half the race, receiving its food and clothes and shelter from the other in return for the performance of [sexual] functions." Characteristically, Charlotte reassured her audiences by acclaiming the "racial ideal of pure lasting monagamous love," and by condemning "morbid fickleness" and "morbid and excessive indulgence." But she placed her major emphasis on being free: sexual love "must be wholly free to be healthful, to be natural, to be right. By 'free' I do not mean promiscuous, but free between those who belong together." The real sinner, then, was not the individual who followed his "natural instincts," but the pompous moralist who constructed "preposterous acrobatics for the soul, and then called them virtues," who enslaved people with "those heaviest weights a soul can bear—Fear and Shame." "Why—stop it!" says the sage. "Don't do it! Control those instincts! Use your will power! Pray!" And sarcastically Charlotte quipped, "Shall we pray? Pray to God to save us from the workings of his own laws?" Attitudes toward human sexuality could be likened to attitudes toward a growing plant, Charlotte continued, with a richer symbolism than she may have realized. First, there was the small green shoot, innocent enough, with its "bud of exquisite hue." Then there was the flower, "large, radiant, glorious in beauty and fragrance—this is virtue with a large V—bow down and worship. Then there is a fruit—a thing with ugly pods, slimy inside, foul smelling, poisonous—ah! this is vice—sin—crime—down with it! [out?] upon it! Don't raise that! But how can you help it when you raise the plant? You can pick it off—but the tree only grows stockier and fruits fuller next time." So much for symbolic celebrations of female sexuality—that fertile, nauseous, ripened fruit.

Classic symbolism notwithstanding, Charlotte loved to mock the unctuous pious prudes. For dress reform lectures, she would take a dressmaker's dummy, a sketch of a corseted horse, or a copy of the

Venus de Milo to liven up her jibes: "the body without clothes is a thing as foreign and unknown in our mental universe, as a bird without feathers, a turtle without his shell." The human soul itself suffers from the indignities of dress, from the inability to see, to feel, and to know the body.

> [If] anyone doubts it let him or her, in well warmed and well locked apartments, sit down garmentless to any daily task or amusement. . . . The very chair is meant for clothes, and does not fit without them. The "feel" of every familiar object is strange to us. Unusual heats and chills come from objects we thought we understood. You cannot settle to your sewing or painting or writing—you cannot settle at all. Your whole body is as full of perturbation as an uncovered ant-hill. It is not that you are not *dressed*—you are not done—you are not whole—you are not *you*.
>
> You only *are* when clothed.
>
> Charlotte Perkins Stetson*

* This lecture, entitled "The Dress and the Body" was probably written in 1891.

Chapter Ten

Heathen Goddess 1893-1894

If Charlotte's lectures were not designed to endear her to San Francisco's straight-laced ladies, they were quite acceptable to some of the spirited politically oriented literati she was more attracted to: Ina Coolbrith—later poet laureate of California; Joaquin Miller—swashbuckler "poet of the Sierras"; Hamlin Garland—"paladin knight" of Populist fiction; Edwin Markham—later to become famous for his poem "The Man with the Hoe." Charlotte's full-pace lecture-writing efforts, which continued despite her personal traumas, had brought her into contact with some of the most avant-garde thinkers and doers of the San Francisco area, the "bohemians," the radical intellectuals with their unconventional lifestyles, literary talents, and recalcitrant political beliefs. Most of her friends were enthusiasts of western culture, explorers of the western terrain, and champions of the California tourist "renaissance." Most, at one time or another, would appear as luminaries on the masthead of Charles Lummis' *Land of Sunshine* magazine,* consort at Lummis' soirées ("noises," as he called them), or drink whisky and talk of protest at soirées of their own.

Writers, lecturers, nonconformists, Charlotte's friends launched a three-pronged campaign: to denounce plutocrary in the name of egalitarianism, to rebuke New England literary traditions in prefer-

* For years, Lummis served as impresario, editor, and mentor for many California protest writers, though he did not assume editorship of the *Land of Sunshine* until 1894. From 1892 through 1894, he spent much of his time traveling in South America.

ence for the élan of local color realists, and to condemn bourgeois sexual and social mores in preference for freer, more experimental, ways of living. At times their writing reflected disillusionment and anger—with politics, with literature, and often with their lives. But it also reflected idealism; it expressed optimism and confidence as well as sensitivity to ugliness and exasperation with the dislocations of modern industrial life.

In some respects theirs was a literature of discovery, an affirmation of a geographical and cultural milieu very different from the one writers had traditionally respected. Beginning with an earlier California "renaissance" connected with the *Overland Monthly*, western writers often viewed themselves as literary pioneers, explorers of a new, exotic, undiscovered physical environment. Charles Lummis was more dramatic about it than most, trekking by foot some 3,507 miles across the continent, and then publishing—in vivid, sometimes startling detail—the story of his ventures in *A Tramp across the Continent*. But works by other members of Charlotte's literary circles had a parallel intent. Ina Coolbrith's *Songs from the Golden Gate* (1895), Adeline Knapp's *This Then Is Upland Pasture* (1897), some of Charlotte's poems in *In This Our World* (1893)—all these were not only nature-loving works, ardent, if sometimes sentimental tributes to the scenic grandeur of the West; they were also, at least indirectly, well-calculated jabs at the ignorance, the misplaced arrogance, the cultural dominance of easterners.*

But it was not only the picturesque western scenery that such writers championed. More importantly, they supported western cultural traditions which in their view had been condescendingly dismissed, despised, or in the case of Indians, ruthlessly despoiled.

* Some of Grace Channing's essays (many of them published in *Out West*) were within this western tradition. Having spent a number of years in Italy (in 1890 and several times after 1897), she was fascinated by the "tree for tree, bush for bush, flower for flower" parallels between the southern Pacific coast and the eastern Mediterranean area, but she felt Californians, particularly transplanted easterners, did not know how to enjoy nature's beauty as fully as the Italians did. She wrote, "One who walks dreaming through these Italian gardens which have been so many centuries the delight of mankind, seeing beyond their vistas California's larger spaces, her far more rapid growth of vegetation, her deeper skies and more splendid color—such a one must feel that he can in truth *but* dream what gardens here might be, and what their influence upon a race growing up amid these 'thoughts of God'" (quoted in Edwin R. Bingham, *Charles F. Lummis: Editor of the Southwest* [San Marino, Calif.: The Huntington Library, 1955], p. 175).

Charles Lummis was one of the major pioneers of western study, incorporating into his books of history, fiction, essay, and verse vivid accounts of the language, folklore and customs of native populations. For years he had lived among Indian tribes in New Mexico, Peru, and Bolivia; he had returned to southern California to become editor of the *Land of Sunshine* magazine, an active promoter of historical, archeological, and ethnological studies of the southwest, and eventually a founder of the Southwest Museum in Los Angeles. Even more flamboyant and outspoken in his celebration of western living—the world of miners, gamblers, and border ruffians as well as Indians—was "bearded sage" Joaquin Miller. He was not always well respected, apparently, cultivating his eccentricities as religiously as he did his literary talents. But his "unmoral treatment of immoral subjects," his "unconscionable" accounts of "commoners" with their incorrect speech, their illiteracy, their uncultivated manners, was yet another expression of disdain for the profit- and status-oriented codes of pious prissies of the East.

If much of the writing of Charlotte's literary friends—their celebrations of scenic beauty, of Indian culture, of western living—was designed to affirm the value of their own cultural milieu, and to snipe at easterners along the way, much of it was also inspired by issues which concerned protest writers all across the country: the immorality of the new industrial order, the approaching exhaustion of natural resources, the corruption of business and government, the exploitation of the common man. None of these were new literary themes of course. They dated back to Bellamy's *Looking Backward*, to George's *Progress and Poverty*, and to farm and labor protest writing of the past several decades. But in the 1890s, as economic pressures intensified, so also did the torrent of "realistic" poetry and fiction—nationally as well as locally. For many writers, the economic depression was becoming the primary focus of attention, the major provocation not only for literary work, but for active political involvement as well. Many writers attended the St. Louis labor convention of 1892, for example, or the Populist Party's convention that same year. Many openly supported Populist demands—for free and unlimited coinage of silver, for the graduated income tax, for government ownership of railroads and public services, for the reclamation of alienated lands. For the most part, they seemed to share the Populists' impassioned explanation of the causes for national discontent. As one contemporary spokesman put it:

> We meet in the midst of a nation brought to the verge of moral, political, and material ruin. Corruption dominates the ballot-

> box, the Legislatures, the Congress, and touches even the ermine of the bench. The people are demoralized; most of the States have been compelled to isolate the voters at the polling places to prevent universal intimidation and bribery. The newspapers are largely subsidized, homes covered with mortgages, labor impoverished, and the land concentrated in the hands of capitalists. The urban workmen are denied the right to organize for self-protection; imported pauperized labor beats down their wages, a hireling standing army, unrecognized by our laws, is established to shoot them down, and they are rapidly degenerating into European conditions. The fruits of the toil of millions are boldly stolen to build up colossal fortunes for the few, unprecedented in the history of mankind; and the possessors of these, in turn despise the Republic and endanger liberty. From the same prolific womb of governmental injustice we breed the two great classes—tramps and millionaires.

Circulating among Charlotte's literary coterie sometime during 1893, the year following the Omaha Populist convention, was one of the leading champions of the "People's Party," Hamlin Garland. A cross-country lecturer at Farmers' Alliance and Populist meetings and conventions, a major proponent of "realistic" fiction at the Congress of Authors of the Chicago Exposition, Garland was perhaps best known for his 1891 fictional portrait of rural life, *Main Travelled Roads*. It reflected the angry mood of many, the protesters' outrage at the living conditions of "men who hopelessly and cheerlessly make the wealth that enriches the alien and the idler." Garland's fiction was directly and intentionally designed to promote the Populists' campaign: to inspire a "heart of gold" perception of the common man, to condemn the plutocrat, and to articulate a faith in the possibility of progressive social change. He summarized the "realistic" fiction writer's purpose this way: "The realist or verist is really an optimist, a dreamer. He sees life in terms of what it might be, as well as in terms of what it is; but he writes of what is, and suggests what is to be, by contrast."

Another strong proponent of this kind of protest literature, and a friend and admirer of Hamlin Garland, was aspiring "revolutionary" poet Edwin Markham. Markham was in fine feather in the fall of 1893—about the time Charlotte knew him best—full of tales of his summer travels with Hamlin Garland, his visit to the Chicago Columbian Exposition (Charlotte had hankered for the chance to go), his contacts with writers and publishers in Boston, New York, and Montreal. Markham was still not yet widely known by contemporary writers; "The Man with a Hoe" would not be published for several years. But his fiery socialist and labor verses, his spirited attacks on bourgeois sexual and social mores, his enthusiastic ruminations on the works of Marx, Kropotkin, Mazzini, Whitman—literally dozens more—brought him warm acceptance in California literary circles. By the time Charlotte met him, Markhim was serving as principal of the Tompkins School of Oakland, living near Joaquin Miller's estate, "The Heights," frequenting Ina Coolbrith's soirées, and very likely testing on his friends versions of the poetry which would later bring him fame.

> Bowed by the weight of centuries he leans
> Upon his hoe and gazes on the ground,
> The emptiness of ages in his face,
> And on his back the burden of the world.

Markham wrote just the sort of verse—poignant, compassionate, defiant—that Charlotte loved to hear, and just the sort she wrote herself. Already she had published some of her protest pieces in the *Woman's Journal* and the *Nationalist*: "In Duty Bound," for example, or her 1890 literary triumph, "Similar Cases." In the same year that she was hobnobbing with Hamlin Garland, Edwin Markham, Ina Coolbrith, and their friends, she published her first anthology of poetry, *In This Our World*, no doubt with their encouragement. Essentially, it was Populist campaign poetry, an expression of outrage against the conditions of the unemployed, the destructiveness of charity, the political irresponsibility of the "looker on." "I don't call it a book of poems," she wrote; "I call it a tool box. It was written to drive nails with," to inspire political commitment, to condemn the "coolly smiling wretch" who ignored the current crisis:

> We have no place for lookers on
> When all the world's at war!

She called for more action, more struggle.

> Louder, my brother! Let us wail no longer
> Like those past sufferers whose hearts did break.
> We are a wiser race, a braver, stronger—
> Let us not ask, but take!

Her poem "To Labor" demanded that workers fight and conquer.

> Then rise as you never rose before!
> Nor hoped before!
> Nor dared before!

And show as was never shown before,
 The power that lies in you!
  Stand all as one!
  See justice done!
Believe, and Dare, and Do!

Some of the poems of *In This Our World* paralleled Ina Coolbrith's celebrations of western scenic beauty ("A Nevada Desert," for example); some had a Reform Darwinist evolutionary cast ("The Survival of the Fittest," or "Poor Human Nature"); almost all were poems of "vivid purpose" such as William Dean Howells urged ("How Many People Poor"); but many reflected a "vivid purpose" that was motivated by a rather different kind of anger and experience.

Go ask the literature of all the ages!
Books that were written before women read!
Pagan and Christian, satirists and sages,—
  Read what the world has said!

There was no power on earth to bid you slacken
The generous hand that painted her disgrace!
There was no shame on earth too black to blacken
  That much praised woman-face!

Eve and Pandora!—always you begin it—
The ancients called her Sin and Shame and Death!
"There is no evil without woman in it,"
  The modern proverb saith!

Another poem decried the hollow victory of love.

And some have Love's full cup as he doth give it—
Have it, and drink of it, and, ah,—outlive it!
Full fed by Love's delights, o'erwearied, sated,
They die, not hungry—only suffocated.

If Charlotte's poetry, like her lectures and her fiction, can sometimes be viewed as autobiographical as well as political reflection, it seems that by 1893 she was concerned not only with the pain of suffocating love such as she had known with Walter, but also with the pain of loveless living following her loss of Delle: "No human soul can ever suffer more/The devastating grief of loneliness." So grim had Charlotte sometimes found that loneliness, and so intense had been the alternating feelings of anger and despair she shared with many protest writers, that she openly acknowledged her occasional preoccupation with suicide and death.

What power can stir these heavy limbs?
  What hope these dull hearts swell?
What fear more cold, what pain more sharp,
  Than the life we know so well? . . .

No human death would be worse to feel
  Than the life that holds us here.
But this is a fear no heart can face—
  A fate no man can dare—
To be run to earth and die by the teeth
  Of the gnawing monster there!

* * *

The years 1890–1893 were ones of deepening nationwide economic depression and of intensifying protest efforts by writers and organizers associated with the Populist and Nationalist movements. For Charlotte personally, they had been traumatic years: she had endured the final separation from Walter, the lingering illness and then the death of her mother, the termination of a love relationship that she had hoped would last for life. Throughout those years, she had been politically assertive—writing, lecturing, expanding contacts with left-wing California protest groups. But she had also been quite personally aloof from men, relying heavily on her one-to-one or group relationships with women for support. By the fall of 1893, however, Charlotte's personal-political interactions were changing. She was starting to move about more freely, to socialize with Edwin Markham, Ina Coolbrith, Joaquin Miller, and their friends, and even to plan some soirées of her own at her boarding house. She formed a "sort of salon," Harriet Howe recalled. "People of all sorts happened in on these evenings, a local labor leader, a society woman, some friendly newspaper men and women, a poet, a lawyer, and once came a minister who smiled benignly." Apparently a wide range of questions were discussed—"psychological, philosophical, economic, biological, and ethical"—"sometimes heatedly, sometimes descending in rapid cascades of wit to the humorous, in the clash of minds and the flow of words." From Harriet Howe's idolizing point of view, Charlotte was the heroine on these evenings, the iconoclast who could confound and outwit everyone: "The group labored to break down her opposition. She would not yield an iota; she could not be shaken." In any case, she "seemed to thrive on these occasions," to enjoy the "mental duel of strongly contested opinions"—"her favorite pastime."

The accelerating pace of Charlotte's social life may have resulted in part from the prodding and encouragement of her literary mentor, Ina Coolbrith. For years, Ina Coolbrith had been at the forefront of the California "renaissance," a heroine to many San Francisco protest writers, purportedly a lover to more than one. Feminist writer Mary Austin would later describe Ina as a "tall, slow woman, well-filled out, a pretty woman," with a "low pleasant voice," a "matter-of-fact" manner, and a "look of one accustomed to uninhabited space and wide horizons." At about the time Charlotte met her, Ina Coolbrith had just been ignominiously dismissed from her position at the Oakland Free Library—after almost eighteen years of service. For her, this was a period of transition as well, one in which she had time not only to reassess her own literary goals, but also to advise, coax, and work with younger writers. Charlotte may have met her through the Pacific West Coast Women's Press Assocation, but she got to know her—well and fast—by living just across from her on Webster Street in Oakland. According to reputation in polite San Francisco society, there was only the "virginal Ina Coolbrith," careful, circumspect, always proper, and "highly respected by all who knew her." But privately she was as unconventional as any of her friends and even more painfully aware than some of them of the hypocrisy of many social-sexual bourgeois moral codes. She had learned the hard way: fleeing from a pathologically jealous husband after he had tried to kill her, changing her name to escape social scorn, and finding, later, her only real experiences of love outside of marriage. Since such effrontery contrasted starkly with her pristine pure facade, Ina Coolbrith, not surprisingly, balked when she was asked to write her memoirs: "Were I to write what I know, the book would be too sensational to print; but were I to write what I think proper, it would be too dull to read."

Charlotte exhibited similar discretion when she wrote about her own experiences with California literati. For instance, she described her fight against the Southern Pacific Railroad—with Markham, Coolbrith, Miller, etc.—as though personal involvements mattered not a whit, and as though the sexual liberation issues usually associated with the 1920s were never part of her campaign. She had simply joined her friends in insisting—"as if the fly should try to bite the cartwheel"—that the Southern Pacific Railroad's monopolistic shenanigans should stop: it had "merciless power in the legislature, in the press, in the courts, even in the churches through wealthy patronage," so that a "whole generation of young men grew up in California who had never seen freedom or honesty in public affairs under the conscienceless tyranny of this powerful Common

Carrier." Charlotte's autobiography discusses the monopoly politics of the Southern Pacific, her diaries obliquely suggest that sexual politics were involved as well: "Am roused to new enthusiasm against the S.P. Speak to Ina Coolbrith about a new crusade against it." September 16: "Talk late. Mr. M. stays all night." "Mr. M.," presumably, was Edwin Markham. The next day, one of her friends (Ina Coolbrith?) came by: "she and Mr. Markham stay to breakfast—fine breakfast." Then they proceeded to Joaquin Miller's home, "The Heights." "We women call on Miller in bed. Dirty person that he is! All cigar ashes on the floor beside him. I try to rouse him on the S.P. question. Dubious success. Climb the hills behind." The next day: "plan further for the S.P. crusade." Those plans happened to coincide rather nicely with a Pacific Coast Women's Press Association convention Charlotte and her friends were having—luncheons, meetings, heated discussions on Southern Pacific crimes. "I am made President," she recorded, "wear black silk" and they "give me a floral tribute!" The following day: "My Darling over night. [Markham again, most likely.] Joaquin calls early." The following day it was again a very enjoyable Markham who won recognition in her diary—this time after a visit to his home—for good talks, good food, good fun. In her autobiography, Charlotte acknowledged that she had provoked a scandal, but claimed that she could not imagine why.

> What the creeping slanders were I never knew. There never were any distinct "charges," never the least hint of anything against my "character," in the usual line. There I was, with my boarders to bear witness, working my head off, doing what I could for mother and child while I had them, wearing clothes that were given me, writing, lecturing and preaching as opportunity offered. I knew well the ordinary risks of a woman in my position among San Francisco–minded people, and took extreme precautions to give no least handle for criticism in behavior. For instance I made it a point to be seen nowhere with any man, to receive no slightest "attention." I remember once Edwin Markham, then a school-teacher in Oakland, not yet known as a poet, asked me to take a soda in a drug-store, and I wouldn't, so absurdly careful was I.

Absurdly careful indeed, though perhaps it is not hard to understand her autobiographical reticence (or deceit, depending on one's point of view). For one thing, she always tried to preserve privacy in her personal relationships, even to the point of mentioning her thirty-four-year marriage to Houghton Gilman in just a sentence or two.

More importantly, by the time Charlotte wrote her memoirs, the flapper generation had emerged. Her choice, politically as well as personally, was to oppose the younger women's views on sex, apparently hoping they would think she never shared them. She warned the 1920 flappers how easily they could be burned in "love relationships," and argued that their fight for sexual freedom was destructive and misplaced. Though her involvement with Markham had been casual, she clearly had been burned several times herself.

At the very least, Charlotte may have been embarrassed and annoyed that she had ever trusted Markham in the first place. Twice married, he was a man of "passion and imagination" but also of deep-seated "neurosis under the solid and increasingly well-esteemed exterior." Here was the ecstatic rebel poet, the champion of the underdog, yet a man—she may have learned—who had been cited by the Society for the Prevention of Cruelty to Children for "too" harshly beating a student in his school. Quick with his well-practised declarations of love, quick with poetic expressions of his heartfelt need to find yet another woman to sustain him, he was "as psychologically dependent on women as any man could be." After the first stage of infatuation, Charlotte may have learned Markham's game, or at least that is the implication of her friends' opinion of Markham's hero, Joaquin Miller. Markham worshipped Miller, chose a home as close to "The Heights" as possible, fraternized with Miller when he got the chance, and even kept scrapbooks of Miller's machismo feats. Yet, as Harriet Howe explained, Miller was viewed by many as a fool.

> Joaquin was already famous for splendid poetry and equally famous for gallantry with the ladies, also for amiable ostentation and affectation in dress. Possibly he fancied himself as a knight of olden time. But to see him, bending low over the hand of a beautiful woman, kissing it ceremoniously, with the well-known bear-skin jauntily festooned across his shoulders, did not produce quite the romantic effect he imagined, on account of the tobacco stained whiskers.

At a dinner party Charlotte gave for Joaquin Miller and Ina Coolbrith, Harriet Howe remembered feeling "like a molecule" herself, but enjoying the repartee immensely:

> Apparently Joaquin was in a mood for sympathy, and began to lament his dark and dreary life, with no affection, no understanding, no love, no anything. After some moments of self-pity he paused expectantly, and Mrs. Stetson spoke, gravely,

gently, "I am surprised to hear of your great lack, for I had always understood that you were surfeited with devotion."

In point of fact, Charlotte was rather "surfeited with devotion" herself in 1893, though presumably she was not in Joaquin Miller's league. Her diary provides only thinly scattered clues, but a certain Mr. Eugene Hough is mentioned often enough to assume that he was more than just a friend. Eugene Hough was a political activist in the California radical community, another champion of the labor movement, a co-worker in the anti-railroad fight, and a "thoroughly nice fellow," she decided. "Mr. Hough" appeared and reappeared (replaced only temporarily by Edwin Markham) in diary entries throughout most of 1893. There were reports of his recurrent Sunday visits, their discussions on municipal politics and Southern Pacific Railroad campaigns, and his help with chores around the house. In 1894, he would make explicit overtures for Charlotte's attentions and affections, but for the moment he very likely was content with less.

Meanwhile, Charlotte still had her countless meetings to attend, her professional and personal commitments to the women's movement, her involvement in Populist and socialist campaigns. The Woman's Alliance, the Pacific Coast Women's Press Association, the local Parents' Association, the State Council of Women, the "Economic Club"—these served as some of Charlotte's contact points for lectures, friendships, political repartee, and animated fun. The more she spoke, the more confident she became, not only of her abilities as a lecturer, but of her unconventional views about lifestyles as well. For instance, after a Women's Christian Temperance Union meeting she wrote, "Am so much moved by the needs of the women that I write a new paper. Speak in the evening. A very trying occasion—so much to say and so much I must not say to them." Or after another politically charged session: "Such questions! Was not as great as I should have been—as wise—as calm—as patient, as loving. Let my irritation show. Such paltry people! Such feeble minds! Such ignorance!" (And such astuteness she was proudly claiming for herself.)

One of the ventures Charlotte enjoyed most at about this time was her work with the Pacific Coast Women's Press Association (PCWPA). An organization of essayists, novelists, poets, and aspiring literary women, it had been founded in 1890 by Mrs. Emily Parkhurst of San Francisco in response to women writers' need for social contact and exchange, for advice about their work, for discussion and consolidated effort on their reform-oriented goals. Along with

California suffrage worker Sarah Cooper, Charlotte was elected vice-president of the PCWPA in 1893. She began helping with their organizational campaigns and writing and editing for their monthly magazine the *Bulletin* (later the *Impress*). She seemed to like the work immensely. From the outset, the *Bulletin* was a magazine of Charlotte's San Francisco literary friends. It reported on women's efforts in suffrage and labor organizations throughout the state, on their educational and dress reform campaigns, on their publications in fiction and poetry. It enthusiastically reviewed or reprinted some of Ina Coolbrith's poetry, some selections from Charlotte's *In This Our World*, some of Adeline Knapp's writings; it acclaimed the work of one of Charlotte's favorite writers, Olive Schreiner—"that wonderful seer of our time"; and consistently and openly, it avowed its quasi-Populist intent. The central purpose of the *Bulletin*, the editors declared, was to promote "the interests of reform on this coast; presenting a monthly summary of news of reformatory progress, and recent thought upon the subject."

By 1893, the *Bulletin* (now the *Impress*) was not only reflecting Charlotte's political perspectives and alliances, but also providing a glimpse of some of her family affairs. One of the magazine's recently acquired mentors, the *Impress* announced, was Charlotte's father, Frederick Beecher Perkins, guest lecturer on press reform at a recent PCWPA social meeting: "It is not often that such wide scholarship and experience are brought to bear on this subject [press reform]; and still seldomer is it so ably and happily presented." According to the *Impress* Perkins condemned the "disgusting license" of the current California press, called for a "public remonstrance" against it, and "closed by showing that the practical way to compel improvement was by withdrawal of patronage from the offending sheets."

Apparently, Charlotte had not only invited her father to speak to her friends, but past resentments notwithstanding, had also enthusiastically applauded him; perhaps she had even written the rave review herself. In any case, a change—not sudden or absolute, but telling—seemed to be occurring in their relationship. Charlotte seemed to be less angry with her father, less disappointed, and was able to feel more pride and warmth instead.

To understand the extent of change, it seemes appropriate to review some of their past interactions—or lack thereof. Charlotte had had almost no contact with her father for several years, and she was irritated. When she had separated from Walter and brought Kate to California in 1888, Frederick had not even bothered to visit. When he finally came, three years later, she wrote in her diary: "Father calls to see me in the morning, and meets his granddaughter for the first time. No emotion amongst us." Some time later, she crossed out the diary entry, possibly to emphasize the coldness, or possibly because she realized there had in fact been "emotion amongst us." In any case, when Frederick refused to visit Mary on her deathbed, Charlotte became even more enraged. The more time Charlotte had spent with her mother, the closer she had felt, and the more estranged she felt from her father.

After Mary's death, however, some form of reconciliation with Frederick had occurred. It was as though Mary's illness intensified a sense of mother-daughter loyalty, while Mary's death provided a release, an opportunity to cast aside some of the tensions which had blocked affection for her father. Charlotte had always wanted his attention and approval. Perhaps at the time of mourning, he felt freer to acknowledge his concern, his sympathy, his respect. For whatever reasons, Frederick began to offer more support. He endorsed and joined some of Charlotte's political campaigns, the press reform and anti-railroad fights in particular; he helped financially (though not even enough to pay Charlotte's debts for Mary's nurses' fees); and he began calling on her more often. She in turn began visiting him at the San Francisco Library; and, by the end of 1893, she was enthusiastically introducing him among her friends.

As though to celebrate the reconciliation, Charlotte invited Frederick to a Christmas party she and her friends were having at her boarding house. Harriet Howe reported: "To our delight, he accepted and came, and thus I met the father of Mrs. Stetson. He was of portly carriage, serene dignity, kindly, very impressive, of few words, but oozing knowledge unconsciously, at every pore." Everyone had been asked to bring a fifteen-cent "joke gift," accompanied by a humorous verse "appropriate to the gift" for each of the others—"seventeen people, ranging from 5 to 55"—and Frederick was asked to serve as "master of ceremonies." He "officiated beautifully, with a twinkle in his eye, but never once losing dignity," Harriet wrote. "I think I remember that he made a short preliminary speech which was applauded. Then he distributed the gifts. At once the room was filled with merriment over the comicality of the gifts and verses. . . . The result was a great success and never before, nor since, have I known such a joyous Christmas." *

That was probably Charlotte's feeling too. Boarding-house ten-

* Harriet Howe implied, but did not state, that the Christmas party was in December 1892, not 1893 as I have suggested here. However, because of Mary's critical condition, such a fun-filled Christmas celebration, with Frederick presiding, would have been extremely unlikely in 1892.

sions had mostly disappeared. Work was going nicely. Friendships were flourishing. And for one of the first times since her separation, Charlotte could view the New Year's prospects rather optimistically. Her diary entry for January 1, 1894 reads: "Desired for this year. Less words and better. More love for people, with concomitant Health."

* * *

In point of fact, 1894 brought a sense of heightened confidence on a number of issues in Charlotte's private life, and, concerning each, Frederick's support may have been a major factor. First, the divorce suit was quietly successful. Not only did Frederick help her find a lawyer, but chances are he also talked to her about his own divorce. Since Frederick's experiences to some extent parallelled Charlotte's, such discussions no doubt relieved some of her sense of guilt and anger. Second, it was some time during the winter or spring of 1894 that Charlotte decided to send her daughter Kate to live with Grace and Walter. That, too, Frederick probably supported. He was planning to travel East; at the very least, he agreed to take Kate with him. As soon as the divorce suit was settled, Walter and Grace planned to be married. Charlotte felt their family situation would be happier for Kate, her own life less encumbered. Given the public condemnation Charlotte expected (and received), to say nothing of her own anxieties, even practical cooperation from her father was a help; but it may be that he (unwittingly?) offered emotional support as well. Charlotte had always regretted her own separation from her father, yet in 1894, she found it necessary to put her daughter through a parallel experience, perhaps an even more painful one, since by most people's standards a child's separation from a mother is worse than a father's absence. It took courage to defy conventions, to consider her own needs as well as Kate's, to insist that a separation from her daughter did not mean denying her love. As Charlotte worked through her own choices and the reasoning behind them, she may have come to a better understanding of her father's past behavior. If so, that helped her to love him more and to feel more confident about herself.

Both of the personal issues that Charlotte faced in 1894—the divorce and the separation from Kate—helped bring her closer to her father. But there was another significant factor affecting their relationship as well. That same spring of 1894, Frederick planned to marry Frankie Johnson Beecher, the "love of his youth." Frankie Beecher's husband, James Chaplin Beecher (Frederick's uncle), had died some years before, and after Mary's death, Frankie agreed to marry Frederick. Again, Charlotte's image of her father had to change. If she still viewed him as a model of professional ambition and achievement, at least he was no longer quite the model of stoic loveless living he may once have seemed to be, a man rejecting emotional involvements with women in preference for his work. Before, Charlotte had probably viewed him as hostile to Mary, to women, and, by extension, to herself. She had responded with her own style of coldness—to her father and, by extension, to other men she knew. But as the relationship with Frederick improved, particularly now that she had some professional success, her attitude toward other men changed also. In fact, as she began to love and trust her father more, she began to feel more love and trust for other men as well, and perhaps also to learn better how to love and trust herself.

* * *

It was early in March of 1894 that Charlotte, inspired by Edwin Markham and Eugene Hough, first began to articulate a changed perception of herself. On March 7 she wrote, "Mr. Hough spends the evening. For the first time in my life I am conscious—faintly—of what I take to be the standing condition of 'lovely women.' A recognition of the possession of sex attraction. But this is no place to use it." The following day a friend said she looked like George Sand; "that makes another," Charlotte noted proudly, "George Elliot, Rachel, Christina Rosetti, a noble list." And twelve days later: "My Fate seems turned. Within two days I receive two declarations of love!!! Rather late change—rather hopeless. Gratifying nonetheless. One brings hope, strength, and joy. I needed it, and thank God for it."

"Hopeless" but "gratifying nonetheless"—that sounded rather dull. She seemed flattered, but not particularly excited, certainly not transported with the kind of rapture she had felt in other love relationships (with Martha and Delle, anyway). She liked the attentions of Markham and Hough, but either they did not meet her expectations, or she was too entrenched in her habits of self-denial and self-depreciation to involve herself as yet. "If it be that I may not have—as indeed I have never had, personal happiness; or rather, happiness in personal relation; it follows that I must ensure as far as may be, happiness in general relation." Characteristically, she then proceeded to review her standard resolutions to secure the "unremittingly demanded virtues": "cheerfulness, courtesy, justice, patience, humility, truthfulness, loving kindness always." But she added another objective as well that in recent years was not quite so typical. She wanted to be pretty: "Now as to material conditions. My most peremptory need is clothing; good, beautiful, sufficient. I must make it a matter of honor to provide these."

Whatever the reasons that Charlotte rejected the relationships with Markham and Hough,* 1893–1894 had marked a turning point. As she later put it to Houghton Gilman: "Three [men] since '93—none since '95. . . . Come to think of it, it was about one a year since I took that queer turn and became 'attractive.'"†

That she was attractive to men was what Charlotte found so "queer," for all along she had viewed herself as attractive to women. Perhaps the traumas with both Martha and Delle had left her embittered about female love relationships; perhaps she had partially accepted the derogatory socially imposed attitudes toward women's love. In any case, it is striking that a woman-supporting woman would assert that "convincing proof" of her attractiveness had come from love relationships with men. That was a strange self-perception, a strange choice of words. Apparently, she sometimes felt she had been "queer" and "unfeminine" during the friendship years with Martha, a "morbid, strange cold sort of monster" while she was passionately involved with Delle, and "more woman than most" when she entered love relationships with men. At times she seemed to forget how much her female friendships had meant, to delight in her "heathen goddess" triumphs instead, and to enjoy immensely the public hoax she perpetuated along the way.

> Queer unfeminine girl that I was, there was first the long devoted love of him who called himself my husband; then, when I thought myself a morbid strange cold sort of monster—no real woman at all—came the convincing proof that I was more woman than most—the strong lasting love of more than

* At least one source of tension in both relationships may have been the "creeping scandal" that her behavior caused. Her autobiography suggests that possibility with Edwin Markham, as does her diary with Eugene Hough. On July 19, 1894, she wrote, "Complaint of a slanderous member [probably of the PCWPA] and serious action decided upon." Only six days later, Eugene Hough was brushed aside: "Alas—he will not do." It seems possible that Charlotte resented Hough partly because of public criticism; but it is also possible that the "slanderous member" spoke about other issues, and that a scandal about Mr. Hough had not occurred at all.

† The first two men were Edwin Markham and Eugene Hough, and the third was probably Paul Tyner, a close friend of Helen Campbell's and a co-worker on the *Impress*.

one man and the knowledge of—of—well, sometimes I feel like "a heathen goddess come again," a wonderful struggling mixed feeling, half shame, half pride, of being—to most people's knowledge a stern cold thinker, a calm pleasant friend of men, dearly loved by women, the favorite of children—a widow—a celibate, a solitary—and inside—Ashtoreth! *

* * *

Meanwhile, during this same protean winter of 1893–1894, Charlotte was still fighting for a settlement of her divorce. Publicly, she was the circumspect married lady, well above reproach, and, privately, the "heathen goddess" fraying with the martyred saint. Walter's divorce suit in Rhode Island had been unsuccessful, so Charlotte began to try the California courts again, this time with her father's practical and emotional assistance, and with Grace Channing's as well. Grace had just come back to California to visit briefly with her parents; but she also hoped to renew her friendship with Charlotte and to ease whatever tensions her plans to marry Walter may have caused. Actually, Charlotte seemed to feel almost no tensions at all. In fact, she seemed pleased. In February she wrote: "Nice long day in the city with Grace. . . . Call on father twice—time to get name of a lawyer to undertake divorce if possible. A wonderful pleasure to be with Grace again—dear queen!" And then, several months later: "Find letter from Walter telling about his wedding with Grace. I feel so glad." Partly it may have been the years of solid friendship with Grace that forestalled feelings of envy or resentment; partly it may have been that Charlotte hadn't really loved Walter anyway. But, as she openly acknowledged, it may also have been that Grace and Walter's marriage helped to soothe her conscience: "Having made the painfully frequent mistake of an untenable marriage, we were at last free from its legal bonds, and before the year was over my conscience was finally relieved of much regret for his sake by Mr. Stetson's happy marriage to my life-long friend, Grace Channing."

Perhaps Charlotte felt pleased for another reason as well: now it might be fair to let Grace and Walter share some of the responsibilities for Katharine. It must have been some time during Grace's visit, or possibly in letters during the months that followed, that Grace and Charlotte first broached the question of having Kate move East. Grace had plenty of worries and needs of her own to

* Ashtoreth was an ancient Semitic fertility goddess.

consider: ill health, aging parents, her professional writing goals. But she was also, characteristically, a strikingly self-sacrificing soul. Besides, she had weathered too many of Charlotte's emotional torrents, too many of her despondent "grey fog" moods, not to fear for Charlotte's health, possibly her sanity. Grace knew that Charlotte's situation had been improving recently, but not, she may have felt, in ways which were particularly good for Katharine. Greater professional success or more satisfying friendships—either one meant Charlotte had less time for Kate. Moreover, Charlotte was making plans to move to San Francisco. Professionally, this would be an important step: she would join Helen Campbell and Paul Tyner in the management of the PCWPA *Impress* magazine. But for Kate this would mean another move, another school, another group of transient adults to learn to trust. Possibly from Grace's point of view (from Charlotte's as well?), Katharine needed two parents instead of one, stability instead of constant moves, a quiet family life instead of boarding-house confusions, and a home-based mother instead of one preoccupied with outside work.* In any case, Grace and Walter presumably wanted (or consented) to have Katharine come live with them.† As Charlotte put it in her autobiography, Grace would make a fine "second mother . . . fully as good as the first, better in some ways perhaps." Walter "longed for his child and had a right to some of her society; and since the child had a right to know and love her father—I did not mean her to suffer the losses of my youth—this seemed the right thing to do."

* * *

From the very outset, Charlotte's relationship with Katharine had been marred by strains and tensions. Warm playful times had been hindered by the frustrations of her marriage and by competing professional ambitions; or, as she preferred to put it, "unmeasured joy and hope" had been undermined by an "aching emptiness of mind." At times, she viewed herself as a complete failure: "No good as a wife, no good as a mother, no good at anything. And you did it all yourself." Yet at other times she saw herself as a model of suc-

*Despite her arguments against sex-role stereotypes, and despite the feminist implications of her separation from Kate, Charlotte probably knew that Grace, not Walter, would assume primary child-care responsibility.

†Katharine later believed that Charlotte sent her to Grace and Walter without consulting them. Though that is possible, I believe it to be unlikely, particularly since Grace visited Charlotte only several months before Katharine went East.

cess—sweet, reasonable, gentle always. "Something of my mother's passion for children I had inherited," Charlotte wrote. "Always I loved children and children loved me." By her own account, she had avoided Mary's faults in mothering, and copied only Mary's strengths: "In my own childhood and youth, I had well learned that 'love' by no means ensures understanding or appreciation." Katharine, Charlotte decided, would experience all that she had missed. Katharine would learn "self-control," not blind obedience to "stern authority," and receive tenderness and warmth, not constant carping disapproval. Since arbitrary commands "would have meant a contest of wills, punishments, bitter unhappiness," Charlotte wrote, from "her earliest years I always made a steady habit of mentioning a reason for an action," rather than insisting that Kate "mind" under compulsion. The "method of suggestion" had worked wonders: "there was never any difficulty in these first years of education." Kate "never gave trouble or caused anxiety by her behavior" —or so Charlotte liked to remember.

Simplistic sentimentalism aside, Charlotte knew she had loved Katharine deeply. She had enjoyed reading to her, playing games, writing and reciting child verses. Katharine, she recalled, had been a "heavenly baby," an "exquisite baby, healthy, intelligent, and good." She had even somehow understood her mother's suffering: "that lovely child would come 'hitching' . . . across the room to bring me a handkerchief because she saw my tears." Even when she was sick, Kate handled matters "philosophically." When she had the measles, Charlotte remembered, "I heard her swearing softly after the fashion of her beloved Arabian Nights—as she rubbed her poor eyes—'O Moses! O Aaron! O Ezra's Ass!'" Or when Katharine was told not to enter a neighbor's yard, she was "an amenable darling" once again: "I can see now that small, disconsolate figure, in its blue apron and little sunbonnet, standing with little bare toes touching the dividing line, looking at Paradise and never going in." Charlotte's affectionate sensitivity to Kate's point of view, even to some of the "wild" frustrations she remembered from her own childhood, are apparent in her 1893 poem, "If Mother Knew." Since Mary had died just several months before, Charlotte may have been particularly alert to how it felt to be a child.

If mother knew the way I felt,—
  And I'm sure a mother should,—
She wouldn't make it quite so hard
  For a person to be good!

I want to do the way she says;
   I try to all day long;
And then she just skips all the right,
   And pounces on the wrong!

A dozen times I do a thing,
   And one time I forget;
And then she looks at me and asks
   If I can't remember yet?

She'll tell me to do something,
   And I'll really start to go;
But she'll keep right on telling it
   As if I didn't know.

Till it seems as if I couldn't—
   It makes me kind of wild;
And then she says she never saw
   Such a disobliging child.

Charlotte knew perfectly well that there had been problems as well as pleasures in her relationship with Katharine, just as in her own relationship with Mary, but in her autobiography she preferred to emphasize, almost exclusively, the positive experiences instead. It was as though she felt she had to prepare her readers for her decision to separate from Katharine not by pointing to any frustrations of the mothering experience, certainly not by suggesting that any self-interest had been involved, but rather by describing only the mutually happy and affectionate rapport that had preceded the decision: "We had happy years together, nine of them, the last four she was mine alone. . . . When I came home from my work anywhere, toward supper-time, I could see that little red-capped figure on the gate-post, watching for me, and she would come, running."

There is a strange irony in Charlotte's autobiographical account, a strange contrast between some of the theories she preached and the ways she chose to explain her own behavior. For instance, publicly she insisted that children needed professional child care, that most women had neither the know-how nor the patience to raise them properly. Yet, rather than describe irritating difficulties with Kate, or complicated maneuverings to make suitable arrangements, she wrote as though she had been a well-trained expert herself. She could argue theoretically that fathers should take some responsibilities for children, and practically that Walter could and should; but she nonetheless seemed to feel the need to apologize for her own decisions. In public writings she argued that mothers should not sacrifice themselves to motherhood, but in private life she seemed to say that she had sacrificed herself by giving up the joys of motherlove. It was the pain of separation from Katharine that Charlotte chose to emphasize, not the pride in testing her feminist convictions. And it was Katharine's needs, not her own, Charlotte's insights as a mother, not her disabilities, love, not frustration, which had motivated the decision.

There are contradictions in Charlotte's later feminist theories, however, that to some extent reflect her personal ambivalence. On the one hand, she assumed an innate similarity of potential in males and females; she argued that socially imposed domestic responsibilities, including child care, had both caused and perpetuated women's status as the second sex. But on the other hand, like so many feminists of her generation, she asserted the natural superiority of the female sex; she emphasized women's mothering and nurturing abilities, their "instincts" of love and service, the glories of mother love. The "ideology of motherhood" can be viewed in a number of ways, but two seem particularly relevant here. In some respects, such mother-worshipping is not "feminist" at all; biological determinism or assertions about "innate differences" serve to validate the separation of males and females into their respective public-private spheres and thus to nullify women's claims to real equality. Charlotte's glorification of female nurturant capacities, together with her defensiveness about her own behavior, suggest an insecurity about, perhaps even a rejection of, her equality-based feminist convictions. She asserted women's right to independence from too much mothering responsibility, but she then glorified the "eternal Mother" as central to the feminine identity, had the women of her utopian novel *Herland* worshipping the "Goddess of Mother Love," and romanticized and sentimentalized her relationship with Katharine as though she regretted any time spent apart. Certainly that represents a conflict, and one with some negative implications: sentimentalism, biological determinism, claims to female nurturant superiority, undermined her emphasis on human qualities women shared with men. But there are some positive self-affirming implications of the "ideology of motherhood" as well. Many women, of course, express pride in mothering experiences, not because of guilt, not because they accept a biological inferiority to men, but because mothering provides them with fundamental sources of self-respect and worth. Such an argument can be used against women, to prod them to go home and stay there, but to deny it is to neglect their culture and experience. Even feminists who argue, as Charlotte often did, that mothering responsibilities tend to inhibit, sometimes to obliterate, women's opportunities in other spheres, can still justifiably emphasize women's strengths as well as their status as victims, the rewards of mothering as well as the burdens. Charlotte's emphasis on her positive experiences with Kate and the pain of separation (however sentimentally expressed) reflect not only insecurity, inconsistency, and a sense of guilt, but also sadness. She was breaking a relationship which thus far had been among the most important of her life. She had attacked directly what Adrienne Rich would later call the "institution of motherhood," the requirement that women display "'instinct' rather than intelligence, selflessness rather than self-realization, relation to others rather than creation of self." And she had done so practically, not just theoretically. Understandably, the decision was a hard one. About two weeks after Katharine had gone East, Charlotte wrote in her diary, "Go to Dr. Kellog. She says *I am all right*. This on top of all I've done lately is remarkable, and most encouraging for entire recovery and establishment of my former health." But even several years after the separation from Katharine, Charlotte was still struggling with the same question: "I tried to reassure myself last night in the dark—that after all my real personal duty, biggest of all, was to speak and write. Not at the expense of my child surely—but it has not been."

Charlotte's autobiographical description of her separation from Kate might be viewed as a call for sympathy, but it was also a very poignant description of the pain which the break with Katharine caused.

> I took her to the uptown station in Oakland, where the Overland trains stopped for passengers; her grandfather appeared; she climbed gaily aboard. She hurried to the window and looked out, waving to me. She had long shining golden hair. We smiled and waved and threw kisses to each other. The train went out, farther and farther till I couldn't see her any more. . . .
>
> That was thirty years ago. I have to stop typing and cry as I tell about it. There were years, years, when I could never see a mother and child together without crying, or even a picture of them. I used to make friends with any child I could so as to hold it in my arms for a little.

Charlotte's account suggests a kind of lifelong mourning, an intensity of sadness not apparent even at the time of Mary's death. Katharine would visit her mother for several months every year, but it was almost as though Charlotte had experienced an emotional death nonetheless, not a temporary separation. A number of writers have suggested recently that women's struggle for creative independence, particularly when it is so desperately intense, sometimes has an unacknowledged violent dimension: death and liberation become sadly juxtaposed. In a recent piece, "The Heroine as Her Author's Daughter," Judith Gardiner writes, "The mothers in all these novels are what the daughters fear and must kill in themselves in order to achieve a positive female identity." Or, as Tillie Olsen puts it, "It took family deaths to free more than one woman writer into her own development." Charlotte's separation from Katharine, emotionally and symbolically, was a self-affirming grasp for freedom as well as a guilt-producing form of death. She would later write to Houghton Gilman that she could not afford to think of Katharine often, "in the foreground in the sense I mean—of intimacy and interrelation. For to keep open and thrillingly responsive to *the thought of her* would be, to my temperament, death. Or a mind unhinged. I cannot bear any more leaks and losses and pains." She was willing to share Katharine's affection with Walter and Grace, but she also recognized her loss: "Of course she does not care much for me; and does for them." Perhaps that was the worst fear of all, that she would lose Katharine's affection entirely: "I have some hopes of Kate—but no surety. She is a strong character. Perhaps when she has lived and suffered she may come to understand. But if she stays happy and prosperous maybe she never will."

* * *

Katharine Beecher Stetson Chamberlin, Charlotte's daughter, was, at the time of my interviews with her in 1975, a sprightly ninety-year-old independent woman living in Pasadena, California. A mother of two children, formerly a painter, sculptor, and professional genealogist, she was most certainly a "strong character," happy, if not particularly prosperous, respectful of her mother, if not entirely sympathetic. Generously willing to share memories and reflections, she spoke with both affection and irritation, admiration and disappointment, concerning what she viewed as her mother's triumphs and fiascos.

Katharine's recollections of Charlotte suggest a repetition of themes of mother-daughter history Charlotte described with Mary. So often, as mothers, both Mary and Charlotte had been exhausted by economic and emotional responsibilities, and both Katharine and Charlotte criticized their mothers for being churlish and mean. Each single mother, preoccupied with work and friends outside the family, allowed her daughter space to develop confidence and independence, but each daughter viewed herself as unnecessarily and inexcusably alone. In both cases, the balance between affectionate concern and necessary distance was precarious, at best.

Yet, while both daughters viewed their mothers as simultaneously too domineering and too aloof, Charlotte emphasized the pathos of her mother's life and her own resulting sadness and remorse. Katharine, by contrast, recalled no lonely desolation in her early childhood. Viewing her mother as a somewhat irresponsible and selfishly distracted "Amazon," she saw no need for sympathy. With self-assertion, never mournful pity, she expressed irritation and resentment with her mother's "brilliant" indiscretions: "You can do anything if you have holes in your head!" But she also acknowledged, albeit reluctantly, profound respect.

Katharine seemed convinced that as a child in Pasadena and Oakland (ages four through nine), she had been for the most party happy, confident, and self-sufficient. She was not lonely. She was not whipped or treated harshly (as Charlotte felt she'd been). She had simply been neglected too often while Charlotte was "lying around in the hammock . . . enjoying nervous prostration." With considerable relish, Katharine elaborated on her childish capers with the neighbors, her kerosene fires in the basement and the henhouse, her frolics in her favorite playground—the freightyard. But that, she somberly explained, had simply not been a healthy, safe environment for "inexperienced young children." Look at the "baggy eyes," she exclaimed, as she pointed to her early photographs. Look how "undersized" because of sleeping irregularly and eating ginger nuts and "nothing else for lunch." "Ostensibly" she was living with her mother, but in reality she was "turned loose" on the neighborhood since Charlotte was either ill or "always on the run." "Mama was always scurrying," always "too tired or too distracted" to provide restful healthy meals, to get the tangles from her hair, or to care about the way she looked. To make matters worse, Charlotte called her "Kate," and that Katharine still associated "with someone being a little cross, quick, hasty."

All Charlotte's claims to the contrary, Katharine thought her mother was an awful teacher. Childish paintings, little essays or stories, Charlotte had laughed at and ridiculed, and Katharine apparently never quite forgave her. Charlotte's "theory was to make fun of something that was a little queer in one's childish drawings," instead of offering support. A bit defensively Katharine added, "My writing efforts quite bored her." Or, "My mother had not the ability of putting herself into the place of another person." She "thought she understood people" (with a strong emphasis on "*thought*"), "but I don't think she began to understand them or even to understand me." So while to Charlotte, Mary had seemed cold, stern, and irrational, to Katharine, Charlotte seemed arrogant and selfishly preoccupied: "She was too absorbed in expressing *herself*, making a career for herself, or in her causes" to take good care of her.

Not surprisingly, Katharine insisted that she felt absolutely no regret for having lived so many years with Grace and Walter. In fact, perhaps as a form of retribution, she often spoke as though her deepest loyalty and affection had always been for Grace; she would describe her mother only with the coolness, distance, and indifference she unequivocally deserved. As Charlotte had predicted, in some ways feared, Katharine felt she had found a second mother "fully as good as the first and better in some ways." Repeatedly Katharine endorsed the Stetsons' style of living, their "more elaborate meals," their thoughtful generosity, their unpretentious intellectual vitality. Grace's quiet excellence she preferred to Charlotte's eccentricity: Grace was the sensitive and more successful teacher,* the superior fiction writer, the original and innovative thinker, the more compassionate and impressive human being. Charlotte was flamboyant, strong-minded, and highly principled, but theatrical to the point of being "barbaric," absurdly inconsiderate, and remarkably forgetful. Despite the fact that Grace and Charlotte had been lifelong friends, Katharine repeatedly placed the two in opposition—perhaps in part because she was jealous of their friendship, or perhaps because she recognized resentments sometimes felt by Grace. In any case, Katharine spoke as though Grace had been not only a mother-substitute but also an ideal to try to emulate and a sympathetic friend who sometimes helped her skirmish with her mother.

One of the most serious sources of antagonism had been Charlotte's decision to send Katharine to live with Walter and Grace in 1894. Katharine seemed not only critical and sarcastic, but rather baffled at her mother's stupidity and selfishness: "That was one of those brilliant things my mother did. . . . Of all the funny things, you know," she "seized the opportunity to get her freedom by shipping me East" without even consulting Walter or Grace.† To make matters worse, Walter and Grace were not even married at the time.‡

* Grace was a kindergarten teacher for a number of years; in fact, at eighteen she taught in one of the first kindergartens of Providence.

† I have suggested earlier that this was probably not the case.

‡ Katharine's trip was in May; Walter and Grace were married June 11, 1894.

Walter was living in a one-room studio apartment, and, from Katharine's point of view, he was much too busy with his painting to be asked to spend time with her: "It is harder for a man to take over a nine-year-old child and take care of her than it is a woman." "To have a nine year old child plumped down on him, no matter how much you love the child, if you are an artist or writer and need your time, it isn't exactly opportune." Unfortunately, Katharine didn't mention Charlotte's need for time for her professional commitments, nor apparently did she appreciate the double-standard implications of her attack.

There was another double standard involved in the decision which Katharine did realize, however, and resented strongly: Charlotte wanted time for her career, but she won it by placing child-care responsibilities on Grace. One woman's freedom at another's expense, the classic bind. As Katharine put it, Grace "had to come and fetch me because she knew my father could not take care of me in a studio and do any painting." Grace may have been as enthusiastic about her writing as Walter was about his painting, but she busied herself with Katharine anyway, taking her to the park, keeping her entertained, helping her adjust. Several weeks after Grace and Walter were married, Grace took Katharine on a vacation in Connecticut, Walter visiting only on weekends so that he would not suffer interruptions in his work. And that pattern apparently continued, Katharine sympathizing with Grace, resenting Charlotte, and feeling no irritation whatsoever about her father's aloofness from what everyone apparently assumed was "women's work." For the next several years, Grace was caring not only for Katharine, but also for a niece, for her aging parents, and for, as Katharine put it, "all those demands of one kind and another that a housekeeper *had* to attend to." Grace did find some time for her reading and writing in the evening, but from Katharine's point of view, she was "infinitely" more busy than Charlotte could have been; yet "this was the way Grace's married life began, with me dumped on her."

Katharine may have resented Charlotte partly because she felt abandoned, and partly because she sometimes felt she had been a burden to Grace. Without meaning to, Grace may have even coaxed Katharine to feel that way, indirectly and subtly, despite her self-sacrificing inclinations, and despite all her fondness for Charlotte. Katharine did not directly speak of resentments Grace may have felt: Grace never criticized Charlotte's "very inconsiderate" behavior, Katharine assured me. "I felt the way I was brought up was *the way*, of course. I never remember at any time in my life feeling the least bit envious of other children or the way they did things." After all, a child's view is dependent on parental attitudes, and "there was no talking down in either family of the other family." But such disclaimers notwithstanding, some of Charlotte's letters suggest that Walter and Grace felt piqued, and said so. For instance, when Charlotte was visiting them at Christmas time one year (1900), she described a "deep bitterness of feeling as to my 'free' life for these years. . . . I can see how it must look to them." "Because 'the mother' is necessarily the best companion for the child, therefore nothing excuses my 'giving' her up. . . . They feel I have shirked a duty." Given Grace and Walter's conventional attitudes that a stepmother should tend to the child while the father works, their expectations of Charlotte as a real mother must have been conventional as well, and their resentment almost inevitable. Undoubtedly, Grace tried to be supportive of Charlotte; undoubtedly, she usually was. But her tendency to deny her own needs in preference for Charlotte's, to be uncomplaining and altruistic always, was bound to create tensions in the friendship.

Underlying resentments may have clouded perceptions on another issue as well: whether Charlotte encouraged Katharine to live with her after her marriage to Houghton Gilman in 1900. Charlotte claimed she did: "I want to have her come with me more than ever," but Katharine "expresses herself strongly in favor of going abroad with them." Whatever the reality, Katharine remembered the facts quite differently: "when my mother was about to marry . . . Grace asked if she would like to take me with her, and my mother said, 'Oh no! It wouldn't be fair to Houghton.' . . . Well, she had done the same thing with Grace in shipping me East just before her marriage and that never crossed her mind. She just forgot completely. I mean she was absolutely fair. She would have seen it if presented to her. But she forgot. And she had a great capacity for forgetting lots of things and a great capacity for remembering certain others that annoyed her, which is of course characteristic of all of us."

Katharine's descriptions of her mother were alternately respectful and condemnatory, affectionate and angry, perhaps reflecting love and hate dichotomies apparent in many mother-daughter relationships. Charlotte was highly principled, but too overbearing, too willing to preach her own ideas "which she felt were superior. . . . Mama was *always* encouraging" and supportive and "felt I had a right to my independence." But "very politely" she would "put me down with a good strong argument that I was all wrong. . . . She was perfectly convinced that her ideas were the right ideas." She was a powerful and successful preacher and lecturer, but not a good listener. She would "talk to people, but it was more in the form of giving than thinking that they had anything to give her." Still, whatever her faults, from Katharine's point of view Charlotte was most certainly "not to blame." She had been inconsiderate of Grace and Walter, but was "entirely unconscious" of the difficulties they faced. She had not "remembered things straight" in her autobiography, but she was never intentionally dishonest. "She had very strong principles and was very honest, which does not mean that she always saw herself as others saw her. But I think she would go to the stake if necessary rather than tell a lie. . . . And she of course never never would have willingly hurt anyone. I think she did at times, probably, because if you are pretty honest and you do disagree with people there is always a good chance of hurting their feelings." But "she was of course by nature very generous of her time and her possessions."

Chapter Eleven

The Impress Years 1894-1895

In May 1894, almost immediately after Katharine left Oakland to join her father and "second mother" in the East, Charlotte moved to San Francisco to live with an "adopted mother" of her own, Helen Campbell, some twenty years her senior. The last several years had been emotionally wearing, to say the least. She had experienced "the most ingenious combination of patent miseries and afflictions," chronic "nervous weakness," and persistent "grey fog" moods ranging "all the way from depression of spirits to devouring melancholia." Or, as Charlotte later put it, "I had lost home and husband, my mother was dead, my father, never close at all, was now removed across the continent. My recent 'best friends' had, as it were, soured on my hands, I had no money at all—I had borrowed again to pay for Katharine's ticket and to move, and left failure behind me, and debt." Charlotte felt she needed security, respite from responsibilities, some mothering for herself, so she turned to Helen Campbell. Passionately committed, gentle, loving, "Mother Campbell" was a fiery lecturer, novelist, muckraker, and champion of the cause of working women. "We became the closest friends," Charlotte wrote; "she was one of my adopted 'mothers.'"

Charlotte had first known Helen Campbell as Helen Weeks,* au-

* She was born Helen Campbell Stuart in 1830, married army surgeon Grenville Mellon Weeks in 1860 (the year Charlotte was born), and after her separation and divorce, took her own middle name (her mother's maiden name), and thereafter called herself Helen Stuart Campbell.

thor of the famed "Ainslee Series," a four volume set of children's stories initially published in *Our Young Folks, St. Nicholas*, and *Riverside* magazine, some of Charlotte's early favorites. There was humor, but also pathos in Helen Campbell's work, a compassionate intensity that was expressed first in her children's fiction, and later in more politically oriented writing. By the 1880s, Helen Campbell's major concern was the contemporary home economics movement, which to her meant mostly "survival economics" for the poor. The low wages, the tough living conditions, the nightmare home life of working women in the slums inspired her to continue writing, but with a different end in view: to discover and describe the kind of homemaking techniques—in health care, diet, sanitation, and budgeting—that might improve the quality of life for people in the ghettos.

Helen Campbell considered questions of household economics to be urgent and compelling: What does it mean to try to exist on three dollars a week? What is the cost, in human terms, of industrial competition, of bargain hunters' quests for always cheaper prices, of capitalists' demands for higher profits? *Mrs. Herndon's Income* (1886) was her fictional expression of these concerns. But by the 1880s she had also helped found a diet kitchen and mission school in Washington, D.C., written a widely read textbook on *The Easiest Way in Housekeeping and Cooking* (1881), served as literary and household editor for *Our Continent* magazine, and briefly managed a "Woman's Work and Wages" column for *Good Housekeeping*. After that work, along with a series of articles on New York sweatshops, she was offered a position with the New York *Tribune* to continue her investigation and exposure of the living and working conditions of wage-earning women in New York. She wrote *Problems of Poverty* in 1887, and, after an eighteen-month sojourn in Europe—in England, France, Italy, and Germany—she published its sequel, *Prisoners of Poverty Abroad* (1889). In 1893, Helen Campbell went to the University of Wisconsin, studied under the famed economist Richard Ely, and subsequently won an American Economic Association award for her monograph "Women and Wages," published with an introduction by Ely.

Helen Campbell was not only a prolific writer and pioneer muckraker, but a vigorous lecturer and organizer besides. In 1893, just before she came to California, she helped establish the National Household Economics Association, one of the major achievements of the Woman's Congress of the World Columbian Exposition. She became a leading campaigner for the National Consumers' League, and was a keen, well-informed promoter of factory legislation to protect women and children. In short she was a political dynamo—promoting socialist objectives, dispatching exposés, and in the process causing a "profound and widespread sensation respecting the life of wage-earning women."

With her "abundant vitality, great imagination, power of dramatic expression and a profoundly sympathetic nature," Helen Campbell was a woman Charlotte could easily turn to as a mentor as well as a "closest friend." In fact, Charlote and Helen had a lot in common. Both were not only incisive speakers and politically committed journalists, but also alternately assertive and despondent rebels. Both were convivial yet factious, demonstrative yet insecure, exuberant yet often lonely and depressed. Charlotte wrote of Helen, "I never knew a nobler woman—unless Grace—and Grace has not had to bear what this one has." "She is the bravest creature—and the lovingest and forgivingest I ever knew." Likewise, Helen wrote of Charlotte sympathetically ("my child," Helen called her): Charlotte was a woman with "sarcasm keen as her wit and her intense human sympathy,—sharp as bees' stings the one, sweet as their honey the other. . . . Antagonized at every turn, listened to because her wit compelled, derided because her fiery protests counted simply as the word of a 'crank,'" Charlotte was, in Helen's view, a woman of "quality" and "promise." Apparently respect and sympathy were mutual—respect for each other's political achievements, sympathy for one another's grief. And if there was a touch of martyr in each of them, there was generosity as well, the more affirmative basis of their friendship.

Charlotte's contact points with Helen Campbell were many—the California Woman's Congress, PCWPA activities, Populist and labor organizations, and common circles of literary and academic friends. Both were contributors to Lummis' *Land of Sunshine* magazine, to *Kate Field's Washington*, to *Worthington's Illustrated* magazine. In 1894, both decided to join forces on the *Impress*, official journal of the Women's Press Association. Charlotte had been writing and editing the *Impress* (formerly called the *Bulletin*) for quite some time. And the more work she did, the more influence and control she wanted. A May 1894 issue of the magazine reported that she had "made a proposition with regard to the *Impress*, stating that she would be unable to carry it indefinitely on its present basis, and that hardly any member could give the time and strength necessary to so conduct it; but that if the association would give it to her at the end of their present year, she had plans for its continuance as a high-class weekly of twice the size, to be conducted, if successfully arranged, by Mrs. Helen Campbell and herself; said paper to retain its present name, and to reserve one page for the W.P.A. news for three years, free."

After arrangements for the *Impress* had been made, Charlotte and Helen began to live together (the winter of 1894–1895). "I shall never forget that she fed me all winter in S[an] F[rancisco]," Charlotte wrote. "Her work brought in our only steady income—she paid for all our food *and cooked it*—in real illness and awful discouragement and intense personal suffering which I did not dream of then." That was just the beginning of the lifelong bond. In late 1895, they briefly worked together again at the United Settlement House in Chicago (later called the Eli Bates House, and closely associated with Jane Addams' Hull House) and lectured and conferred together at various socialist and suffragist conventions. They still maintained their mother-daughter-type relationship even after Helen became too ill to continue with her public work. "Mmm! I'd love to make a comfortable background for her old age," Charlotte wrote, but "I'm rather mixed up between my honest love for her and desire to help her; and the undeniable usefulness of having her near." "She can do wonders, and likes to. Herself, she eats small doses of vegetarian stuff. For me she delights to cook exquisite viands; she could take a green German damsel and train her—do all the managing—and glory in it. Her room and board wouldn't be a circumstance, I should feel glad to have her at a salary!" As it turned out, Helen Campbell did, in effect, sometimes serve as Charlotte's maid, running her household while Charlotte sported off on lecture tours, but just as often she needed and received Charlotte's emotional as well as financial assistance. This kind of personal and professional interaction continued sporadically until about 1912, when Helen Campbell moved to Massachusetts, where she died in 1918.

* * *

Charlotte and Helen started their friendship in 1894 not only with common political perspectives but with at least three other connecting links as well: a joint Women's Press Association project, the *Impress*; a shared house on Powell Street in San Francisco; and an affectionate tie with a mutual friend, Paul Tyner, Helen's "adopted son," possibly Charlotte's lover.* The PCWPA now had a "home of its own," the *Impress* announced: "Sunny, quiet, and easily acces-

* Charlotte later wrote Houghton Gilman, "Once I thought I should marry this worthy man. Then I found his weakness of character" (CPS to GHG, Oct. 12, 1898, AESL).

sible, we hope to find here real comfort and convenience, such as we have spoken of and wished for so long." The *Impress* headquarters and the PCWPA stomping grounds were also the Campbell-Stetson-Tyner home.

Professionally as well as personally, the collaboration worked rather nicely. Paul Tyner "did the political stuff, theatrical notes, and so on." Charlotte did "articles, verses, ethical problems—a department, and reviews"; and Helen Campbell initiated a "Household Economics" column, later called "The Art of Living," which culled and refined principles she had been working on for years. Helen Campbell pleaded for efficiency, economy, and scientific management of the home, a variation on the Progressives' goal of efficiency in government and business, and a middle-class formulation of techniques she had devised when working on home conditions of the poor. "The home today is not only a synonym for sentiment but for science," she told her readers. They must study home economics seriously, treat cooking like a profession such as medicine or law, and rely on more than just instincts and common sense. "The women's movement of today," she stated, "consists of the progress of woman from her special position as female to her general position as human." According to *Impress* articles, the goal was not that women should reject domestic functions, but that they should be more scientific, more efficient about them, and thus more human.*

Charlotte's responsibilities with the *Impress* were rather vaguely defined. According to her autobiography, she haphazardly filled in where she could.† For instance, the *Impress* needed stories: "I could

*As though to assure readers that the *Impress* was not too "feminist," most of the "Art of Living" columns were introduced with a long quotation from John Ruskin, showing how, by using "English thoroughness, French art and American hospitality" good "ladies (loaf givers)" could assure that "everybody has something nice to eat." See, for example, "The Art of Living," *Impress* II, no. 1 (Oct. 6, 1894), 8. Helen and Charlotte may not have been aware that Ruskin also believed that vestal virgin ladies should complement doing-thinking men, but know better than to question the perfection of their own separate "sacred place."

†It is possible that Charlotte wrote more of the articles and did more of the editing and managing work for the *Impress* than she claimed in her autobiography. There is a letter written to her cousin, Marian Whitney, in which she states, "I send you with this some copies of *The Impress*, our W.P.A. paper. . . . I edit it, write most of it with my own fair hand, and attend to the business management also—an arduous task this last. It takes most of my

not write a good story every week, much less buy one. So I instituted a series of 'Studies in Style,'" offering readers an "avowed imitation" of well-established authors and asking them to guess the source. Also, she wrote essays on "Everyday Ethical Problems." They expressed her "hope for a clear and scientifically based system of ethics, which shall be capable of proof and illustration, like any other science"; but they also expressed her affinity for quite pragmatic rules: "Let your New Year's resolutions be few—one good one thoroughly carried out is better than five failures." Finally, Charlotte used *Impress* columns to explain some of her feminist convictions, though usually rather mildly. "Do women dress to please men?" she asked. "What do women want with all this excessive attractiveness?" What they need is stronger bodies and "freer muscular activity." The coming "change in woman's dress must be preceded by a change in her activity."

Articles on dress reform, suffrage, household economics, and the kindergarten movement, reports on women's club activities, the Woman's Congress, and WCTU campaigns—all these identified the *Impress* as a "woman's paper." But it was also a protest journal in a larger sense, the editors insisted. It was a "woman's paper in so far as women are human," but it was also dedicated to the "ideal of human brotherhood," which to Helen and Charlotte meant essentially the Populist-Nationalist ideal. Responding to whispers that the magazine might be too radical for certain PCWPA faint-hearted souls, the editors simply stated that the Populists currently seemed to have a monopoly on truth: "Some anxious member queries whether the Populist leaning of the Impress is the idea of the association [the PCWPA] or the editor. Said member should read the current magazines freely and see how general has been the Populist color in these later issues. Populism, dear member, is a large present movement, noticed at length by wise political observers, and reviewed in proper season by the Impress as part of current literature. Should another party rise on American soil, from as wide a foundation, strike root as quickly and grow as fast, the Impress will review it at equal lengths."

Without further to-do, the *Impress* editors proceeded to develop the Populist line: to report on current Populist meetings, to acclaim

---

time, and so far has brought in no money, but it's good for the Association, good for the best interests of the state, good for women, and, if I should make it 'pay' would be good for me. Even as it as it has taught me lots" (Charlotte Perkins Stetson to Marian Whitney, March 19, 1894, VCL).

the progress of labor organizations, to applaud protest heroes—Eugene Debs, Hamlin Garland, Jacob Riis, Edward Bellamy, Henry Demarest Lloyd—and to damn the corruption, fraud, and conspiracy of political tycoons. Grover Cleveland's position on currency was discussed this way: "The conspiracy marches on!" Cleveland's policies would "inevitably . . . place the commerce and industry of the country, absolutely at the mercy of a combination of money mongers."

Governmental chiselers, industrial monopolists, unbridled money mongers—these were the *Impress* villains: "seventy-one percent of the wealth of the United States is owned by nine percent of the families, while twenty-nine percent of the wealth is all that falls to ninety-one percent of the population." And statistics must be viewed in human terms. "Nearly two million children are employed in American mines, mills, factories and shops or stores: about a tenth of the nation's working population robbed of childhood, stunted, starved, prematurely aged and worn out." Or again: "Fifty thousand school children in London go to school habitually hungry. But the School Board is concerned chiefly with theological issues." One editorial quipped that Andrew Carnegie had reduced "the wages of his employees twenty percent" and enhanced his personal prestige by giving "$50,000 out of his increased profits to a public library." Another suggested that the Rothschild family had "built a hospital but first . . . made the poor to fill it." And finally (paraphrasing the words of one of Charlotte's current mentors, Stanford economist Edward A. Ross*): "Today there are more than two thousand millionaires in the country and the billionaire will appear in the near future, while among the masses thousands are constantly on the verge of starvation."

The *Impress* reflected, then, the diverse left-wing perspectives of its diverse left-wing friends, PCWPA associates, socialist and labor

* Only temporarily was Edward Ross a "Stanford economist." He was best known for his work in sociology at the University of Wisconsin. He wrote, "I met annually with economists and shared in their discussions until the founding of the American Sociology Society in 1903 gave me a chance to hobnob with Sociologists." In 1906, he began teaching at the University of Wisconsin, serving as the chairman of the sociology department there from 1929–1937.

Ross was also a personal friend of Charlotte's. He wrote, she "was a dear intimate of ours. She was the most brilliant woman I have known and had the most beautiful head I ever laid eyes on" (Edward Alsworth Ross, *Seventy Years of It: An Autobiography of Edward Alsworth Ross* [New York: Appleton-Century, 1936], pp. 56–60).

activists, and Charles Lummis and his *Land of Sunshine* colleagues. Also, it reflected the views of some "new school" academics, some "scientific muckrakers," economists, and sociologists connected with nearby Stanford University, and some academics from other universities as well (particularly Johns Hopkins, Chicago, and Wisconsin). At least some academic institutions were tolerating rebels, and David Starr Jordan, the president of Stanford, was certainly among them. A close family friend of impresario Charles Lummis, Jordan wrote for the *Land of Sunshine* magazine, supported *Impress* efforts, lectured at socialist-oriented meetings, and, philosophically as well as pragmatically, promoted a flexible, humanistic, community approach to learning.

One of Charlotte's early contacts with Jordan and some of the young Stanford faculty, may have come during her three-day visit to the campus in mid-March 1894. She wrote, "Drop in on President Jordan. He invites me to lecture there, . . . afternoon tea is given in my honor." Several days later she travelled back to Oakland from San Francisco: "By great good fortune President Jordan goes up too, and I talk with him most eagerly all the way up. My objections disappear—he has a great active honest open mind; I like him." The next month she went back to Stanford to give her lecture, stayed with Earl Barnes and his family, lunched with the Jordans, had "quite a reception in the evening," and this—she may have gloated just a bit—without any university-conferred credentials.

Another member of the Stanford faculty Charlotte met at about this time was the attractive six-and-a-half-foot-tall economist Edward Ross—crusader for free silver, for trade unionism, for Populist-Progressive causes. Probably she got to know him through Helen Campbell. For one thing, both Helen Campbell and Edward Ross were former students of Wisconsin economist Richard Ely, founder of the American Economic Association, and a leading proponent of the "new school of political economy." For another, they both promoted Ely's academically "seditious" views: that current inequalities were ethically unjust and economically unsound; that economic theory should be responsive to human needs; that academics should and could make pragmatic proposals for progressive social change. Edward Ross and Helen Campbell, then, had parallel political perspectives, mutual friends, and, to some extent at least, corresponding intellectual achievements as economists, lecturers, writers, and teachers, but with some differences. Ross, having received his Ph.D. under Ely's supervision at Johns Hopkins, had secured a teaching post at Stanford. Helen Campbell, having received Ely's blessing, but not a Ph.D., while studying with him at Wisconsin, had secured the *Impress* post—unstable, short-lived, and unremunerative. Subsequently, both Helen Campbell and Edward Ross were invited to teach at the University of Wisconsin, again with Ely's backing. But while Ross stayed there over twenty years, Helen Campbell gave only two lectures courses—"Social Science" and "Household Science"—just after leaving her *Impress* work in 1895. Well-respected publications notwithstanding, she was never offered the permanent Wisconsin academic post she apparently hoped for and to some extent expected.

However serious the affront, the fact remains that both Charlotte and Helen were having some influence on certain academic institutions in ways which reflected national trends toward more acceptance of women in the professions, toward more academic involvement in political reform, and toward a "revolt against formalism" in learning. Left-wing academics joined left-wing political activists in fighting *for* a more experimental, politically inspired education, and *against* conservative pundits, whose politics as well as educational philosophy they scorned. For instance, in the San Francisco area, Stanford scholars bragged about their homespun manners and Populist convictions, scoffed at Berkeley high-brow profs with a bit of reverse snobbism, and acclaimed David Jordan's Populist intent. Jordan wrote:

> It is not brick and mortar, books and laboratories that make a university. These are its vegetative organs. Its spirit is given by its teachers. It is not what is their fame, what their degrees, what have they published, but *what can they do*? . . . The best teacher, other things being equal, is the one most human. The ultimate end of education is the regulation of human conduct. Its justification is the building up of an enlightened common sense. It is to help make right action possible and prevalent that the university exists.

The association of academics with radicals in San Francisco was only a local manifestation of what was in fact a national phenomenon with John Dewey at its head. Just recently appointed chairman of the department of philosophy, psychology, and education at the University of Chicago (disciplines were not as specialized in 1894), John Dewey was immersed in the reform campaigns of Jane Addams and her Hull House friends—organizers, writers, radicals of all descriptions. Dewey's educational philosophy parallelled his political concerns. Problems of poverty, urbanization, trade unionism, immigration—these were central issues in his fight for educational reform, his attack against excessively rigid and formal learning, his demand that learning serve as a reformer's tool. With optimism as well as analytic verve, he argued that the teacher should encourage people's cooperative and humanistic impulses, stimulate their innate capacity for creative and socially progressive work, and inspire them to apply scientific methods to the problems of human life. In short, the teacher should undermine the "scandalous" separation of reason from moral value.

That kind of thinking suited Charlotte exactly. She would always stay on the fringes of academia. But she was well-read enough, intellectual and political enough, and also close enough to academic renegades—Ross, Jordan, Barnes, and later John Dewey as well*—to formulate some astute, sometimes fiery, educational proclamations of her own. Moreover, since she'd been exposed for years to her father's jibes against the universities (also she had no job at stake†) sharp quips came easily. Conservative academics had made of teaching a "dreary narrow hide-bound monotonous profession," she scoffed, "hampered by Ideas that were not only mummies, but fossils." The more absurd such intellectual conservatives could be made to look, the better; they were just as baneful as any other status-quo supporting sorts. Comfortably secure in their elite ivory-tower positions, unconcerned about and unaware of the "old-time wail" from "crowded street, from boundless hill and vale," they cultivated "knowledge for the sole purpose of teaching it to others—that they may teach it to others—forever and ever, none of this knowledge ever touching earth as it were. . . . It merely flows on from mind to mind, like endless generations of unborn children."‡

Such quips aside, Charlotte was in fact promoting educational perspectives which many 1890s dissenters shared: Conservative academic institutions were responsible for perpetuating human suffering rather than responding to human needs. They socialized people to accept inequities rather than push for change. They used schools for class advantage, for glorifying the "high and mighty,"

* It is certain that Charlotte read at least portions of Dewey's work, and it is very likely that she met and talked with him while visiting Jane Addams at Hull House. John Dewey, interestingly enough, was almost exactly the same age as Charlotte.

† Other radicals had a good deal less immunity. For instance, Edward Ross was fired from Stanford, seven of his colleagues felt compelled to resign in protest, and progressive scholars all across the country found that a fight for academic freedom often simultaneously involved fighting for their jobs.

‡ This quotation and others in the concluding chapters of this book are taken from Charlotte's later writings on the assumption that she held (or was developing) such views in the mid-1890s.

and for teaching everyone else to accept inferiority as a result of nature. They taught students to conform rather than rebel, absorb rather than express, and memorize rather than think. John Dewey wrote, "When the whole civilized world is giving its energies to the meaning and value of justice and democracy, it is intolerably academic that those interested in ethics should have to be content with conceptions already worked out." As a basis of progressive education, he encouraged pragmatic learning, experimentation, and action-oriented knowledge.

Charlotte's educational goals were similar: to teach students to use their "own power—to observe, deduce, and act accordingly." Naturally, conservatives would try to stop them. Once students begin to use their "precious mental capacities," they inevitably threaten the hallowed institutions where pompous pundits ply their trade. But good teachers—socialist-oriented ones, that is—should be delighted. They should stop the fear-motivated kind of learning, the "nerve-exhausting treadmill," the "mere transmission of what people used to believe." They should abolish the grading system, which leads to dull indifference, and eliminate examinations, which, like "stomach pumps," call for regurgitated truths. Competitive education simply reflects the contemporary "combat theory of life," Charlotte wrote, "the same old 'Vae Victic,' the same down-turned thumbs for the vanquished." Once the "young mind" is "set free to find out what is to be known," education can be for life, not death.

* * *

Charlotte's sardonic blasts against universities reflected goals many other Populist-Progressives shared—to challenge paternalism in the name of fraternalism, to use learning to promote the brotherhood of man. Still, since feminist issues seemed to her so critically important, yet so alien to many academics and left-wing males, the women's movement continued to occupy most of Charlotte's time. She hobnobbed with male intellectuals more than she used to, but she still felt more comfortable, probably more useful, with women —local associates and national celebrities as well.

In California, 1894–1895, the place to find these women was at the statewide annual Woman's Congresses, in Golden Gate Hall, on Sutter Street in San Francisco. Suffragists and feminists, professionals, aspiring professionals, and housewives, local and national women's movement leaders—over 2,000 women attended these congresses. One of Charlotte's projects was to help to plan them, working out general logistics and hospitality arrangements, organizing speakers' schedules, writing and conferring with preceptors themselves. These Woman's Congresses were to be the high-points of Charlotte's California political career.

Purportedly, the Woman's Congresses were not meant to be politically offensive, that is, reformist or radical, suffragist or feminist. Instead, ostensibly, the object was to interest "women in matters which tend to improve moral and social conditions." Or, as one writer nobly put it, "These congresses bring women together in great numbers, not for religion, not for reform, not for entertainment, but to study together the questions of the day, that they may better understand and do their real work in the world. To see and hear each other, to listen to papers from the platform and answers from the floor, to know what others are thinking and doing—it makes life richer and wiser and sweeter, and builds up the womanhood of the State."

The Woman's Congress lecture topics also sometimes sounded innocent enough. "Woman and the affairs of the world as they affect and are affected by her," was the general theme of 1894. If sessions on "Elementary Education" and "Higher Education" were relatively quiet, others on "Economics and Industry," "Civil Reform," and "Social Reform" provided occasion for rather heated Populist debates. At least some of the controversy may have been triggered by Charlotte and her friends: Dr. Kellog Lane spoke on "Social Purity," Adeline Knapp on the problems of unemployed women, Helen Campbell on the "General Conditions of Working Women and Children," and Charlotte on "What Socialism Is."

In 1895, the planners decided that the Woman's Congress of that year would be "devoted to the study and discussion of the Home, in its deepest and widest relations." Helen Campbell spoke on "Skilled Labor or Domestic Service," Dr. Kellog Lane on "City Mothers," Susan B. Anthony on "The Relation of the Home to Education," and Dr. Anna Howard Shaw on "The Educational Influence of Home Life on Men and Women." With these women in the lead, the congress of that year was both strident and rebellious. Susan B. Anthony, national suffragist campaigner, charismatic, forceful, and defiant, probably set the tone.*

* Although these statements of Susan B. Anthony and Dr. Anna Shaw were not given at the 1895 Woman's Congress, but in the 1900s, they are nonetheless representative of the kind of speeches Anthony and Shaw often made on their countless cross-country suffragist campaigns.

> My friends, what is a man's idea of womanliness? It is to have a manner which pleases him—quiet, deferential, submissive, approaching him as a subject does a master? He wants no self-assertion on our part, no defiance, no vehement arraignment of him as a robber and a criminal. While the grand motto, "Resistance to tyrants is obedience to God," has echoed and re-echoed around the globe; . . . while every right achieved by the oppressed has been wrung from tyrants by force; while the darkest page on human history is the outrages on women—shall men still tell us to be patient, persuasive, womanly?

Dr. Anna Howard Shaw may have voiced similar views, only a bit more quiescently:

> The assumption that women have neither discernment nor judgment and that any man is superior in all the qualities that make for strength, stability and sanity to any woman, simply because he is a man and she is a woman, is still altogether too common. The time has come when women must question themselves to learn how far they are personally responsible for this almost universal disrespect and then set about changing it.

That, of course, was precisely what many women wanted—to shed their fears, their passivity, their deferential stance, to expose men's arrogance and reject men's power in the home. Charlotte would later offer some sophisticated theoretical analyses of goals such as these, but at the 1895 Woman's Congress she may have been content with some brief though poignant comments. Cooking, sewing, nursing, washing, caring for children, house-cleaning—"not only do we undertake to have all these labors performed in one house, but by one person." Woman was not even marginally "prepared for her herculean tasks (Hercules was never required to perform twelve labors *all at once*!)." Why should women face such impossible burdens? "Why is that which is so palpably false of a man held to be true of a woman? 'Because men and women are different!' will be stoutly replied. Of course they are different—in sex, *but not in humanity*. In every human quality and power they are alike; and the right service of the home, the right care and training of the child, call for human qualities and powers, not merely for sex-distinctions." Just consider "what any human business would be in which there was no faintest possibility of choice, of exceptional ability, of division of labor." In any other business you would hardly combine the "Restaurant and Laundry," the "Bakery and Bath-house," the "Kindergarten and Carpet-Cleaning Establishment." And yet "we carry on all these contradictory trades in one small building, and also live in it." "No men, with practical sense and trained minds, would put up for a week with the inchoate mass of wasted efforts in the home; and when women have the same trained minds and practical sense, they will not put up with it much longer. . . . If each man did for himself the work he expects of his woman, there would be no wealth in the world; only millions and millions of poor tired men, sweeping, dusting, scrubbing, cleaning, serving, mending, cooking, washing, ironing—and dying for lack of food." In fact, "if all men kept house too, there would be no human world."

These were not Charlotte's words in 1895. They are quotations from her later writings. But whatever variations on these themes she offered at the Woman's Congress, even the San Francisco *Examiner* noticed that women were impressed: "It was the American wife who was put under the scalpel. Charlotte Perkins Stetson told her that the cherished belief in woman's instinctive sense of beauty was a pleasant fairy tale." Even the home was not beautiful, and the "American wife took it all good-humoredly, even humorously. She laughed aloud. She liked the picture and she recognized it." In fact, women seemed eager to share such views, and to acknowledge restive feelings they had been harboring. This congress was the "most marvelous gathering I ever saw," Dr. Anna Howard Shaw said. Another woman, remembering times when "the very word 'suffrage' was uttered almost with bated breath, [when] blackguards of the press . . . reviled and insulted its advocates," urged readers to appreciate how remarkable the congress had been: "those packed audiences listening with breathless attention and the words of the noble women whose names were once a by-word and scorn among them. . . . In point of numbers, interest, and enthusiasm, there has been nothing like these meetings in the history of the city."

The California Woman's Congress was a stirring event to be sure —politically, intellectually, emotionally. An organizational coup for local women, it also provided an exhilarating sense of alliance with the national women's movement. Suffrage was finally becoming "respectable," which, for many, meant that middle-class "ladies" were involved—writers, professionals, women of substantial means. Women's issues could no longer be considered the province of eccentrics and crackpots. No longer could women be politically and intellectually ignored—or so, for a time, it seemed. Even the national mood was changing, as were women's organizational techniques. Small local women's groups had been proliferating for years, but by the mid-1890s there was more unity among them, more purpose, more drive. Their national associations showed it. For instance, both the National Council of Women and the General Federation of Women's Clubs were coordinating women's efforts, facilitating communication, linking women's clubs together, encouraging local autonomy, but at the same time ensuring women's involvement with reform and suffrage goals. Most importantly, the two main branches of the suffrage movement had just been reunited; on non-suffrage issues they agreed to disagree. They had been divided since 1869, Elizabeth Cady Stanton and the New York-based National Woman Suffrage Association voicing more diverse and radical political concerns through a journal called the *Revolution*; Lucy Stone, Henry Blackwell, and the Boston-based American Woman Suffrage Association confining their writings in the *Woman's Journal* to more exclusively women-oriented goals.* By 1890, the two groups had merged into the National American Woman Suffrage Association (NAWSA). They held national suffrage conventions, inspired countless state conclaves (of which the California Woman's Congress was one), sponsored speaking tours for their celebrities, barnstormed the country with their suffrage "propaganda," and began to make—or so it seemed—substantial dents in the male political preserve. Two states had already granted women suffrage by 1893. Two more would do so by 1896. And although no more states would concede women voting power until 1910, an irreversible commitment to suffrage had been made within the women's movement itself.

Symbolically as well as politically, the suffrage issue provided many women with a rallying point: an organizational purpose, a common focus for their anger, a compelling human rights appeal.†

* The National Woman Suffrage Association was more concerned with inequities resulting from class and race than was the American Woman Suffrage Association (referred to as National and American hereafter). Also, the National's approach to women's issues was more diverse: they hammered more frequently on questions of divorce, unemployment, wage discrimination, and anti-woman religious views. A born and bred New England Beecher, Charlotte's early contacts had been with the relatively more conservative Boston-based American Suffrage group.

† Historians have pointed out, however, that many suffragists of the post-1890 period were more conservative than their abolitionist-suffragist counterparts earlier in the century. To the extent that turn-of-the-century women advocated suffrage for middle-class whites only, the "human rights" appeal was seriously compromised.

As Charlotte later put it, for women there was no "democracy at all, but a semi-democracy, one half of the race ruling over the other half;" and "never yet has any special class been raised up to do the governing of other people and proved competent to do it with a dispassionate appreciation of other people's needs." But from Charlotte's viewpoint (and that of countless other women too), it was a mistake to view suffrage as a panacea. She was disturbed by those who did: "Are we not somewhat blinded by the undeniable truth that the use of the ballot is the best way to promote progress and so fail to see that there are others? . . . After all, the ballot is not an end—it is a means."

That was precisely how many women felt: suffrage was just one of many issues to consider. Marriage, motherhood, divorce, domestic strain and isolation, economic disability, child labor, unemployment and wage discrimination, factory work and tough urban living—these were among the issues women debated at the California Woman's Congress, and all across the country. Although Charlotte merely joined them, she often posed such questions so incisively, so poignantly (and so rarely spoke of suffrage issues by themselves), that already many of her co-workers recognized her potential as a defiant, compelling, and charismatic radical. As one contemporary put it, "Your work will be a help to the movement. What you ask for is so much worse than what we ask for that they will give us the ballot to stave off further demands."

* * *

Whether Charlotte heard such backhanded compliments in 1895 or later, it was probably the praise and prodding of women at the California Woman's Congress that encouraged her to seek a larger political arena, to become a feminist "at large." Susan B. Anthony urged her to, and Jane Addams even invited her to stay at Hull House for a while. Charlotte liked the idea of encountering and debating national celebrities, of attending national and international conventions, of meeting with and lecturing to countless women's groups; and, since a network of hospitality for suffrage speakers was already fairly well established, she would have the chance to stay in (and observe) the homes of different women across the country. Besides, Helen Campbell would be leaving the *Impress* to teach several courses at the University of Wisconsin and most of Charlotte's friends and family—Katharine, Grace and Walter, Frederick, Martha Lane—were living in the East. As to money, California lecturing paid little, the *Impress* paid even less, so she must have figured that bigger audiences would mean better pay.

Charlotte was attracted by the prospects and confident of having reasonable success. Californians had praised her work; "Similar Cases" had been reprinted and acclaimed all across the country; and *In This Our World* had received mostly positive reviews. William Dean Howells wrote her:

> I am ashamed not to have said long ago how much pleasure we have all taken in your book of poems. They are the wittiest and wisest things that have been written this many a long day and year. You are not only the prophetess of the new [era?] . . . but you speak with a tongue like a two edged sword. I rejoice in your gift fearfully and wonder how much more you will do with it. I can see how far and deep you have thought about the things at hand; and I have my bourgeois moments when I could have wished you for success's sake to have been less frank. But of course you know that you stand in your own way! . . . My wife joins me in thanking you for your book.

It was also encouraging to know that the *Impress*, though it did not pay, was reasonably well respected. Charlotte's uncle Edward Everett Hale supported it of course: "I think The Impress is brilliantly written, and full of good things." And Stanford president David Starr Jordan also gave his blessings: "I, of course, find the paper bright, fresh and clean; it contains much matter of value, especially to the women of the coast." Even the local press supported it, at least according to quotations *Impress* authors chose to print. The San Francisco *Report* noted: "The Impress is a model of typographical elegance, and in literary tone is admirable. The publishers may readily count on public support." Other papers praised the "intellectual" content, the "bright, brave and independent writing," as well as the "bright and radical personality of Charlotte Perkins Stetson." The San Francisco *Town Talk* stated: "The editorials in The Impress are bright, forcible and full of purpose. . . . It is the only journal of its kind published on this coast and should receive the support of every thinker and literary worker—whether amateur or professional." The San Francisco *Star* was also encouraging: "When we state that [the *Impress*] editor is Mrs. Charlotte Perkins Stetson, of this city, it should be sufficient alone to ensure its favorable reception."

Since the *Impress* had been well received, in some circles at least, and since both Helen Campbell and Charlotte had enjoyed rather favorable reactions to their other California efforts, it seems likely that both decided to leave San Francisco partly because they had prospects for more satisfying kinds of work. But there were other less pleasant reasons for leaving which Charlotte found easier to describe. In fact, so miserable were her memories of her last few California years—the hellish decision about Katharine, the bouts of depression, the public criticism—that her autobiographical account sometimes makes it sound as though she had had no support or self-confidence at all. For whatever reasons, she implied that the failure of the *Impress* had inspired in her a sense of ignominious defeat. When Helen Campbell began making "inquiries as to the rather surprising lack of support," this is what she heard:

> "Nothing that Mrs. Stetson does can succeed here," and, "You risk your own reputation in joining her." Said a prominent woman doctor, "Yes, it is a brilliant paper, an interesting paper, but after what Mrs. Stetson printed in her first issue no self-respecting woman could have it on her table."

"And what was the marvel of iniquity which so shocked as immoral a city as the country owned?" Charlotte continued. "It was a beautiful poem, of a nobly religious tendency—by Grace Ellery Channing! Such was the San Francisco mind."

In point of fact, there were many "marvels of iniquity" for California matrons to abhor: the separation and divorce, imaginatively embellished by the San Francisco *Examiner*; the separation from Kate; the *menage á trois* at 1004 Powell Street, to say nothing of lingering suspicions about former liaisons in Oakland. Of course, the publication of Grace Channing's poetry had not helped the situation, nor had warm praise of Walter's *Impress* border designs and illustrations. San Franciscans could accept hate-filled separations, apparently, more readily than genial or thoughtful ones. As Charlotte put it, "continued friendship was what the pure-minded San Franciscans could not endure. Hatred, jealousy, preliminary misdemeanors, they would have accepted as quite natural." But that she, Grace, and Walter "should have remained in friendly correspondence, with mutual understanding, affection and respect, through these hard years, was to them incomprehensible."

Most "scandalous" of all, however, was Charlotte's failure as a mother, not just because she had sent Kate East, but also because she had been so permissive, so irresponsible. Charlotte wrote, "Discipline and obedience were still the ideal then. My ideas looked to them not only wrong in principle, but impracticable." For instance, neighbors "thought it scandalous that I should so frankly teach her the simple facts of sex." One of the "good mamas" said she would admit that "Katharine was the best child she ever saw, but it was no credit to her mother—she would have ruined any other child by her system!" So for her eccentric discipline techniques, for sending Kate away—"For all this I was harshly blamed, accused of 'neglecting my child,'" for being an "unnatural mother." *

Occasional autobiographical exaggerations notwithstanding, Charlotte had in fact "affronted public opinion hopelessly by this 'unnatural motherhood.'" † Charles Lummis had "sprung valiantly" to the rescue; Mary Austin had been "for her" all the way, and "for the freedom from convention that left her the right to care for her child in what seemed the best way to her." But public condemnations grated nonetheless, so much so that Charlotte used the *Impress* pages for redress. In early 1895, less than a year after Katharine left, Charlotte published a short story entitled "An Unnatural Mother." She may have written it partly to bolster her spirits; but she also wrote it to urge other women to align themselves against the narrow-minded San Francisco gossip mongers, and to defy, once again, the conventional sentimental codes of motherhood.

In the story, the "unnatural mother" was not "like other girls —she never seemed to care for dress and company and things girls naturally do." Disapprovingly, "the worthy matrons" of the town "shook their heads and prophesied no good of a girl who was 'queer.'" When she married they said, "We all thought she never would, but she did. And a mighty queer husband she got too. He was an artist or something like that—made pictures for the magazines

* Several years later, Charlotte was even criticized by California "friends." While visiting Pasadena in 1898, she wrote to Houghton Gilman, "I've just made a fool of myself. Went across the way to call on some old neighbors, and—I foolishly supposed—friends, and got violently slapped in the face. . . . I've been so used of late to friendship—affection—honor; that it was painfully surprising. It's the "unnatural mother" racket—the same old thing. Dear, dear! I haven't felt so uncomfortable inside for ever so long. The same kind of bitter swollen chockey[?] feeling I had when reproved as a child" (to Houghton Gilman, Dec. 25, 1898, AESL).

† Charlotte apparently affronted at least one historian as well. In his Ph.D. dissertation William Doyle wrote, "It is possible that she was popular because she was addressing other frustrated women who were also unsuccessful mothers." Her writing at times "undoubtedly was partly an attempt to justify her own conduct as wife and mother." See William Doyle, "Charlotte Perkins Gilman and the Cycle of Feminist Reform," unpub. Ph.D. diss., University of California, Berkeley, 1960, pp. 211–212.

and such as that." The woman of the story has a daughter, "'and it was just shockin' to see how she neglected that child from the beginnin'. She never seemed to have no maternal feelin' at all! . . . Why,'—here the speaker's voice sank to a horrified hush, 'she never made no baby clo'se for it! Not a single sock.'" Somewhat melodramatically, the protagonist is killed after saving the lives of friends and neighbors by warning them of a flash flood. Yet despite her "noble sacrifice," the neighbors respond: "It's a mercy to the child that she lost her mother, I do believe! How she ever survived that kind of treatment beats all!" One younger woman modestly protests: "It does seem to me that she did her duty." But another answers quickly, "I'm ashamed of you! . . . No mother ought to leave her child, whatever happens. . . . A mother's duty is to her own child! . . . She was an unnatural mother!"

Charlotte of course had different feelings about her unconventional behavior, alternately penitent and defiant, but either way she felt compelled to emphasize her suffering. The fictional "unnatural mother" was the martyred heroine. The real "unnatural mother" was morbidly depressed. In a poem, "The Duty Farthest," published just several months before, she again seemed to ask her *Impress* readers for sympathy-provoked respect.

THE DUTY FARTHEST

Finding myself unfit to serve my own,
I left them, sadly, and went forth alone
    Unto the world where all things wait to do—
    The harvest ripe—the laborers but few.
I studied long to find the wisest way,
Proved every step, worked on day after day
    In those great common tasks that need us all
    But where one's own part is so brief and small
That no one counts the labor one has spent
Yet I could see good grow and was content.
    Ah me! I sighed, for home served lovingly.
    And lo! the whole round world was home to me.

Charlotte's recent years in Oakland and San Francisco had brought moments of success and confidence, but also disappointments: loneliness, scandal, debt, and several painful setbacks in her love-life as well. Even the relationship with "Mother Campbell" had its ups and downs—whether because of work pressure, financial strains, Paul Tyner complications, whatever. In any case, Charlotte assumed (albeit somewhat proudly) that once again the fault was her own. Several years later she wrote, "What I maintain is that I am 'trying' and 'wearing' to live with permanently." Even "dear Mother Campbell found me something of a trial only three winters ago! You see I am very busy 'being me'—it is engrossing, and I expect other people to be as interested in the process as I am, and they are not!"

Chapter Twelve

Mothers of Civilization, Daughter of Eve 1896

As she began her train ride East Charlotte reminded herself, "Be glad! Be free!" After all, she was a strong independent woman, a reformer with a mission and message at last. Sometimes bitter-sweet reflections marred the newfound sense of freedom: "I don't wear well," she would grumble. Or "I'm not good to live with." But she was more proud than ashamed of the temperamental restlessness she thought would ultimately bring success: "I said many years ago—in girlhood—that I was like a big bird without legs. As long as I could fly it was all right; but when I attempted to sit down it was painful and awkward." For years she had dreamed of being on the move. As early as 1881, she had described to Martha Luther the "mounting ambition" which seemed to drive her, the "wild delicious sense of boundless strength," the desire to become "*myself as a self* you know, not merely as a woman or that useful animal a wife and mother." Now, in 1896, she finally had her chance. She had more direction, and more freedom to pursue opportunities that would further her political-professional success. She would attend her first National Woman's Suffrage Convention in Washington, visit Jane Addams at Hull House in Chicago, participate in the International Socialist and Labor Congress in London—and those would only be the highlights. She would move from local to national and international political arenas, meet with social and intellectual reformers, and expand her reputation in the process. She would compare current goals and strategies, clarify her own ideals, and confirm preferences and prejudices that fit her needs and marked her times. She was still learning, still looking for her place, still questioning: How to be a suffrage worker who found the suffrage issue unappealing? a reformer who found organizational pragmatic politics a bore? an egalitarian who preferred WASPS to immigrants, celebrities to commoners, and middle-class pleasantries to ghetto noise and dirt?

At this point, Charlotte felt confused as well as excited by the challenge of her "wander years." She was confronting disparate philosophies and political perspectives when she wanted unifying truths, and she was pursuing round-robin friendships when she wanted the security of home-based love. When someone asked her, "Don't you feel very much at sea?" she responded simply. "I do. Like a sea-gull at sea."

* * *

One of Charlotte's first stops as an itinerant lecturer was the twenty-eighth annual Woman's Suffrage Convention, held in Washington, D.C., in January 1896.* As a representative of the Pacific Coast Woman's Congress and the California Suffrage Association, she would address the convention, preach in local churches, testify before the House Judiciary Committee, and, momentarily at least, join other delegates—138 from all but thirteen of the states and territories—in fighting for the cause of woman's suffrage.

While political unity was the goal of some women at the 1896 convention, fractious debate was the predictable reality. As president of the National American Woman Suffrage Association, Susan B. Anthony was the presiding officer, coaxing, soothing nerves, but also raising hackles by saying what she thought; and as author of the *Woman's Bible*, Elizabeth Cady Stanton was a central focus of debate. Under the circumstances, it was somehow telling that Susan B. Anthony opened the convention not with a prayer but with a précis: "The thought that brought us here twenty-eight years ago was that, if the Federal Constitution could be invoked to protect black men in the right to vote, the same great authority could be invoked to protect women. The question has been urged upon every Congress since 1869."

* Charlotte's first stop was Jane Addams' Hull House in Chicago, where she would stay for about three months. Because most of the visit (Feb. through March 1896) was after the Washington convention, however, the Hull House experiences are discussed later in this chapter.

Understandably, patience was wearing thin, old guard leaders were tiring, and suffrage appeals in the name of justice had a ring of *déjà vu*. As Elizabeth Cady Stanton put it, even the most eloquent "logical arguments," ones based on "justice, science, morals and religion, are all as light as air in the balance with old theories, creeds, codes and customs." Yet, whereas to Stanton the solution was to broaden the campaign and fight for women's rights across the board, to others the solution was to consolidate the effort and demand one right alone. To them, the purpose of the convention was to "build a great organization based upon the one platform of the enfranchisement of women." They wanted to organize more efficiently, update tactics, raise more money, excite each other with progress reports (the admission of Utah as a state with full suffrage for women, for instance), and determine exactly what needed to be done. It was time to discard, even repudiate, extraneous debate and to precipitate political action.

To many of the delegates, however, the women's issue was much broader than the right to vote, and convention responsibilities more substantial than devising plans to win it. As a suffrage worker only casually interested in suffrage, Charlotte was, of course, among these delegates. She had come to the convention looking for new arguments, not old ones, for theories, not pragmatic plans, for controversy as well as politically expedient debate. From her point of view, the two convention experiences that were most exciting—apart from the celebrity whirl itself—were the sessions on Stanton's *Woman's Bible* and the contacts with sociologist Lester Ward. Both piqued her curiosity and helped shape her thought.

To Charlotte, the debate on the *Woman's Bible* was a highlight of the convention, and she relished the fight. Many other delegates saw it, however, as an unfortunate distraction. After all, just by organizing on suffrage alone, women were showing their mettle. They were stepping out of their homes and into the public arena, jeers and opposition notwithstanding. They were rebels against prevailing codes of passivity and piety. They were developing an effective sophisticated political campaign. Leave religious issues alone, some of the delegates warned, and concentrate on suffrage. To far too many people, Stanton's *Woman's Bible* would seem threatening, even blasphemous. It would alienate church fathers with their money and influence, pious ladies with their wagging tongues, friends and foes alike. Supporters would stop working, block the flow of funds, squash the chance of victory. True, Elizabeth Cady Stanton had written the *Woman's Bible* as an individual statement, not a suffrage tract. But it was up to the convention delegates to say so, to tell the world publicly and formally that her views were not theirs. After a heated debate they passed a resolution disavowing any responsibility for the *Woman's Bible*. The vote was fifty-three to forty-one.

Some of the delegates considered the decision a shocking mistake. As Susan B. Anthony put it, Elizabeth Cady Stanton had "stood for half a century as the acknowledged leader of progressive thought and demand in regard to all matters pertaining to the absolute freedom of women." Stanton had helped initiate the Seneca Falls Convention back in 1848, served as the president of the National Woman Suffrage Association for twenty-one years, launched and co-edited the militant woman's paper, the *Revolution*, and emerged, some argued, as one of the most incisive and inspiring theorists in the nineteenth-century women's movement in America. Of course Stanton had not confined her interest to the vote. She had fought against the institution of slavery, against prevailing marriage and divorce laws, against economic injustices, and now against orthodox religious views which degraded women. Her determination to confront questions of class and race as well as sex, to integrate political, religious, and economic concerns, had inspired middle-class women to feel political compassion for groups unlike themselves and to coordinate their efforts with broadly based movements for reform. Now suffrage delegates were, in effect, denouncing her and narrowing their political concerns. In Susan B. Anthony's view, the *Woman's Bible* resolution not only gave a sharp rebuff to a long-established leader, but also provided strong evidence of a turn toward narrow-minded bigotry: "I shall be pained beyond expression if the delegates here are so narrow and illiberal as to adopt this resolution. . . . Ten women educated into the practice of liberal principles would be a stronger force than 10,000 organized on a platform of intolerance and bigotry."

It was a strange sort of intolerance at that: suffragists were disavowing a *Woman's Bible* that gave religious arguments and Biblical support for the view that women are the equals of men. For many suffragists—publicly anyway—it was one thing to fight for voting power, but quite another matter to suggest that they address their prayers to God the Mother. The *Woman's Bible* begins with a quotation from Genesis:

> So God created man in his *own* image, in the image of God created he him; male and female created he them. [Genesis 1:27]

Elizabeth Cady Stanton commented:

> The first step in the elevation of woman to her true position, as an equal factor in human progress, is the cultivation of the

> religious sentiment in regard to her dignity and equality, the recognition by the rising generation of an ideal Heavenly Mother, to whom their prayers should be addressed, as well as to a Father.
>
> If language has any meaning, we have in these texts a plain declaration of the existence of the feminine element in the Godhead, equal in power and glory with the masculine. The Heavenly Mother and Father!

Whether Charlotte had heard or read such views before, she liked them now, spoke forcefully in support of Stanton's book, and joined the delegates voting against the *Woman's Bible* resolution. Stanton had hit a responsive chord. Her Biblical analysis, her female-affirming religious imagery, her condemnation of male religious power—these had inspired Charlotte to sit up, take notice, and consider such questions herself. It was many years later that Charlotte would publish her own analogous (albeit less impressive) religious tract, *His Religion and Hers*, some twenty-seven years later, in fact. But her belief in the value of God the Mother imagery reflected Stanton's influence, as did her decision to consider the feminist implications of religious faith.

Charlotte already recognized that women's deferential stance and derogatory self-perceptions could be attributed to their isolation in the home, their political and economic impotence, their intellectual privation. Perhaps spurious religious imagery was another cause. There were plenty of reasons women should be proud; surely God the Mother images could be used to support them: as mothers, women loved and served and sacrificed; as mothers, they were more cooperative and compassionate, less competitive and violent than men. These were rather standard nineteenth-century arguments; what was needed was religious faith to buttress them. In some respects then, a loving God the Mother image was a religious corollary of the secular mother ideal, which many suffragists supported, and which evolutionary theorists (particularly Lester Ward) tried to ground in fact.

In her religious-political writings, Charlotte tried to integrate Reform Darwinist evolutionary "knowledge" with contemporary feminist ideals, and thereby explain the origin of human faith. Naturally as well as historically, man was the warrior-hunter for whom "death was the impressive crisis"; when he created God, it was a "proud, angry, jealous, vengeful" one much like himself. Woman, by contrast, was the "eternal Mother," naturally as well as historically. For her, birth was the "impressive crisis." If only she had had the opportunity to create or imagine God. Woman's God would have been "the Life-giver, the Teacher, the Provider, the Protector," not only equal to man's God of Battles, but "much more in line with social progress." Man's religion had taught people to submit and obey. It negated their power to think, to confront life situations realistically and constructively. It encouraged intolerance and fatalism. Perhaps most importantly, it "implanted in our minds the concept of our essential unworthiness." All this, Charlotte concluded, could be traced "to that one cause, to the monopolization of religious thought and doctrines and the establishment of creeds by men alone."

Whether Elizabeth Cady Stanton's *Woman's Bible* had directly or indirectly inspired her, Charlotte came to view religious imagery as a critical issue of the feminist campaign. Like many later feminists, she regarded a self-affirming spiritual vision not only as a needed antidote to androcentric power, but also as a precondition for women's self-respect. At times she spoke of God as a Force, the *Process* of being, creating, becoming, what Mary Daly calls God the Verb.* And like Elizabeth Gould Davis, Charlotte urged women not only to reject derogatory lessons of patriarchal theology, history, and anthropology, but, even more importantly, to find strength and inspiration from a faith in the matriarchal primal force.†

If Charlotte's religious writings were at least partly inspired by her experiences at the 1896 Woman's Suffrage Convention, some of her secular "woman-as-superior" arguments may have been inspired there as well. For at this convention she not only heard the debate on Stanton's *Woman's Bible,* she also dined and debated with evolutionary theorist Lester Ward. To some extent at least, Stanton and Ward had overlapping messages. Stanton provided religious documentation of the Heavenly Mother ideal. Lester Ward provided evolutionary documentation of its secular counterpart: eternal mother nourishes and sustains the race. Uncle of her Stanford friend Edward Ross, friend of Helen Campbell and Richard Ely, sociologist, paleontologist, psychologist, and "handsome and virile" gentleman besides, Lester Ward became Charlotte's lifelong mentor. Perhaps it was because Ward argued—scientifically—that "the grandest fact in nature is woman."

Charlotte's first meeting with Lester Ward occurred on the opening day of the suffrage convention. She wrote in her diary, "Prof. Lester Ward calls, enjoyed seeing him." January 26: "Preach A.M. in People's Church. Prof. Ward and wife come to hear me. . . . Sup and

* See Mary Daly, *Beyond God the Father* (Boston: Beacon Press, 1973).
† See Elizabeth Gould Davis, *The First Sex* (New York: Putnam, 1971).

spend evening with Prof. Ward. Beautiful rich day." January 28: "Speak before the Judiciary Committee of the House of Representatives. Attend afternoon session and fight the resolution disavowing the 'Woman's Bible.' It went through, hotly and closely contested. Go to a reception given me by Prof. and Mrs. Ward."

It greatly pleased Charlotte not only that Ward had initiated their contact, but also that he had made it clear how impressed he was with her work, particularly with her 1890 poem "Similar Cases." For good reason, he remarked, "Similar Cases" had been "read by nearly everybody in this country": it was "the most telling answer that has ever been made" to Darwinian conservatives. So pleased had he been that he had quoted it in a public lecture, tried adding a stanza of his own—in "faint imitation," he modestly remarked—and then personally requested a copy of *In This Our World*. Not surprisingly, Charlotte was elated. She wrote him, "I am exceedingly proud that you should want my book. . . . Nothing has ever pleased me more in relation to my work, than the use which I heard you made of 'Similar Cases' in a recent lecture." Several days before the suffrage convention Ward wrote her saying that he hoped to give a reception in her honor while she was staying in Washington: "Please say you will [come] and confer a great pleasure on your appreciative admirer."

The admiration was mutual. In fact, for Charlotte the 1896 convention marked the beginning of a lifelong hero-worshipping respect. Ward was "quite the greatest man I have ever known," she wrote. "He was an outstanding leader in Sociology, familiar with many sciences, and his Gynaecocentric Theory, first set forth in a *Forum* article in 1888, is the greatest single contribution to the world's thought since Evolution."* When asked what works she had relied on when writing *Women and Economics* two years later, she

* Lester Ward has been regarded as one of the "giants of nineteenth-century sociology," as the "Father of Sociology," or, as one writer put it, "the American Aristotle." (See particularly Samuel Chugerman, *Lester F. Ward, the American Aristotle: A Summary and Interpretation of His Sociology* [Durham, N.C.: Duke University Press, 1939].) Though Ward may well deserve his reputation, biographer Clifford Scott explains it a bit more circumstantially: "The eventual publication of *Dynamic Sociology* in 1883 became the first American work with 'sociology' in its title; and Ward, willy-nilly, had become a 'founding father' of the newborn discipline in North America" (Clifford Scott, *Lester Frank Ward* [Boston: Twayne, 1976], p. 106). Charlotte would eventually view herself as a sociologist, and share some of Ward's views on social problems generally, but that will be discussed in another context.

answered that there had been only two: Geddes and Thompson's *Evolution of Sex*, and an 1888 *Forum* article by Lester Ward.† Dedicating a later work, *Man-Made World* (1911), to Ward "in honor and gratitude for his gynaecocentric theory of life," she wrote: "nothing more important to humanity has been advanced since the theory of evolution, and nothing more important to women has ever been given to the world."

†Charlotte was considerably more casual about the influence of Ward's theories in her private letters than she would be publicly. On June 5, 1897, just before starting on *Women and Economics*, she wrote Houghton Gilman, "If you like heavy reading why don't you sail in on Ward's 'Dynamic Sociology' and 'Psychic Factors of Civilization' etc. Perhaps you have. I mean to read 'em when my head is equal to it." July 10, 1897: "Ward I don't fully know—I wish I did—but I have looked at his chapters that touch women and this is not his position at all." July 22, 1897: "I wrote the Brood Mare long before I read Ward. I've been thinking those things—and much more—for many years." Sept. 18, 1897: "Is there no place you can find Ward? You seem to have very hard luck with him. Haven't you any professional friends of whom you could borrow the thing? I am quite anxious to know if I ought to read it before publishing my book" (AESL).

Despite Charlotte's efforts to popularize Ward's gynaecocentric theory in her own writings, Ward only reluctantly acknowledged her support, and that after considerable prodding. In his *Pure Sociology* (1903) he complained that his gynaecocentric theory had not received the attention it deserved: "The idea has not wholly escaped the human mind, but it is never presented in any systematic way" (Lester F. Ward, *Pure Sociology: A Treatise on the Origin and Spontaneous Development of Society* [New York: Augustus M. Kelley, 1970; 1st pub., 1903], p. 298). On reading that, Charlotte was "grieved" (annoyed?): "I was a little grieved in reading your statement that no one had taken up your theory—for I had stoutly defended it in my book Women and Economics. But perhaps you didn't consider that book of sufficient importance to mention. Or perhaps you haven't read it." Still, she chose to praise him. "[I] hasten to tell you that I am no[w] well enough to read your books; with no more pleasure than before, for I always enjoyed them; but with an ease I have not known for twenty years!" (June 30, 1903, JHL). Or again the next year, "I grow stronger from year to year and my head clears up, I read your work with more and more pleasure" (Jan. 20, 1904, JHL). Several years later, however, Charlotte still wanted more acknowledgment from Ward than he had been willing to give. She complained that he must not have noticed her "explicit reference" to his *Forum* article, "because you say that to your knowledge no one has ever advocated your theory; and I've done my humble best at it, in lecture book and article these many years" (to Lester Ward, March 15, 1906, JHL). The next year, she decided to send him a copy of her book, *Human Work*. "I truly think it will

Lester Ward first presented his gynaecocentric theory in a lecture to an 1888 dinner meeting in Washington, D.C. (with Elizabeth Cady Stanton in attendance), and then in an article, entitled "Our Better Halves," published the same year. The central tenet of his argument was that "in the economy of organic nature the female sex is primary, and the male a secondary element": "Woman is the unchanging trunk of the great genealogic tree; while man, with all his vaunted superiority, is but a branch, a grafted scion, as it were." That did not mean, Ward explained, that contemporary women could claim equality with men. A combination of environmental and hereditary forces had crushed their talents and temporarily destroyed many of their naturally productive inclinations. But it did mean that opportunities should be opened to women across the board, and that they should be allowed and encouraged to resume their natural role in the vanguard of reform: "it becomes clear that it must be from the steady advance of woman rather than from the uncertain fluctuations of man that the sure and solid progress of the future is to come."

Lester Ward offered just the kind of arguments many suffragists made themselves—women deserved power and respect because of (not despite) their nurturing "feminine instincts"—and he was marshalling "scientific" arguments to prove them. Evolutionary study showed, Ward argued, that the first function of the male was

---

interest you to see how largely I have followed the same lines of thought you have covered so much more fully." She still complimented him, but also let him know, perhaps because of her irritation, that his influence may not have been so great after all: "one of the big pleasures long deferred is reading your books. So far—except for the Phylogenic forces in Pure Sociology; and some of the shorter papers—. . . I have not really read you at all" (to Lester Ward, Jan. 2, 1907, JHL). This time Ward responded—and in a hurry: "I have read your book. I could hear my own voice all the time. But, of course, it was not an echo. It is pitched much higher than I can strike and differs also entirely in *timbre*. I have always told Dr. Ross that all I could do was to block out the statue from the slab in rough strokes, and he must finish it up. Now you come along and touch it up with a fine-pointed chisel" (Ward to Gilman, Feb. 9, 1907, AESL). Ward may have been pleased (or was he annoyed?) that at least through Charlotte's work his ideas would reach a far wider audience than they otherwise would have. *Women and Economics* would go through seven printings over a twenty-five–year period, and be translated into at least six languages, whereas one of Ward's best-known works, *Dynamic Sociology* (1883), sold no more than five hundred copies in ten years.

simply to enable the female to reproduce, and that the female, the primary source of life, was therefore of superior importance. True, males had changed more through time than females had. They had become stronger and larger than women. But that was because selection of a mate was "naturally" a female function, because of survival laws, not because nature intended the male to dominate or protect the female. The male had to adapt to win the female's favor and had to fight battles with other males in order to reproduce. Consider evolutionary evidence, Ward continued. In almost all species below the vertebrates in evolutionary development—bees, moths, and mosquitoes, for example—"female superiority is well-nigh universal." Certain spider species manifest the point unmistakably: "the miniature lover is often seized and devoured during his courtship by the gigantic object of his affections." What then happened to the human male and female power balance? It was "widely abnormal," Ward decided; it was "warped, and strained by a long line of curious influences": Men won the right to select their mates (the female's natural right), began choosing women for beauty not brains, and subverted nature's intent. Hereditary influences enfeebled women; male dominance crippled them still more; and women thus lost equality with men. If reformers would study the laws of nature, they would understand their imperative responsibility to support the cause of suffrage.

Given the Reform Darwinist perspective she had adopted anyway, to say nothing of "eternal mother" images that had an understandable appeal, it is not surprising that Charlotte found Ward's gynaecocentric theory not only intellectually persuasive, but delightfully expedient as well. She admired his scholarly research, his calm, cool, scientific denunciation of the spurious power and bogus self-conceit of men. She liked his evolutionary illustrations: the "tiny male" common spider, for instance, "tremblingly achieves his one brief purpose, and is then eaten up by his mate." And she liked his sex-selection theory, his notion that nature planned for woman to be decision-maker in the courting game. (That suited Charlotte temperamentally as well as theoretically.) After all, she quipped with a characteristic humor Ward could rarely match, "if there is a race between males for a mate—the swiftest gets her first; but if one male is chasing a number of females he gets the slowest first." Charlotte sometimes varied the language slightly, but essentially she left Ward's arguments intact—and no wonder. Despite the usual self-righteous justifications for male dominance and power, Ward finally had proved how transient men really were, how dispensable, how second-rate.

Ward's gynaecocentric theory supported what suffragists were asking for and more. In many of her later books and articles, Charlotte would try to popularize it and explain its implications: that women were naturally altruistic, nurturant, and thus superior to innately aggressive warlike men; that they were the originators of socially useful work, since it was "founded in mother love, in the anti-selfish instinct of reproduction"; that they could have governed the world more effectively than men since their natural inclinations were to love, serve, and cooperate; and that their "influence would have been toward more peaceful industrial development" rather than toward the competitive violent methods men preferred. In fact, Charlotte would later write,

> The whole feminine attitude toward life differs essentially from the masculine, because of [woman's] superior adaptation to the service of others, her rich fund of surplus energy for such service. Her philosophy will so differ, her religion must so differ, and her conduct, based on natural impulses, justified by philosophy and ennobled by religion, will change our social economics at the very roots.

Female superiority, Charlotte asserted, was a fact of Natural Law.

> The innate, underlying difference [between the sexes] is one of principle. On the one hand, the principle of struggle, conflict, and competition, the results of which make our "economic problems." On the other, the principle of growth, of culture, of applying services and nourishment in order to produce improvement.

For any number of reasons, Ward's work pleased suffragists enormously. He offered evolutionary arguments to support the suffrage cause, and scholarly reasons why women should enjoy self-respect and expand their power. Moreover, unwittingly and indirectly, he seemed to endorse, even promote, some anti-male convictions which many suffragists, at times at least, liked asserting anyway. (Occasionally Charlotte's anger was so intense that some of her writings sound like myopic anti-male assaults.) No wonder Ward managed to attract a whole "group of women admirers." His celebration of women's sexual superiority was not original (though his hypothesis concerning its evolutionary base was); most certainly, he had not "initiated" the feminist fight;* but his kind of intellectual

* Samuel Chugerman wrote, Ward's "studies in sex were therefore only a prelude to the feminist movement which his writings initiated in America"

ammunition was just what many suffragists thought they needed; and his generous personal attention (such as the private reception he gave to Charlotte) was just what many women liked. In fact, as one biographer notes, "more than half of the letters he received came from married and from professional women who for various reasons, but especially because of his free thought and women's rights views, found him interesting company." Suffragist Emily Palmer Cape, one of his "unconventional" devotees for several years (and later his personal biographer), said much the same thing: "Women wanted to meet him to express their admiration, I might almost say adoration. He found it difficult to respond to some of the letters he received without hurting the feelings of the writers."

Whatever the reasons underlying Charlotte's adoration-admiration for Lester Ward, she had some credentials that could win his respect—a feminist charisma, an incisive message, a vivacious style—at least if a *Woman's Journal* report can be believed.

> Those of us who have for years admired Mrs. Stetson's remarkably bright poems were delighted to meet her, and to find her even more interesting than her writings. She is still a young woman, tall, lithe and graceful, with fine dark eyes, and spirit and originality flashing from her at every turn like light from a diamond. She read several poems to the convention, made an address one evening and preached twice on Sunday; and the delegates followed her around, as iron filings follow a magnet.

Not everyone responded quite so positively, of course. Nellie Bly reported for the New York *World*:

> Charlotte Perkins Stetson has a long name, a large vocabulary, a good voice, an attractive smile and magnificent thinking faculties. . . . I never remember hearing a more pleasant speaker. . . . As I looked at Mrs. Stetson I mourned. She has an ideal

---

(Chugerman, *Lester Ward, the American Aristotle*, p. 378). William Doyle also perhaps credited Ward with more than he deserves. Doyle believed that he could demonstrate that "every word Gilman wrote on the woman question was informed by the sociology of Lester Frank Ward." Or again, "To place her views in their proper position in the history of ideas, however, it must be stressed that her approach to the woman question was derived essentially from Lester Ward" (William Doyle, "Charlotte Perkins Gilman and the Cycle of Feminist Reform" [Ph.D. diss., University of California, Berkeley, 1960], pp. 175, 161). It would seem that the intellectual as well as the experiential bases of Charlotte's views (and of those of her contemporaries) were so rich and varied that Lester Ward should be viewed as only one important influence among them.

> face, clear cut and poetic. She parts her hair and combs it smoothly back over her ears, which is a very becoming style for her.
>
> But oh, how she dresses! I fear she is daft on dress reform or some other abomination. She was decidedly wider at the waist than she was below it. We did not need to be told that she was corsetless, and, I fear, petticoatless! Her suit was a mud-colored cloth, . . . and the short scant skirt hung every way but pretty.*

Attractive, magnificent, or daft, Charlotte marched up to the convention platform willing to display more about her brand of nonconformity than just her corsetless shape. Ward's type of argument was probably the one most commonly heard at the convention, and Charlotte reassured her audience that she agreed with it.† But in her own message to the delegates she chose to take a somewhat different line, one that was less flattering to women, less concerned with a mother's loving instinct than with a mother's need for activity beyond the home: "We have heard much of the superior moral sense of women. It is superior in spots but not as a whole." Women are too involved in "purely personal relations," she complained, to be either morally sensitive or politically alert; they are simply too involved in mothering. A woman "will not neglect" her children if she does outside work; she "will be better to them and of more worth as a mother." Her responsibility is to step out into the world, and serve children everywhere. Just "because you began in the cradle is no reason why you should always stay there. Because charity begins at home is no reason why it should stop there, and because woman's first place is at home is no reason why her last and only place should be there."

That was the same idea Charlotte had been developing for years, that mothering did not require sacrificing humanness. For even

* Nellie Bly was discouraged by the appearance of Alice Stone Blackwell also: "She wore a broadcloth coat of a style fully six years old. It was double-breasted, with two rows of enormous pearl buttons. And her black cashmere skirt was shocking. I never saw a skirt hang worse or one more badly made. It was short and showed her common-sense shoes, which was far from inspiring to those in front. And I judged without hesitation that Alice Stone Blackwell does not believe in containing the waist or encouraging any one part of the human body to a greater development than the other" (New York *World*, Jan. 26, 1896).

† This is not meant to imply that suffrage delegates discussed Ward or his evolutionary theories directly, but rather that most of them accepted the nurturant woman assumptions which he was trying scientifically to prove.

while she was acclaiming Ward's theories and celebrating women's genius, she was still concerned with the fact of sexual inequality, the causes of "artificial" differences, and the human right to live, love, and work in freedom. As she later put it,

> That is masculine which belongs to the male sex as such; to any and all males *without regard to species*. . . . That is feminine which belongs to the female sex, as such, *without regard to species*. . . . That is human which belongs to the human species as such, *without regard to sex*. . . . Every step of social development, every art, craft, and science . . . these have to do with humanity, as such, and have nothing to do with sex.

Still, there was a strange sort of inconsistency in Charlotte's view. At times, she emphasized biological differences and celebrated, even worshipped, the eternal mother. At other times, she acclaimed human equality and condemned the spurious effects of mothering responsibilities. To some extent, this was a reflection of what one writer calls "an intellectual milieu permeated by evolutionism and Lamarckianism." It was characteristic of Reform Darwinians to blur the distinction between acquired and inherited traits, and "to assume the physical inheritance of quite complex mental characteristics which we understand today in cultural terms." Also, it was a reflection of inconsistencies apparent in suffragist debates for years. But in Charlotte's case, and doubtless in other women's as well, there were personal worries hovering in the not-too-distant background to confuse matters even more. How to pursue work without missing Kate or feeling guilty about her own mothering responsibilities? How to experience love and keep independence intact? How to squash doubts and insecurities and establish herself as a strong-minded woman? As she later put it to Houghton Gilman, "for all the invulnerable self-belief and self-reliance which I have to have to live at all, you've no idea how small potatoes I think of myself at heart. . . . Being so many times marked n.g. [no good] it has sort of stuck in." Doubtless a lot of other women felt that way as well; perhaps they too sometimes used "eternal mother" theories to combat their fears and affirm their self-respect.

* * *

After leaving California, Charlotte had gone first to Chicago, where she had established Jane Addams' Hull House as her base, and then to Washington, D.C., for the suffrage convention. Now she was ready to enjoy a longer stay at Hull House, at the corner of Halsted and Polk Streets, Chicago. "It stood, quite literally, between drink and death; at one side of the house was an undertaker's; and at the other, a saloon." In a neighborhood of immigrants and poorly paid workers, of tenement houses, of sweatshops, of churches and saloons—7 of one, 255 of the other—it was not the kind of setting most native middle-class Americans found appealing or familiar. "Greeks slaughtered sheep in basements, Italian women and children sorted rags collected from the city dump, in courtyards thick with babies and vermin; bakers made bread in dirty holes under the sidewalks, and distributed it to their neighbors." This, as one writer viewed it, was Ward Nineteen, the setting Jane Addams had chosen for her home, Hull House. Built as a private dwelling some thirty years before by Charles J. Hull, then used as a factory, later a furniture house, by 1896 Hull House had become a "City of Refuge" and a social settlement training ground. The goals, the co-founders stated, were to "provide a center for a higher civic and social life; to institute and maintain educational and philanthropic enterprises; and to investigate and improve the conditions in the industrial districts of Chicago."

If the stated goals seem idealistic and vague, the number and scope of the programs the co-founders sponsored were extraordinary. Hull House was teeming with activity. Jane Addams, Florence Kelley, Julia Lathrop, and their cohorts responded like an emergency corps to countless crisis situations all over West Side Chicago. They washed newborns, laid out the dead, served as midwives, nursed the sick, cared for toddlers, provided meals and housing for the unemployed, and discussed social theories, but always in the context of here-and-now pragmatic needs. By 1896, Hull House was conducting almost forty different kinds of programs. It was at one and the same time an unemployment agency, a battered-wives shelter, a day care center, a lending library, a recreational site, a cooking school, a savings bank, and a reformers' meeting ground. In 1891, Hull House workers had started a public kitchen to provide cheap, healthy, carry-out meals for housewives and workers. The same year they helped to sponsor the "Jane Club," a cooperative self-supporting boarding club for factory girls. By 1896, they had organized boys' clubs, girls' clubs, college extension courses and summer-school programs, kindergarten training classes, workshops for arts, crafts, music, and theater. Social work had not even been established as a profession when Jane Addams and her friends began Hull House in 1889. They were shaping the needed precedents themselves, gaining experience the hard way, and then teaching by example instead of by how-to-do-it books. Almost fifty-thousand visitors came to Hull

House during the first year alone. By the second year, the average was a steady two thousand a week. Some came only for a brief perusal, others, like Charlotte, for a three-month stay.

Hull House was regarded as a "City of Refuge" not only for those oppressed by poverty and miserable social conditions, but for those oppressed "by riches and responsibilities" as well. Moral enthusiasts, reformers, and radicals, "prime ministers of Europe, philosophers of all doctrines, labor leaders and great capitalists and unpopular poets and popular novelists and shabby exiles from half the kingdoms of the world visited Hull House." They ran the house together, cooperatively tackled the practical work that needed to be done, and theorized, wrote, and argued about almost everything. Long, heated debates at breakfast would be renewed at dinner time, at scores of meetings, at informal get-togethers all over the house. There were plenty of strong characters, heady ideals, and massive disagreements. But there were also important unifying goals—to give pragmatic meaning to contemporary theories of social democracy, and to do so with the most highly qualified and best-trained minds around. John Dewey led discussions on educational techniques, for example, Richard Ely on national economic trends, Governor Altgeld on state and local politics, while Jane Addams served as inspiration, listening, prodding, picking brains. Celebrities shared their expertise, neighbors and residents their know-how and experience, co-founders their coordinating skills, their aspirations, and their remarkably divergent talents.

Hull House was fired and engineered largely by women, and, some said, by as brilliant a corps of women as could have been found: Ellen Gates Starr, organizer of wage-earning women, and activist in the Women's Trade Union League; Alice Hamilton, doctor and scientist, later to become professor of pathology at the Women's Medical College of Northwestern, and then professor of industrial medicine at Harvard; Julia Lathrop, pioneer sociology researcher and major inspiration behind *Hull-House Maps and Papers*, and later the head of the United States Children's Bureau; Florence Kelley, first English translator of Friedrich Engels' *The Condition of the Working Class in England*, a lawyer, a chief factory inspector for the state of Illinois, and an organizer for the National Consumer's League for over thirty years. As one writer put it, these women "did more than any other group of women in American History to improve the position of women in general, and social legislation and administration in particular."

Best known of the Hull House heroines, of course, was Jane Addams, the principal executive director, perhaps the central driving force. She was, as Charlotte put it, "a truly great woman. Her mind had more 'floor space' in it than any other I have known. She could set a subject down, unprejudiced, and walk all around it, allowing for every one's point of view." She was a creative thinker and efficient organizer. She put supporters to work on Hull House concerns: tenement house conditions, child labor, factory inspection, compulsory school attendance, labor organization, juvenile courts, minimum-wage and maximum-hour legislation. In her books, *Democracy and Social Ethics* (1902), for example, and *Twenty Years at Hull House* (1910), she explained her reform philosophy. In her countless administrative posts she tried to make it work. She was the first woman president of the National Conference of Charities and Correction, the first head of the National Federation of Settlements, the first vice-president of the National American Woman Suffrage Association, a chairperson of the Woman's Peace Party, a president of the International Congress for Women at the Hague, and first president of the Woman's International League for Peace and Freedom.

While Jane Addams was probably best known as a pragmatic social reformer, Charlotte as a radical feminist theorist, the two women had much in common. In fact, there were some striking parallels in their lives as well as in their thought. Both were born in 1860 and died in 1935. Both grew up in a society where women's opportunities outside the home were few, and in a middle-class environment which encouraged introspection, high idealism, and moral fervor. During their early twenties, both suffered disabling illnesses, convalesced in Dr. S. Weir Mitchell's hospital (Jane Addams for a spinal ailment, Charlotte for melancholia), and both strained restlessly to design some kind of work to suit their needs. Jane Addams founded Hull House when she was twenty-nine, roughly the same time Charlotte published her first successful works. And in the 1890s, before their national reputations were well established, they each admired the other's work. When Charlotte realized that Houghton Gilman had never even heard of Jane Addams, she wrote him: "Not know Jane Addams! . . . Jane Addams of Hull House! Not know Hull House & Jane Addams. Behold the deficiencies of a college education. Why Jane Addams is one of the noblest, wisest, strongest, sweetest women in the world, and Hull House is the greatest 'Social Settlement' in America. Get 'Hull House Maps and Papers' right off, and improve your mind."

Most of Jane Addams' concerns were ones Charlotte already shared through contacts with California Nationalists, but the experience in the Chicago ghetto gave them a more solid base. In fact, that was one of Jane Addams' goals, to prod middle-class reformers to smell and feel and experience city life themselves. Charlotte found the atmosphere unforgettable, and, no doubt, depressing as well: "The loathly river flowed sluggishly near by, thick and ill-smelling; Goose Island lay black in the slow stream. Everywhere a heavy dinginess; low, dark brick factories and gloomy wooden dwellings often below the level of the street; foul plank sidewalks, rotten and full of holes; black mud underfoot, damp soot drifting steadily down over everything."

Despite the heavy gloominess—Charlotte's gloomy spirits as well as the gloomy streets—she was excited by her Hull House friends. They were not spinning abstract theories, or moralizing or pining either. John Dewey talked about learning by doing, Jane Addams about learning from life itself. Like some of the Stanford professors she had known, they were pragmatic teachers, not erudite ones, and expressed the kind of common-sense views she shared. "No one needs special knowledge to see the basic needs of mere physical humanity," she would write, "as good air, good food, good housing, good clothing, good education, and good employment," and obviously it was the responsibility of society to provide them.

There are such splendid things to do—
So wonderful—so many!
But one can't do the things he feels
Till after he has had his meals,
And got his clothes on—can he? . . .

The Powers of human life today
Are wonderful and many
But when a man's whole strength must pour
To stave the wolf off from the door
He can't do much else—can he?

While the Hull House experience seemed to strengthen Charlotte's pro-labor stance, it may well have unleashed some of her anger as well, or at least given it a better focus. Almost certainly there was personal animus festering behind her political campaigns; reformers (or human beings generally) often find social outlets for anger which has a private base, and the effects can be productive. In any case, from Charlotte's viewpoint, poverty and needless human suffering were reason enough to harbor bitterness, and hope for progressive social change reason enough to express it: This "civilized nation" has plenty of resources, but it misuses and wastes them; it produces disease instead of happiness, universal poverty instead of universal wealth. So many people say poverty is a "spur" to strengthen character. It is not, Charlotte would quip. It is a "deadly anaesthetic" wrecking hearts and brains and bodies instead. Reformers have every reason to feel "bitter."

> People who are awake to a world-old, world-wide, hideous injustice; people who realize that to this very hour men are driven to death, women to shame as well as death (having always their own special miseries to bear as well as the common load of humanity) and even children, little children, to premature death from under-nourishment and overwork—such people are apt to become bitter.

In Charlotte's view, such bitterness had a constructive purpose: Hull House friends were devising schemes to combat injustice and finding ways to implement them. And although Charlotte would not become a settlement-house organizer herself, the least she could do was support their work through lecturing and writing. In point of fact, many of the practical reform suggestions that appeared in her later utopian novels, how-to-do-it articles, and even larger analytic works, were ones originally designed and tested in Ward Nineteen. She would recast them to be sure; sometimes her proposals were more radical, more uncompromising, some would say bizarre (e.g., kitchenless houses). But for the most part, they parallelled Hull House projects she had seen. She suggested, for instance, that professionals be hired to prepare healthy family meals; Hull House had a public kitchen. She advocated professionally run day-care centers to free women for outside work; Hull House already had established one. She wrote about cooperative living and training centers for working-class women and domestic servants; Hull House had a cooking school, a kindergarten training program, a self-supporting cooperative for women factory workers. She wanted community recreational centers; Hull House provided one—with music, art, a library, a theater, a gymnasium, the works. She wrote articles on "Making Towns Fit to Live In," on problems of city dirt, political graft and corruption, unemployment, child labor—all major Hull House concerns.

These, in fact, were concerns of social feminists generally, and show the kind of social philosophy many of them shared. As Progressives, most believed that problems of "industrial anarchy" should be approached by pragmatic, peaceful, well-planned programs; that social justice required a hard-headed commitment to reason, legality, and common sense; that class conflict was counterproductive, and Marxist revolutionary theories wrong. Like most Progressives, both Charlotte and Jane Addams believed that more could be accomplished by understanding and cooperation than by warfare. Like most social feminists, they believed women's unique function was to love, serve, and keep the peace—whether in the home, the ward, or the world. Because of their nurturing instincts, what Jane Addams called their "moral energy," women could become "Mothers of Civilization." Perhaps, as one historian suggests, they too often viewed themselves as the "social charwomen" of the industrial system, trying to soften the blows of industrial exploitation with their domestic charm. But political compassion, which they called motherly compassion, nonetheless inspired these "Mothers of Civilization" to fight inequalities they thought were wrong, to devise and conduct pragmatic campaigns in the still largely male-controlled political arena, and thus make important contributions to the reformers' cause.

Charlotte approached her Hull House work just as she approached her mentor Lester Ward, by agreeing with such "nurturant mother" ideals even while they sometimes angered her, or made her feel depressed. It was difficult to glorify motherhood and, at the same time, fight against mothering responsibilities herself, or, on a more theoretical level, condemn the oppressive limitations which mothering typically entailed. As she would write some years later, "the human female, the world over, works at extra-maternal duties for hours enough to provide her with an independent living, and then is denied independence on the ground that motherhood prevents her working!"

Even at the outset then, Charlotte probably felt some disagreement with Jane Addams' social-feminist approach. Jane Addams worked on programs to help women with domestic responsibilities when necessity forced them to seek outside work. Charlotte thought such services should be used to eliminate women's domestic responsibilities entirely. True, Jane Addams worked with people for whom basic necessities—food, health, housing—were predominant concerns, Charlotte with those fortunate enough to hope for other things as well—satisfying work and economic independence, for instance. Yet Jane Addams' goal was to strengthen the family and celebrate the beauty of women's motherly service within it, while Charlotte attacked the patriarchal family as an oppressive institution in itself, indeed as a fundamental source of oppression in society at large. In the family, she would later write, there "is neither freedom nor equality. There is ownership throughout; the dominant father, the more or less subservient mother, the utterly dependent child." Thus with "eternal mother" imagery still hovering not too subtly in the background, she would come to believe that the emancipation of the "subservient" mother was a first-priority concern: "Nothing will conduce so much to the right growth of society in body and spirit as the progress of women from their prehistoric sex-bound egoism and familism to their rightful share and place in the vital processes of society."

Charlotte took a more radical stance than Jane Addams on the needs and rights of women, but not on every issue. For instance, Jane Addams would join the minority of reformers and radicals opposing American entry into the First World War, but Charlotte would spend her energies attacking German "homicidal mania" instead. Moreover, Jane Addams was among the few turn-of-the-century reformers who chose to live and work in immigrant neighborhoods and devote her energies to improving the immigrants' quality of life. For a time Charlotte tried to emulate her, but in later years chose to revile immigrants instead, and to preach the racist-ethnocentric credos more common to her generation. By the time of the war, Charlotte would conclude that America had "stuffed" itself "with the most ill-assorted and unassimilable mass of human material that ever was held together by artificial means," and that the invasion of foreigners would have to stop.

> Let us by all means welcome and help a steady stream of incoming new-made Americans; but let us, before it is too late, for the sake of those splendid visions of the past, and our own more splendid visions of the future, protect ourselves from such a stream of non-assimilable stuff as shall dilute and drown out the current of our life, and leave this country to be occupied by groups of different stock and traditions, drawing apart, preserving their own nationality, and making of our great land merely another Europe.

That was Charlotte's view of immigrants in 1915. If nothing else she was candid about it. But in the winter of 1896, she may have

* As late as 1903 Charlotte perhaps still had more understanding of minority rights than many suffragists. At the National American Woman's Suffrage Convention held in Washington, D.C. that year, she was one of the few delegates to oppose establishing educational qualifications for voting. Upper-class women often argued their natural superiority qualified them for the vote, whereas the inferiority of immigrants, the working class, and blacks justified exclusion. Charlotte disagreed. "Will the exclusion from suffrage educate and improve the illiterate masses more quickly than the use of it?" (*The History of Woman Suffrage*, vol. V, ed. Ida Husted Harper [New York: J. J. Little and Ives, 1922], 78). She felt people should have the vote to improve as well as to protect themselves.

been more tolerant, or at least was trying to be. She admired settlement-house workers enormously, and she probably wanted to admire neighborhood immigrant families as well. For instance, in one of her Hull House lectures she argued that the "'lower class' we so condemn as immigrants are healthier grafts upon our body politic than more highly specialized branches would be," and gave "facts to prove their rapid assumption of citizenship." In fact, so enthusiastic was Charlotte about the importance of Hull House work, that her first inclination was to become a settlement-house worker herself. She wrote, "Here was companionship, fellow feeling, friendly society. My verse was known and liked, new friends were made, there were lecture engagements, and presently I was asked to be the head of another settlement, on the North Side, in a place called 'Little Hell.'" Almost immediately she wrote Helen Campbell asking her to become the director instead, and suggesting that they work and live together there. Helen Campbell agreed. By February they had found two young Harvard men to join them, George Virtue and Hervey White, and had started making plans for a more permanent arrangement. After a long talk with "Mother Campbell," Charlotte wrote in her diary, "The settlement becomes sure and real for next year." Several days later: "Glorious days—the work very clear." By March 1896: "Brace up and write things out for myself—make plans etc. . . . Meeting of Trustees. They are willing we should go on with the work—raise money and spend it."

But the plans collapsed almost as soon as they were made. The settlement-house projects seemed challenging, the friends warm, yet something about the atmosphere—or Charlotte's psyche anyway—triggered another "grey fog" depression, a relapse of her earlier "mental illness." She felt too miserable even to be cordial, much less to pitch in and work. On March 14 she wrote, "Very bad day. Mother [Campbell] feels very badly about my behavior. I know that my behavior is my condition—that I am not well." The next day: "Am so bad that Mother sends me over to Dr. McCracken's. They take me in joyfully and keep me. Also they recognize that I am in a serious condition." March 16: "Sit down in office to talk to Dr. and weep dismally. It is really the beginning of melancholia. Am very weak—can hardly sit up—low appetite. Mind a heavy dark grey."

What caused the relapse? Facing the dull grey streets when she preferred open-spaced patrician ones? Trying to feel compassion when she felt animosity instead? Straining to believe what she thought she should? Those seem likely enough reasons, and common enough as well. A troubling mixture of depression, frustration, and anger occur so often as preferences interfere with stated goals, prejudice erodes reason, or feelings conflict with political convictions. She simply disliked the "flux of disconnected people" at Hull House, and the "noisome neighborhood," as well. She admired "wonderful Miss Addams handling it all so well and meeting the thousand calls upon her so gently and effectively—it is magnificent, but it tires me very much." *

Perhaps another problem was involved as well, again one not unique to Charlotte: trying to confine anger to political concerns when anger on the home front was so explosive. Whether it was anger against Martha, Walter, or Delle, against her mother for dying, against her father for deserting her, or against Katharine for having been born at all—whatever the reasons for the rage, the times she busied herself denying it were probably the times she felt most depressed, most desperate and lonely. In any case, Charlotte was pleased that the McCrackens had "rescued" her from "that black house in Little Hell": They "welcomed me in their own pleasant home on the south side, and the wife-and-mother doctor slept on the lounge downstairs and gave me her own bed, with her little girl in it. She well knew what it meant to me to have a child in my arms again, a little girl child, about the age of mine when I had her in Pasadena."

A fine predicament. Charlotte must have winced at the irony. She was telling mothers at least to supplement mothering responsibilities with outside work, yet here she was an independent mother too sick to work at all. She was pushing for the rights of women, yet regretted missing the experience most women said was central to their lives. A poem, "In Mother-Time," written just several weeks before the "Little Hell" illness suggests such thoughts were bothering her. In it, she spoke of women passing through "the years of holy maidenhood, with motherhood" as the goal; she spoke of "White-robed mothers, flower-crowned mothers, in the splendor of their youth," "In the grandeur of maturity and power." However sentimentally expressed, it was that "eternal mother" theme again, the one she had been hearing about all year: Elizabeth Cady Stanton's "Heavenly Mother," Lester Ward's "Mother of the Race," Jane Addams' "Mothers of Civilization" ideal.

Charlotte must have felt as though she were the "daughter of Eve" instead, or the "devil's daughter," as she had warned Martha

* The quotations of this paragraph are taken from letters written while Charlotte was visiting Jane Addams in 1900, not in 1896, the year of the first visit. I am assuming, however, that they reflect feelings she had all along.

years before. In 1881 she had told Martha, "the mother side of me is strong enough to make an interminable war between plain duties and inexpressible instincts. I should rage as I do now at confinement and steady work, and spend all my force in pushing two ways without getting anywhere." By 1896, she had freed herself from some of the emotional responsibilities for Katharine. Now she seemed to feel the need to free herself from other emotional ties as well. About a week before she left "Little Hell," and just about the time her depression was beginning, Charlotte wrote: "Things are a little thick. I am too close to people. My own work gets no attention. . . . I feel Mrs. Campbell too much. I think I feel Mr. Virtue too much. What should I do? My own life opens up duly in literature and lecturing. I should more fully follow these lines. I should see to it that I have more time alone. I must learn to maintain my own integrity even among others."

Chapter Thirteen

On the Celebrity Circuit 1896

CHARLOTTE'S characteristic approach to life was to seek comfort in moving on, breaking ties, and exploring new terrain. From April through July 1896, she travelled. She stopped for several brief visits at the settlement houses in Chicago; otherwise she arranged to deliver sermons and lectures where she could: Boston, Providence, Hartford, Kansas City, Topeka, Madison, Milwaukee, Detroit, Washington, Philadelphia, New York. On July 8, 1896, too depressed to remain settled, yet too full of energy to allow herself to rest, Charlotte set off for England to attend the International Socialist and Labor Congress. At first she intended to go as a socialist. Then she read the membership card, found she disagreed "with both theory and method as advanced by the followers of Marx," and decided to go as a delegate for the Alameda County Federation of Trades instead.

She left Chicago by train, went by boat from Toronto down the St. Lawrence, through the Thousand Islands and the rapids, leaving Montreal on the S.S. *Mongolian* for the hefty fee of fifty dollars. "The steamer was a 'whaleback' cattle-boat, one 'class,' pleasant people enough. Our bovine passengers grew steadily more perceptible as days passed, until the dining-room port-holes had to be closed, to keep them out, as it were."

After arriving in London, Charlotte's first heady introduction to the English political environment was through "A Great Peace Demonstration," which preceded the Socialist and Labor Congress, on July 26, 1896. It was an unforgettable experience—feeling the excitement of the enormous Hyde Park procession; rubbing shoulders with celebrities ("I was in one of the speaker's wagons, with August Bebel, Herbert Burroughs, and, as I remember, George Bernard Shaw"); proving her mettle through a "drenching rain" ("I was the last speaker on the last platform to stay out"); and being moved by the spirit and intent of the demonstration resolution, if not agreeing with everything it said. The resolution read in part:

> That this International Meeting of Workers (recognising that peace between the nations of the world is an essential foundation of International Brotherhood and human progress, and believing that wars are not desired by the peoples of the earth, but are caused by the greed and selfishness of the ruling and privileged classes with the single view to obtain the control of the markets of the world in their own interests and against all the real interests of the workers) hereby declares that between the workers of different nationalities there is absolutely no quarrel, and that their one common enemy is the capitalist and landlord class, and that the only way of preventing wars and ensuring peace is the abolition of the capitalist and landlord system of society in which wars have their root, and it therefore pledges itself to work for the only way in which that system can be overthrown—the socialisation of the means of production, distribution and exchange.

The resolution called further for universal suffrage (because "large numbers of working men and all working women do not possess the vote and cannot take part in political action"), for international arbitration of disputes rather than "the brutality of force of arms," and for the "establishment of an International Eight Hours Day for all workers."

Charlotte was elated not only by the ideas and demands of the congress, but also by the sense of common purpose, the contacts, the moods. She liked hearing the French socialist Jaurès, for example, with his "rising storm of eloquence" (though she "did not know a word he said"). She was fascinated by the Anarchists as well—Prince Kropotkin, Elisee Reclus, Louise Michel—"desperately earnest souls," she called them. And lastly, she enjoyed hobnobbing with the Fabians, "that group of intelligent, scientific, practical and efficient English Socialists" with their "knee-breeches, soft shirts, woolen hose and sandals."

The Fabians, it seems, attracted Charlotte most—their politics as well as their casual demeanor. Unlike some of the Marxist-Socialists she met at the congress, the Fabians were peaceful revolutionaries—in theory, in organizational policy, in personal style. They saw no need for violent political upheaval, or even for "revolutionary opposition to the main course of development." The socialist state was already on its way, they argued, through the force of evolution, and through the kind of pragmatic peaceful efforts Charlotte was accustomed to: arranging meetings, editing short-lived weekly papers, writing, speaking, articulating visions, dreaming dreams. To be sure, the Fabians were radical critics of contemporary society—inordinately effective and constructive ones. But they felt compelled to write a separate report for the Labor Congress nonetheless, making very clear their own commitment to peaceful social change: "The object of the Fabian Society is to persuade the English people to make their political constitution thoroughly democratic and so to socialize their industries as to make the livelihood of the people entirely independent of private Capitalism. . . . Democracy, as understood by the Fabian Society, means simply the control of the administration by freely elected representatives of the people." Only a peaceful democracy, they continued, would respond to the people's needs. Fabian resolutions called for equal opportunity and equal pay for men and women, the establishment of sanitary and safe working conditions, minimum-wage and maximum-hour regulations, universal suffrage, the abolishment of child labor, the nationalization and municipalization of industry—all preconditions, in their view, for the "complete abolition of the competitive system."

For Charlotte, the goals of the Fabians seemed practical, eminently reasonable, profoundly just: that the means of production and exchange be publicly controlled, that "each and every industry . . . change from an individualistic to a socialistic basis," that business "be managed and run in the interests of the whole community instead of in the interests of the present small class of private owners." As she liked to put it, competition "is no more part of the business than a combat between cooks is party of cooking." "Society is not somebody else dominating over us. Society is us—taking care of ourselves." The Fabians were right, Charlotte concluded, just as Edward Bellamy had been. For with "right economic belief and right action there would be no division of Producer and Consumer, no Leisure Class, no Working Class, no divided ranks of Capital and Labour. All would produce, all would consume; all would work and all would have leisure; all would share in the social capital and social labour,—both elements of social advantage." Thus the socialist state would be established naturally, without violence and bloodshed, and without class conflict as well. For the natural force called evolution would be "always pushing, pushing, upward and onward through a world of changing conditions. You can count on it. It is always there. It is 'the will to live,' and behind that is 'the will to improve.'" By definition, "life means progress."

It was views such as these, humorously, boldly, compassionately expressed in public lectures and published poems,* that gave Charlotte a foothold among intellectuals in England—socialists, feminists, and Fabians alike. She admired them all. William Morris, that "gray and glorious" thinker; May Morris Sparling, "a dear and lasting friend"; J. Ramsay MacDonald, "a handsome, brilliant young fellow"; Gertrude Roecliff, who treated Charlotte "like a sick princess"; Alfred Russel Wallace, "that world-renowned intellect"; Harriot Stanton Blatch, a "very advanced" feminist indeed—these were only some of the English politicos Charlotte singled out for consultation, debate, or sometimes a chess game or two.†

One of the more eccentric of Charlotte's Fabian acquaintances was Edward Carpenter, upper-class Cambridge University Fellow turned socialist, naturalist, vegetarian, sandal maker, and (according to some) prolific troublemaker besides. Like his close friends Havelock Ellis and Olive Schreiner (Charlotte's mentor since California days), Carpenter advanced the familiar Fabian views, and others also. He spoke of personal as well as political imperatives, of the need to improve the quality of social-sexual interactions as well as to satisfy basic economic needs. Make divorce and trial marriages easier, Carpenter demanded. Allow more joyous love, freer sex, and all "the wealth and variety of affectional possibilities." Abolish the perverse distinction between legitimate and illegitimate children. And in all love relationships be independent and free. To be sure, Carpenter sometimes enthusiastically applauded marriage; but his idea of a successful one was not quite of the usual sort.

> A marriage, so free, so spontaneous, that it would allow of wide excursions of the pair from each other, in common or even in separate objects of work and interest, and yet would hold them all the time in the bond of absolute sympathy, would by its very freedom be all the more poignantly attractive and by its

*When *In This Our World* was published in England by T. Fisher Unwin, it received positive reactions from the Fabians. Charlotte was particularly pleased that Beatrice Webb asked her to read some of the poems to a group of Fabians visiting together for a week-end, and that they had "listened attentively" (*The Living of Charlotte Perkins Gilman: An Autobiography* [New York: Harper & Row, 1975; 1st pub., 1935], p. 204).

†Charlotte wrote Lester Ward, "Stayed a few days with Alfred Russel Wallace and enjoyed it immensely. He arranged some lectures for me, and took the chair. I felt so small—to stand up and lecture before that great man" (to Lester Ward, Dec. 10, 1896, JHL). In her autobiography, she also men-

> very scope and breadth all the richer and more vital—would be in a sense indestructible; like the relation of two suns which, revolving in fluent and rebounding curves, only recede from each other in order to return again with renewed swiftness into close proximity—and which together blend their rays into the glory of one double star.

Carpenter's best-known work, *Love's Coming of Age*, was published in 1896, and it was in September of that year that Charlotte visited him at his country retreat near Sheffield. Her diary entry reads simply, "see Edward Carpenter . . . beautiful soul." Since he advocated views she shared, and elegantly defended her independent lifestyle in the process, Charlotte admired him a lot. Even in a letter written (a year or so later) to the man she would subsequently marry, Charlotte put Carpenter's books at the head of her list of recommended reading. "I think very highly of Carpenter's works on 'marriage' and 'sex love,'" she wrote Houghton Gilman, "more highly than of any I ever read on those lines. Read 'em carefully, and tell me what you think—some time—if you want to." Given Carpenter's association with 1890s free-love thinking, and her own inclinations along those lines as well, Charlotte's later autobiographical reflections sound dull, or perhaps we should say cautious: "Some [of the Fabians'] sandals were made by Edward Carpenter, who lived in a small cottage in the country, near a little brook which served as a bathtub, and 'Worked with his hands.' I was taken to see him, later, and he measured my feet and made me a pair of those strong leather sandals, still in working order."

Although circumspection must have motivated Charlotte's autobiographical account of Edward Carpenter, one needs another explanation for a rather different fictional sketch she made of him in the early 1890s and published, years later, in the *Forerunner*. In a parody entitled "The Unexpected," free-love spokesman "Edouard Charpentier" stands as protagonist.

The fictional Edouard Charpentier is a painter, a man as enthusiastic in his coquettish love for beautiful and charming models as he is ambitious in his work. Then he meets his true love, Mary Greenleaf. "What a figure!" No, he decides, not a "figure." "She has a body, the body of a young Diana." In rather chauvinistic style, however, Charpentier decides that Mary is the prudish New England

tioned her "unforgettable visit" with Alfred Russel Wallace. "This was one of the rare occasions on which I have felt modest and inferior, that world-renowned intellect was an overpowering presence. We played two games of chess, one he won, one was a draw—which was better than I expected" (*Living*, p. 211).

type. She is the pure, pious kind of lady who still holds naively and tenaciously to the "usual woman's faith in [marital] conventions." So he gallantly proposes, pleads, and ultimately marries her, only to discover to his horror that she is enjoying a lively, surreptitious love-life on the sidelines. To make matters worse, she chooses artists and bohemians, the worst kind of men around. "I know them—I am a painter myself." He becomes so enraged that he decides to murder the artist he thinks is his wife's lover. Melodramatically he awaits the suspect's arrival at their "den of Bohemians" meeting spot, only to discover that he has been duped once again. His wife is not the pious, passive princess he once adored, nor the disgrace he more recently imagined. She is a painter in her own right, in fact a better one than he. She hires her own models, rents a studio in the artist quarter, and claims for herself the freedom, independence, and creative genius he associates exclusively with men.

Undoubtedly Charlotte liked and admired some of Carpenter's views on sex and marriage. Possibly she liked his marriage metaphors as well—the "two suns" receding from each other and returning "richer and more vital," the "double star" blending of independent rays. But she was suspicious as well. For if she found his "double star" image elegant in writing, she must have assumed the double-standard marriage was what he actually preferred. In any case, even before Charlotte met him, she chided him not for advocating too much freedom, but for thinking that freedom was beyond woman's ken.

* * *

Most of the Fabians Charlotte met were more circumspect, more traditionally "political" than Edward Carpenter, at least in their publicly expressed concerns. For however eccentric their lifestyles may have been, or however colorfully they bantered love-life matters privately between them, they were inclined to keep the gossip down, the socio-economic issues paramount. In some respects, the political-literary coterie Charlotte found in England must have seemed reminiscent of the one she had known in California, except that the Fabians were even more impressive. What she felt about them, however, or how she experienced them, is hard to say.* For instance, her autobiography refers to Beatrice and Sidney

*The chapter in Charlotte's autobiography concerning her trip to England reads like a dull travelogue, a brief compendium of sights and celebrities, none of which excited her at all. One should keep in mind, however, that this chapter (in fact, most of the second half of her autobiography) was prob-

Webb simply as "distinguished Fabians," a rather dull characterization for one of the most vital and influential marriage teams in British history. For even by the time Charlotte met them, the Webbs had established their reputation as high-powered intellectuals. *The Co-operative Movement* (1891) by Beatrice Webb, *Fabian Essays in Socialism* (1889) and the classic *History of Trade Unionism* (1894) by the two of them together—these are just some of the highlights of their notorious careers. As political activists as well as writers, they helped found London's secondary and technical school system, create the London School of Economics, and reorganize the University of London. They conducted non-stop political campaigns—for communalized ownership of economic institutions, for nationally established minimum standards of health, housing, and income. In short, they were in the vanguard of the Fabian movement which Charlotte admired and emulated for years. All of this is barely discernible, however, in Charlotte's autobiography. She simply noted the Webbs' distinction, acknowledged that she met them, and otherwise said nothing at all.

Charlotte treated their friend George Bernard Shaw only slightly better. She had enjoyed his banter while she was visiting the Webbs at their country place near Saxmundham.

> Conversation, where Mr. Shaw took part, was bitterly brilliant. He made jokes about his sister's grave. Just once I answered him successfully. We were at dinner, and the talk drifted into animadversions on the U.S.A. Presently Mr. Shaw turned to me as I sat quietly beside him and caustically remarked that he supposed I would put all this into the newspapers when I reached home. I assured him that I did not write for the papers, and was not that kind of writer, anyway.
>
> "Then what were you thinking about?" he demanded. To which I peacefully replied, "About the effect of geography on the mind."

Obviously Charlotte was more pleased to record having met and talked with Shaw than she was impressed with the quality of what he said. "Shaw's work is always clever and good reading," she wrote. "But I do not love the man. He has an evil spirit." Whether it was Shaw's character or his intimidating, cryptic manner that Charlotte disliked, she still appreciated his "very good and useful [literary] criticism," and admitted, albeit reluctantly, that she enjoyed his

ably written in the difficult months immediately following the death of her husband Houghton Gilman, and immediately before her own.

wit. "More talk with Shaw—interesting rather. . . . All these men are funny all the time."

That was written on August 6, 1896, when Charlotte was in good spirits. She was enjoying the contacts, the recognition, the sense of shared political concerns. Unfortunately, however, her mood suddenly began to change. Perhaps the trip wore her down, or the endless meetings, or possibly news of a problem at home. Whatever the reasons, several days after her visit with Shaw and the Webbs, Charlotte began to feel painfully depressed. Her diary shows the all-too-familiar symptoms. August 12, 1896: "Find that I am really very low again. O dear! It is so long." August 13–16: "very weak," "miserable," "very blue and weepy." August 17: "Still miserable. Cannot write or anything." August 18: "Still miserable. I am alarmed at it." August 22: "This illness seems more physical than usual. Doubtless a sympathetic collapse internally." August 28: "Try to write—can not. Brain will not work. I notice, gradually in the past month or two, a loss of my ready control of words."

Whether because she was anticipating such a relapse, or simply responding to a deep-seated need, Charlotte began to look for supportive sympathetic "mothers" (Helen Campbell substitutes) at almost every stopover she made. Since coming abroad, she had managed to "adopt" one several times—Amie Hicks in London, for instance, or Annie Dowie during an Edinburgh stay. But however much comfort and understanding they may have offered, Charlotte floundered. As she put it in her autobiography: "If I had been well and clear-headed all this would have been a vivid and wonderful time. But I was still dragging up from that last collapse, and often had hardly wit enough to get about. Once, while unable to do any kind of work, I was riding on an omnibus, painfully conscious of the minimum of intelligence left me, and had this horrible thought: here were the other people beside me, also able to sit up and ride on an omnibus—perhaps they had no more brains than I did."

* * *

On November 19, 1896, after some five months of carousing about England, Charlotte boarded the *Furnessia*—with $9.25 in her pocket—and started the trip back home. She was discouraged by her last week's efforts ("A week of foregone failure, hard work and heavy sledding"), was seasick constantly ("I'm unable to take my clothes off"), and characteristically assumed the role of "philosophic invalid." "I cannot eat nor drink," she wrote, "but then I do not want to. I cannot do anything whatever, but again, I have nothing whatever to do."

When the ship landed, the first thing Charlotte did was to go "home," or the closest proximity of a home she had, her step-mother's New York boarding house.* As though she didn't have troubles enough already, her father, she learned, was very ill. After marrying Frankie Johnson Beecher several years before, he had travelled around looking for a job, become increasingly depressed, and gradually lost his health. By the time Charlotte returned from England, he had "broken down completely," and his wife had just recently taken him to the Delaware Water Gap Sanatorium.

Charlotte must have been acutely saddened and disappointed by Frederick's situation. If she had heard news of it several months before, it had probably caused her August relapse, her inability to work effectively or travel comfortably, in short the depression that spoiled her English trip. Clearly, she felt conflicting emotions toward her father: resentment for the years he had rejected her; anger for the countless times he let her down—emotionally, intellectually, economically; warmth for the reassurance he had finally shown in recent years. The turning point had occurred in 1893, about the time of Mary Perkins' death. After that, he had seemed more like a father, erratic to be sure, but congenial and respectful. He had encouraged her last years' work in California, for instance, had helped with Katharine's trip back East, and probably had even taken some pride in the Beecher-Perkins stubbornness with which she shunned conventions and shaped her life. Frederick's illness, however, produced a radical shift in their relationship and, in Charlotte, a stinging regret. For, however satisfying their reconciliation, it had been too brief, too poorly grounded, too quickly followed by a debilitating illness and by an unsettling reversal of child-parent roles. Still craving Frederick's reassurance and approval, Charlotte suddenly had become the nurturer and comforter instead. The "brilliant intellect" was sinking gradually into "idiocy"; the iconoclast-reformer-father was dying "slowly, hideously," from a "softening of the brain."†

Understandably, Charlotte's first reaction was to become depressed. But her response to the crisis may have been more stoic as well—reinforcing her commitment to her father's goals as free-lance

* Charlotte had gone there once before after a serious depression, just after finishing her settlement-house work the preceding April. "It was literally the first time I had ever been in my father's house since infancy," she wrote; it was a comforting experience, apparently, even though Frederick wasn't there. He had been in Washington, "probably trying to arrange for some employment" (*Living*, p. 191).

† Charlotte's visits with her father over the next several years, and also her feelings at the time of his death in 1899, will be treated in a subsequent volume.

intellectual, renewing her determination to succeed even where he failed. Whatever the intensity of Charlotte's emotional-intellectual struggle, however, and whatever the nature of the "uplifting" resolutions she enlisted for the fight, her diary entries sketch only surface events in a cool, stark way. On December 3, 1896, she wrote, "Go down to see [father] at sanatorium, Delaware Water Gap. He is much better and seems glad to see me." The next day, "Little talk with father. Give him $5.00."

Besides making these sad treks to see her father, however, Charlotte spent most of her time during these first few adjustment weeks getting reacquainted with her father's family, with Frankie Johnson Perkins and her three adopted daughters in their New York boarding house. With them, she could feel somewhat closer to her father, talk about his situation, perhaps catch an anecdote or two about his life. In no time at all she found she liked them. Frankie Perkins was an "affectionate" and "charming little lady," Charlotte wrote, "with curly hair and dimples, the kind which attains vivid attractiveness at sixteen and remains permanently at that period." Moreover, Frankie Perkins' three adopted daughters were "cordial" and "pretty" as well—"step-adopted-sisters-in-law-by-marriage," Charlotte called them. Characteristically, she loved the genealogical absurdity of the family situation—"my father became my great-uncle, my great-aunt became my mother, and I became my own first-cousin-once-removed." But what she also craved was a "settled residence for a while," and a restful congenial "family atmosphere." On November 30, 1896, Charlotte wrote, "Arrive. . . . Drive up to my 'Mama's,' 20 W. 32nd St. They are glad to see me. . . . Little upstairs room—will be $7.00 a week. Visit for a while first. Very comfy."

Charlotte used most of the month of December for rest—her own active kind of rest, that is. She played battledore and shuttlecock with fellow boarders, spent hours sewing some new clothes, and gradually began to scan the New York scene for modestly remunerative work. Her best contacts were at women's-club or social-reform-club meetings. There she was sometimes asked to read her poems. Sometimes she even sold copies of her book (*In This Our World*, her poetry anthology). Perhaps the most important breakthrough after her English trip, however, was an invitation to become a contributing editor of the *American Fabian*, official organ of a recently established group of American socialist, feminist, and labor movement activists whom Charlotte had known about or worked with for years. As the journal modestly stated, the group had "received its initiative from the Fabian Society of London—an association of brilliant young thinkers and writers. . . . We think it clear that not only must progress move" in the directions outlined by the English Fabians, "but that it is unconsciously doing so all the time. We wish to use our efforts in spreading the gospel of the new order as widely as we can."

Charlotte was undoubtedly as committed to "spreading the gospel" as any of her colleagues, but she was realistic enough to know she had to sell herself as well. The *American Fabian* suited her needs exactly. For not only could she send in pithy articles to demonstrate her political convictions; she could also enjoy the publicity efforts of her friends. An article by one colleague especially pleased her. Co-worker and former suitor Eugene Hough sent in a glowing report of her California work.

> The energy and sacrifice contributed to the labor movement must at all times be gratuitous to be effective. . . . It was seen by some earnest trade unionists that [Charlotte Stetson] was, potentially, a force that could be used for the everlasting good of their class. She responded readily to their requests for aid in their effort to mould a just public sentiment toward their aims. She went here and there and everywhere, in season and out of season, carrying a fund of information and inspiration to each body before whom she appeared, giving to this one a comforting and strengthening touch, and to that one a stunning and bewildering blow. She carried our cause into church societies, press clubs and women's associations, set up our banner before the doors of the universities, and compelled moss-covered educators to see the fundamental principle of society is an economic principle.
>
> . . . Who can number the able men and women whom she has influenced? Who can weigh the power of her satire, the force of her logic, the power of her individuality? I will tell you who can so weigh, number and measure: it is he whose hands have been soiled and calloused with hard labor ever since he can remember; he who, by his economic condition, is stunted and deformed and impoverished in every part save aspiration. Such are numerous in the labor movement. Such, without adulation or sentimentalism, know and love and appreciate their ablest, bravest and most unselfish friend and leader, Charlotte Perkins Stetson.

While Eugene Hough's glowing report clearly reflected personal ties with Charlotte, it also showed genuine respect. For whatever his private disappointments may have been, he gave just the kind of public boost she needed for the next year's work. His tribute would stir readers' interest, facilitate contacts with reformers, and bring some national attention to her local California work. The last several years had been ones of preparation: securing independence from family responsibilities, from Katharine, from relationships she thought detracted from her work. In the next few years she would make her mark. According to her diary, she approached the New Year optimistically. On December 31, she wrote, "Upstairs at 11:50 and received the New Year alone as usual. Health and Work." *

* She also noted that her total debts outstanding were $4,034.50.

Afterword

"THIRTY-FIVE hundred words I wrote this morning, in three hours!" A book's chapter in one sitting; a steady six-week pace of morning writing; an explosive blending of reflections and insights she had been accumulating for years; and thus in 1898 *Women and Economics* was dashed into print. It was Charlotte Gilman's single most important work, the beginning of her rapid climb toward notoriety as one of the major feminist theorists in turn-of-the-century America. Jane Addams of Hull House thought *Women and Economics* a "masterpiece." Her co-worker Florence Kelley believed it was "the first real, substantial contribution made by a woman to the science of economics." As one contemporary reviewer put it, "Since John Stuart Mill's essays on *The Subjection of Women*, there has been no book dealing with the whole position of women to approach it in originality of conception and brilliancy of exposition."

One of the major themes of *Women and Economics*, and one which Charlotte had already developed in unpublished lectures and writings, was that women have the right and need for economic independence, for satisfying and socially useful work, and for personal relationships based on love rather than necessity. Drawing on contemporary thinking in the fields of anthropology, history, philosophy, and social ethics, and committed to a socialist vision of equality for all, Charlotte attempted to trace the historical roots of current social and economic dislocation, and to project viable programs of reform. With sarcasm, wit, and keen analysis, she argued that the degradation of women must be viewed as an issue of preeminent concern. Women's isolation in the home, the thwarting of their energies in the mundane domestic tasks of cooking, cleaning, and personal service, the sexual division of labor artificially imposed by the institution of the family—these were not only some of the most socially destructive phenomena historically, but they were also currently some of the most pernicious obstacles to social change. In order to become fully human and, even more importantly, in order to free their energies to enrich the quality of human life, women must have the opportunity to engage visibly and effectively in public work. They must learn to communicate their visions, to articulate their needs, to shape and define their experiences in ways that would be publicly and creatively shared. In short, women must become participants in the making of history, in the building of a better future world.

Charlotte had conducted her own life according to the tenets of her faith, and by 1898, at the age of thirty-eight, she had become an inspiring and effective public figure herself. She had produced work of lasting value, had secured modest economic independence, and with remarkable gall and ingenuity had redefined the commonly accepted norms of womanhood—the dutiful daughter, the loving wife, the natural mother. Clearly, Charlotte's "new woman" ideals pertained to more than merely lifestyle. Professionally, she had prodded other women to bolster their confidence, break domestic molds, and show their mettle in the public world; and, personally, she had secured for herself the opportunity for travel, the time and energy for self-discovery, the autonomy for creative public work.

Charlotte knew perfectly well, however, that the price for nonconformity was high. She had learned the hard way. She had suffered from intellectual isolation in a society which characteristically still degraded women, still named and defined contemporary issues according to the needs of men. She had endured public condemnation for her unconventional behavior—her divorce, her separation from her daughter, her personal relationships, her uncompromising commitment to her work. And she had experienced painful alienation from her family, indeed often also from her closest friends. Perhaps even more serious than outside pressures such as these, however, were the conflicts still raging in herself, her anxieties, her inability to retain a sense of confidence and worth. For as is so often the case in women's history, it is not only the instances of societal prejudice that dampen women's spirits, but also the prejudice they direct against themselves. Taught from childhood to accept "feminine" responsibilities, to defer passively to other people's needs, women often find it hard to respect themselves, much less to recognize, accept, and respect authenticity and purpose in their work. Like so many professional women even today, Charlotte was unable to feel consistently the self-assurance she publicly projected. Exceptional though she clearly was, she still had not been able to free herself completely of the "feminine" dilemmas, the "burden of our common womanhood" that she so brilliantly described.

At midpoint in her life, Charlotte still struggled with two major goals: to communicate her insights more effectively and to find a greater measure of peace and happiness within herself. To read her autobiography, one would think that by 1896 Charlotte had resolved most of her internal conflicts. She acknowledged that she was still occasionally bothered by inexplicable depressions, but otherwise implied that she happily and confidently (indeed almost exclusively) attended to her public work. Yet, for all of her determination throughout her life to project an image of herself as the undistracted "stern cold thinker," Charlotte continued to provide a private record that shows an intense personal confrontation with almost every woman's issue her public writings theoretically discuss. For in 1897, the same year she was writing *Women and Economics*, she began a passionate three-year correspondence with Houghton Gilman, the man who, in 1900, became her second husband. She wrote him twenty- to thirty-page letters almost daily, introducing herself, reviewing past achievements, bemoaning past mistakes, and candidly confronting the contradictions in herself. At the time, Charlotte urged Houghton not to keep her letters. "If you save all this stuff it'll be trotting out biographically some day—and then you'll be sympathized with," she warned him. "I pray thee, mark these letters 'Please Destroy.'" But she did not insist even then, Houghton did not comply, and in later life she saved them purposely. It was as though, once again, she realized that her published writings would be one type of legacy. Another would be the record of her life—compelling, disquieting, and very real.

Notes

Citations in the notes are listed by page number and, where necessary, by opening words of the passage quoted. Publication information for works cited can be found in the bibliography. The following abbreviations will be used:

AESL Arthur and Elizabeth Schlesinger Library, Charlotte Perkins Gilman Collection
BL Bancroft Library, Charles Walter Stetson correspondence
CAP Charlotte Anna Perkins
CPG Charlotte Perkins Gilman
CPS Charlotte Perkins Stetson
CWS Charles Walter Stetson
FBP Frederick Beecher Perkins
GHG George Houghton Gilman
JHL John Hay Library, Charlotte Gilman–Lester Ward correspondence
ML(L) Martha Luther (Lane)
RIHS Rhode Island Historical Society, Charlotte Gilman's correspondence with Martha Luther (Lane)
SD Stowe Day Foundation, correspondence of Mary Westcott Perkins and Isabella Beecher Hooker
VCL Vassar College Library, Charlotte Gilman's correspondence with Martha Whitney

INTRODUCTION

3 *"We ourselves, by maintaining . . ."* CPG, *Women and Economics*, p. 331.

"To prove that a woman . . ." AESL, CPS to GHG, July 26, 1899.

4 *"Marx and Veblen"* Andrew Sinclair, *The Emancipation of the American Woman*, p. 272.

"most original and challenging . . ." Mary Gray Peck, *Carrie Chapman Catt: A Biography*, p. 454.

"leading intellectual . . ." Alice Rossi, ed., *The Feminist Papers*, p. 568.

5 *"Of women especially have been required . . ."* CPG, *His Religion and Hers*, p. 134.

7 *"Gentle reader, wouldst . . ."* AESL, Diary, Jan. 1, 1879.

8 *"Incidental thought . . ."* RIHS, CAP to ML, Aug. 13, 1881.

"well, sometimes I feel . . ." AESL, CPS to GHG, Dec. 16, 1898. The commonly held view is that Charlotte was hostile to men, or at least unhappy in emotional, sexual relationships. See, for instance, William O'Neill, *Everyone was Brave*, pp. 130–133; David Kennedy, *Birth Control in America*, p. 132; Carl Degler, Introduction to *Women and Economics*; Alice Rossi, ed., *The Feminist Papers*, pp. 566–572.

CHAPTER I

13 For a discussion of nineteenth-century ideas of "true womanhood," see Barbara Welter, "The Cult of True Womanhood."

14 *"world servers . . ."* CPG, *Living*, p. 3.

"splendid physique . . ." William Blaikie, *How to Get Strong*, p. 58.

"God has intended . . ." Quoted from Henry Ward Beecher in Eric Goldman, *Rendezvous with Destiny*, p. 69.

15 *"A little river ran near it . . ."* AESL, unpublished autobiography, p. 15.

"charming water color studies" CPG, *Living*, p. 15.

16 *"clog the wheels of progress . . ."* Quoted from Victoria Woodhull in William O'Neill, *Everyone was Brave*, p. 26. For Catharine Beecher's philosophy, see Kathryn Kish Sklar, *Catharine Beecher: A Study in American Domesticity*.

18 *"the greatest scandal . . ."* William O'Neill, *Everyone Was Brave*, p. 260.

19 *"What a sad dark life . . ."* AESL, CPS to GHG, Feb. 1, 1899.

"So able a man . . ." Ibid., Feb. 9, 1899.

"smug, fat, young divine" FBP, "The Un-Manufactory," in *Devil Puzzlers*, pp. 42–96.

"recklessness, dishonesty . . ." FBP, *The Station and Duty of American Teachers as Citizens, in View of the Materialism of the Age*, p. 13.

"The reason of the . . ." Ibid., pp. 22–24.

20 *"honest good Government . . ."* FBP, *Boston Daily Globe*, Oct. 18, 1887.

"an anomaly, she was the only . . ." Lyman Beecher Stowe, *Saints, Sinners and Beechers*, p. 152.

"still I constantly feel . . ." FBP, "Childhood: A Study," in *Devil Puzzlers*, pp. 137–38.

21 *"satisfy imperfectly . . ."* FBP, "The Station and Duty," p. 2.

"Her eyes are much . . ." SD, Isabella Beecher Hooker to John Hooker, June 3, 1857.

"Delicate and beautiful . . ." CPG, *Living*, p. 7.

"when being a Baptist . . ." Ibid., p. 6.

"was too good for him" SD, Isabella Beecher Hooker to John Hooker, June 3, 1857.

22 *"we hear however . . ."* Ibid.

"idolized youth . . ." CPG, *Living*, pp. 7–8.

"Engagements were made . . ." Ibid.

"The doctor said that . . ." Ibid., p. 15.

23 *"A species of fearful contortion . . ."* FBP, "My Forenoon with the Baby," in *Devil Puzzlers*, p. 200.

"I often ask . . ." Ibid., p. 215.

24 *"instinct for living . . ."* FBP, "Childhood: A Study," in *Devil Puzzlers*, pp. 136–140.

"I, who have a loving heart . . ." FBP, "The Compensation Office," in *Devil Puzzlers*, pp. 167–169.

25 *"Father agreed to pay . . ."* AESL, "Autobiography of C. A. Perkins," Jan. 14, 1880.

For a discussion of Frederick and Mary, see CPG, *Living*, pp. 8–9.

"forced to move . . ." CPG, *Living*, p. 8.

26 For Charlotte's descriptions of Mary Perkins, see AESL, CPS to GHG, Oct. 14, Sept. 16, 1898, and March 12, 1899.

"violently well brought up" CPG, *Living*, p. 14.

CHAPTER II

28 *"I used to put away . . ."* CPG, *Living*, pp. 10–11.

"Mother loved us . . ." Ibid., p. 23.

"both love and disappointment . . ." Adrienne Rich, *Of Women Born*, p. 11.

"lovely tales . . ." Ibid., pp. 6, 18, 22; AESL, unpublished autobiography, pp. 13–15.

29 *"'over and over' . . ."* AESL, unpublished autobiography, pp. 13–15.

"the evening chorus . . ." AESL, Thomas Adie Perkins to CPG, Oct. 17, 1926.

"years of healthy . . ." AESL, unpublished autobiography, p. 28.

"small handfuls of sand . . ." Ibid., p. 15.

29–30 For Charlotte's childish pranks, see AESL, unpublished autobiography, p. 19; CPG, *Living*, p. 15.

30 *"The effect on me . . ."* AESL, unpublished autobiography, p. 30.

"I know that a secret consciousness . . ." AESL, Thomas Addie Perkins to CPG, Oct. 17, 1926.

"light shot-gun . . ." AESL, unpublished autobiography, p. 29.

"the gun, and his traps . . ." Ibid.

31 *"Dear Father . . ."* AESL, CAP to FBP, undated [probably 1872].

"A whipping inflicted . . ." FBP, "Childhood: A Study," in *Devil Puzzlers*, p. 108.

32 *"If you were a mischievous child . . ."* CPG, *Living*, pp. 15–16.

"His father was so angry . . ." CAP, "The Story of a Good Girl and a Bad Boy," in AESL, "The Literary Vurks of Princess Charlotte."

33 AESL, "A Fairy Tale."

34 *"thirst for glorious loveliness"* CPG, *Living*, p. 20.

"Influenced by a friend . . ." Ibid., pp. 23–24.

"To this day . . ." AESL, unpublished autobiography, pp. 31–32.

35 *"childish prayers . . ."* CPG, *Living*, pp. 7, 25.

"Irish servant . . ." Ibid., p. 25.

35–36 For parental attitudes toward adolescence, see Joseph Kett, *Rites of Passage*, chs. 5–7.

36 *"I did not want . . ."* CPG, *Living*, p. 10.

"stern restrictions . . ." Ibid., p. 20.

37 *"floating and wallowing . . ."* Ibid., pp. 26–27.

"I have always loved God . . ." SD, Mary Westcott Perkins to Isabella Beecher Hooker, May 15, 1879.

38 *"identify more with daughters . . ."* Nancy Chodorow, "Family Structure and Feminine Personality," in Michelle Zimbalist Rosaldo, ed., *Woman, Culture, and Society*, p. 48.

"one of the major events . . ." CPG, *Living*, pp. 33–34.

"If I was a free agent . . ." Ibid., p. 35.

39 *"Dear Father . . ."* AESL, CAP to FBP, undated [probably 1875].

"'*Unstable as water' . . .*" Ibid.

40 *"I kissed my father . . ."* AESL, CPS to GHG, Feb. 1, 1899.

"appetite for petting . . ." CPG, *Mag-Marjorie*, in *Forerunner*, III (Jan. 1912), 11.

41 *"Saw father . . ."* AESL, Diary, Feb. 18, 1876.

"most enlivening way . . ." Edward E. Hale, "The Choice of Books," in Lyman Abbott, ed., *Hints for Home Reading*, pp. 63–69.

"my total schooling . . ." CPG, *Living*, pp. 18, 27; also, AESL, folder no. 1. See also Thomas Woody, *A History of Women's Education in the United States*, 544–546.

42 *"A tendency to . . ."* CPG, *Living*, p. 27.

"Here was Law . . ." Ibid., p. 29.

"took to 'dress reform' . . ." Ibid., p. 28.

43 *"strangledst . . ."* Ibid., pp. 28, 31.

CHAPTER III

44 *"Sixteen, with a life . . ."* CPG, *Living*, p. 44.

45 *"As I look over . . ."* Ibid.

"Girlhood, in the usual sense . . ." AESL, unpublished autobiography, p. 53.

"happy, peaceful periods of time . . ." Gordon Allport, *The Use of Personal Documents in Psychological Science*, p. 78. Nancy Chodorow offers an argument which may help explain the intensity of Charlotte's indictment of her mother. Chodorow points out that very commonly a daughter "projects what she defines as bad within herself onto her mother and tries to take what is good into herself" (Nancy Chodorow, "Family Structure and the Feminine Personality," in Michelle Zimbalist Rosaldo, ed., *Woman, Culture, and Society*, p. 59).

46 *"two opposing natures . . ."* RIHS, CAP to ML, July 30, 1881.

"Within this book . . ." AESL, Diary, Dec. 25, 1875.

"By the way . . ." Ibid., Jan. 1, 1876.

"Thomas is more than . . ." Ibid., Jan. 2, 1876.

"just unbearable . . ." Ibid., Jan. 4–17, April 14, July 3–17, 1876.

47 *"Oh be joyful! . . ."* Ibid., April 29, May 9, Dec. 24, Dec. 31, 1876.

"We leave here . . ." Ibid., Feb. 7, 1876; March 6, 1876.

"Oh dear! . . ." Ibid., April 18, 1877.

"One of mother's cousins . . ." CPG, *Living,* pp. 51–52.

48 *"submission to a tutelage . . ."* Ibid., pp. 69–70; AESL, unpublished autobiography, p. 50.

"fight fire with fire . . ." Ibid., p. 51; AESL, unpublished autobiography, p. 53.

49 *"The first step . . ."* Ibid., pp. 56–60, 32.

"But you don't believe it . . ." Ibid., pp. 56–60.

"What do I want to do . . ." CPG, *Benigna Machiavelli,* in *Forerunner,* V (March 1914), 73; V (Jan. 1914), 11.

50 *"Gentle reader . . ."* AESL, Diary, Jan. 1, 1879.

"remain in her mother's . . ." CPG, *Living,* p. 45.

"I Mary A. Perkins . . ." AESL, Diary, Oct. 1878.

"Go to the School . . ." Ibid., Sept. 23, 1878.

"As for writing letters . . ." AESL, FBP to CAP, undated [probably 1878].

51 *"two miles' walk . . ."* CPG, *Living,* pp. 64, 46.

"Oh! TOMMIS IS COME! . . ." AESL, Diary, Jan. 29, 1878; Feb. 9, 1878.

"Thomas comes. And . . ." Ibid., Nov. 23, 1878.

52 *"Having after much toil . . ."* Ibid., Diary, Feb. 4, 1879.

"If it were not for mother . . ." Ibid., Diary, Feb. 7, 1879.

"Mother is scared and blue . . ." Ibid., Feb. 14, 1879.

"Mother is very cross . . ." Ibid., Feb. 17, 1879.

53 *"Postman with letter . . ."* Ibid., March 3, 1879.

"How blind people are! . . ." Ibid., March 6, 1879.

"We were both permeated . . ." Ibid., March 8, 1879.

"weep and snivel . . ." Ibid., March 30, 1880.

"I break down . . ." Ibid.

54 *"to help humanity . . ."* CPG, *Living,* p. 36.

"Have taken a fancy . . ." AESL, Diary, March 26, 1877.

"Let us call good reading . . ." Ibid., June 23, 1877.

"logic and important . . ." CPG, *Living,* pp. 35–43.

55 *"God was Real . . ."* Ibid.

"innate incredulity . . ." Ibid., p. 40.

"reading all men's opinions . . ." AESL, FBP to CAP, Oct. 15, 1878.

"holding communion . . ." RIHS, CAP to ML, Aug. 19, 1879.

56 *"Hurrah! Go to the Essay Club! . . ."* AESL, Diary, Feb. 22, 1879.

57 *"There are three ways . . ."* Caroline Hazard, *Some Ideals in the Education of Women*, p. 10.

"We understand each other . . ." AESL, Diary, June 27, 1879.

"I am feeling very lonesome . . ." Ibid., June 19, 1878.

"He came, he saw . . ." Ibid., Aug. 1878.

58 *"I never was so courted . . ."* Ibid., Jan. 1, 1880.

"What joys were mine! . . . AESL, CAP to GHG, Jan. 5, 1880.

"reign supreme . . ." AESL, Diary, Sept. 15, 1879; March 11, 1880.

"notify mother . . ." Ibid., Jan. 17, 26, 1879.

"little fight . . ." Ibid., Jan. 21, 1880; Aug. 16, 1880.

"Mother introduces her . . ." Ibid., Jan. 4, 1880.

"Mother smiling . . ." Ibid., Dec. 13, 1880.

"uproarious jollification" Ibid., Oct. 1, 1880.

"My greatest fault . . ." Ibid., Dec. 31, 1878.

59 *"all call me . . ."* Ibid., Sept. 20, 1878.

"Pleasing epistle . . ." Ibid., May 17, 1878; March 23, 1880.

60 *"I suppose I ought . . ."* SD, Mary A. Perkins to Isabella Beecher Hooker, Nov. 11, 1879.

"Up in the broad bright . . ." AESL, Diary, Jan. 15, 1881; Feb. 20, 1881.

"I am no sort of good . . ." Ibid., Feb. 24–28, March 1, 1881.

61 *"on account of . . ."* Ibid., March 2, March 5, 1881.

"Dear Father . . ." AESL, CAP to FBP, April 10, 1881.

CHAPTER IV

65 *"I never knew . . ."* RIHS, CAP to ML, Sept. 5, 1881.

"My health was splendid . . ." CPG, *Living*, p. 71.

66 *Follow Blaikie every night . . ."* AESL, Diary, Oct. 27, 1879.

"to sanity and mental power . . ." William Blaikie, *How to Get Strong*, p. 272.

"Among American women running . . ." Ibid., p. 230.

"each day I ran a mile . . ." CPG, *Living*, p. 67.

"with 'facilities' wherein . . ." RIHS, CAP to ML, Aug. 1, 1881.

67 *"No long-tutored heir . . ."* CPG, *Living*, pp. 69, 72.

"wasted [her] *substance . . ."* Ibid., p. 98.

"gentle, lovely . . ." Ibid., p. 48.

"What horrid stuff . . ." RIHS, CAP to ML, July 31, 1881.

"Incidental thought . . ." Ibid., Aug. 13, 1881.

"Martha comes . . ." AESL, Diary, May 14, 1881.

68 *"As for me . . ."* Ibid., May 2, 1881.

"compact of mutual understanding" CPG, *Living*, p. 48.

"lovely little red . . ." AESL, Diary, May 14, 1881.

"agreed that neither . . ." AESL, unpublished autobiography, p. 54.

"Those years with you . . ." RIHS, CPS to MLL, Jan. 20, 1890.

"'Well' said my aunt . . ." RIHS, CAP to ML, July 17, 1881.

"didn't stand the ghost . . ." Ibid., July 18, 1881.

"Boasted to Sam . . ." Ibid., undated letter.

69 *"'Why,' said I . . ."* Ibid., Aug. 3, 1881.

"I asked him point-blank . . ." Ibid., Aug. 2, 1881.

"But I declare . . ." Ibid.

70 *"And truly I bethink me . . ."* Ibid., Aug. 15, 1881.

71 *"Look you—I do not want . . ."* Ibid.

"What sayeth the Sage? . . ." Ibid., Aug. 25, 1881.

"You've no idea how . . ." Ibid., Aug. 29, 1881.

"luxuriated in dear Sam . . ." Ibid., July 29, 1881.

"with a most deeply interested expression . . ." Ibid., July 29, 1881.

72 *"The man free, the woman . . ."* CPG, *The Home*, p. 6.

"frightful incompatibility . . . my rebellion . . ." RIHS, CAP to ML, July 29, 1881.

"And what do you think . . ." Ibid.

"And so further . . ." Ibid.

73 *"They all opened . . ."* Ibid., undated letter.

74 *"I am really getting glad . . ."* Ibid., July 24, 1881.

"How do you make me out lonely? . . . " Ibid., July 30, 1881.

"I know you want . . ." Ibid.

75 *"care I don't want . . ."* Ibid.

"do great things . . ." Ibid.

"Now I shall descend . . ." Ibid.

"O my little love! . . ." Ibid.

76 *"half from personal love . . ."* Ibid., Aug. 1, 1881.

"Don't ever think . . ." Ibid.

"I wouldn't change with Shakespeare! . . ." Ibid., Aug. 4, 1881.

"The curtain wavers . . ." Ibid., Aug. 13, 1881.

"to hang on to preconceived ideas . . ." Ibid., Aug. 9, 1881.

"I look forward . . ." Ibid., Aug. 10, 1881.

77 *"As for you . . ."* Ibid., July 24, 1881.

"As for your heart . . ." Ibid., July 30, 1881.

"It's a long lane . . ." Ibid., July 18, 1881.

78 *"Go ahead and enjoy yourself . . ."* Ibid., July 29, 1881.

"I think you misunderstand me . . ." Ibid.

79 *"And if Halicarnassus* doesn't . . ." Ibid.

"Little kitten, little kitten . . ." Ibid., July 24, 1881.

"Look you, I haven't . . ." Ibid., July 29, 1881.

"I'm disappointed. That mean . . ." Ibid., Aug. 2, 1881.

80 *"O you dear bewitching lovely . . ."* Ibid., Aug. 4, 1881.

81 *"I* am *certain . . ."* Ibid., Aug. 10, 1881.

82 *"giving to the woman the home . . ."* CPG, *Women and Economics*, p. 225.

"our steady insistence . . ." Ibid., p. 51.

"integrity and dignity . . ." Carroll Smith-Rosenberg, "The Female World of Love and Ritual: Relations Between Women in Nineteenth-Century America," pp. 9–10.

"deep personal happiness" CPG, *Living*, p. 48.

"The freedom of it! . . ." RIHS, CAP to ML, Aug. 13, 1881.

83 *"Glad she likes you . . ."* Ibid.

"Look here. Some sort of club . . ." Ibid.

"I think it highly probable . . ." Ibid., Aug. 15, 1881.

84 *"Seems to me my letters . . ."* Ibid.

"Suppose you love that man . . ." Ibid., Aug. 16, 1881.

"O my prophetic soul! . . ." Ibid.

85 *"And here's encouragement . . ."* Ibid.

86 *"we live in our big house . . ."* Ibid., Aug. 23, 1881.

"Say, I feel ever . . ." Ibid.

"what fun it was . . ." Ibid., Aug. 2, 1881.

"brought me 7 pairs . . ." AESL, Diary, Sept. 24, 1880.

"Lace, finer than finest tulle . . ." RIHS, CAP to ML, July 27, 1881.

87 *"Do women dress to please men?"* CPG and Alexander Black, "Do Women Dress to Please Men?"

"dressed up yesterday . . ." RIHS, CAP to ML, July 24, 1881.

"He's devoted to you . . ." Ibid., Aug. 29, 1881.

"That shawl device . . ." Ibid.

88 *"Just open your big eyes . . ."* Ibid.

"Say pussy, you've no idea . . ." Ibid., Sept. 4, 1881.

"Now if I were . . ." Ibid.

"It is rather . . ." Ibid.

89 *"'If I had a lover . . .'"* Ibid., Sept. 5, 1881.

"Go to Martha's . . ." AESL, Diary, Oct. 18, 1881.

"Martha there . . ." Ibid., Oct. 27, 1881.

"Am closeted with Mrs. L[uther] . . ." Ibid., Oct. 29, 1881.

"sermon of which I heard . . ." Ibid., Oct. 30, 1881.

"Martha over . . ." Ibid., Nov. 1, 1881.

"Pleasant, to ring . . ." Ibid., Nov. 5, 1881.

"Letter from Sam . . ." Ibid., Nov. 9, 1881.

"Go home with Mrs. Luther . . ." Ibid., Nov. 13, 1881.

90 *"Spend an hour in . . ."* Ibid., Nov. 15, 1881.

"Walk in the dark . . ." Ibid., Nov. 16, 1881.

"Jim comes home . . ." Ibid., Dec. 18, 1881.

"A grand jolly . . ." Ibid., Dec. 28, 1881.

"Some books and things . . ." Ibid., "Poem for Martha," Dec. 30, 1881.

"A year of steady work . . ." Ibid., Dec. 31, 1881.

CHAPTER V

91 *"My watchword at 21 . . ."* AESL, Diary, 1882, flyleaf.

"I have a twilight . . ." Ibid., Jan. 14, 1882.

"Mr. Stetson calls . . ." Ibid., Jan. 22, 1882.

92 *"poor New England pastor's . . ."* Nelson M. Stetson, *Stetson Kindred of America, no.* 4, p. 13.

"He was quite the greatest man . . ." CPG, *Living*, p. 82.

"dark-haired and dark-eyed . . ." AESL, Thomas Adie Perkins to CPG, Oct. 17, 1926.

93 *"I have this day . . ."* AESL, Diary, Jan. 29, 1882.

"An Anchor to Windward" Ibid., Jan. 31, 1882.

94 *"[I] said that I had . . ."* CPG, *Living*, pp. 82–83.

95 *"Sam comes . . ."* AESL, Diary, Feb. 17, 1882.

"Mr. Stetson arrives . . ." Ibid., Feb. 19, 1882.

"The impetus is slackening . . ." RIHS, CAP to ML, Aug. 10, 1881.

"In Duty Bound" *Living*, pp. 76–77.

96 *"O my Friend! . . ."* AESL, CAP to CWS, Feb. 13, 1882.

"if I am the devil's child . . ." RIHS, CAP to ML, Aug. 1, 1881.

97 *"The difference between our lives . . ."* AESL, CAP to CWS: Feb. 13, 1882.

"I am thinking deeply just now . . ." Ibid., Feb. 20, 1882.

99 For a discussion of "flight from womanhood," see Karen Horney, "The Flight from Womanhood: The Masculinity Complex in Women as Viewed by Men and Women," in Jean Baker Miller, ed., *Psychoanalysis and Women*, pp. 5–20. Although I have made no attempt to offer a psychoanalytic interpretation of Charlotte's life, my work is influenced by the writings of Karen Horney, Juliet Mitchell, and other feminist-oriented authors who offer useful insights into ways in which women internalize patriarchal norms. They suggest that since women's search for fatherly affection encourages a passive identification with the mother, and a rejection of aggressive tendencies within themselves, the resolution of the Oedipus complex involves an acceptance of the position of subordination in a heterosexual relationship with a man.

"Three Women," *Forerunner*, II (May 1911), 119, 134.

"I have just spent . . ." AESL, CAP to CWS, Feb. 21, 1882.

100 *"How can I offer . . ."* Ibid., Feb. 22, 1882.

"proud and joyful . . ." AESL, undated poem [probably 1882].

101 *"And I think of . . ."* Ibid.

"I am beginning . . ." AESL, CAP to CWS, March 6, 1882.

"thinks me queer among women . . ." AESL, CAP to Charlotte Hedge, March 26, 1882.

"I've been a good little girl . . ." Ibid.

102 *"Because t'is Spring . . ."* AESL, CAP to CWS, May 1, 1882.

"With body & heart . . ." Ibid., June 15, 1882.

"Yours of the 9th received . . ." AESL, CAP to FBP, June 19, 1882.

103 *"namely, the embodiment . . "* FBP, *My Three Conversations with Miss Chester*, pp. 30–50, 62, 82–84.

104 *"As my reward there came . . ."* AESL, Diary, Sept. 8, 1882.

"The Oval Portrait," in Edgar Allan Poe, *The Complete Poems and Stories of Edgar Allan Poe*, pp. 382–384.

105 *"These many days I've . . ."* AESL, CWS to CAP, Sept. 22, 1882.

106 *"Really enjoyed myself . . ."* AESL, Diary, Oct. 5, 1882.

"My lips are my lover's . . ." Ibid., Oct. 27, 1882.

107 *"long happy evening . . . My last act . . ."* Ibid., Dec. 31, 1882.

"She thinks we'd . . ." Ibid., Oct. 17, 1882.

"Mother proposes a grand . . ." Ibid., Feb. 11, 1883.

"If I have any personal volition . . ." Ibid., Feb. 15, 1883.

"O God I wish to do . . ." Ibid., April 1, 1883.

108 *"I am obliged to decline . . ."* Ibid., April 5, 1883.

"is not coming any more . . ." Ibid., April 8–April 29, 1883.

"Call on Connie Pitman . . ." Ibid., May 14, 1883.

"A Grand Pleasure; . . ." Ibid., April 13, April 15, 1883.

"O my God! . . ." AESL, CAP to CWS, May 13, 1883.

109 *"I always think of you . . ."* AESL, CAP to Thomas Adie Perkins, May 13, 1883.

"Walter calls! . . ." AESL, Diary, May 14–May 17, 1883.

110 *"Write note to Walter . . ."* Ibid., May 15, May 17, 1883.

"demanded a year's complete . . ." CPG, *Living*, p. 83.

"the grandest preaching . . ." AESL, Diary, May 20, 1883.

"After that, in spite of . . ." CPG, *Living*, p. 83.

"Belief in God . . ." AESL, see unpublished "sermons," 1883–1884.

111 *"As you know . . ."* Ibid.

"Boy's Room . . ." AESL, Diary, Jan. 20, March 24, June 3, 1883.

"received with disapprobation . . ." Ibid., May 24, 1883.

112 *"The men folks fish . . ."* RIHS, CAP to MLL, Sept. 6, 1883.

"The people here have grown . . ." Ibid., Sept. 16, 1883.

113 *"take it on trust . . ."* Ibid.

"I confess I'm . . ." Ibid., Sept. 14, 1883.

"I'm glad you want . . ." Ibid.

114 *"Don't you think really dear . . ."* Ibid., Sept. 16, 1883.

"Whereas I, Charlotte A. Perkins . . ." AESL, "Thoughts and Fingerings," Nov. 3, 1883.

"1st Absolutely unselfish . . ." Ibid.

115 *"And this year gone? . . ."* AESL, Diary, Dec. 31, 1883.

"With no pride . . ." Ibid., Jan. 1, 1884.

116 "Conway Brown shot himself . . ." Ibid., Jan. 1, 1884.

117 *"course of diet . . ."* Ibid., Jan. 2, 1884.

"run *with her easily . . ."* Ibid., Jan. 11, 1884.

"40 laps . . ." Ibid., Feb. 20, 1884.

"Good air *and* plenty of it . . ." AESL, CAP to Thomas Adie Perkins, May 13, 1883.

"exercise hilariously . . ." AESL, Diary, Jan. 30, Jan. 11, March 24, 1884.

"Sit and sew demurely . . ." Ibid., Feb. 11, 1884.

118 *"Carrie's black silk . . ."* Ibid., March 4, 1884.

"Walter. Am lachrymose . . ." Ibid., March 9, 1884.

"stop and see Walter . . ." Ibid., March 12, 1884.

"not for lack of thought . . ." Ibid., March 25, 1884.

"lovely curtain stuffs" Ibid., April 23, 1884.

"stop and see Walter . . ." Ibid., Feb. 13, 1884.

"joying in my little house . . ." Ibid., Feb. 29, 1884.

"Stop in and see . . ." Ibid., March 14, 1884.

119 *"first step . . . the entering . . ."* Ibid., Dec. 13, 1884.

"All that life held . . ." CAP, "One Girl of Many."

120 *"intensive self-denial . . . there was no natural . . ."* CPG, *Living*, p. 82.

"marriage is the woman's . . ." CPG, *Women and Economics*, p. 37.

"One is not born . . ." Simone de Beauvoir, *The Second Sex*, p. 249.

CHAPTER VI

121 *"Aunt C[aroline] was hearty . . . I install Walter . . ."* AESL, Diary, May 2, 1884.

"Up at 8:20 or so . . ." Ibid., May 3, 1884.

122 *"Then loaf a bit . . ."* Ibid., May 5, 1884.

"most delectable . . ." Ibid., May 6–May 7, 1884.

"I hereby take my solemn oath . . ." Ibid., the oath was written on loose paper and signed Charles Walter Stetson, Oct. 22, 1882.

"rudely breaks in upon . . ." CPG, *Women and Economics*, p. 219.

"I suggest he pay me . . ." AESL, Diary, May 9, 1884.

123 *"Realizing the great need . . ."* AESL, Thomas Addie Perkins to CPS, May 26, 1884.

"vast accumulation of dishes . . ." AESL, Diary, May 16, 1884.

"Bed. Am disgusted . . ." Ibid., May 24, 1884.

"on foreordination . . ." Ibid., June 7–9, 1884.

"Scrub out house . . ." Ibid., June 3, 1884.

"Feel sick. . . . Walter gets breakfast . . ." Ibid., June 13–14, 1884.

"Am sad: last night . . ." Ibid., June 15, June 25, June 26, 1884.

124 *"Purity . . . is that state . . ."* AESL, "Thoughts and Fingerings," Nov. 3, 1883.

"One of the most pitiful . . ." CPG, "Divorce and Birth Control," p. 131.

"Gaily to the gate . . ." CPG, "Parlor-Mindedness," *Forerunner*, I (March 1910), 9.

"feel sick . . ." AESL, Diary, Aug. 3, 1884.

"Sick still . . ." Ibid., Aug. 8, 1884.

"Dear kind thoughtful . . ." Ibid., July 24, 1884.

125 *"Dismal evening . . ."* Ibid., Sept. 4, 1884.

"I go up to mother's . . ." Ibid., Sept. 18, 1884.

"sicker than I've been . . ." Ibid., Sept. 21, 1884.

"My journal has been . . ." Ibid., Dec. 31, 1884, Jan. 1, 1885.

126 *"I get so tremulous . . ."* Ibid., Jan. 15, 1885.

"very hot and . . ." Ibid., Jan. 29, 1885.

"Bed in blanket . . ." Ibid., Jan. 30, 1885.

"I must be strong . . ." Ibid., Feb. 2, 1885.

"Am very very tired . . ." Ibid., Feb. 4, 1885.

"So hysterical . . ." Ibid., Feb. 17, 1885.

"A wellnigh . . ." Ibid., Feb. 19, 1885.

"This day, at about five . . ." Ibid., March 23, 1885.

"The experience of mothering . . ." Nancy Chodorow, "Family Structure and Feminine Personality," in Michelle Zimbalist Rosaldo, ed., *Woman, Culture, and Society*, pp. 47, 59. There is an abundance

of literature available on the subject of the psychobiology of pregnancy and postpartum depression, the issue of the connection between the physiological and psychological response. Clearly there is a substantial increase in the frequency of depression or "mental illness" among women during and immediately following pregnancy, but the complex medical and psychiatric debates on the subject are far beyond the scope of treatment here.

127 *"as a mother suddenly . . ."* Adrienne Rich, *Adrienne Rich's Poetry*, p. 109.

"pretty well used up . . ." AESL, Diary, May 1, 1885.

"The first anniversary . . ." Ibid., May 2, 1885.

"She starts . . ." Ibid., May 3, 1885.

"am very tired . . ." Ibid., May 9, 1885.

"Mother over early . . ." Ibid., May 10, 1885.

"So nice to have . . ." Ibid., May 11, 1885.

128 *"Here was a charming home . . ."* CPG, *Living*, pp. 89–92.

"paragon of Victorian . . ." Alexandra Symonds, "Phobias after Marriage," in Jean Baker Miller, ed., *Psychoanalysis and Women*, p. 299.

"Every morning the same . . ." AESL, Diary, Aug. 30, 1885.

"I let Walter read . . ." Ibid., Aug. 30, 1885.

129 *"Cry more after breakfast . . ."* Ibid., Sept. 14, 1885.

"Dreary days these . . ." Ibid., Sept. 25, 1885.

"I could not read nor write . . ." CPG, *Living*, pp. 90–91, 101.

"Feeling the sensation fear . . ." Ibid.

130 *"genuine sympathy and appreciation . . ."* CPS, "On Advertising for Marriage," p. 7.

"If a man . . ." Ibid.

131 *"We propound discuss . . ."* AESL, Diary, Oct. 8, 1885.

"He came to the door . . ." CPG, *Living*, p. 92.

132 *"had been scalped . . ."* Ibid., p. 93.

"took me across to a room . . ." Ibid.

"The vivid beauty . . ." AESL, unpublished autobiography, p. 69.

"Callas bloomed . . ." CPG, *Living*, p. 94.

"Kind and congenial . . ." Ibid.

133 *"I have not written . . ."* RIHS, CPS to MLL, Jan. 4, 1886.

"are all very kind to me . . ." Ibid.

"I wish he was near enough . . ." Ibid.

134 *"delicate, shrinking . . ."* AESL, *The Literary Development of California*, Jan., 1891.

"You can see I am . . ." RIHS, CPS to MLL, March 13, 1886.

"Have painted . . ." Ibid.

135 *"Am trying to get accustomed . . ."* AESL, Diary, April 1, 1886.

"Baby exasperating about . . ." Ibid., April 27, 1886.

"Manage to paint . . ." Ibid., Aug. 31, 1886.

"Do not feel well . . ." Ibid., Sept. 19, 1886.

"always the pain . . ." Ibid., Sept. 13, 1886.

"Allegory," AESL, unpublished short story, Sept. 1886.

136 *"laughed at him . . ."* Ibid.

"A maid was asked in marriage . . ." CPS, "The Answer," p. 313.

137 *"lovely motherly sweet . . ."* AESL, Diary, Oct. 6, 1886.

"Why Women Do Not Reform Their Dress?" p. 338.

138 *"makes an ass of himself . . ."* AESL, Diary, Oct. 22, 1886.

"so harshly from a moral point . . ." Ibid., Oct. 9, 1886.

"I leave behind me tonight . . ." Ibid., Dec. 31, 1886.

139 *"good talk . . ."* Ibid., Feb. 20, 1887.

"advocate co-operation . . ." *People*, Dec. 5, 1885.

141 *"since the vast majority . . ."* Ibid., March 5, 1887.

"woman can take . . ." Ibid., March 19, 1887.

"Men have for so long . . ." Ibid., March 26, 1887.

"In Massachusetts . . ." Ibid., Aug. 27, 1887.

"Twenty thousand . . ." Ibid., Sept. 10, 1887.

142 *"is what you are born for . . ."* Ibid., April 16, 1887.

"Every woman has rights . . ." Ibid., June 18, 1887.

"the marriage ceremony the bride . . ." Ibid., July 23, 1887.

CHAPTER VII

143 *"Kate tires me out . . ."* AESL, Diary, Jan. 9, 1887.

"Am horrified to find . . ." Ibid., Sept. 1, 1886.

"Still feel poorly . . . depart at 6 . . ." Ibid., Jan. 17, 1887.

144 *"jolly time at the gym . . ."* Ibid., Feb. 7, Feb. 21, 1887.

"was hardly a socially acceptable . . ." Ann Douglas Wood, "'The Fashionable Diseases': Women's Complaints and their Treatment," p. 7.

145 *"Thro all the surging sound . . ."* AESL, A Valentine poem from CWS to CPS, Feb. 1887.

146 *"was more near the verge . . ."* CPG, "Making a Change," *Forerunner*, II (Dec. 1911); 312.

"A very hard night . . ." AESL, Diary, March 7, 1887.

"I have a crying fit . . ." Ibid., March 13, 1887.

"Bad day. Getting back . . ." Ibid., March 20, 1887.

147 *"Try the spare room . . ."* Ibid., March 22, 1887.

"Walter breaks down . . ." Ibid., April 5, 1887.

148 *"I have kept . . ."* Ibid., April 18, 1887.

149 *"long letter giving . . ."* CPG, *Living*, p. 95.

"Live as domestic . . ." Ibid., p. 96.

150 *"case of nervous breakdown . . ."* Ibid., p. 119.

150–151 "The Yellow Wall-paper."

152 *"Finally, in the fall . . ."* CPG, *Living*, p. 96.

"If I had been of the slightest . . ." Ibid., p. 97.

153 *"her feminism emerged as a product . . ."* Margaret George, *One Woman's Situation: A Study of Mary Wollstonecraft*, p. 7.

154 *"Freedom is not merely a means . . ."* Grace Ellery Channing, ed. *Dr. Channing's Notebook: Passages from the Unpublished Manuscripts of William Ellery Channing*, p. 7.

155 *"Love is not giving . . ."* Ibid., pp. 10, 43–46.

"Are we not to . . ." Ibid., p. 46.

"All that winter . . ." CPG, *Living*, pp. 104–105.

156 *"So I set forth . . ."* Ibid., p. 105.

"little wood-and-paper . . ." Ibid., pp. 107–108.

"preliminary necessity . . ." Ibid., pp. 108–110.

157 *"agreed to separate . . ."* Ibid., p. 96.

"Katharine is just blooming . . ." BL, CWS to Rebecca Steer Stetson, Dec. 28, 1888.

"Charlotte is very busy . . ." Ibid., Jan. 8, 1889.

"combine and dine . . ." Ibid., April 29, 1889.

158 *"Charlotte is better . . ."* Ibid., May 27, 1889.

"Charlotte wrote her mother . . ." Ibid., June 7, 1889.

"some ten or twelve . . ." RIHS, CPS to MLL, March 16, 1889.

"Charlotte is doing good work . . ." BL, CWS to Rebecca Stetson, July 12, 1889.

"There is almost always . . ." Ibid., July 9, 1889.

"Walter is very happy . . ." RIHS, CPS to MLL, March 16, 1889.

"By Christmas . . ." CPG, *Living*, p. 109.

"the weakness of brain . . ." RIHS, CPS to MLL, Aug. 15, 1889.

159 *"No one has ever . . ."* Ibid.

"almost cruel . . ." BL, CWS to Rebecca Stetson, July 23, 1889.

"No, Kate and Charlotte . . ." Ibid., Oct. 30, 1889.

"Charlotte is full of the new . . ." Ibid., Nov. 4, 1889.

"I have been rather . . ." Ibid., Nov. 30, 1889.

"I have learned . . ." Ibid., Dec. 4, 1889.

"called suddenly to the bedside . . ." CPG, *Living*, p. 109.

160 *"Walter has gone East . . ."* RIHS, CPS to MLL, Jan. 20, 1890.

"I haven't any heart . . ." Ibid.

161 *"You knew and loved me once . . ."* Ibid.

162 *"strong, free, self-reliant . . ."* AESL, Grace Ellery Channing and CPS, "A Pretty Idiot," unpublished play.

163 "The Test Case," AESL, unpublished. Later published, with some changes, as "Circumstances Alter Cases," *Forerunner*, V (April 1914), 85–88.

164 *"first year of freedom": "I wrote . . ."* CPG, *Living*, p. 111.

CHAPTER VIII

167 See Thomas C. Cochran and William Miller, *The Age of Enterprise*; Harold U. Faulkner, *Politics, Reform and Expansion: 1890–1900*; Samuel P. Hays, *The Response to Industrialism*; Edward C. Kirkland, *Industry Comes of Age*; Ray Ginger, *The Age of Excess*; Alexander B. Callow, ed., *American Urban History*; Henry Pelling, *American Labor*; Robert Bremner, *From the Depths*; Robert Wiebe, *The Search for Order: 1870–1920*.

168 *"The march of invention . . ."* Henry George, *Progress and Poverty*, pp. 7–8.

169 *"Cherry Street . . ."* Jacob Riis, *How the Other Half Lives*, p. 43.

"It is doubtful . . ." W. D. P. Bliss, *American Fabian*, IV (June 1898), 1. See also, Edward Bellamy, *Looking Backward*; and Arthur Morgan, *Edward Bellamy*.

170 *"Nationalism means essentially . . ."* W. D. P. Bliss, "Christianity and Socialism," p. 99. For further discussion of American socialism see Howard Quint, *The Forging of American Socialism*; Daniel Bell, *Marxian Socialism in the United States*; G. D. H. Cole, *A History of Socialist Thought*, vol. III; Ira Kipnis, *The American Socialist Movement, 1897–1912*; David Herreshoff, *American Disciples of Marx*; C. Howard Hopkins, *The Rise of Social Gospel in American Protestantism, 1865–1915*.

171 *"no style . . . not invented much . . ."* RIHS, CPS to MLL, April 15, 1890.

"largeness of thought . . ." CPS, *Impress*, II, no. 15 (Jan. 12, 1895), 3.

"artificial habits of life . . ." AESL, "Nationalism and Love," unpublished lecture, Dec. 20 and 21, 1890.

"everybody would share . . ." AESL, unpublished lectures, June 15, and Dec. 20 and 21, 1890.

172 *"Being born without . . ."* Ibid., Dec. 20 and 21, 1890.

173 *"The tradesman naturally . . ."* Ibid.

"Army discipline . . ." AESL, "Socialism and Morality," unpublished lecture, Jan. 11, 1893. For Charlotte's views on blacks, see also CPG, "A Suggestion on the Negro Problem."

174 *"The human race . . ."* CPG, "Old Religions and New Hopes," *Forerunner*, VI (Feb. 1915), 35–36. See also, CPG, *His Religion and Hers*, pp. 193, 220.

"The 'will of God' means . . ." CPG, "A Socialist Prayer," *Forerunner*, II (May 1911), 124.

175 *"thrust at the spirit . . ."* The quotation is from the editor in a reprint of "Similar Cases," *New England Magazine*, III (Sept. 1890), 134.

"I have been dying to write you . . ." AESL, Edward Everett Hale to CPS, July 15, 1890.

"I have been wishing, ever since . . ." AESL, William Dean Howells to CPS, June 9, 1890.

"It may be essential . . ." RIHS, CPS to MLL, April 15, 1890.

176 *"Here is a long neglected . . ."* Ibid., June 17, 1890.

"never was a favorite . . ." Ibid., July 27, 1890.

177 *"What you say of . . ."* Ibid.

"I guess I told you . . ." Ibid.

178 *"I shall never forget . . ."* Harriet Howe, "Charlotte Perkins Gilman," p. 211.

"steady undying force which urges . . ." AESL, unpublished lecture, June 15, 1890.

"We know, I say . . ." Ibid.

"To my delight . . ." Harriet Howe, "Charlotte Perkins Gilman," p. 211.

179 *"Wise Mr. Steward . . ."* Ibid.

"The women in this . . ." Ibid.

For information on declining birth rates, see W. H. Grabill, C. V. Kiser, and P. K. Whelpton, *The Fertility of American Women*; also Peter Laslett and Richard Wall, eds., *Household and Family in Past Time*. For women's changing position in the work force, see Elizabeth Baker, *Technology and Women's Work*. For rising divorce rates, see William O'Neill, *Divorce in the Progressive Era*; Mary Ryan, *Womanhood in America*; William Chafe, *The American Woman*; Robert Smuts, *Women and Work in America*; Lucy Maynard Salmon, *Domestic Service*. For an excellent study of the relationship between socialists and feminists in the early twentieth century see Mari Jo Buhle, "Women and the Socialist Party, 1901–1914," in Edith Altbach, ed., *From Feminism to Liberation*, pp. 65–86.

181 *"In large generalization . . ."* CPG, *Man-Made World*, pp. 35–36; CPG, *The Home*, p. 316.

For discussion of the social purity movement, see Linda Gordon, "Voluntary Motherhood: The Beginnings of Feminist Birth Control Ideas in the United States" in Mary S. Hartman and Lois Banner, eds., *Clio's Consciousness Raised*, pp. 54–71; David Pivar, *Purity Crusade: Sexual Morality and Social Control, 1868–1900*; Linda Gordon, *Woman's Body, Woman's Right*.

182 *"If there is any real law . . ."* CPS, "Custom and the Line of Modesty."

"Now I am helping . . ." RIHS, CPS to MLL, July 27, 1890.

"Nationalism has struck . . ." AESL, unpublished lectures, June 15, 1890; Dec. 20, 21, 1890.

"causes and cures . . ." Ibid., June 26, 1890; Dec. 20, 21, 1890.

183 *"Jealousy, suspicion, infidelity . . ."* Ibid., June 26, 1890.

"On the rightnesss . . ." Ibid.

"[G]reat success . . ." AESL, Diary, Jan. 21, 1891.

"And they call . . ." Ibid., Jan. 23, 1891.

"Her object was to . . ." Harriet Howe, "Charlotte Perkins Gilman," p. 211.

184 *"Now some of you are squirming . . ."* AESL, unpublished lecture, Feb. 4, 1891.

"We hear a great deal . . ." Ibid., Jan. 21, 1891.

185 *"Am pretty miserable . . ."* CPG, *Living*, pp. 114–115.

186 *"overdose of acid phosphate . . ."* AESL, Diary, Sept. 1, 1890.

"When my awful story . . ." RIHS, CPS to MLL, July 27, 1890.

"Grace has left me . . ." Ibid., Sept. 4, 1890.

"A very quick but very hard year . . ." AESL, Diary, Dec. 31, 1890.

CHAPTER IX

187 *"will go down in history . . . And have any . . ."* AESL, unpublished lecture, Feb. 17, 1891.

188 *"united as a class . . ."* Ibid., Jan. 21, 1891.

"She walketh veiled and sleeping . . ." The poem was written in 1889, read to her class in March 1891, and published in *In This Our World*, p. 125.

189 *"That is but a brief expression . . ."* AESL, unpublished lectures, March 10, 13, 1891; Oct. 1, 1891.

"Women are human . . ." AESL, CPS to GHG, May 22, 1898.

"Was introduced . . ." AESL, Diary, May 11, 1891.

"Go and lunch . . ." Ibid., May 21, 1891; also May 23, May 26, June 1, June 2, June 7, July 14, July 18, 1891.

"most fully the really passionate . . ." AESL, CPS to GHG, March 7, 1899.

190 *"I told you that . . ."* Ibid.

"certainly did love me . . ." CPG, *Living*, p. 143.

"Two dear letters . . ." AESL, Diary, July 24, 1891; also July 25, Aug. 3, Aug. 25, Aug. 27, 1891.

"most generously kind . . ." CPG, *Living*, p. 143.

"Call on Dr. Lummis . . ." AESL, Diary, June 11, 1891.

191 *"Then I write to my love"* Ibid., June 15, 1891.

"Letter from Walter . . ." Ibid., Dec. 10, 1891.

"wrote that he could . . ." CPG, *Living*, p. 132.

"I have a lovely room . . ." AESL, Diary, Sept. 1891.

"On Friday, September 18th . . ." quoted from CPG, *Living*, p. 133. Charlotte used "Dora" in her autobiography instead of Adeline Knapp (Delle).

192 *"not yet mellowed . . ."* Ella Sterling Cummis Mighels, *The Story of the Files: A Review of California Writers and Fiction*, p. 390.

"Delle is beginning . . ." AESL, Diary, Nov. 6, 1891.

"A lovely evening . . ." Ibid., Oct. 29, Oct. 30, Nov. 6, Nov. 14, Nov. 18, Nov. 26, Dec. 25, Dec. 26, Dec. 27, 1891.

193 *"I am by no means . . ."* Ibid., Dec. 31, 1891.

"For this new year . . ." CPG, *Living*, pp. 135–136.

"a large and pleasant . . ." Ibid., p. 137.

194 *"9 people in the house . . ."* AESL, Diary, Feb. 29, 1892.

"Measles galore . . ." Ibid., March 14, 1892.

"Just work and measles" Ibid., March 16–17.

"She likes her room . . ." Ibid., April 2, 1892.

"I did all the housework . . ." CPG, *Living*, p. 140.

"She concludes to . . ." AESL, Diary, Sept. 13, 1892.

"It is difficult . . ." Harriet Howe, "Charlotte Perkins Gilman," pp. 212–213.

195 *"Up till 12:30 . . ."* AESL, Diary, Sept. 30, 1892.

"Am feeling first rate . . ." Ibid., Oct. 25, 1892.

"The mother has other children . . ." AESL, unpublished lecture, early 1890s, undated.

197 *"This was more honest . . ."* CPG, *Living*, p. 142.

"She hath willfully deserted . . ." AESL, Application for Divorce, Charles Walter Stetson, Oct. 1, 1892.

"simple facts . . ." CPG, *Living*, pp. 142–143.

"It appears that . . ." Ibid., p. 141.

"Gave out in . . ." AESL, Diary, Dec. 29, 1892.

"Yesterday morning's dispatches . . ." *San Francisco Examiner*, Dec. 19, 1892.

198 *"The fact that . . ."* Ibid.

"When two grown persons . . ." AESL, newsclipping from an unidentified Philadelphia paper, Dec. 20, 1892.

"she had too much literary . . ." *Boston Globe*, Dec. 19, 1892.

"In the name of . . ." AESL, newsclipping from an unidentified New York paper, Dec. 18, 1892.

"Do not deceive yourself . . ." *Los Angeles Times*, Dec. 22, 1892.

"I am pained . . ." AESL, newsclipping from an unidentified Philadelphia paper, Dec. 24, 1892.

"I have always . . ." *San Francisco Examiner*, Dec. 20, 1892.

"There are not many women . . ." *San Francisco Examiner*, Dec. 25, 1892.

199 *"It has been a year of great . . ."* AESL, Diary, Dec. 31, 1892.

"The bells and horns . . ." Ibid., Jan. 1, 1893.

"There were six sick . . ." CPG, *Living*, p. 139.

"Up at three . . ." AESL, Diary, Jan. 29, Jan. 8, Jan. 13, Jan. 16, Jan. 17, Jan. 31, 1893.

"very interesting . . ." Ibid., Jan. 4, Jan. 31, 1893.

200 *"Unless I learn . . ."* Ibid., Feb. 5, 1893.

"Divorced or not . . ." CPG, *Living*, p. 9.

"her mother's death reinforces . . ." Judith Gardiner, "The Heroine as Her Author's Daughter," pp. 244–253.

201 *"Sit up til two . . ."* AESL, Diary, March 3, 1893.

"giving reasons for . . ." Ibid., March 4, 1893.

202 *"quiet sunny afternoons . . . this beautiful . . ."* Harriet Howe, "Charlotte Perkins Gilman," pp. 212, 216.

"Sleep with Hattie" AESL, Diary, March 14, 1893.

"Mother sinking all day . . ." Ibid., March 6, 1893.

"Father over in the afternoon" Ibid., March 7, 1893.

"And tomorrow . . ." Ibid., April 4, 1893.

"The dear girl . . ." Ibid., April 4, April 5, May 5, 1893.

203 *"Trouble with Delle . . ."* Ibid., May 3, May 11, May 12, May 14, 1893.

"Age—near 33 . . ." Quoted from CPG, *Living*, pp. 165–167.

204 *"Rise at six . . ."* Ibid.

"Delle comes up . . ." AESL, Diary, July 6, July 12, July 13, 1893.

"Her behavior . . ." Ibid., July 15, 1893.

"Talk with Hattie . . ." Ibid., July 27, 1893.

"Says my behavior . . ." Ibid., Aug. 7, 1893.

205 *"one of those literary vampires . . ."* CPG, *Living*, p. 143.

"There seemed to creep . . ." Harriet Howe, "Charlotte Perkins Gilman," p. 212.

206 *"exactly what had been . . ."* Ibid., p. 213.

"The kindest thing . . ." CPG, *Living*, pp. 143–144.

"I left Mrs. Stetson's house . . ." AESL, note from Adeline Knapp, May 16, 1893.

"To most people . . ." AESL, CPS to GHG, Oct. 12, 1897.

208 *"right conduct on our part . . ."* AESL, "Socialism and Morality," unpublished lecture, Jan. 11, 1893.

"racial ideal of pure . . ." Ibid.

209 *"the body without clothes . . ."* AESL, unpublished lecture, probably written April 1891.

CHAPTER X

212 *"We meet in the midst . . ."* Quoted from Ignatius Donnelly in Harold Faulkner, *Politics, Reform, and Expansion: 1890–1900*, p. 129.

213 *"men who hopelessly . . ."* Quoted from William Dean Howells in Jean Holloway, *Hamlin Garland, A Biography*, p. 62.

"The realist or verist . . ." Ibid., pp. 90–91.

214 *"Bowed by the weight of centuries . . ."* Edwin Markham, *The Man with the Hoe*, p. 15.

"I don't call it . . ." An interview with CPS, quoted from the *Topeka State Journal*, June 18, 1896.

"We have no place . . ." "The Looker-On," *In This Our World*, p. 184.

"Louder, my brother! . . ." "The Old-Time Wail," ibid., p. 186.

"Then rise . . ." "To Labor," ibid., p. 194.

215 *"Go ask the literature . . ."* "Reassurance," ibid., p. 139.

"And some have . . ." "Too Much," ibid., p. 58.

"No human soul . . ." "Our Loneliness," ibid., p. 61.

216 *"What power can stir . . ."* "The Wolf at the Door," ibid., pp. 177–178.

"sort of salon. . . . People of all sorts . . ." Harriet Howe, "Charlotte Perkins Gilman," p. 214.

217 *"tall, slow woman . . ."* Mary Austin, *Earth Horizon*, p. 231.

"virginal Ina Coolbrith . . . highly respected . . ." Franklin D. Walker, *San Francisco's Literary Frontier*, p. 64.

"Were I to write . . ." Ibid., p. 63.

"as if the fly . . ." CPG, *Living*, p. 150.

"merciless power . . ." Ibid., p. 145.

218 *"Am roused to new . . ."* AESL, Diary, Sept. 17, 1893; also Sept. 16, Sept. 22, Sept. 23, 1893.

"What the creeping . . ." CPG, *Living*, p. 171.

219 *"passion and imagination . . . neurosis . . ."* Louis Filler, *The Unknown Edwin Markham: His Mystery and Its Significance*, pp. 71, 92.

"Joaquin was already . . ." Harriet Howe, "Charlotte Perkins Gilman," p. 214.

220 *"thoroughly nice fellow"* AESL, Diary, March 15, 1893.

"Am so much moved . . ." Ibid., July 20, 1893.

"Such questions! Was not . . ." Ibid., March 27, 1893.

221 *"that wonderful seer . . ."* *Impress*, I, no. 7 (Dec. 1893), 5.

"the interests of reform . . ." *Bulletin*, Sept. 1893.

"It is not often . . ." *Impress*, I, no. 7 (Dec. 1893), 1.

"Father calls to see me . . ." AESL, Diary, March 19, 1893.

222 *"To our delight . . ."* Harriet Howe, "Charlotte Perkins Gilman," p. 213.

223 *"Desired for this year . . ."* AESL, Diary, Jan. 1, 1894.

224 *"Mr. Hough spends . . ."* Ibid., March 7, 1894.

"that makes another . . ." Ibid., March 8, 1894.

"My Fate seems turned . . ." Ibid., March 20, 1894.

"If it be that . . ." AESL, "Thoughts and Fingerings," March 26, 1894.

225 *"Three [men] since '93 . . ."* AESL, CPS to GHG, May 23, 1898.

"Queer unfeminine girl . . ." Ibid., Dec. 16, 1898.

226 *"Nice long day . . ."* AESL, Diary, Feb. 10, 1894.

"Find letter from . . ." Ibid., June 18, 1894.

"Having made the painfully . . ." CPG, *Living*, p. 167.

227 *"second mother . . ."* Ibid., p. 163.

"unmeasured joy . . ." Ibid., pp. 91, 153–154.

228 *"Something of my mother's . . ."* Ibid., pp. 138–159.

"If mother knew . . ." Quoted from CPG, *In This Our World*, pp. 150–152; originally in AESL, Diary, Sept. 8, 1893.

229 *"We had happy . . ."* CPG, *Living*, p. 162.

231 *"'instinct' rather than intelligence . . ."* Adrienne Rich, *Of Woman Born*, p. 42.

"Go to Dr. Kellog . . ." AESL, Diary, June 15, 1894.

"I tried to reassure myself . . ." AESL, CPS to GHG, Jan. 20, 1900.

"I took her to the uptown station . . ." CPG, *Living*, pp. 163–164.

232 *"The mothers in all these . . ."* Judith Gardiner, "The Heroine as Her Author's Daughter," p. 248.

"It took family deaths . . ." Tillie Olsen, "Silences: When Writers Don't Write," in Susan Koppelman Cornillon, ed., *Images of Women in Fiction: Feminist Perspectives*, p. 107.

"in the foreground . . ." AESL, CPS to GHG, Oct. 1, 1897.

"Of course she does not care . . ." Ibid., Jan. 5, 1900.

"I have some hopes . . ." Ibid., March 26, 1899.

232–237 Personal interviews with Katharine Stetson Chamberlin, July 1976.

236 *"deep bitterness of feeling . . ."* AESL, CPS to GHG, Jan. 20, 1900.

CHAPTER XI

238 *"the most ingenious . . ."* VCL, CPS to Marian P. Whitney, March 19, 1894.

"I had lost . . ." CPG, *Living*, p. 164.

"We became the . . ." Ibid., pp. 142, 171.

240 *"profound and widespread . . ."* Frances Willard and Mary A. Livermore, eds., *A Woman of the Century*, p. 148.

"I never knew . . ." AESL, CPS to GHG, May 9, 1900.

"She is the bravest . . ." Ibid., Nov. 15, 1899.

"sarcasm keen as . . ." AESL, Helen Campbell, "Charlotte Perkins Stetson—A Sketch," *Time and the Hour*, April 16, 1898.

"made a proposition . . ." *Impress*, I, no. 11 (May, 1894), 5.

"I shall never forget . . ." AESL, CPS to GHG, Nov. 15, 1899; May 9, May 19, 1900.

"home of its own . . ." *Impress*, I, no. 12 (June 1894), 4.

242 *"did the political stuff . . ."* CPG, *Living*, pp. 172–173.

"The home today . . ." *Impress*, vol. II, no. 2 (Oct. 13, 1894); vol. XI, no. 10 (Dec. 8, 1894).

"I could not write a good story . . ." CPG, *Living*, p. 173.

243 *"hope for a clear . . ."* *Impress*, II, no. 13 (Dec. 29, 1894), 3.

"woman's paper in so far . . ." *Impress*, II, no. 2 (Oct. 13, 1894), 2.

"Some anxious member queries . . ." *Impress*, I, no. 14 (Aug. 1894), 1.

244 *"The conspiracy marches . . ."* *Impress*, II, no. 10 (Dec. 9, 1894), 2.

"seventy-one percent . . ." *Impress*, II, no. 8 (Nov. 24, 1894), 3.

"Nearly two million . . ." *Impress*, II, no. 12 (Dec. 22, 1894), 2; II, no. 11 (Dec. 15, 1894), 1; II, no. 8 (Nov. 24, 1894), 3.

245 *"Drop in on . . ."* AESL, Diary, March 16, 1894.

"By great good fortune . . ." Ibid., March 19, 1894.

"quite a reception . . ." Ibid., April 18, 1894.

246 *"It is not brick and mortar . . ."* Quotation of David Starr Jordan in Edwin Bingham, *Charles F. Lummis: Editor of the Southwest*, p. 170. See also John Dewey, *School and Society*; John Dewey and James H. Tufts, *Ethics*; Morton White, *The Origins of Dewey's Instrumentalism*.

247 *"dreary narrow . . ."* CPG, "Two Great Pleasures," *Forerunner*, III (April 1912), 103.

"old-time wail" CPG, *In This Our World*, p. 185.

"knowledge for the sole purpose . . ." CPG, *Our Brains and What Ails Them*, in *Forerunner*, III (Aug. 1912), 218.

248 *"When the whole civilized . . ."* John Dewey and James H. Tufts, *Ethics*, p. v.

"own power . . ." CPG, "Wholesale Hypnotism," *Forerunner*, I (Aug. 1910), 6.

"mere transmission . . ." CPG, *Our Brains and What Ails Them*, in *Forerunner*, III (Aug. 1912), 219; CPG, "Growth and Combat," *Forerunner*, VII (Sept. 1916), 251; CPG, *Human Work*, pp. 32–33.

249 *"women in matters . . ."* AESL, Notice of the Second Annual Meeting of the Woman's Congress of the Pacific Coast.

"These congresses bring women . . ." AESL, "Woman's Congress," article from an unidentified San Francisco newspaper.

"devoted to the study . . ." AESL, Notice of the Second Annual Meeting of the Woman's Congress of the Pacific Coast.

250 *"My friends, what is a man's idea . . ."* *History of Woman Suffrage*, IV, 165.

"The assumption that women . . ." *History of Woman Suffrage*, V, 159. Dr. Anna Howard Shaw's speech was delivered in 1909.

"not only do we . . ." CPG, "Domestic Economy," *Independent*, LVI (June 16, 1904), 1,359–1,360; CPG, *The Home*, p. 314.

"what any human business would be . . ." CPG, "The Normal Social Group To-day," *Forerunner*, IV (July 1913), 175; CPG, *Women and Economics*, p. 225; CPG, "What Do Men Think of Women?"

Forerunner, III (Jan. 1912), 15; CPG, "Her Own Money: Is a Wife Entitled to the Money She Earns," pp. 5–7.

251 *"No men . . ."* CPG, "How Home Conditions React Upon the Family," p. 598.

"It was the American wife . . ." *San Francisco Examiner*, May 29, 1895.

"most marvelous gathering . . ." *History of Woman Suffrage*, IV, 253.

"the very word 'suffrage' . . ." Reda Davis, *California Women: A Guide to their Politics, 1885–1911*, p. 90.

253 *"democracy at all . . ."* *History of Woman Suffrage*, IV, 277.

"Are we not somewhat . . ." CPG, "Suffrage Work," *Woman's Journal*, XXXV (March 5, 1904), 74.

"Your work will be . . ." CPG, "A Summary of Purpose," *Forerunner*, II (Nov. 1916), 287.

254 *"I am ashamed not to have said . . ."* AESL, William Dean Howells to CPS, July 11, 1894.

"I think The Impress . . ." *Impress*, II, no. 10 (Dec. 8, 1894), 15; II, no. 11 (Dec. 15, 1894), 15; II, no. 15 (Jan. 12, 1895), 15.

255 *"inquiries as to . . ."* CPG, *Living*, pp. 173, 167.

"Discipline and obedience . . ." Ibid., pp. 158–161.

256 *"Katharine was the best . . ."* Ibid., pp. 160–161.

"affronted public opinion . . ." Mary Austin, *Earth Horizon*, p. 293.

"An Unnatural Mother," *Impress*, II, no. 20 (Feb. 16, 1895), 4–5.

257 *"'and it was just . . .'"* Ibid.

"The Duty Farthest," *Impress*, II, no. 7 (Nov. 17, 1894), 5.

258 *"What I maintain . . ."* AESL, CPS to GHG, Dec. 21, 1898.

CHAPTER XII

259 *"Be glad! Be free!"* CPG, *Living*, p. 180.

"I don't wear well . . ." AESL, CPS to GHG, Aug. 23, 1897.

"I said many years . . ." Ibid., Aug. 8, 1897.

"mounting ambition . . . wild delicious sense . . ." RIHS, CAP to ML, July 31, 1881.

"myself as a self . . ." Ibid., July 24, 1881.

260 *"Don't you feel very much . . ."* CPG, *Living*, p. 181.

"The thought that brought us . . ." *History of Woman Suffrage*, IV, 252.

261 *"Logical arguments . . . justice . . ."* Ibid., p. 335.

"build a great organization . . ." Ibid., p. 256.

262 *"stood for half a century . . ."* Ibid., p. 264.

"I shall be pained . . ." Ibid., p. 264.

"So God created man . . ." Elizabeth Cady Stanton, *The Woman's Bible*, pp. 14–15.

263 *"death was the impressive crisis . . ."* CPG, *Man-Made World*, p. 226; CPG, *His Religion and Hers*, pp. 51, 5–7.

264 *"the Life-giver . . ."* CPG, *His Religion and Hers*, p. 51.

"implanted in our minds . . ." Ibid., pp. 112–114, 227.

"handsome and virile" Clifford Scott, *Lester Frank Ward*, p. 39.

"the grandest fact . . ." Lester Ward, "Our Better Halves," p. 275.

"Prof. Lester Ward calls . . ." AESL, Diary, Jan. 23, 1896.

"Preach A.M. . . ." Ibid., Jan. 26, 1896.

265 *"Speak before the Judiciary Committee . . ."* Ibid., Jan. 28, 1896.

"read by nearly everybody . . ." Lester Ward, *Glimpses of the Cosmos*, pp. 336–339.

"I am exceedingly proud . . ." JHL, CPS to Lester Ward, Jan. 1, 1896.

"Please say you will . . ." AESL, Lester Ward to CPS, Jan. 17, 1897.

"quite the greatest man . . ." CPG, *Living*, p. 187.

"He was an outstanding . . ." Ibid.

266 *"in honor and gratitude . . ."* CPG, Dedication to *Man-Made World*. See also CPG, *Living*, p. 259.

267 *"in the economy . . ."* Lester Ward, "Our Better Halves," pp. 266–275.

268 *"female superiority is . . ."* Ibid.

"tiny male . . . tremblingly achieves . . ." CPG, *Women and Economics*, p. 129.

"if there is a race . . ." CPG, *His Religion and Hers*, pp. 270, 30.

269 *"founded in mother love . . ."* CPG, *The Man-Made World*, pp. 182, 234–235.

"The whole feminine attitude . . ." CPG, *His Religion and Hers*, p. 270.

"The innate, underlying difference . . ." Ibid., p. 271.

"group of women admirers" Clifford Scott, *Lester Frank Ward,* pp. 39–40.

270 *"more than half of the letters . . ."* Ibid.

"Women wanted to meet him . . ." Emily Palmer Cape, *Lester Ward*, p. 78.

"Those of us who have for years . . ." Quoted from *Woman's Journal* in *Historv of Woman Suffrage*, IV, 256.

"Charlotte Perkins Stetson has a . . ." Nelly Bly, *New York World,* Jan. 26, 1896.

271 *"We have heard . . ."* *History of Woman Suffrage*, IV, 266–267.

"because you began in the cradle . . ." Ibid.

272 *"That is masculine . . ."* CPG, "Masculine, Feminine, and Human," p. 18.

"an intellectual milieu . . ." George W. Stocking, Jr., *Race, Culture and Evolution*, p. 251.

"for all the invulnerable self-belief . . ." AESL, CPS to GHG, May 11, 1897.

273 *"It stood, quite literally . . ."* Margaret Tims, *Jane Addams of Hull House*, p. 43.

"Greeks slaughtered sheep . . ." James Weber Linn, *Jane Addams,* p. 168.

"provide a center for . . ." Margaret Tims, *Jane Addams of Hull House*, p. 49.

274 *"City of Refuge . . . by riches . . ."* James Weber Linn, *Jane Addams,* p. 132.

"prime ministers of Europe . . ." Ibid., p. 140.

275 *"a truly great woman . . ."* CPG, *Living*, p. 184.

"Not know Jame Addams! . . ." AESL, CPS to GHG, July 27, 1897.

276 *"The loathly river . . ."* CPG, *Living*, pp. 184–185.

"No one needs special knowledge . . ." CPG, *His Religion and Hers,* p. 281.

"There are such splendid things . . ." CPG, "Food and Clothes," *Forerunner*, IV (Sept. 1913), 234.

277 *"People who are awake . . ."* CPG, "This Bitterness," *Forerunner,* III (Dec. 1912), 317.

278 *"social charwomen"* See Mary Ryan, *Womanhood in America*, pp. 139–191.

"the human female . . ." CPG, *Women and Economics*, pp. 20–21.

"is neither freedom nor equality . . ." CPG, *The Home*, p. 171.

279 *"Nothing will conduce . . ."* CPG, *Human Work*, p. 133.

"homicidal mania" CPG, "Comment and Review," *Forerunner*, VI (Aug. 1915), 223.

"stuffed . . . with the most . . ." CPG, *With Her in Our Land*, in *Forerunner*, VII (June 1916), 153.

"Let us by all means welcome . . ." CPG, "Let Sleeping Forefathers Lie," *Forerunner*, VI (Oct. 1915), 263.

280 *"'lower class' we so condemn . . ."* AESL, CPS to GHG, Dec. 4, 1898.

"Here was companionship . . ." CPG, *Living*, p. 184.

"The settlement becomes sure and real . . ." AESL, Diary, Feb. 28, 1896.

"Glorious days . . ." Ibid., March 1, 1896.

"Brace up and write . . ." Ibid., March 13, 1896.

"Very bad day . . ." Ibid., March 14, 1896.

"Am so bad that Mother . . ." Ibid., March 15, 1896.

"Sit down in office . . ." Ibid., March 16, 1896.

281 *"flux of disconnected people . . . noisome neighborhood"* AESL, CPS to GHG, May 15, 1900.

"wonderful Miss Addams . . ." Ibid., May 15, 1900.

"rescued . . . that black house . . ." CPG, *Living*, p. 190.

"In Mother-Time," *In This Our World*, pp. 144–145. Charlotte's diary indicates that "In Mother-Time" was written on Feb. 26, 1896.

282 *"the mother side of me . . ."* RIHS, CAP to ML, July 24, 1881.

"Things are a little thick . . ." AESL, "Thoughts and Fingerings," March 7, 1896.

CHAPTER XIII

283 *"with both theory . . ."* CPG, *Living*, pp. 198–199.

"The steamer was . . ." Ibid., p. 199.

284 *"I was in one . . ."* Ibid., p. 201.

"That this International Meeting . . ." AESL, "Resolution," Hyde Park Demonstration in Favor of International Peace.

"rising storm of eloquence . . ." CPG, *Living*, pp. 202–203.

285 *"revolutionary opposition to . . ."* G. D. H. Cole, *A History of Socialist Thought*, III, Pt. I, p. 210.

"The object of the Fabian Society . . ." AESL, *Report on Fabian Policy and Resolutions*, pp. 3–5.

"each and every industry . . ." CPG, *His Religion and Hers*, p. 148.

"is no more part of the business . . ." CPG, "Growth and Combat," *Forerunner*, VII (Oct. 1916), 276–277.

"Society is not . . ." *Moving the Mountain*, in *Forerunner* II (Aug. 1911), 223.

"right economic belief . . ." CPG, *Human Work*, pp. 355–356.

"always pushing, pushing . . ." CPG, "Having Faith in Evolution," *Forerunner*, VI (Nov. 1915), 299.

286 *"life means Progress"* CPG, *Women and Economics*, p. 208.

"gray and glorious . . ." CPG, *Living*, pp. 208–211.

"the wealth and variety . . ." Edward Carpenter, *Love's Coming of Age*, p. 121.

287 *"A marriage, so free . . ."* Ibid., p. 121.

"see Edward Carpenter . . ." AESL, Diary, Sept. 28, 1896.

"I think very highly of . . ." AESL, CPS to GHG, June 4, 1897.

"Some [of the Fabians'] sandals . . ." CPG, *Living*, p. 203.

"The Unexpected," orig. pub. May 21, 1890, in *Kate Field's Washington*, pp. 335–336; later published in *Forerunner*, IV (Nov. 1913), 280–284.

288 *"usual woman's faith . . ."* Ibid.

"distinguished Fabians" CPG, *Living*, p. 203.

289 *"Conversation, where Mr. Shaw . . ."* Ibid., p. 204.

"Shaw's work is . . ." AESL, CPS to GHG, Aug. 1, 1897.

"very good and useful . . ." AESL, Diary, Aug. 3, 1896.

290 *"More talk with . . ."* Ibid., Aug. 6, 1896.

"Find that I am . . ." Ibid., Aug. 12–Aug. 28, 1896.

"If I had been well . . ." CPG, *Living*, p. 209.

"A week of foregone failure . . ." Ibid., pp. 213–214.

291 *"broken down completely . . ."* Ibid., p. 215.

"brilliant intellect . . ." Ibid.

292 *"Go down to see . . ."* AESL, Diary, Dec. 3 and 4, 1896.

"charming little lady . . ." CPG, *Living*, p. 191.

"Arrive . . . Drive up . . ." AESL, Diary, Nov. 30, 1896.

"received its initiative . . ." *American Fabian*, II, no. 8 (Dec. 1896), 4.

293 *"The energy and sacrifice . . ."* Eugene Hough, "The Work and Influence of Charlotte Perkins Stetson in the Labor Movement," *American Fabian*, II, no. 9 (Jan. 1897), 12.

294 *"Upstairs at 11:50 . . ."* AESL, Diary, Dec. 31, 1896.

AFTERWORD

295 *"Thirty-five hundred words . . ."* AESL, CPS to GHG, Sept. 2, 1897.

"masterpiece" AESL, Jane Addams to CPS, July 19, 1898.

"the first real, substantial . . ." AESL, Florence Kelley to CPS, July 26, 1898.

"Since John Stuart Mill's essays . . ." *London Daily Chronicle*, June 26, 1899. *Women and Economics* was widely reviewed in both the United States and England. Several examples follow.

"The most significant utterance on the subject since Mill's *Subjection of Women*." *Nation*, June 8, 1899.

"This book unites in a remarkable degree the charm of a brilliantly written essay with the inevitable logic of a proposition of Euclid. It deals of course with the woman question, but in a manner so striking, from a standpoint so novel, with a wit so trenchant yet void of offence, that no apology is needed for its publication in England after making something of a sensation in the United States. Nothing that we have read for many a long day can approach in clearness of perception, in power of arrangement, and in lucidity of expression." *Westminster Gazette*, London, Aug. 29, 1899.

"[*Women and Economics*] has been considered by feminists of the whole world as the outstanding book on Feminism." *New York City Review of Literature*, Aug. 19, 1933.

"It lacks beauty; it is too clever, one suspects that it is glib rather than profound; it stirs no deep reverberations of the soul, as Ellen Key would say—but you can quote it, and remember its points." *Chicago Tribune*, May 24, 1914.

297 *"stern cold thinker"* AESL, CPS to GHG, Dec. 16, 1898.

"If you save all this stuff . . ." Ibid., May 25, 1897.

Bibliography

PRIMARY SOURCES

Manuscript Collections

Arthur and Elizabeth Schlesinger Library on the History of Women in America, Radcliffe College, Cambridge, Mass. The Charlotte Perkins Gilman Collection.

Bancroft Library, University of California, Berkeley, Calif. The Charles Walter Stetson correspondence.

John Hay Library, Brown University, Providence, R.I. The Charlotte Gilman–Lester Ward correspondence.

Rhode Island Historical Society, Providence, R.I. Charlotte Gilman's correspondence with Martha Luther (Lane).

Stowe Day Foundation, Hartford, Conn. Correspondence of Mary Westcott Perkins and Isabella Beecher Hooker.

Vassar College Library, Vassar College, Poughkeepsie, N.Y. Charlotte Gilman's correspondence with Marian Whitney.

Selected List of Published Works by Charlotte Gilman and Magazines with Which She Was Closely Affiliated

American Fabian, Vol. II, nos. 1–20 (Oct. 6, 1894–Feb. 16, 1895).

"The Answer," *Woman's Journal*, XVII, no. 40 (Oct. 2, 1886), 313. (As Charlotte Perkins Stetson.)

Benigna Machiavella. Serialized in *Forerunner*, vol. V (1914).

Bulletin, I (Sept.–Oct. 1893). *Impress Magazine*, I–II (Nov. 1893–Feb. 1895).

Concerning Children. Boston: Small, Maynard, 1900.

The Crux. Serialized in *Forerunner*, vol. II (1911).

"Custom and the Line of Modesty," *Kate Field's Washington*, Sept. 17, 1890. (As Charlotte Perkins Stetson.)

"Divorce and Birth Control," *Outlook*, CXLVIII (Jan. 25, 1928), 130–131, 153.

"Do Women Dress to Please Men?" *Century Magazine*, CIII (March 1922), 651–659. (With Alexander Black.)

"Domestic Economy," *Independent*, LVI (June 16, 1904), 1,359–1,363.
Forerunner, I–VII (1910–1916).
"Her Own Money: Is a Wife Entitled to the Money She Earns?" *Mother's Magazine*, VII, no. 2 (Feb. 1912), 5–7.
Herland. Serialized in *Forerunner*, vol. VI (1915).
His Religion and Hers: A Study of the Faith of Our Fathers and the Work of Our Mothers. New York: The Century Company, 1923.
The Home: Its Work and Influence. New York: McClure, Phillips, 1903.
"How Home Conditions React Upon the Family," *American Journal of Sociology*, XIV (March 1909), 592–605.
Human Work. New York: McClure, Phillips, 1903.
In This Our World: Poems. New York: Arno, 1974; 1st pub., 1893. (As Charlotte Perkins Stetson.)
"The Labor Movement." A prize essay read before the Trades and Labor Unions of Alameda County, Sept. 5, 1892. Oakland, Ca.: Alameda County Federation of Trades, 1893. (As Charlotte Perkins Stetson.)
The Living of Charlotte Perkins Gilman: An Autobiography. New York: Harper & Row, 1975; 1st pub., 1935.
Mag-Marjorie. Serialized in *Forerunner*, vol. III (1912).
"Making Towns Fit to Live In," *Century Magazine*, CII (July 1921), 361–366.
The Man-Made World: Our Androcentric Culture. New York: Charlton, 1911.
"Masculine, Feminine, and Human," *Woman's Journal*, XXXV (Jan. 16, 1904), 18.
Moving the Mountain. Serialized in *Forerunner*, vol. II (1911).
"On Advertising for Marriage," *Alpha*, II, no. 1, (Sept. 1, 1885), 7. (As Charlotte Perkins Stetson.)
"One Girl of Many," *Alpha*, IX (Feb. 1, 1884), 15. (As Charlotte A. Perkins.)
Our Brains and What Ails Them. Serialized in *Forerunner*, vol. III (1912).
The Punishment That Educates. Cooperstown, New York: Crist, Scott, and Parshall, 1907.
Social Ethics. Serialized in *Forerunner* V (1914).
"Suggestion on the Negro Problem," *American Journal of Sociology*, XIV (July 1908), 78–85.
"The Unexpected," *Kate Field's Washington*, May 21, 1890, pp. 335–336. (As Charlotte Perkins Stetson.)
What Diantha Did. Serialized in *Forerunner*, vol. I (1909).
"Why Women Do Not Reform Their Dress?" *Woman's Journal*, XVII (Oct. 23, 1886), 338. (As Charlotte Perkins Stetson.)
With Her in Our Land. Serialized in *Forerunner*, vol. VII (1916).
Woman's Journal, XVI–XXXVI (1886–1906).
Women and Economics: A Study of the Economic Relation Between Men and Women as a Factor in Social Evolution. New York: Harper & Row, 1966; 1st pub., 1898. (As Charlotte Perkins Stetson.)
Women and Social Service. National American Woman Suffrage Association, 1907.

"The Yellow Wall-paper," *New England Magazine*, V (Jan. 1892), 647–659, (as Charlotte Perkins Stetson); rpt., New York: Feminist Press, 1973.

SECONDARY SOURCES

Unpublished Works

Allen-Robinson, Polly Wynn. "The Social Ethics of Charlotte Perkins Gilman." Ph.D. diss. Harvard University, 1978.

Doyle, William. "Charlotte Gilman and the Cycle of Feminist Reform." Ph.D. diss., University of California, Berkeley, 1960.

Porter, Mary A. (Mary A. Hill.) "Charlotte Perkins Gilman: A Feminist Paradox." Ph.D. diss., McGill University, 1975.

Potts, Helen Jo. "Charlotte Perkins Gilman: A Humanist Approach to Feminism." Ph.D. diss., North Texas State University, 1975.

Published Works

Abbott, Lyman, ed. *Hints for Home Reading*. New York: G. P. Putnam's Sons, 1880.

Addams, Jane. *Democracy and Social Ethics*. New York: Macmillan, 1902.

———. *Twenty Years at Hull House*. New York: Macmillan, 1966; 1st pub., 1910.

Allport, Gordon. *The Use of Personal Documents in Psychological Science*. Bulletin 49. New York: Social Science Research Council, 1942.

Altbach, Edith, ed. *From Feminism to Liberation*. Cambridge, Mass.: Schenkman, 1971.

Anthony, E. J., and Benedek, Therese. *Parenthood: Its Psychology and Psychopathology*. Boston: Little, Brown, 1970.

Austin, Mary. *Earth Horizon: An Autobiography*. Boston: Houghton Mifflin, 1932.

Baker, Elizabeth. *Technology and Woman's Work*. New York: Columbia University Press, 1964.

Beals, Carlton. *The Great Revolt and Its Leaders: The History of Popular American Uprisings in the 1890's*. New York: Abelard-Schuman, 1968.

Beard, Mary. *Woman as Force in History*. New York: Collier-Macmillan, 1946.

Beauvoir, Simone de. *The Second Sex*. Trans. H. M. Parshley. New York: Knopf, 1953.

Bell, Daniel. *Marxian Socialism in the United States*. Princeton: Princeton University Press, 1952.

Bellamy, Edward. *Looking Backward, 2000–1887*. Boston: Ticknor, 1888.

Bingham, Edwin. *Charles F. Lummis: Editor of the Southwest*. San Marino, Calif.: The Huntington Library, 1955.

Blaikie, William. *How to Get Strong and How to Stay So*. New York: Harper & Brothers, 1898; 1st pub., 1879.

Blassingame, John W. *The Slave Community: Plantation Life in the Antebellum South*. New York: Oxford University Press, 1972.
Bliss, W. D. P. "Christianity and Socialism," *Nationalist*, I (Aug. 1899), 99.
Bremner, Robert. *From the Depths: The Discovery of Poverty in the United States*. New York: New York University Press, 1956.
Brown, Cheryl L., and Karen Olson. *Feminist Criticism: Essays on Theory, Poetry and Prose*. Metuchen, N.J.: Scarecrow Press, 1978.
Callow, Alexander, ed. *American Urban History: An Interpretive Reader with Commentaries*. 2nd ed. New York: Oxford University Press, 1973.
Campbell, Helen. *The Easiest Way in Housekeeping and Cooking*. New York: Fords, Howard, & Hulbert, 1881.
———. *Household Economics*. New York: G. P. Putnam's Sons, 1897.
———. *Prisoners of Poverty*. Boston: Roberts Brothers, 1887.
———. *Prisoners of Poverty Abroad*. Boston: Roberts Brothers, 1889.
———. *The Problems of the Poor*. New York: Fords, Howard, & Hulbert, 1882.
Cape, Emily Palmer. *Lester Ward*. New York: G. P. Putnam's Sons, 1922.
Carpenter, Edward. *Love's Coming of Age*. London: George Allen & Unwin, 1896.
Carroll, Berenice, ed. *Liberating Women's History: Theoretical and Critical Essays*. Urbana, Ill.: University of Illinois Press, 1976.
Chafe, William H. *The American Woman: Her Changing Social, Economic, and Political Role, 1920–1970*. New York: Oxford University Press, 1977; 1st pub., 1972.
Channing, Grace Ellery, ed. *Dr. Channing's Notebooks: Passages from the Unpublished Manuscripts of William Ellery Channing*. Boston: Houghton Mifflin, 1887.
———. *Sister of a Saint and Other Stories*. Chicago: Stone & Kimball, 1905.
Channing, William H., R. W. Emerson, and J. F. Clarke, eds. *Memoirs of Margaret Fuller Ossoli*. Boston: Roberts Brothers, 1874.
Chesler, Phyllis. *Women and Madness*. New York: Avon, 1972.
Chodorow, Nancy. *The Reproduction of Mothering: Psychoanalysis and the Sociology of Gender*. Berkeley, Calif.: University of California Press, 1978.
Chugerman, Samuel. *Lester Ward, The American Aristotle: A Summary and Interpretation of His Sociology*. New York: Octagon Books, 1965; 1st pub., 1939.
Cochran, Thomas and William Miller. *Age of Enterprise: A Social History of Industrial America*. New York: Harper & Row, 1968.
Cole, G. D. H. *A History of Socialist Thought*. Vol. III. New York: St. Martin's Press, 1953–1958.
Cole, Margaret. *The Story of Fabian Socialism*. Rev. ed. New York: Wiley, 1961.
Conway, Jill. "The Woman's Peace Party and the First World War." In *War and Society in North America*, ed. J. L. Granatstein and R. D. Cuff, pp. 52–65. Toronto: Thomas, Nelson & Sons, 1971.
———. "Women Reformers and American Culture, 1870–1930," *Journal of Social History*, V (Winter 1971–1972), 164–177.

Cornillon, Susan Koppelman, ed. *Images of Women in Fiction: Feminist Perspectives*. Rev. ed. Bowling Green, Ohio: Bowling Green University Popular Press, 1973.

Cott, Nancy. *The Bonds of Womanhood: "Woman's Sphere" in New England, 1780–1835*. New Haven: Yale University Press, 1977.

Croly, Herbert. *The Promise of American Life*. New York: Macmillan, 1909.

Dalla Costa, Mariarosa. *The Power of Women and the Subversion of the Community*. 2nd ed. Bristol, England: Falling Wall Press, 1973.

Daly, Mary. *Beyond God the Father: Toward a Philosophy of Women's Liberation*. Boston: Beacon Press, 1973.

Davis, Allen. *American Heroine: The Life and Legend of Jane Addams*. New York: Oxford University Press, 1973.

Davis, Elizabeth Gould. *The First Sex*. New York: G. P. Putnam's Sons, 1971.

Davis, Reda. *California Women: A Guide to their Politics, 1885–1911*. San Francisco: California Scene, 1968.

Degler, Carl. "Charlotte Perkins Gilman on the Theory and Practice of Feminism," *American Quarterly*, VIII (Spring 1956), 21–39.

———. *Is There a History of Women?* Oxford: Clarendon Press, 1975.

———. "What Ought to be and What Was: Women's Sexuality in the Nineteenth Century," *American Historical Review, LXXIX* (Dec. 1974), 1,467–1,490.

Deutsch, Helene. *The Psychology of Women*. Vols. I and II. New York: Grune and Stratten, 1944, 1945.

Dewey, John. *School and Society*. Chicago: University of Chicago Press, 1961; 1st pub., 1899.

Dewey, John, and James H. Tufts. *Ethics*. New York: Holt, 1908.

Dorfman, Joseph. *Thorstein Veblen and His America*. New York: Kelly, 1934.

Drinnon, Richard. *Rebel in Paradise: A Biography of Emma Goldman*. Boston: Beacon Press, 1970.

Faulkner, Harold. *Politics, Reform, and Expansion: 1890–1900*. New York: Harper & Row, 1963; 1st pub., 1959.

Filene, Peter. *Him/Her/Self*. New York: Harcourt Brace Jovanovich, 1975.

Filler, Louis. *The Unknown Edwin Markham: His Mystery and Its Significance*. Yellow Springs, Ohio: The Antioch Press, 1966.

Fine, Sidney. *Laissez Faire and the General-Welfare State: A Study of Conflict in American Thought, 1865–1901*. Ann Arbor: University of Michigan Press, 1964.

Firestone, Shulamith. *The Dialectic of Sex: The Case for Feminist Revolution*. New York:Bantam, 1971.

Flexner, Eleanor. *Century of Struggle: The Women's Rights Movement in the U.S.* New York: Atheneum, 1971; 1st pub., 1959.

Franklin, Margaret Ladd. *The Case for Woman Suffrage: A Bibliography*. New York: National College Equal Suffrage League, 1913.

Friedman, Jean, and William Shade, eds. *Our American Sisters*. Boston: Allyn & Bacon, 1973.

Gardiner, Judith. "The Heroine as Her Author's Daughter." In *Feminist Criticism: Essays on Theory, Poetry and Prose*, ed. Cheryl L. Brown and Karen Olson, pp. 244–253. Metuchen, N.J.: Scarcrow Press, 1978.

George, Henry. *Progress and Poverty: An Inquiry into the Cause of Industrial Depression, and of Increase of Want with Increase of Wealth—The Remedy*. New York: Appleton, 1880.

George, Margaret. *One Woman's Situation: A Study of Mary Wollstonecraft*. Chicago: University of Illinois Press, 1970.

Ginger, Ray. *Age of Excess: The United States from 1877–1914*. 2nd ed. New York: Macmillan, 1975.

Goldman, Eric. *Rendezvous with Destiny*. New York: Vintage, 1961; 1st pub., 1956.

Gordon, Linda. *Woman's Body, Woman's Right: A Social History of Birth Control in America*. New York: Grossman, 1976.

Gordon, Michael, ed. *The American Family in Social and Historical Perspective*. New York: St. Martin's Press, 1978.

Grabill, W. H., C. V. Kiser, and P. K. Whelpton. *The Fertility of American Women*. New York: Wiley, 1968.

Gutman, Herbert. *The Black Family in Slavery and Freedom, 1750–1920*. New York: Pantheon, 1976.

Hale, Edward E. *Roland Hazard Memorial*. Peacedale, R.I., 1891.

Haller, J. S. and Robin M. Haller. *The Physician and Sexuality in Victorian America*. Urbana, Ill.: University of Illinois Press, 1974.

Hamilton, Mary A. *Sidney and Beatrice Webb: A Study in Contemporary Biography*. Boston: Houghton Mifflin, 1933.

Hamilton, W. J. J., J. O. Boyd, and W. H. Mossman. *Human Embryology*. Baltimore: Williams & Wilkins, 1962.

Hammer, Signe. *Daughters and Mothers, Mothers and Daughters*. New York: Quadrangle, 1975.

Hartman, Mary S., and Lois Banner, eds. *Clio's Consciousness Raised: New Perspectives on the History of Women*. New York: Harper & Row, 1974.

Hays, Samuel P. *Response to Industrialism*. Chicago: University of Chicago Press, 1957.

Hazard, Caroline. *Some Ideals in the Education of Women*. New York: Thomas Y. Crowell, 1900.

Henry, Alice. *Women and the Labor Movement*. New York: George H. Doran, 1923.

Herreshoff, David. *American Disciples of Marx: From the Age of Jackson to the Progressive Era*. Detroit: Wayne State University Press, 1967.

History of Woman Suffrage. Vols. I–III ed. Elizabeth Cady Stanton, Susan B. Anthony, and Matilda J. Gage. Rochester, N.Y.: Charles Mann, 1881, 1882, 1886. Vol. IV ed. Susan B. Anthony and Ida Husted Harper. Indianapolis: Hollenbeck Press, 1902. Vols. V and VI ed. Ida Husted Harper. New York: J. J. Little & Ives, 1922.

Hofstader, Richard. *Social Darwinism in American Thought*. Boston: Beacon Press, 1964; 1st pub., 1944.

Holloway, Jean. *Hamlin Garland: A Biography*. Austin: University of Texas Press, 1960.

Hopkins, C. Howard. *The Rise of Social Gospel in American Protestantism, 1865–1915*. New Haven: Yale University Press, 1967.

Hough, Eugene. "The Work and Influence of Charlotte Perkins Stetson in the Labor Movement," *American Fabian*, III, no. 9 (Jan. 1897), 12.

Howe, Harriet. "Charlotte Perkins Gilman—As I Knew Her." *Equal Rights: Independent Feminist Weekly*, II, no. 27 (Sept. 5, 1936), 211–216.

Howells, William Dean. *The Rise of Silas Lapham*. Boston: Houghton Mifflin, 1884.

Irwin, Inez Hayes. *Angels and Amazons: A Hundred Years of American Women*. Garden City, N.Y.: Doubleday, Doran, 1933.

Jones, Mary. *The Autobiography of Mother Jones*. New York: Arno, 1969; 1st pub., 1925.

Kanter, Rosabeth Moss. *Work and the Family in the United States*. New York: Russell Sage Foundation, 1977.

Katzman, David M. *Seven Days a Week: Women and Domestic Service in Industrializing America*. New York: Oxford University Press, 1978.

Kennedy, David. *Birth Control in America: The Career of Margaret Sanger*. New Haven: Yale University Press, 1970.

Kett, Joseph. *Rites of Passage: Adolescence in America, 1790 to the Present*. New York: Basic Books, 1977.

Kipnis, Ira. *The American Socialist Movement: 1897–1912*. New York: Columbia University Press, 1952.

Kirkland, Edward. *Industry Comes of Age: Business, Labor and Public Policy*. Alexandria, Va.: Time Books, 1967.

Knapp, Adeline. *An Open Letter to Carrie Chapman Catt*. Berkeley, Calif.: New York State Association Opposed to the Extension of the Suffrage to Women, Nov. 10, 1899.

———. *One Thousand Dollars a Day: Studies in Practical Economics*. Boston: Arena Publishing Company, 1894.

Kraditor, Aileen. *Ideas of the Woman Suffrage Movement, 1890–1920*. New York: Columbia University Press, 1965.

Kreps, Juanita, ed. *Women and the American Economy*. Englewood Cliffs, N.J.: Prentice-Hall, 1976.

Laslett, Peter, and Richard Wall, eds. *Household and Family in Past Time*. Cambridge: Cambridge University Press, 1972.

Lazarre, Jane. *The Mother Knot*. New York: McGraw-Hill, 1976.

Lerner, Gerda. "Placing Women in History: Definitions and Challenges," *Feminist Studies*, III, no. 1/2 (Fall 1975), 5–14.

Linn, James Weber. *Jane Addams: A Biography*. New York: D. Appleton-Century, 1935.

Lippmann, Walter. *Drift and Mastery*. New York: M. Kennerley, 1914.

Maccoby, Eleanor E., and Carol N. Jacklin, eds. *The Psychology of Sex Differences*. Stanford: Stanford University Press, 1974.

MacKenzie, Norman, and Jeanne MacKenzie. *The Fabians*. New York: Simon & Schuster, 1977.

Markham, Edwin. *The Man with the Hoe and Other Poems*. Garden City, N.Y.: Doubleday, Page, 1917.

Mighels, Ella Sterling Cummis. *The Story of the Files: A Review of California Writers and Fiction*. World's Fair Commission of California, Columbian Exposition, 1893.

Miller, Jean Baker, ed. *Psychoanalysis and Women*. Middlesex, England: Penguin Books, 1973.

Millett, Kate. *Sexual Politics*. New York: Doubleday, 1970.

Mitchell, Juliet. *Psychoanalysis and Feminism*. New York: Pantheon, 1974.

———. *Woman's Estate*. New York: Random House, 1973.

Mitchell, S. Weir. *Roland Blake*. New York: Houghton Mifflin, 1886.

Money, John, and Anke A. Ehrhardt. *Man and Woman, Boy and Girl: Differentiation and Dimorphism of Gender Identity*. Baltimore: Johns Hopkins University Press, 1972.

Morgan, Arthur. *Edward Bellamy*. New York: Columbia University Press, 1944.

Noble, David. *The Paradox of Progressive Thought*. Minneapolis: University of Minnesota Press, 1958.

Oakley, Ann. *Woman's Work: The Housewife Past and Present*. New York: Random House, 1976.

O'Neill, William. *Divorce in the Progressive Era*. New Haven: Yale University Press, 1967.

———. *Everyone Was Brave: The Rise and Fall of Feminism in America*. Chicago: Quadrangle, 1969.

Parsons, Alice Beale. *Woman's Dilemma*. New York: Thomas Y. Crowell, 1926.

Peck, Mary Gray. *Carrie Chapman Catt: A Biography*. New York: H. W. Wilson, 1944.

Pelling, Henry. *American Labor*. Chicago: University of Chicago Press, 1960.

Perkins, Frederick Beecher. *Devil Puzzlers, and Other Studies*. New York: G. P. Putnam's Sons, 1877.

———. *My Three Conversations with Miss Chester*. New York: G. P. Putnam's Sons, 1877.

———. *The Station and Duty of American Teachers as Citizens, in View of the Materialism of the Age*. Hartford, Conn.: Association of the Alumni of Connecticut State Normal School, Oct. 7, 1857.

Pivar, David J. *Purity Crusade: Sexual Morality and Social Control, 1868–1900*. Westport, Conn.: Greenwood Press, 1973.

Poe, Edgar Allan. *The Complete Poems and Stories of Edgar Allan Poe, with Selections from His Critical Writings*. New York: Knopf, 1946.

Quint, Howard. *The Forging of American Socialism: Origins of the Modern Movement*. New York: Bobbs-Merrill, 1953.

Rabb, T. K., and Robert I. Rotberg, eds. *The Family in History: Interdisciplinary Essays*. New York: Harper & Row, 1973.

Reed, James. *From Private Vice to Public Virtue: The Birth Control Move-*

ment and American Society Since 1830. New York: Basic Books, 1977.
Report on Fabian Policy and Resolutions. Presented by the Fabian Society to the International Socialist Workers and Trade Union Congress. London: The Fabian Society, 1896.
Rheingold, Joseph C. *The Fear of Being a Woman: A Theory of Maternal Destructiveness*. New York: Grune and Stratten, 1964.
Rich, Adrienne. *Adrienne Rich's Poetry*. Selected and edited by Barbara Charlesworth Gelpi and Albert Gelpi. New York: Norton, 1975.
———. *Of Woman Born: Motherhood as Experience and Institution*. New York: Norton, 1976.
Riegel, Robert. *American Feminists*. Lawrence, Kansas: University of Kansas Press, 1968.
Riis, Jacob. *How the Other Half Lives: Studies among the Tenements of New York*. New York: C. Scribner's Sons, 1903.
Robbins, Caroline. *Poems and Anti-Slavery Drama in Prose and Verse*. Providence: J. A. & R. A. Reid, Printers, 1876.
Rosaldo, Michelle Zimbalist, ed. *Woman, Culture, and Society*. Stanford, Calif.: Stanford University Press, 1974.
Rosenberg, Charles E. "Sexuality, Class, and Role in Nineteenth-Century America," *American Quarterly*, XXV (May 1973), 131–153.
Ross, Edward Alsworth. *Seventy Years of It: An Autobiography of Edward Alsworth Ross*. New York: D. Appleton-Century, 1936.
Rossi, Alice, ed. *The Feminist Papers: From Adams to de Beauvoir*. New York: Bantam, 1978; 1st pub., 1973.
Rowbotham, Sheila. *Woman's Consciousness*. Middlesex, England: Penguin Books, 1973.
———. *Women, Resistance, and Revolution*. New York: Random House, 1974.
Ryan, Mary. *Womanhood in America*. New York: Franklin Watts, 1975.
Salmon, Lucy Maynard. *Domestic Service*. 2nd ed. New York: Macmillan, 1901.
Sampson, Ronald. *The Psychology of Power*. New York: Pantheon, 1966.
Schreiner, Olive. *Dreams*. Boston: Roberts Brothers, 1891.
———. *The Story of an African Farm*. Boston: Little, Brown, 1883.
———. *Woman and Labour*. London: T. F. Unwin, 1911.
Scott, Anne Firor. *The Southern Lady: From Pedestal to Politics, 1830–1930*. Chicago: University of Chicago Press, 1970.
Scott, Clifford. *Lester Frank Ward*. Boston: Twayne Publishers, 1976.
Scott, John A. *Woman against Slavery: The Story of Harriet Beecher Stowe*. New York: Thomas Y. Crowell, 1978.
Sherfey, Mary Jane. *The Nature and Evolution of Female Sexuality*. New York: Random House, 1972.
Shorter, Edward. *The Making of the Modern Family*. New York: Basic Books, 1975.
Sicherman, Barbara. "American History: A Review Essay," *Signs*, I, no. 2 (Winter 1975), 461–485.

Sinclair, Andrew. *The Emancipation of the American Woman*. New York: Harper & Row, 1965.
Sklar, Kathryn Kish. *Catharine Beecher: A Study in American Domesticity*. New Haven: Yale University Press, 1973.
Smith-Rosenberg, Carroll. "The Female World of Love and Ritual: Relations Between Women in Nineteenth-Century America," *Signs*, I, no. 1 (Autumn 1975), 9–10.
———. "The Hysterical Woman: Sex Roles and Role Conflict in Nineteenth-Century America," *Social Research*, XXXIX, no. 4 (Winter 1972), 652–678.
———. "The New Woman and the New History." *Feminist Studies*, III, no. 1/2 (Fall 1975), 185–198.
Smuts, Robert. *Women and Work in America*. New York: Columbia University Press, 1959.
Stanton, Elizabeth Cady. *Eighty Years and More (1815–1897): Reminiscences of Elizabeth Cady Stanton*. London: T. F. Unwin, 1898.
———. *The Woman's Bible*. New York: Arno, 1972; 1st pub., 1895.
Stanton, Theodore, and Harriot Stanton Blatch, eds. *Elizabeth Cady Stanton as Revealed in Her Letters, Diary and Reminiscences*, 2 Vols. New York: Harper & Bros., 1922.
Stetson, Nelson M. *Stetson Kindred of America, No. 4*. Rockland, Mass.: Press of A. I. Randall, 1914.
Stocking, George W., Jr. *Race, Culture and Evolution: Essays in the History of Anthropology*. New York: The Free Press, 1968.
Stowe, Lyman Beecher. *Saints, Sinners and Beechers*. Indianapolis: Bobbs-Merrill, 1934.
Strasser, Susan M. "Mistress and Maid, Employer and Employee: Domestic Service Reform in the United States, 1897–1920," *Marxist Perspectives*, I, no. 4 (Winter 1978), 52–67.
Tims, Margaret. *Jane Addams of Hull House, 1860–1935*. New York: Macmillan, 1961.
Tylor, Edward Burnett. *Primitive Culture*. 1st American ed. Boston: Estes and Lauriat, 1874.
Veblen, Thorstein. *The Theory of the Leisure Class*. New York: Macmillan, 1899.
Walker, Franklin D. *The Literary History of Southern California*. Berkeley, Calif.: University of Washington Press, 1950.
———. *San Francisco's Literary Frontier*. New York: Knopf, 1939.
Ward, Lester. *Dynamic Sociology*. New York: D. Appleton, 1883.
———. *Glimpses of the Cosmos*. New York: G. P. Putnam's Sons, 1917.
———. "Our Better Halves," *Forum*, VI (Nov., 1888), 266–275.
———. *Pure Sociology: A Treatise on the Origin and Spontaneous Development of Society*. Rpt. of 2nd ed. New York: Augustus M. Kelley, 1970; 1st pub., 1903.
Webb, Beatrice. *The Co-operative Movement of Great Britain*. London: S. Sonnenschein, 1891.

Webb, Sidney, and Beatrice Webb. *History of Trade Unionism*. London: Longmans, Green, 1894.

———, Beatrice Webb, George Bernard Shaw, and others. *Fabian Essays in Socialism*. London: Fabian Society, 1889.

Welter, Barbara. "The Cult of True Womanhood," *American Quarterly*, XVIII (Summer 1966), 151–174.

Wiebe, Robert. *The Search for Order: 1870–1920*. New York: Hill & Wang, 1967.

Willard, Frances, and Mary A. Livermore, eds. *A Woman of the Century*. Buffalo, New York: C. W. Moulton, 1893.

White, Morton. *The Origins of Dewey's Instrumentalism*. New York: Columbia University Press, 1943.

———. *Social Thought in America*. Boston: Beacon Press, 1957.

Wilson, R. J. *Darwinism and the American Intellectual*. Homewood, Ill.: Dorsey Press, 1967.

Wood, Ann Douglas. "The Fashionable Diseases: Women's Complaints and Their Treatment," *Journal of Interdisciplinary History* IV (Spring 1973–1974), 25–52.

Woody, Thomas. *A History of Women's Education in the United States*, Vol. I. New York: Science Press, 1929.

Zaretsky, Eli. *Capitalism, the Family, and Personal Life*. New York: Harper & Row, 1976.

Index

Works by Charlotte Perkins Gilman are cited as "Gilman" whether or not they were published under that name. Readers wishing complete bibliographical information should consult the Bibliography.